GERMAN-AMERICAN
HANDBOOK

GERMAN-AMERICAN
HANDBOOK

A collection of current idioms, colloquialisms, familiar quotations, localisms, dialectal and slang expressions, and words not generally found in German-English dictionaries

BY

EDMUND P. KREMER

University of Oregon

J. B. LIPPINCOTT COMPANY
CHICAGO   PHILADELPHIA   NEW YORK

PRINTED IN THE UNITED STATES OF AMERICA

TO MY MOTHER

Preface

The object of this handbook is to supply English-speaking students of German with a ready reference for the English equivalents of many German colloquial and slang terms. These expressions commonly occur in modern German novels, newspapers, and magazines, and are frequently heard in the ordinary course of conversation. Without a comprehension of such terms, the student's knowledge of German cannot help being more or less artificial.

What student, on being exposed to a new language, is not confronted with such "trouble spots"? How much do relatively advanced students lose by their inability to grasp the color and meaning of the terse idiom or the slang expression? This handbook endeavors to furnish the service necessary in such cases. Its scope includes much information that would otherwise have to be gleaned from various sources, many of which are not readily accessible.

Although brevity has been an objective of this volume, at no time has clarity been sacrificed to terseness. It should be remembered, however, that slang expressions and idioms are the most changeable segment of a language. "Much of it is so ephemeral that it is never recorded. All of it is in a constant state of flux, with a rate of change much more rapid than in any other kind of language. An expression that is obsolete in one region is just gaining currency in another. To one person a certain expression is 'old stuff'; to another person, even in the same region or in the same group, this expression is the newest of the new. And though the wording may be identical, the real meaning and the special application may be very different in the various regions and groups. Sometimes the meaning differs even among individuals in the same region or group." [1] In addition to being the most changeable part of a language, such expressions often transcend a single connotation. The effort has been made here to present key meanings. Often the actual connotation of a phrase may be derived from an illustration and developed specifically in terms of the direct context in which it happens to appear.

Because such words and phrases often transcend their literal meanings, a

---

[1] M. H. Weseen, *A Dictionary of American Slang;* p. v. Thomas Y. Crowell Co., New York, 1934.

volume of this kind must give equivalents rather than definitions. For this reason, and also to illustrate phrases in context, a form has been prepared that not only isolates such terms but also illustrates their usage in actual sentence construction. To facilitate reference to them, key words have been arranged in alphabetical order.

The author wishes to extend special thanks for encouragement and advice on many details to H. L. Mencken of Baltimore, Dr. Ernst Rose of New York University, and Dr. Otto Koischwitz of Hunter College; also to Helene E. Hoffmann of New York for a careful revision of the text and numerous valuable contributions of an editorial nature. He wishes further to acknowledge his indebtedness for the many helpful suggestions received from his students, colleagues, and friends; and to those writers, journalists, and scholars—known and unknown—whose works he drew upon liberally.

In a work of this character it is inevitable that there be omissions and mistakes. For any inadequacy, the author can only offer his apologies.

E. P. K.

Bibliography

The following are some of the principal books and the leading periodicals consulted in the preparation of this work.

A. BOOKS

German

Bergman, M.: *Spracheigenheiten.* Leipzig, F. Hirt, 1921.

Borchardt-Wustmann: *Die sprichwörtlichen Redensarten im deutschen Volksmund.* Leipzig, F. A. Brockhaus, 1925.

Danton and Danton: *Wie sagt man das auf Deutsch?* New York, F. S. Crofts and Co., 1936.

Depenbrock, J.: *Deutsche Redensarten.* Münster, Aschendorff, 1932.

Duden: *Der große Duden, Stilwörterbuch.* Leipzig, Bibliographisches Institut, 1934.

Duden: *Rechtschreibung der deutschen Sprache.* Leipzig, Bibliographisches Institut, 1935.

Genthe, A.: *Deutsches Slang.* Straßburg, K. J. Trübner, 1892.

Kluge, F.: *Unser Deutsch.* Dritte Auflage. Leipzig, Quelle & Meyer, 1914.

Lange, F.: *Deutsche und englische Idiome.* Heidelberg, J. Groos, u.d.

Lipperheide, F.: *Spruchwörterbuch.* Berlin, J. Dörner, 1934.

Loewe-Breul: *Deutsch-englische Phraseologie.* Berlin-Schöneberg, Langenscheidt, 1926.

Muret-Sanders: *Enzyklopädisches Wörterbuch der englishen und deutschen Sprache.* Berlin, Langenscheidt, 1910.

Paul, H.: *Deutsches Wörterbuch.* Vierte Auflage. Halle, M. Niemeyer, 1935.

Petrun, R.: *Das deutsche Wort.* Leipzig, G. Dollheimer, 1933.

Richter, A.: *Deutsche Redensarten.* Leipzig, F. Brandstetter, 1930.

Toussaint-Langenscheidt: *Der kleine Toussaint-Langenscheidt, Englisch.* Berlin, 1901.

Wasmuth, Hans-Werner: *Slang bei Sinclair Lewis.* Doctor's dissertation. Hamburg, 1935.

Wykeham, Reginald: *1000 idiomatische englische Redensarten.* Berlin, Langenscheidt, 1936.

English

Craigie, Sir William, and Hulbert, James R.: *A Dictionary of American English on Historical Principles*. Chicago, The University of Chicago Press, 1936.

Dixon, J. M.: *English Idioms*. London, Thomas Nelson and Sons, 1927.

Empey, Arthur Guy: *Over the Top*, by an American soldier who went, together with *Tommy's Dictionary of the Trenches*. New York, G. P. Putnam's Sons, 1917.

Farmer, John Stephen, and Henley, W. E.: *A Dictionary of Slang and Colloquial English*. New York, E. P. Dutton and Co., 1905.

Fowler, Henry Watson: *A Dictionary of Modern English Usage*. Oxford, The Clarendon Press, 1926.

Hauch, Edward F.: *German Idiom List*, selected on the basis of frequency and range of occurrence. New York, The Macmillan Co., 1929.

Holt, Alfred H.: *Phrase Origins*, a study of familiar expressions. New York, Thomas Y. Crowell Co., 1936.

Horwill, Herbert William: *A Dictionary of Modern American Usage*. Oxford, The Clarendon Press, 1935.

Irwin, Godfrey: *American Tramp and Underworld Slang*, words and phrases used by hoboes, tramps, migratory workers, and those on the fringes of society, with their uses and origins. New York, Sears Publishing Co., 1930.

Lambert, M. B.: *Handbook of German Idioms*. New York, Henry Holt and Co., 1910.

Mathews, M. M.: *The Beginnings of American English*. Chicago, The University of Chicago Press, 1931.

Mencken, H. L.: *The American Language*, an inquiry into the development of English in the United States. New York, Alfred A. Knopf, Inc., 1936.

Murray, Sir James, chief editor: *A New English Dictionary on Historical Principles*. Oxford, The Clarendon Press, 1893.

Nock-Mutschmann: *Spoken American*. Leipzig and Berlin, Teubner, 1930.

Partridge, Eric Honeywood: *Slang Today and Yesterday*, with a short historical sketch and vocabularies of English, American, and Australian slang. London, George Routledge and Sons, Ltd., 1933.

Roget: *Roget's Thesaurus of English Words and Phrases*. New York, Grosset and Dunlap, 1933.

Rörig, H.: *Brighter German*. London, G. Bles, 1934.

Rose, Howard N.: *A Thesaurus of Slang.* New York, The Macmillan Co., 1934.

Schoch-Kron: *The Little Yankee.* Ettlingen and Leipzig, J. Bielefield, 1930.

Smith, Charles Alfonso: *New Words Self-Defined.* New York, Doubleday, Doran and Co., 1934.

Smith, Logan Pearsall: *English Idioms.* Oxford, The Clarendon Press, 1923.

————: *Words and Idioms*, studies in the English language. Boston, Houghton Mifflin Co., 1925.

Tindall, S.: *Progressive German Idioms.* Oxford, The Clarendon Press, 1916.

Tucker, Gilbert M.: *American English.* New York, Alfred A. Knopf, Inc., 1921.

Webster's New International Dictionary. Second edition. Springfield, Massachusetts, G. and C. Merriam, 1934.

Weekley, Ernest: *An Etymological Dictionary of Modern English.* New York, E. P. Dutton and Co., 1921.

Weseen, Maurice Harley: *A Dictionary of American Slang.* New York, Thomas Y. Crowell Co., 1934.

Williams, Guy: *Logger-Talk*, some notes on the jargon of the Pacific Northwest woods. Seattle, The University of Washington Book Store, 1930.

Wyld, Henry C. K.: *Colloquial English.* London, T. E. Unwin, Ltd., 1925.

————: *The Universal Dictionary of the English Language.* London, George Routledge and Sons, Ltd., 1932.

B. PERIODICALS

American Speech, a quarterly of linguistic usage. New York, Columbia University Press.

Dialect Notes, publication of the American Dialect Society. Norwood, J. S. Cushing Co.

Words, a monthly publication devoted to the origin, history, and etymology of English words. Los Angeles, California.

A:
> Dies ist das A und O des Problems.

This is the problem from A to Z; this is the whole problem in a nutshell.

> Wer A sagt, muß auch B sagen.

You made your bed—now lie in it!; you'll have to pay the piper (*or* suffer the consequences).

Aal:
> Es hieße den Aal beim Schwanz fassen, schenkte man seinen Worten Glauben.

You can't believe a word he says.

aalen:
> Er aalte sich vor Behagen.

He felt like a million dollars; he felt on top of the world.

Aas:
> Das ist aber ein Aas!

Isn't he the rascal (*or* a smart guy)?; there's a devil for you!

> Kein Aas ließ sich sehen.

There wasn't a soul there (*or* in sight).

aasen:
> Er hat mit seinen Kräften nur so geaast.

He was burning the candle at both ends.

ab:
> Ab!

Scat!; scram!; vamoose!; beat it!
> Er ist ganz ab.

He's all washed up (*or* played out).
> Er schreibt ab und an.

He writes now and then.
> Sie kommen ab und zu.

They come occasionally (*or* once in a while).
> Draußen geht einer auf und ab.

Someone is walking back and forth outside.

Abbau:
> Der Abbau von Beamten und Gehältern wurde verschoben.

The discharge of employees and the cut in salaries were postponed.

abbauen:
> Ich baue ab.

I'll be going now; I quit.
> Er wurde abgebaut.

He was discharged.

abberufen:
> Er wurde aus diesem Leben abberufen.

He cashed in his checks; he kicked the bucket; he passed away.

abbiegen:
> Sie haben es ihm abgebogen.

They cramped his style; his activities were curbed.

abblasen:
> Der Streik wurde abgeblasen.

The strike was called off.

abblitzen:
> Sie hat ihn abgeblitzt.

She gave him the icy mitt (*or* cold shoulder); she turned him down.

abbrechen:
> Brich dir nur keinen ab!

Don't put on the dog!; don't be high-hat!

Abc:
    Man lobte sie durchs Abc.   They praised her to the skies.

abdampfen:
    Wann dampfen Sie wieder ab?   When are you pulling out of here?; when are you going to leave?

abdrücken:
    Es drückte ihr fast das Herz ab.   It almost broke her heart.

Abend:
    Es ist noch nicht aller Tage Abend.   Time will tell; we haven't seen the last of it.
    Man soll den Tag nicht vor dem Abend loben.   Don't crow too soon; praise a fair day at night!

Abendmahl:
    Sie können das Abendmahl darauf nehmen!   You can bet your life (*or* take an oath) on that!

aber:
    Ach nein!   On the contrary!
    Nein aber!   I say!; not really!
    Nu aber!   Is that so!
    Oder aber lassen Sie uns das tun!   Or else let's do that!; how about letting us do that?

Aber:
    Die Sache hat ein Aber.   There's a catch (*or* hitch) to it.

abessen:
    Er hat bei ihnen abgegessen.   They've given him the gate (*or* air); they're through with him.

abfallen:
    Er ließ sie gründlich abfallen.   He turned them down flat.

abfertigen:
    Er fertigte ihn kurz ab.   He sent him packing (*or* about his business).

abfinden:
    Er hat sich abgefunden.   He returned the compliment.
    Sie kann sich damit nicht abfinden. She can't take (*or* put up with) it.

Abfuhr:
    Er hat sich eine schwere Abfuhr geholt. He took an awful beating; he suffered a reversal.

abgeben:
    Ich warne dich, sonst gibt's noch was ab. I'm warning you, you'll be in for it.
    Er will sich damit nicht abgeben. He won't have anything to do with it.

abgeblaßt:
    Das sind abgeblaßte Ausdrücke.   Those are rubber-stamp (*or* conventional) expressions.

abgebrannt:
    Er war vollkommen abgebrannt.   He was flat broke.

abgebrüht:
    Er ist ein abgebrühter Gauner.   He's a hard-boiled swindler.

abgedroschen:
    Sie ergingen sich in abgedroschenen Redensarten. They used bromides (*or* hackneyed expressions).

abgefeimt:
    Er ist ein abgefeimter Spitzbube.   He's crooked as a dog's hind leg; he's an out-and-out crook.

abgegolten:
Damit ist sein Anspruch abgegolten. — That settles his claim.

abgegriffen:
Er erging sich in abgegriffenen Schlag= wörtern. — He used platitudes (*or* dull commonplaces).

abgehen:
Dafür geht ihm das rechte Verständnis ab. — That's beyond him; he can't appreciate it; he doesn't understand that.

Wann geht der nächste Zug ab? — What time does the next train leave?

Alles ging gut ab. — Everything turned out all right.

Man hat ihn abgegangen. — He was frozen out (*or* left out in the cold).

Ich fürchte, das wird nicht ohne Schlägerei abgehen. — I'm afraid it will come to blows (*or* there'll be a fight).

Sie lassen sich nichts abgehen. — They live well; they deny themselves nothing.

abgejachert:
Er kam abgejachert nach Hause. — He came home tuckered (*or* washed) out.

abgekämpft:
Er ist gänzlich abgekämpft. — He's all run down (*or* played out).

abgekartet:
Es ist eine abgekartete Sache. — It's in the cards; it's a put-up job.

abgeklärt:
Er ist ein abgeklärter Mensch. — He's a seasoned (*or* mellowed) person; he has poise.

abgelauscht:
Die Geschichte ist dem Leben abgelauscht. — The story is true to life.

abgelebt:
Er sieht abgelebt aus. — He looks worn out.

abgemacht:
Abgemacht! — That's o. k. with me; it's a go!; it suits me; shake (hands) on it!

abgerackert:
Er ist jetzt schon abgerackert. — He's bushed (*or* run down) already.

abgerissen:
Er sah abgerissen aus. — He was down at the heel; he looked shabby (*or* like a bum).

abgescheuert:
Der Mantel ist abgescheuert. — The overcoat is threadbare.

abgeschieden:
Er lebt ganz abgeschieden. — He's a hermit (*or* recluse).

abgeschlossen:
Er verfügt über eine abgeschlossene Bildung. — He has a well-rounded education.

abgespannt:
Sie fühlte sich abgespannt. — She felt tired (*or* washed) out.

abgestellt:
Der Vertrag ist auf Treu und Glauben abgestellt. — It's a gentlemen's agreement.

abgestimmt:
Es ist ein fein abgestimmtes Urteil. — It's a very wise decision.

abgeſtuft:
Die Gehälter ſind abgeſtuft.

Salaries are on a graduated scale.

abheben:
Wer abhebt, gibt nicht.

Whoever cuts, doesn't deal; you can't have your cake and eat it too.

abhelfen:
Dem iſt leicht abzuhelfen.

That's easily done (*or* fixed).

abholen:
Er holte ſie von der Bahn ab.

He met them at the station.

abkanzeln:
Er kanzelte ſie ab.

He delivered a sermon (*or* lecture); he bawled them out.

abkaufen:
Man muß ihm jedes Wort abkaufen.

It's like pulling teeth to make him talk; every word has to be wheedled (*or* coaxed) out of him.

abklabaſtert:
Er war ganz abklabaſtert.

He was all tuckered out (*or* exhausted).

abklappern:
Er klapperte die ganze Stadt nach Arbeit ab.

He scoured the whole town for a job.

Abklatſch:
Sie iſt der Abklatſch ihrer Mutter.

She's the very image of her mother.

abklopfen:
Der Gefangene klopft ſeine Zeit ab.
Er hat jeden Laden danach abgeklopft.

The prisoner is doing (*or* serving) time.
He knocked at every door; he tried everywhere to get it.

abknapſen:
Man hat ihm zehn Prozent vom Gehalt abgeknapſt.

They cut his salary ten per cent.

abknöpfen:
Sie knöpften ihm fünf Mark ab.

They did him out of five marks.

abknutſchen:
Sie knutſchten das Kind ab.

They petted (*or* hugged and kissed) the child.

abkratzen:
Er iſt gerade abgekratzt.
Der Kranke wird wohl bald abkratzen.

He just left.
The patient will probably kick off (*or* pass away) soon.

abladen:
Er mußte ordentlich abladen.

He had to shell out plenty (of money).

Ablaß:
Das hieße, den Ablaß nach Rom tragen.

That would be carrying coals to Newcastle; that's a waste of time (*or* energy).

ablaſſen:
Laß ab, ihn zu quälen!
Er ließ ihnen zehn Pfund ab.
Er wollte von dem Preis nichts ablaſſen.

Stop bothering him!; leave him alone!
He let them have (*or* sold them) ten pounds.
He didn't want to knock off (*or* come down) a penny.

ablaufen:
    An ihm läuft alles ab.

It runs off him like water off a duck's back; he has a thick skin; nothing bothers him.

    Die Sache lief übel ab.

It came to a sorry pass; it had a sad ending.

    Seine Zeit ist abgelaufen.

He's at his rope's end; his time has come; he must die.

    Er ließ sie schwer ablaufen.

He sent them packing (*or* about their business).

ableben:
    Der Brauch hat sich abgelebt.

It's an outworn custom.

Ableger:
    Das Geschäft ist ein Ableger unsrer Münchner Firma.

The store is a branch of our Munich house.

abluchſen:
    Man hat ihm sein Geld abgeluchst.

He was gypped (*or* swindled) out of his money.

abmachen:
    Machen Sie das mit sich selber ab!

Fight your own battles!

abmurkſen:
    Sie haben ihn abgemurkst.

They bumped him off; they did away with him.

abnehmen:
    Der Kranke nimmt ab.

The patient is on the decline; his strength is failing.

    Der Mond nahm ab.

The moon was on the wane.

Abonnement:
    Im Abonnement ist das Essen billiger.

Meals are cheaper if you buy a meal ticket.

abpaſſen:
    Das hat er gut abgepaßt.

He came at (*or* hit upon) the psychological moment; he timed that perfectly.

Abraham:
    Hier sind wir aufgehoben wie in Abrahams Schoß.

This is pretty soft (*or* just like home); we're leading the life of Riley here; we're living in great comfort.

abrechnen:
    Mit dem werde ich schon noch abrechnen.

He'll get what's coming to him!; I'll pay that fellow off yet!

abreißen:
    Die Arbeit reißt nie ab.

There's never a letup; there's no end of work.

abrücken:
    Sie sind von ihm abgerückt.

They dropped (*or* broke with) him.

abſagen:
    Er ließ ihnen absagen.

He sent word that he couldn't come.

abſägen:
    Man hat ihn abgesägt.

He was given the ax (*or* gate); he was fired (*or* discharged).

Abſatz:
    Die Ware findet einen reißenden Absatz.

The article sells like hot cakes; there's a big market (*or* demand) for it.

abſchätzig:
    Er urteilte abſchätzig über ſie.

He ran her down (*or* razzed her); he spoke disparagingly of her.

abſchieben:
    Schieb ab!
    Man hat ihn als läſtigen Ausländer ab=
    geſchoben.

Scram!; beat it!; move on!
He was expelled from the country as an undesirable alien.

abſchinden:
    Schinde dich doch nicht ſo ab!

Don't kill yourself!; don't work so hard!

Abſchlag:
    Er zahlt auf Abſchlag.

He pays in installments (*or* on the installment plan).

abſchlägig:
    Seine Eingabe wurde abſchlägig be=
    ſchieden.

His petition was turned down.

abſchließen:
    Er hat mit der Welt abgeſchloſſen.

He's done (*or* through) with the world and its concerns; he's retired from active life; he lives in seclusion.

abſchließend:
    Er kann noch kein abſchließendes Urteil
    abgeben.

He can't give a definite opinion yet.

abſchmieren:
    Unſre Mannſchaft wurde abgeſchmiert.

Our team took a beating (*or* was defeated).

abſchneiden:
    Laſſen Sie uns hier abſchneiden!

Let's take this short-cut!

abſchreckend:
    Laſſen Sie ſich das als abſchreckendes Bei=
    ſpiel dienen!

Let that be a warning to you!

abſchreiben:
    Ich muß Ihnen leider abſchreiben.

I'm sorry I can't do it (for you).

abſchüſſig:
    Er iſt auf der abſchüſſigen Bahn.

He's on the skids; he's slipping; he's on the downgrade.

abſchwirren:
    Er ſchwirrte bald ab.

He soon bolted (*or* left).

abſehbar:
    Er kann das in abſehbarer Zeit nicht
    ſchaffen.

He can't do that for a long time.

abſehen:
    Er ſieht es auf Komplimente ab.
    Hat man es darauf abgeſehen?

He's fishing for compliments.
Is that the idea?; is that what they have in mind?

    Sie haben es auf ihn abgeſehen.

They've got him spotted; they've got their eye on him.

    Das Ende iſt nicht abzuſehen.

There's no telling where (*or* how) it will end.

abſetzen:
    Es ſetzte Hiebe ab.

They came to blows.

Abſicht:
    Er hat Abſichten auf ſie.

He's thinking of marrying her.

abfolvieren:
Na, das haben wir glücklich abfolviert! | Well, that's that!; we did it!

abfpeifen:
Er läßt sich nicht derartig abfpeifen. | He won't be put off like that (*or* that easily).

Abfprechendes:
Sie hat etwas Abfprechendes an sich. | Her attitude is intolerable.

abftechen:
Diefes Gemälde fticht vorteilhaft von jenem ab. | This painting contrasts favorably with that.

Er ftach ihn im fiebten Gang ab. | He finished him (*or* knocked him out) in the seventh round.

abfteigend:
Er ift auf dem abfteigenden Aft. | He's on the skids; he's slipping; he's on the downgrade.

abftoßen:
Er ftieß die Ware rechtzeitig ab. | He sold the goods in time.

abftrapazieren:
Strapazier dich doch nicht fo ab! | Take it easy!; don't kill yourself!

abftreiten:
Das läßt er fich nicht abftreiten. | You can't convince him.

abtoffeln:
Er toffelte ihn wie einen dummen Jungen ab. | He spoke to him like a Dutch uncle; he bawled him out as if he were nothing but a kid.

abtragen:
Tragen Sie ab! | Clear the table!
Wie kann ich Ihnen jemals meine Schuld abtragen? | How can I ever repay you?

abträglich:
Das wäre feiner Gefundheit abträglich. | That might injure his health.

abwälzen:
Er fuchte die Schuld von fich abzuwälzen. | He tried to pass the buck (*or* shift the blame).

abwartend:
Er nimmt eine abwartende Haltung ein. | He keeps a neutral course; he lays low (*or* bides his time).

abwickeln:
Der Verkehr wickelte fich glatt ab. | Traffic moved on smoothly.

abwimmeln:
Den hätten wir glücklich abgewimmelt. | We froze him out after all; we managed to get rid of him very nicely.

abwinken:
Als er mich um Geld anging, habe ich fofort abgewinkt. | When he asked for money, I immediately said: nothing doing!

abwürgen:
Er hat den Motor abgewürgt. | He killed the motor (*or* engine).

abzapfen:
Er wollte ihnen fchon wieder Geld abzapfen. | He wanted to bleed them again for money.

abzirkeln:
Er zirkelte feine Worte genau ab. | He weighed his words carefully.

ach:

Ach, was macht das?
> Now I ask you, what difference does that make?

Ach nee!
> You don't say!; you don't mean it!

Ach so!
> Oh, well!; so that's what you mean!; I see!

Ach was!
> Bah!; baloney!; nonsense!; piffle!

Ach wo!
> Oh, no!; not at all!

Ach:

Ein Ach der Bewunderung entfloh ihren Lippen.
> She oh'd and ah'd; she exclaimed with wonder.

Er schrie Ach und Weh, als er das Unglück entdeckte.
> He yelled bloody murder (or shouted for help) when he discovered the disaster.

Er bestand die Prüfung mit Ach und Krach.
> He passed the exam(ination) by the skin of his teeth (or with great difficulty).

acheln:

Sie werden heute spät acheln.
> They'll eat late today.

Achillesferse:

Deutsch ist seine Achillesferse.
> German is his weak spot.

Achse:

Er ist den ganzen Tag auf Achse.
> He's on the go (or running around) all day long.

Achsel:

Er nimmt es auf die leichte Achsel.
> He takes it easy (or lightly).

Er trägt auf beiden Achseln.
> He's on both sides of the fence; he's a hand-shaker (or yes-man).

Er zuckte mit den Achseln.
> He shrugged his shoulders.

Man sieht ihn über die Achsel an.
> He's looked down upon; they give him the cold shoulder.

acht:

Es geschah vor acht Tagen.
> It happened a week ago.

Acht:

Sie wurde von der Gesellschaft in Acht und Bann getan.
> Society gave her the cold shoulder; she was ostracized.

Achtung:

Achtung da!
> Watch your step!; look out!; be careful!

Alle Achtung vor Ihrer Arbeit!
> Congratulations on the good work!

ad acta:

Die Sache ist ad acta gelegt.
> The matter has been put aside (or on the shelf).

Adam:

Er zog den alten Adam aus.
> He turned over a new leaf.

Nach Adam Riese stimmt das.
> That's right as rain; there's no getting away from it.

Ader:

An ihm ist keine falsche Ader.
> He's true-blue; there's nothing false in him.

Er hat keine Ader von seinem Vater.
> He's wholly unlike his father.

Er hat eine leichte Ader.
> He has a devil-may-care attitude; he takes life easy; he makes light of everything.

Adresse:

Er kam an die falsche Adresse.
> He went to the wrong door (or party); he met his master.

Affe:
Ich dachte, mich laust der Affe.   I thought I was seeing things; I was quite surprised (*or* taken aback).

So ein dummer Affe!   Such a big baboon!; what a silly ass!
Sie gaben ihrem Affen Zucker.   They made whoopee (*or* cut loose); they were going strong (*or* making merry).

Sie hat einen Affen an ihm gefressen.   She's sweet on him; she's nuts (*or* crazy) about him.

Er hat sich einen Affen gekauft.   He's lit up (tight *or* high); he's soused.

Affenfahrt:
Er kam in einer Affenfahrt.   He came at top speed.

affenjung:
Er ist noch affenjung.   He's still half-baked; he's only a kid.

Affenkasten:
Das Zimmer ist der reine Affenkasten.   The room is a regular cage (*or* two-by-four).
Hier stinkt's wie in einem Affenkasten.   It smells to high heaven here.

Affenschande:
Es ist eine Affenschande, wie er sich benimmt.   It's a dirty shame the way he carries on; his behavior is scandalous (*or* outrageous).

Affentheater:
Mach doch kein Affentheater!   Cut out that monkey business (*or* funny stuff)!

Agens:
Die Sucht nach Geld war das Agens seiner Handlung.   Avarice was his motive; his act was prompted by avarice.

Ägide:
Das Spiel steht unter seiner Ägide.   He's sponsoring the play.

ägyptisch:
Es herrschte eine ägyptische Finsternis.   It was pitch-dark.

ahnen:
Was ahnt er davon?   What does he know about that?

ähnlich:
Das sieht ihm ähnlich.   That's just like him.

Ahnung:
Haben Sie 'ne Ahnung!   That's where you're all wet (*or* wrong).
Stimmt das?—Ach, keine Ahnung!   Is that correct?—No, sir!; far from it!
Er hat keine Ahnung von Tuten und Blasen.   He doesn't know beans about it; he knows as much about it as the man in the moon.

Akazie:
Es ist, um auf die Akazien zu klettern!   It's enough to drive one batty (*or* make one tear one's hair).

Akkord:
Die Leute arbeiten in Akkord.   The men do piecework.

Akte:
Darüber sind die Akten noch nicht geschlossen.   The matter has not yet been settled.

aktuell:
Die Frage ist aktuell.   The problem is urgent.

Alarmbereitschaft:

Die Polizei ist in höchster Alarmbereit=
schaft.

The police are ready (*or* prepared) to act at
a moment's notice.

all:

Alles eher als das.

Anything but that.

Alles in allem genommen.

Everything considered.

Der Junge ist ihr ein und alles.

The boy is everything to her; she thinks the
world of him.

Er ist auf alles gefaßt.

He's prepared for the worst.

Es geht hier um alles oder nichts.

This is a case of all or nothing.

Er bedankte sich in aller Form.

He expressed his thanks in good and due
form.

Sie reisten in aller Frühe.

They left bright and early.

alle:

Es ist alle.

That's the end.

Die Dummen werden nicht alle.

There's a sucker (*or* fool) born every
minute.

allein:

Es kam ganz von allein.

It came all by itself.

allemal:

Gehen Sie mit?—Na, allemal!

Are you going alone?—You bet I am!

allerhand:

Das ist allerhand!

That's putting it strong!

Das ist allerhand für den Preis.

That's quite a bit for the money.

Allerhand Hochachtung!

Swell!; capital!; congratulations!

Allerweltskerl:

Er ist ein Allerweltskerl.

He's a crackajack (*or* whiz).

alltäglich:

Er ist ein ganz alltäglicher Mensch.

He's just average.

alltags:

Alltags bleibt er daheim.

On weekdays he stays at home.

Alp:

Ihr fiel ein Alp vom Herzen.

A weight was lifted from her mind.

also:

Also doch!

Am I surprised!; you don't say so!

Also passen Sie auf!

Now listen!; mark my words then!

Sie wollen also nicht?

So you won't, eh?

Na also!

That's the boy!; there you are!; didn't I
tell you?

alt:

Jung gewohnt, alt getan.

The child is father to the man; habits
learned in childhood persist throughout
life.

Es bleibt beim alten.

Things remain as they were.

Man hat ihn zum alten Eisen geworfen.

He was thrown on the scrap heap (*or* given
the sack); he was discarded (*or* discharged).

Das ist für den Alten Fritz.

That's labor lost; that's a waste of time.

Es geht alles im alten Gleise fort.

Everything is going on as usual.

Der alte Gott lebt noch.

God is still with us.

Er hat Einfälle wie ein altes Haus.

He gets crazy notions.

Er ist „Alter Herr."

He's a grad(uate); he's an alum(nus).

Er hat den alten Menschen abgelegt.	He turned over a new leaf.
In alter Treue!	As ever!
Er räumte mit dem alten Zopf auf.	He did away with the red tape (*or* petty formality).
Alte:	
Wie die Alten sungen, so zwitschern die Jungen.	The young pigs grunt like the old sow; like father, like son; it runs in the family.
Alter:	
Er steht in reiferem Alter.	He's reached the years of discretion; he's a mature person.
Sie ist im schönsten Alter.	She's in the prime of life.
alters:	
Vor alters war das nicht so.	Things were different in the old days.
Amboß:	
Du mußt Hammer oder Amboß sein.	Either you must be master or servant.
Er ist zwischen Hammer und Amboß.	He's between the devil and the deep blue sea; he's in a tight spot (*or* an embarrassing situation).
Amen:	
Das kommt so bestimmt wie das Amen in der Kirche.	That's as sure as death and taxes.
Ammenmärchen:	
Er erzählte ihnen Ammenmärchen.	He told them cock-and-bull (*or* fish) stories; he strung them along.
Amt:	
Das ist nicht Ihres Amtes!	Paddle your own canoe!; mind your P's and Q's!; that's none of your business!
Er ist in Amt und Würden.	He holds office.
Das Fräulein vom Amt hat eine Nachricht für Sie hinterlassen.	The (telephone) operator left a message for you.
Amtsmiene:	
Er steckte eine Amtsmiene auf.	He became stiff as a poker; he became very officious (*or* businesslike).
Amtsschimmel:	
In der Verwaltung herrscht der Amtsschimmel.	The administration is run by red tape.
an:	
Es ist an dem.	It's so; that's a fact.
Er hat das so an sich.	That's just his way.
Er ist an die dreißig Jahre alt.	He's going on thirty.
Der Gedanke ist an und für sich nicht schlecht.	The idea in itself is not a bad one.
Sie schreibt ab und an.	She writes now and then.
anbändeln:	
Er versuchte, mit ihr anzubändeln.	He gave her a come-hither look; he tried to make (*or* flirt with) her.
anbauen:	
Wo hat er sich angebaut?	Where did he settle down?
Anbeißen:	
Sie ist zum Anbeißen.	She looks good enough to eat; she's a peach (*or* honey).

anbiedern:
Er biedert sich überall an. — He's a yes-man (*or* handshaker); he bows and scrapes.

anbinden:
Binden Sie sich nicht mit dem an! — Don't pick a row with that man!; let him alone!

anbohren:
Er bohrte bei ihnen an, aber sie blieben stumm. — He tried to worm it out of them, but they kept mum (*or* still).

Andenken:
Bewahren Sie uns ein gutes Andenken! — Don't forget us!

ander:
Das ist nichts anderes. — That's all it amounts to.
Er besann sich eines andern. — He changed his mind.
Eins ins andere gerechnet. — Altogether; taken all in all.
Er wiederholte es einmal ums andere. — He repeated it over and over again.
Wenn man eins zum andern nimmt. — If you put two and two together.
Die Gewohnheit ist ihm zur andern Natur geworden. — The habit is second nature with him.
Sie ist in andern Umständen. — She's in the family way (*or* pregnant).

ändern:
Was man nicht kann ändern, muß man lassen schlendern. — What can't be cured must be endured.
Es läßt sich nicht ändern. — It can't be helped.

anders:
Er besann sich anders. — He changed his mind.
Ich denke nicht anders. — I think so too.
Er konnte nicht anders. — He couldn't help it; he had to.

anderthalb:
Auf einen Schelm gehören anderthalbe. — It takes a thief to catch a thief; pay rogues in their own coin!

andichten:
Man hat ihm das angedichtet. — He's been falsely accused of (*or* charged with) it.

andrehen:
Was drehen wir nun an? — Now what are we going to do?
Er drehte es ihnen an. — He palmed it off on them.

anecken:
Er hat bei ihnen angeeckt. — He offended them.

anfangen:
Mit ihm ist nichts anzufangen. — I can do nothing with him.

anfassen:
Er hat die Sache verkehrt angefaßt. — He started at the wrong end; he did it the wrong way.

anfechten:
Was ficht Sie an? — What's come over you?; what's the matter with you?
Er läßt es sich nicht anfechten. — He doesn't care (*or* mind it); it doesn't bother him.

Anflug:
Sie hat einen leichten Anflug von Erkältung. — She has a slight cold.

anführen:
Er läßt sich nicht so leicht anführen. | He's not so easily fooled (*or* taken in).

angeben:
Der gibt aber an! | Doesn't he lay it on thick?; what a bluff he is!

Was gebt ihr heute abend an? | What are you doing tonight?

angeblasen:
Er bekam die Erkältung wie angeblasen. | He caught cold all of a sudden.

angeblich:
Der angebliche Wert ist höher. | The nominal value is higher.

angebracht:
Das ist bei ihm nicht angebracht. | That won't get by with him; you can't pass that off on him; it's out of place here.

angebunden:
Er war kurz angebunden. | He was blunt (*or* to the point).

Angedenken:
Sein Vater seligen Angedenkens. | His late father.

angeflogen:
Ihr kommt alles wie angeflogen. | Things come easily to her; she learns quickly.

angegangen:
Das Fleisch schmeckt etwas angegangen. | The meat tastes a little tainted (*or* spoiled).

angegossen:
Der Rock sitzt ihr wie angegossen. | The coat fits her like a glove.

angegriffen:
Sie sah recht angegriffen aus. | She looked very tired.

angeheitert:
Die ganze Gesellschaft war etwas angeheitert. | The whole party was feeling a little gay (*or* high).

angehen:
Wie geht das Geschäft?—Es geht an. | How's business?—Pretty fair!; so so!; coming along!

Was geht Sie das an? | What business of yours is that?; what do you care?

Er hilft, so gut es angeht. | He does all he can.

angekränkelt:
Er ist nicht von Verbildung angekränkelt. | Education hasn't spoiled him.

Angel:
Er will alles aus den Angeln heben. | He wants to throw everything by the board (*or* make drastic changes).

Er sagte es ihnen zwischen Tür und Angel. | He told them at the last moment (*or* as he was leaving).

angelegen:
Er läßt sich den Plan sehr angelegen sein. | He takes a great interest in the project.

angelegentlich:
Er erkundigte sich angelegentlich nach ihr. | He showed a keen interest in her.

angeleimt:
Er saß wie angeleimt. | He sat there as if he didn't know when to go home; he couldn't be budged.

angeln:
  Nun kann sie sich einen andern angeln. — Now she may set her cap for someone else.
  Den will ich mir einmal angeln. — I'll lay down the law to that fellow; I'll get him yet.

angenagelt:
  Er blieb wie angenagelt stehen. — He remained rooted to the spot.

Angenehme:
  Er verband das Angenehme mit dem Nützlichen. — He combined business with pleasure.

angerichtet:
  Das Essen ist angerichtet. — Dinner is served.

angerückt:
  Da kommt er angerückt! — There he comes!

angesagt:
  Was für Wetter ist auf heute angesagt? — What's the weather forecast for today?

angesäuselt:
  Er war leise angesäuselt. — He was feeling happy; he had a few drinks in him.

angeschleift:
  Sie brachten ihn angeschleift. — They brought him along.

angeschossen:
  Er ist wütend wie ein angeschossener Eber. — He's mad as hops (*or* a wet hen).

angeschrieben:
  Er scheint oben gut angeschrieben zu sein. — He seems to be well liked by (*or* in favor with) his superiors.

angeschwirrt:
  Endlich kam er angeschwirrt. — He finally blew (*or* burst) in.

angestiefelt:
  Sie kam vergnügt angestiefelt. — She came in high spirits.

angestiegen:
  Eben kommen sie angestiegen! — Here they come!

angetan:
  Die Sache ist nicht danach angetan, ihn zu beunruhigen. — That can't disturb him.

angewandt:
  Das ist eine übel angewandte Nachsicht. — That's misplaced sympathy.

angewiesen:
  Sie ist ganz auf sich angewiesen. — She's (thrown) entirely on her own (resources); she takes care of herself.

angreifen:
  Die Krankheit hat ihn angegriffen. — The illness has told (*or* left its mark) on him.
  Er soll fremde Gelder angegriffen haben. — He is said to have embezzled money entrusted to him.

Angriff:
  Die Arbeit ist in Angriff genommen. — Work has been started; the job is under way.

angriffslustig:
  Er war in angriffslustiger Stimmung. — He had a chip on his shoulder; he was on the warpath (*or* in a quarrelsome mood).

angst:
   Ihr war angst und bange.

She was scared stiff (*or* to death).

Angsthase:
   Sie ist ein kleiner Angsthase.

She's chickenhearted; she's a fraidcat.

ängstlich:
   Es ist damit nicht so ängstlich.

No (need to) hurry!; take your time!

Angströhre:
   Lassen Sie doch die Angströhre daheim!

Leave your top (*or* silk) hat at home!

anhaben:
   Was kann er ihnen anhaben?

What (harm) can he do to them?

Anhalt:
   Sie hat keinen Anhalt zu der Vermutung.

Her suspicions are groundless.

anhalten:
   Er hat um sie angehalten.

He popped the question; he proposed to her.

anhaltend:
   Sie haben anhaltende Kälte.

They're having a long spell (*or* siege) of cold weather.

Anhang:
   Sie ist ohne Anhang.

She has no family; her relatives are all dead.

anhängen:
   Er hängt gern jedem etwas an.

He's an old mud-slinger; he enjoys painting everyone black.

Anhänger:
   Im Anhänger ist mehr Platz.

There's more room in the next car.

anhängig:
   Die Sache ist bei Gericht anhängig.

The trial is pending.

anhauchen:
   Er hauchte sie nicht schlecht an.

He sure(ly) told them a thing or two; boy, how he blew up at them!; that was some bawling-out he gave them!

anhauen:
   Lassen Sie uns den nächsten Besten anhauen!

Let's tackle (*or* talk to) the firstcomer!

Anhieb:
   Es gelang ihm auf Anhieb.

He succeeded right off the bat (*or* at once).

anhören:
   Man hört ihm den Deutschen an.

You can tell by his accent that he is German.

ankleben:
   Es klebt ihm noch immer an.

He'll never live it down; he can't get away (*or* escape) from it.

anklingen:
   Ihr Brief läßt viele Erinnerungen in meiner Seele anklingen.

Your letter reminds me of many things.

anklopfen:
   Klopfen Sie mal bei ihm an, was er dazu denkt!

Ask him (*or* See) what he thinks about it!; get his opinion on the matter!

anfommen:

Es kommt ihm sauer an.	It's a bitter pill for him to swallow; it's tough on (or difficult for) him.
Es kommt ihr auf ein paar Minuten nicht an.	A minute more or less won't matter to her.
Das kommt ganz auf Sie an.	That rests entirely with you.
Da kam er schön an.	He surely got a nice reception.
Wollen Sie es darauf ankommen lassen?	Will you take a chance?; will you risk it?

anfönnen:

Sie kann nicht dagegen an.	She can't help it.

anfrallen:

Er hatte die Stirn, uns anzukrallen.	He had the nerve to horn (or crowd) in on us.

Anfraß:

Das Mädel hat viel Ankraß.	The girl's a knockout (or honey); she has "it"; she's very popular.

anlassen:

Der Junge läßt sich gut an.	The boy is doing nicely.
Er ließ sie hart an.	He gave them the cold shoulder; he snubbed them.

Anlauf:

Er besiegte sie im ersten Anlauf.	He beat (or had the jump on) them from the start.

anlaufen:

Damit wird er übel anlaufen.	He'll get the worst of it.

anlegen:

Er legt es darauf an, sie zu ärgern.	He makes it a point to annoy them.

Anlehnung:

Er besprach den Fall in Anlehnung an das Textbuch.	He discussed the case with reference to the textbook.

Anliegen:

Bringen Sie Ihr Anliegen vor!	What's on your mind?; tell me what you want!

anmelden:

Melden Sie das Ferngespräch an!	Call long distance!
Er meldete sich schriftlich an.	He wrote to say that he was coming.

anmerken:

Man merkt ihm den Ausländer an der Sprache an.	One can tell from his speech that he's a foreigner.
Laß dir nichts anmerken!	Don't let on!

anmuten:

Es mutet ihn sonderbar an.	It strikes him as peculiar.

annehmen:

Sie nimmt sich des Hundes an.	She's minding (or looking after) the dog.

anniesen:

Ich fürchte, er wird uns anniesen.	I'm afraid he'll bawl us out.

anno:

Das war anno dazumal.	That was way back (or ages ago).
Es war anno Tobak.	That was way back; it happened in the year one.

anöden:
Er ödete sie mit seinem Geschwätz maßlos an. — He bored them to death with his prattle.
Der Kerl versuchte, uns anzuöden. — The fellow had a chip on his shoulder; he tried to pick a quarrel with us.

Anpfiff:
Er bezog einen Anpfiff. — He was called on the carpet; he got a dressing- (or calling-)down.

Anpflaumen:
Lassen Sie doch das ewige Anpflaumen! — Quit your kidding (or ribbing)!

anpumpen:
Hoffentlich pumpt er uns nicht an! — I hope he won't touch (or ask) us for any money!

anranzen:
Ich möchte nur wissen, warum er sie so angeranzt hat. — I'd just like to know why he high-hatted (or snubbed) her.

anreißen:
Die Firma reißt tüchtig an. — The firm is putting out a lot of bally-hoo; it's carrying on an intensive advertising campaign.

anrempeln:
Er möchte alle Leute anrempeln. — He has a chip on his shoulder; he's ready to pick a quarrel with anyone.

anrichten:
Da haben Sie aber was Schönes angerichtet! — Now you've started something!

anrüchig:
Sein Ruf ist höchst anrüchig. — He has a very bad rep(utation).

Anrudern:
Kommen Sie morgen zum Anrudern? — Will you be at the opening meet of the rowing club tomorrow?

ansagen:
Er hat sich zu Tisch angesagt. — He said he'd come for dinner.

anschicken:
Sie schickt sich nicht gut dazu an. — She can't get into the swing of it; she can't make the grade.

anschlagen:
Bei dem schlägt nichts mehr an. — He's a hopeless case.
Man schlägt sein Talent zu niedrig an. — His ability is underrated.
Nun schlägt sie das Thema schon wieder an. — There she goes harping on the same string; she's bringing up the same old story again.

anschmieren:
Er hat sie tüchtig angeschmiert. — He surely pulled the wool over their eyes.

anschmusen:
Er suchte sich bei ihm anzuschmusen. — He played up to him; he tried to curry favor with him.

Anschnauzer:
Er bezog einen üblen Anschnauzer von seinem Vorgesetzten. — His boss gave him hell (or called him down severely).

anſchneiden:
Laſſen Sie uns die Frage anſchneiden! — Let's broach the subject!

anſchreiben:
Schreiben Sie die Rechnung an! — Put it on the cuff, please!; charge it!

anſehen:
Sieh mal einer an! — What do you know about that!
Man ſieht es ihm an. — You can tell by looking at him; it's written all over his face.
Er konnte es nicht mehr mit anſehen. — He couldn't take (or put up with) it any longer.

Anſehen:
Er gibt ſich gern ein Anſehen. — He likes to show off (or put on the dog).
Er beurteilt die Menſchen ohne Anſehen der Perſon. — He judges people indiscriminately; he's no respecter of persons.

anſetzen:
Wie hoch ſetzen Sie das Haus an? — At what figure do you value the house?

Anſprache:
Das Mädchen hat keine Anſprache. — The girl lacks charm; she isn't very popular; she's a lemon (or unattractive).

anſprechen:
Das Ergebnis iſt als günſtig anzuſprechen. — The result must be regarded as favorable.

anſpringen:
Endlich ſprang der Motor an. — At last the motor began to run.

Anſpruch:
Die Billigkeit ſeines Anſpruchs iſt klar. — That much he's certainly entitled to.
Er iſt ſtark in Anſpruch genommen. — He's up to his neck in business; he's a very busy man.

Anſtalt:
Er machte keine Anſtalten zu gehen. — He made no move to go.

Anſtand:
Er hat keinen Anſtand. — He has no breeding; he's a boor.
Er nahm keinen Anſtand, es ihm zu ſagen. — He didn't hesitate to tell (or mind telling) him.

anſtändig:
Laſſen Sie uns die Sache auf anſtändige Weiſe erledigen! — Let's have fair play!; let's handle this squarely!

Anſtandswauwau:
Sie ſpielte bei dem geſtrigen Tanz den Anſtandswauwau. — At the dance last night she acted as a fire extinguisher (or chaperon).

anſtehen:
Ich ſtehe nicht an, Ihnen das zu ſagen. — I don't mind telling you; I have no qualms about telling you.
Das ſteht ihm wohl an. — That suits him well.
Laſſen wir es damit noch anſtehen! — Let's drop it (or put it off for a while)!

anſtellen:
Stell dich doch nicht ſo an! — Don't make such a fuss!; stop carrying on so!
Was haben Sie denn nun angeſtellt? — Now what have you been up to?

anſtoßen:
Stoßt an! — Here's how!; let's make a toast!
Er möchte nicht anſtoßen. — He wouldn't want to offend anyone.

anstreichen:

Streichen Sie den Tag rot im Kalender an! — Make this a red-letter day!

Das werde ich ihm aber anstreichen. — I'll pay him back for that!; I'll get even with him yet!

anstrengen:

Er will einen Prozeß gegen sie anstrengen. — He plans to take the matter to court; he intends to bring legal action (*or* start suit) against them.

antanzen:

Können Sie heute zum Abendbrot antanzen? — Can you drop in for dinner tonight?

antippen:

Tippen Sie mal bei ihm an, ob er Lust hat mitzugehen! — Just drop a hint (*or* sound him out) to see if he would care to come along!

Antrieb:

Hierzu fehlt jeder Antrieb. — There's no point in (*or* reason for doing) that; the incentive is lacking.

Er kam aus eignem Antrieb. — He came of his own accord (*or* free will).

antun:

Tun Sie uns doch das nicht an! — At least spare us this (humiliation)!

Sie hat's ihm angetan. — He fell for her; he lost his heart to her.

Antwort:

Er muß Rede und Antwort stehen. — He has to explain (*or* account for) himself; he has to submit to a cross-examination.

anwandeln:

Was wandelt Sie an? — What's the matter with you?; what has come over you?

anwerfen:

Wirf den Motor an! — Give her the gas!; start the motor!

Anwesende:

Sehr verehrte Anwesende! — Ladies and gentlemen!

anzapfen:

Er wurde beim Essen schwer angezapft. — They kidded him unmercifully (*or* made much fun of him) during the dinner.

Er wollte uns um drei Mark anzapfen. — He tried to bleed us of three marks.

Apfel:

Der Apfel fällt nicht weit vom Stamm. — Like father, like son; he's a chip off the old block.

Er mußte in den sauren Apfel beißen. — He had to swallow the bitter pill; he had to take his medicine; he had to suffer the consequences.

Aplomb:

Er flog mit Aplomb aus der Firma. — The firm dropped him on the spot (*or* then and there).

Er trat mit großem Aplomb auf. — He was cocksure of himself; he appeared very self-conscious.

Apotheker:

Da haben Sie aber beim Apotheker gekauft! — That dealer must have seen you coming; you certainly paid well (*or* an exorbitant price) for that.

Apparat:
Sie werden am Apparat gewünscht. | You're wanted on the phone.

Appelmus:
Er war gerührt wie Appelmus (=Apfel= | He was quite touched.
mus).

appetitlich:
Das Kind sieht appetitlich aus. | It's a good-looking (or an attractive) child.

April:
Sie ist launisch wie der April. | She's changeable as the weather; she's like the wind.

Er wurde in den April geschickt. | He was taken for a ride; they made a fool of him.

Arbeit:
Arbeit macht das Leben süß. | No sweet without sweat.
Er ist bei ihnen in Arbeit. | He's in their employ.
Er lebt von seiner Hände Arbeit. | He lives by the sweat of his brow.

Arbeitsprozeß:
Mehr Leute wurden in den Arbeits= | More people were given jobs (or hired).
prozeß eingegliedert.

arg:
Das ist doch zu arg! | That's going too far!
Er hat sie arg erschreckt. | He frightened them to death.
Es liegt sehr im argen. | It's a terrible mess (or sorry state of affairs); things have come to a sorry pass.

Er ist in arger Verlegenheit, das zu er= | He can't for the life of him account for it; he's quite at a loss to explain that.
klären.

ärgern:
Mensch, ärgere dich nicht! | Don't let it get you, old boy!; cheer up!

Arkadien:
Der Kerl ist in Arkadien geboren. | He's a regular boor (or hayseed); he comes from the sticks (or backwoods).

arm:
Er ißt uns noch arm. | He'll eat us out of house and home.

Arm:
Er hat einen langen Arm. | He has pull (or great influence).
Er lief uns gerade in die Arme. | He ran right into us.
Nimm die Beine untern Arm! | Shake a leg!; step on it!; make it snappy!
Können Sie mir mit einer Mark unter | Could you help me out with a mark?
die Arme greifen?

Ärmel:
Er schüttelte seine Antworten nur so aus | He had the answers at his fingertips; he always had a ready answer.
dem Ärmel.

Armutszeugnis:
Damit hat er sich selber ein Armutszeugnis | With that he sealed his own doom; he thereby proved his own lack (or incapacity).
ausgestellt.

Art:
Art läßt nicht von Art. | Birds of a feather flock together; every cat to her kind.

Das ist doch keine Art! | You should be ashamed of yourself!; that's no way to do (or be)!

Er schafft, daß es eine Art hat. | He works like sixty (or to beat the band).

Das hat keine Art.	There's no style to that; that's not right; that won't do.
Er verſuchte es auf alle Art und Weiſe.	He tried it every which (or possible) way.
Er iſt aus der Art geſchlagen.	He's a lone wolf (or an outsider).
Der Fall iſt einzig in ſeiner Art.	The case is unique.

artig:

Sei fein artig!	Be good!
Das iſt ſehr artig von Ihnen!	You're being very nice!; that's very kind of you!

Aſche:

Friede ſeiner Aſche!	May he rest in peace!
Es gab ungebrannte Aſche.	The sparks flew; blows fell.

Aſchgraue:

Das geht ins Aſchgraue.	That's going too far.

Aſt:

Damit ſägt er ſich den Aſt ab, auf dem er ſitzt.	He's cutting his own throat; he's cutting off his nose to spite his face.
Er lachte ſich einen Aſt.	He nearly split his sides (or died laughing).
Er iſt auf dem abſteigenden Aſt.	He's on the skids (or slipping); he's on the downgrade.

Atem:

Er ſtieß den letzten Atem aus.	He breathed his last.
Eine ganze Reihe von kleineren Fällen hielt die Polizei in Atem.	A whole slew (or flock) of lesser cases kept the police on the go.
Laſſen Sie ihn ein wenig zu Atem kommen!	Give him a little breathing spell!

a tempo:

Er ging a tempo heim.	He went home at once.

Athen:

Er trägt Eulen nach Athen.	He carries coals to Newcastle; he's wasting his time (or energy).

ätſch:

Ätſch!	See, what did I tell you?; serves you right!

auch:

Auch gut!	Good again!
Iſt es auch ſo?	Is it really so?; is that true?
Haben Sie ihn auch geſehen?	Are you sure you saw him?
Sie haben da einen feinen Hut.—Er hat aber auch genug gekoſtet.	That's a nice hat you've got there.—It ought to be; it cost enough.
Wie dem auch ſein mag.	Be that as it may.
Ohne auch nur zu fragen.	Without so much as asking.
Er hat recht. Ich auch.	He's right. So am I.
Iſt er auch' fort?	Has he gone, too?
Iſt' er auch fort?	Has he really gone?
Er iſt nicht da. Sie auch nicht.	He isn't here. Neither is she.

auf:

Auf der Uhr iſt es acht.	It's eight by that clock.
Es geht auf Mitternacht.	It's almost (or going on) midnight.
Er kam viertel auf drei.	He came at quarter past two.
Er hat das Zimmer auf vierzehn Tage gemietet.	He rented the room for two weeks.

Er ging auf meine Bitte.	He left at my request.
Wie heißt das auf deutſch?	What's this called in German?; how do you say it in German?
Es hat nichts auf ſich.	It's o.k. (*or* all right); it's of no consequence.
Glück auf!	Good luck!
Er lebte dort von klein auf.	He lived there from childhood.
Draußen geht einer auf und ab.	Someone is walking back and forth outside.
Machen Sie ſich auf und davon!	Beat it!; off with you!; begone!

aufbauſchen:

Er bauſchte die Sache mächtig auf. — He made a mountain out of a molehill; he exaggerated the matter.

aufbieten:

Er bot alles auf, die Stelle zu bekommen. — He made every effort to secure the position.

aufbremſen:

Ich werde ihm eins aufbremſen. — I'll sock (*or* hit) him one.

aufdrängen:

Ein Gedanke drängt ſich mir auf. — I've got an idea; it occurs to me.

aufdrehen:

Er hatte mächtig aufgedreht. — He was all pepped up (*or* very much alive).

auffallen:

Es fiel ihm sogleich auf. — He noticed it at once.

auffallend:

Sie ist so auffallend! — She looks a fright!; she's a sight to behold!

auffliegen:

Der Verein flog auf. — The club disbanded.

auffriſchen:

Er will sein Deutſch auffriſchen. — He wants to brush up on his German.

aufgabeln:

Wo haben Sie denn das aufgegabelt? — Where did you pick that up?

aufgeben:

Geben Sie den Brief auf! — Mail the letter!

Aufgebot:

Er arbeitete unter Aufgebot aller seiner Kräfte. — He summoned every ounce of strength to the task; he worked like a horse.

aufgedonnert:

Sie war ſchrecklich aufgedonnert. — She was all decked out (*or* dolled up); she was dressed to kill.

aufgehen:

Er geht ganz in seiner Arbeit auf. — He's all wrapped up in his work.

Das Herz ging ihr auf vor Freude. — Her heart swelled with pride.

aufgehoben:

Der Junge ist da gut aufgehoben. — The boy is in good hands there.

aufgeknöpft:

Er war mächtig aufgeknöpft. — He was very free and easy (*or* jovial).

aufgekratzt:

Sie war sehr aufgekratzt. — She was gay as a lark.

aufgelegt:

Er ist heute zu allem aufgelegt. — He feels his oats today; he's looking for trouble.

aufgeſchmiſſen:

Ohne Geld sind wir aufgeſchmiſſen. — Without money we're out of luck (*or* stuck).

aufgeweckt:

Er ist ein aufgeweckter Junge. — He's a bright, intelligent boy.

aufhalsen:

Sie haben sich da eine schwierige Aufgabe aufgehalst. — You certainly bit off a big chunk (*or* took a load upon yourself); that's a difficult problem you've saddled yourself with.

Er halste ihnen Schund auf. — He palmed rubbish off on them; he stuck them with junk.

aufhalten:

Halten Sie sich doch nicht bei Kleinigkeiten auf! — Don't waste your time on trifles!

Er hielt sich über alles auf. — He kicked (*or* complained) about everything.

aufhängen:

Er hat ihnen schlechte Ware aufgehängt. — He palmed inferior goods off on them.

aufheben:

Sollen wir die Tafel aufheben? — Shall we leave the table?

Aufheben:

Mach doch nicht soviel Aufhebens davon! — Don't make such a fuss about it!

aufhören:

Da hört sich doch alles auf! — That's the limit!; that beats all!

aufkommen:

Er läßt niemand neben sich aufkommen. — He won't brook any rivals.

Dafür müssen Sie nun auch aufkommen! — You'll have to pay the piper!; you'll suffer for that!

aufkriegen:

Sie kriegen doch noch diese Portion auf? — You'll be able to get that down (*or* eat that up), won't you?

aufmerksam:

Das war sehr aufmerksam von Ihnen! — That was very considerate (*or* thoughtful) of you!

aufmucken:

Plötzlich muckte er auf. — He suddenly took the bit in his teeth; he bridled up (*or* got sore).

aufnehmen:

Er nimmt es mit jedem auf. — He's ready (*or* a match) for anybody.

aufpacken:

Da hat er sich was Schönes aufgepackt. — He certainly bit off a big chunk; he took a great responsibility upon himself.

aufraffen:

Er kann sich zu keinem Entschluß aufraffen. — He can't make up his mind (*or* come to a decision).

aufrappeln:

Er hat sich bald wieder aufgerappelt. — He soon pulled through (*or* recovered).

aufräumen:

Er hat mit den Verbrechern nicht schlecht aufgeräumt. — He made a clean sweep of (*or* did away with) the gangsters.

aufreiben:

Die Arbeit reibt ihn auf. — The job is getting him down (*or* wearing him out).

aufrichtig:
Das freut mich aber aufrichtig. | That really pleases me; I'm delighted to hear it.

auffagen:
Sie sagten ihm die Freundschaft auf. | They broke with him.

auffchlagen:
Schlagen Sie Seite zehn auf! | Turn to page ten!
Alles schlägt auf. | Prices are going up.

auffchneiden:
Schneid doch nicht so auf! | Don't blow so hard (*or* lay it on so thick!); don't brag so much!

auffitzen:
Er ließ sie auffitzen. | He put one over on them; he fooled them.

auffpielen:
Sie spielt sich gern auf. | She likes to put on airs (*or* the dog); she likes to show off.

aufftacheln:
Man hatte ihn dazu aufgestachelt. | He was egged on to it.

auffteden:
Stecken Sie's auf! | Give it up (for lost)!
Er hat bei dem Geschäft nichts aufgesteckt. | He didn't make much on that deal.

auffteigen:
Ein Gedanke steigt in mir auf. | I've got an idea; it occurs to me.

aufftöbern:
Wo er das Buch nur aufgestöbert hat? | I wonder where he unearthed (*or* came across) the book?

aufftoßen:
Das könnte ihm noch sauer aufstoßen. | That might have unpleasant consequences for him.

auftifchen:
Tischen Sie doch nicht immer wieder die alten Geschichten auf! | Don't dish up (*or* tell) the same old stories time and again!

auftragen:
Er trägt immer stark auf. | He always lays it on thick; he's an awful bluffer.

auftreiben:
Er ist nirgends aufzutreiben. | He can't be located (*or* found) anywhere.
Er vermochte kein Geld aufzutreiben. | He couldn't raise the money.

auftreten:
Es war höchste Zeit, daß er einmal dagegen auftrat. | It was high time he put his foot down.

Auftrieb:
Er hat keinen Auftrieb. | He has no push (*or* ambition).

auftrumpfen:
Sie sollten ihm einmal auftrumpfen. | You should speak plainly to him; tell him what's what!; give him a piece of your mind!

Aufwafchen:
Das geht in einem Aufwaschen hin. | That's killing two birds with one stone.

aufwerfen:

Er warf sich zum Sprecher auf.	He set himself up as spokesman.
Die Frage wurde aufgeworfen.	The question was raised.

aufzählen:

Er zählte das Geld bar auf.	He planked down the cash.

aufziehen:

Sie zogen ihn auf.	They made fun of him.
Man hatte den Prozeß echt amerikanisch aufgezogen.	The trial was conducted in the usual sensational American fashion.

Aufzug:

Er kann doch nicht in dem Aufzug fort.	He can't go in that getup (or dressed like that).

Augapfel:

Er hütet das Tier wie seinen Augapfel.	The animal is the apple of his eye; he cares for it as he would for himself.

Auge:

Da bleibt kein Auge trocken!	It's enough to make one cry.
Die Augen brachen ihm.	He was dying.
Was die Augen sehen, glaubt das Herz.	Seeing is believing.
Vier Augen sehen mehr als zwei.	Two heads are better than one.
Er drückte ein Auge zu.	He connived (or winked) at it; he let it pass.
Machen Sie die Augen auf!	Snap out of it!; wake up!
Eine Krähe hackt der andern die Augen nicht aus.	There's honor among thieves.
Machen Sie die Augen ein wenig zu!	Take forty winks (or a nap)!
Er hat keine Augen dafür.	He isn't interested.
Er sieht ihr alles an den Augen ab.	He anticipates her every wish.
Er setzte ihnen den Daumen aufs Auge.	He brought pressure to bear upon them; he kept a tight rein on them.
Das paßt wie die Faust aufs Auge.	That's a lot of hooey; it's preposterous (or ridiculous).
Seine Familie steht nur noch auf zwei Augen.	There's only one member of his family left.
Aus den Augen, aus dem Sinn.	Out of sight, out of mind.
Er ist seiner Mutter wie aus den Augen geschnitten.	He's the very image of his mother; he's a chip off the old block.
Man behält ihn scharf im Auge.	They've got him shadowed; they keep close watch on him.
Man gönnt ihm nicht das Weiße im Auge.	They begrudge him the very shirt on his back.
Er hat das im Auge.	He has that in view; he's considering it.
In meinen Augen hat er recht.	In my opinion, he's right.
Die Anzeige fiel ihm ins Auge.	The ad(vertisement) caught his eye.
Er schlug das Kalb ins Auge.	He made a break (or faux pas); he was tactless.
Sie sehen den Tatsachen ins Auge.	They're facing the facts.
Das fällt in die Augen.	That hits one in the eye; it's conspicuous.
Er sah ihr zu tief in die Augen.	He fell in love with her.
Der Hut stach ihr in die Augen.	The hat took her eye (or fancy).
Er kam mit einem blauen Auge davon.	He got off pretty easy; he escaped by the skin of his teeth.
Der Junge schläft mit offnen Augen.	The boy is wool-gathering (or day-dreaming).

Komm mir nicht wieder unter die Augen!	Never let me see your face again!
Sie hatten ein Gespräch unter vier Augen.	They had a *tête-à-tête* (*or* confidential talk).
Da fiel ihm die Binde von den Augen.	Then he saw the light; it dawned on him.
Das liegt vor Augen.	That's apparent (*or* evident).
Es schwamm ihm vor den Augen.	His brain was swimming; his head was in a whirl.

Äugelchen:

Sie machte ihm Äugelchen.	She made eyes at him; she gave him a come-hither look; she flirted with him.

Augenmaß:

Er hat kein politisches Augenmaß.	He has no political acumen.

Augenpulver:

Diese Schrift ist das reine Augenpulver.	This scrawl is hard on the eyes.

Augenschein:

Sie können sich durch Augenschein davon überzeugen.	Just go and see for yourself!

Augenweide:

Sie ist eine rechte Augenweide.	She's a peach (*or* honey); she's a looker (*or* sight for sore eyes).

aus:

Er hat das Buch aus.	He has finished the book.
Mit ihm ist's aus.	He's done for; it's all over with him.
Das Spiel ist aus.	The game is up (*or* lost).
Er ist darauf aus, sie zu betrügen.	He's bent on buffaloing (*or* cheating) them.
Er sah uns vom Fenster aus.	He saw us from the window.
Er weiß weder ein noch aus.	He's at his wits' end; he doesn't know which way to turn.
Er geht bei ihnen ein und aus.	He's a frequent caller at their house.

ausbaden:

Nun kann er die Geschichte auch ausbaden.	Now let him face the music (*or* take the consequences).

ausbeißen:

Lassen Sie ihn die Zähne daran ausbeißen!	Let him try (his teeth on) it!; let him have a try at it!

ausbitten:

Das bitte ich mir aber aus!	I must insist on that.

ausbleiben:

Seine Strafe soll nicht ausbleiben.	He won't get out of his punishment.

ausbrechen:

Jetzt bricht's aber aus!	Now the fun begins!; here we go!

ausbringen:

Sie brachten seine Gesundheit aus.	They drank his health.

ausbuddeln:

Wo haben Sie dieses Buch ausgebuddelt?	I wonder where you dug up this book?

Ausbund:

Er ist ein wahrer Ausbund von Gelehrsamkeit.	He's a walking encyclopedia; he's a bundle of learning (*or* a real scholar).

ausdehnen:

Sie sollten das nicht auf jedermann ausdehnen.	You shouldn't apply that to everybody.

ausdenken:
Die Folgen sind nicht auszudenken.

One can't begin to visualize all the consequences.

ausdienen:
Der Anzug hat ausgedient.

The suit has served its turn.

Auseinandersetzung:
Es kam zu einer scharfen Auseinandersetzung zwischen den beiden.

They exchanged hard words.

ausessen:
Nun kann er auch ausessen, was er sich eingebrockt hat.

Now he must pay the piper (or price); let him suffer the consequences of his action.

ausfallend:
Er wurde ausfallend.

He became insulting (or personal).

Ausflucht:
Er hat immer Ausflüchte zur Hand.

He always has a way out (or an alibi).

Ausfluß:
Es war nur ein Ausfluß seiner schlechten Laune.

He just happened to be sulky (or in the dumps).

ausfressen:
Was hat er jetzt wieder ausgefressen?

What new cain has he raised?; now what has he been up to?

ausführen:
Jemand hat ihm den Hut ausgeführt.

Somebody snatched his hat.

Ausgang:
Die Magd hat heute ihren Ausgang.

The maid has her afternoon off today.

ausgeben:
Er gab sich für einen Schriftsteller aus.

He posed (or passed himself off) as a writer.

ausgebeutelt:
Er ist vollkommen ausgebeutelt.

He's flat broke; he hasn't a cent to his name.

ausgebrannt:
Ihm war die Kehle vor Durst wie ausgebrannt.

He was dry as a gourd; his throat was parched.

ausgedehnt:
Er verfügt über ausgedehnte Kenntnisse.

He's exceedingly well informed.

ausgefallen:
Was für eine ausgefallene Idee das ist!

What a silly idea!

ausgeglichen:
Er ist ein ausgeglichener Charakter.

He has poise.

ausgehen:
Ich fürchte, das geht nicht gut für ihn aus.

I'm afraid it will get him in Dutch (or hot water).

Er geht nur darauf aus.
Das Geld ging ihm aus.

That's just his object.
He ran short of money.

ausgekocht:
Er ist ein ausgekochter Geselle.

He's a sly old codger.

ausgelassen:
Sie war ausgelassen vor Freude.

She was exuberant (or in high spirits); she was beside herself with joy.

ausgelernt:

Er ist ein ausgelernter Spitzbube. | He's a wise guy (*or* an old rascal).

ausgemacht:

Er nahm das als ausgemacht an. | He took that for granted.

Er ist ein ausgemachter Spitzbube. | He's an out-and-out rogue.

ausgepicht:

Der Kerl ist ausgepicht. | He's a tough customer (*or* hard-boiled egg); he's a hard nut to crack.

Er hat eine ausgepichte Kehle. | He's a regular tank (*or* sponge); he can drink enough to float a battleship.

ausgeprägt:

Er besitzt einen scharf ausgeprägten Charakter. | He has a strong character; he's a strong-minded person (*or* an outstanding personality).

ausgerechnet:

Ausgerechnet heute muß der Mensch kommen! | Today of all days he has to come!

ausgeschlossen:

Ganz ausgeschlossen! | Absolutely not!; not on your life!

ausgetauscht:

Der Junge ist wie ausgetauscht. | He's like a new boy.

ausgezeichnet:

Das paßt mir ausgezeichnet. | That's swell; that suits me to a T.

ausgiebig:

Machen Sie ausgiebig davon Gebrauch! | Use (it) all you want!

ausgleichen:

Das gleicht sich auch wieder aus. | It's always tit for tat; it may be your turn next.

ausgucken:

Er hat sich fast die Augen danach ausgeguckt. | He almost wore his eyes out looking for it.

aushaken:

Jetzt hakt's aber aus! | That takes the cake (*or* beats all)!; that's the last straw!

Bei dem hat's ausgehakt. | He's a total flop (*or* failure).

aushalten:

Sie hält den Menschen aus. | She's his meal ticket; she supports him.

Er hält nirgends lange aus. | He never stays (*or* lasts) long in one place.

Er kann viel aushalten. | He can take it; he can put up with a lot.

Mit ihm ist nicht auszuhalten. | Nobody can stand him.

aushecken:

Das kann nur er ausgeheckt haben. | That's just like him; only he could have thought that one up.

ausholen:

Ich muß ihn mal darüber ausholen. | I must sound him out on the matter.

auskennen:

Er kennt sich darin aus. | He knows the ropes; he knows his onions (*or* business).

Er kannte sich nicht mehr aus. | He didn't know which way to turn; he was at his wits' end.

ausklaffen:
    Hoffentlich klafft er nicht aus.   I hope he won't squeal (*or* let the cat out of the bag); I hope he doesn't talk.

auskneifen:
    Unser Hund kniff gestern aus.   Our dog gave us the slip (*or* ran away) yesterday.

ausknobeln:
    Er kann nicht ausknobeln, wie sie das gemacht haben.   He can't figure out how they did it.

auskommen:
    Sie können miteinander nicht auskommen.   They can't get along together.

Auskommen:
    Sie haben ihr knappes Auskommen.   They're just getting by (*or* making ends meet).

auskramen:
    Er kramte allerlei Neuigkeiten aus.   He came out with (*or* divulged) all sorts of news.

auskratzen:
    Der Verbrecher wollte eben auskratzen, als die Polizei eintraf.   The gunman was on the point of skipping out by the time the police arrived.

auskundschaften:
    Versuchen Sie es auszukundschaften!   Try to smoke (*or* find) it out!

auslachen:
    Laß dich nicht auslachen!   Don't make a fool of yourself!

auslegen:
    Er legte den Betrag für sie aus.   He advanced them the money.
    Man wird das übel auslegen.   They'll take it wrong; they'll put an evil construction on it.

ausleiden:
    Er hat ausgelitten.   He gave up the ghost; his sufferings are over; he is dead.

auslernen:
    Man lernt nie aus.   One is never too old to learn.

auslöffeln:
    Was man sich eingebrockt hat, muß man auch auslöffeln.   One must reap what one has sown; now that you've made your bed, you must lie in it; you will have to pay the piper.

ausmachen:
    Machen Sie das miteinander aus!   You may settle that among yourselves!
    Das macht nichts aus.   That's all right; never mind!; it makes no difference.
    Wieviel macht es aus?   How much does it come to?

ausmalen:
    Malen Sie sich das einmal aus!   Imagine that!; just fancy!

ausmären:
    Mären Sie sich nun endlich aus!   Please wind (*or* finish) up now!

ausmünzen:
    Er hat das zu verschiedenen Sachen ausgemünzt.   He made various uses of it.

ausnahmsweise:
Stimmt das?—Ausnahmsweise ja! | Is that correct?—Yes, for once (*or* a wonder)!

ausnehmen:
Das nimmt sich schlecht aus. | That doesn't look so hot (*or* good).

ausposaunen:
Sie brauchen das nicht gleich auszuposaunen. | You don't need to shout that from the housetops; you needn't broadcast it.

ausrangieren:
Er wurde wegen seines Alters ausrangiert. | He was shelved (*or* dismissed) on account of his age.

ausreißen:
Sein Hund ist ihm gestern ausgerissen. | His dog gave him the slip (*or* ran away) yesterday.

ausrichten:
Damit richtet er nichts aus. | That won't get him anywhere; it won't do him any good.

Haben Sie meine Bestellung ausgerichtet? | Did you deliver my order?

Bei ihm können Sie nichts ausrichten. | You can't prevail upon (*or* influence) him.

aussabbern:
Sabber dich aus! | Pipe down!; shut up!

aussaugen:
Er wurde von seinem Gläubiger bis auf den letzten Heller ausgesaugt. | His creditor mulcted him; he squeezed the last penny out of him.

Ausschank:
Kommen Sie herein in meinen Ausschank! | Come in and see my hangout (*or* place)!

ausschauen:
Wie schaut's aus? | How's the world treating you?; how's tricks?; how are you?

ausschiffen:
Der Minister wurde aus dem Kabinett ausgeschifft. | The minister was given the ax (*or* gate); he was ousted.

ausschlachten:
Die Presse hat den Fall weidlich ausgeschlachtet. | The press went to town on (*or* made the most of) this case.

Ausschlag:
Das gab der Sache den Ausschlag. | That turned the tide (*or* decided the issue).

Ausschluß:
Die Sache wurde unter Ausschluß der Öffentlichkeit verhandelt. | The case was heard behind locked doors.

Ausschnitt:
Er sah nur einen Ausschnitt des amerikanischen Lebens. | He saw merely a cross-section of life in America.

Ausschuß:
Sie sahen nur den Ausschuß des Pöbels. | They went slumming; they saw only the riffraff.

ausschütten:
Er wollte sich vor Lachen ausschütten. | He nearly split his sides; he nearly died laughing.

ausschweigen:
   Sie schweigt sich darüber aus.

She shuts up like a clam; she keeps mum (*or* silent) on that point.

aussehen:
   So siehst du gerade aus!
   Er sieht mir nicht danach aus.

You would!; not on your life!
I wouldn't expect him to; he's not that kind of a person.

   Es sieht mir ganz danach aus.

It looks very much like it to me.

äußer:
   Sein äußerer Mensch sah herabgekommen aus.

He was down at the heel; he looked seedy (*or* shabby).

Äußerlichkeit:
   Sie hängt sehr an Äußerlichkeiten.

She stands very much on ceremony; she's a stickler for form.

Äußerste:
   Kampf bis aufs Äußerste!
   Er geht bis zum Äußersten.

War to the finish!; shoot to kill!
He'll go the limit; he won't stop at anything (short of the grave).

   Wenn es zum Äußersten kommt.

If worse comes to worst; if it comes to a showdown.

aussetzen:
   Sie setzen sich dabei einer Zurückweisung aus.

You're asking to be snubbed.

   Er hat an allem was auszusetzen.

He kicks (*or* complains) about everything.

ausspannen:
   Jemand hat ihm das Rad ausgespannt.
   Sie sollten einmal gründlich ausspannen.

Someone copped (*or* swiped) his bicycle.
What you need is a good long rest.

ausspielen:
   Er hat ausgespielt.

He's done for.

ausstechen:
   Er stach alle seine Konkurrenten aus.

He outstripped (*or* outsmarted) all his competitors; he beat them to the draw; his business led the field.

   Lassen Sie uns eine Pulle Wein miteinander ausstechen!

Let's kill (*or* drink) a bottle of wine together!

ausstehen:
   Er hat noch Geld ausstehen.

He still has money coming to him.

aussteigen:
   Berlin, alles aussteigen!

Berlin, all out!

Aussterbeetat:
   Der Anzug steht auf dem Aussterbeetat.

The suit is on its last legs (*or* done for); it will have to be discarded.

austoben:
   Jugend muß sich austoben.

Youth must have its fling; youth will sow its wild oats.

Austrag:
   Wann kommt die Meisterschaft zum Austrag?

When will the championship be decided?

austragen:
   Das trägt nicht viel aus.

That cuts no ice; that makes little difference.

Ausübung:

Er starb in Ausübung seines Berufes. | He died with his boots on (*or* in harness); he died on the job.

Auswachsen:

Es war zum Auswachsen. | It was enough to drive one crazy.

auswärts:

Sie wohnen jetzt auswärts. | They now live out of town.

ausweisen:

Das wird sich schon ausweisen. | We shall see what we shall see; time will tell.

auswischen:

Ich werde ihm gelegentlich eins auswischen. | I'll give it to him some day; I'll land on him sometime.

auszahlen:

Er hat sich dabei tüchtig ausgezahlt. | He gave himself an awful beating; he hurt himself quite badly.

Axt:

Er suchte der Axt einen Stiel. | He looked for a good excuse.

Er versprach, die Axt an die Wurzel zu legen. | He promised to make radical (*or* drastic) changes.

B

B:
Wer A sagt, muß auch B sagen.

You made your bed—now lie in it!; you'll have to pay the piper (*or* suffer the consequences).

Babchen:
Er verlor sein ganzes Habchen und Babchen.

He lost the shirt off his back; he lost everything he owned.

Backe:
Au Backe!
Er nahm die Backen voll.
Man hat ihm die Backen wattiert.
Dem kann man das Vaterunser durch die Backen blasen.

Gosh!; golly!; great Scott!
He blew off (steam); he talked big.
He got his face slapped.
He's nothing but skin and bones.

backenbleiben:
Der Junge ist backengeblieben.

The boy flunked out (*or* was held back) in school.

Backofen:
Er gähnt gegen den Backofen.

He's fighting a losing battle; the odds are too great for him.

Bad:
Er muß das Bad austragen.

He has to pay the piper (*or* suffer the consequences).

Man wird ihm das Bad schon gesegnen.
Er ist ins Bad gefahren.
Er hat das Kind mit dem Bad ausgeschüttet.

They'll make it hot for him.
He went to a spa.
He threw good money after bad; he rejected both the good and the bad; he acted without discretion.

Bader:
Er ist aus einem Bader ein Bischof geworden.

He's risen from corporal to field marshal.

baff:
Sie war baff.

She couldn't say boo (*or* a word); she was dumbfounded.

Bählamm:
Er ist ein richtiges Bählamm.

He's a regular jackass.

Bahn:
Er brach einer neuen Ansicht Bahn.

He was the originator of a new idea; he thought that one up.

Er brachte ein andres Thema auf die Bahn.
Er ist auf der schiefen Bahn.

He introduced another subject.
He's on the skids; he's sliding downhill; he's going to the dogs.

Man brachte sie nach der Bahn.

They saw her off (on the train).

bald:
Bald spricht er so, bald so.
First he's for it and then against it; he straddles the fence.

Ich hätte bald was gesagt!
Well, I never!

Das ist bald getan.
That's easily done.

Balken:
Er lügt, daß sich die Balken biegen.
He lies like a trooper; he's a shameless liar.

Wasser hat keine Balken.
Praise the sea but keep on land!; keep your feet on the ground!; play safe!

ballfähig:
Sie ist gerade erst ballfähig.
She's still in her teens.

Ballon:
Er hat den Ballon voller Sorgen.
He's up to his neck in worry.

Sein Chef hat ihm eins auf den Ballon gegeben.
His boss jacked him up (or bawled him out).

Bammel:
Sie haben mächtig Bammel davor.
They're scared to death of it.

Band:
Der Junge geriet über das Geschenk außer Rand und Band.
The boy went wild over the present; he was crazy about (or thrilled with) it.

Bändel:
Er hatte seine Aufgabe am Bändel.
He had the lesson at his fingertips.

Sie führt ihn am Bändel herum.
She leads him around by the nose; he's tied to her apron strings.

Bandwurm:
Das ist ein wahrer Bandwurm von einem Satz.
That's a whale of a sentence; it's terribly involved.

Bangbüchs:
Er ist eine große Bangbüchs.
He's a jellyfish (or a big clamface); he has no guts; he's yellow (or chickenhearted).

bang(e):
Dem Jungen war bang nach der Mutter.
The boy longed for his mother.

Ihr war angst und bange.
She was scared stiff (or to death).

Bangen:
Es war eine Zeit des Hangens und Bangens.
It was an anxious (or harrowing) time.

Bank:
Er schob es auf die lange Bank.
He kept putting it off.

Sie taten es alle durch die Bank.
They all did the same.

Er zog sie durch die Bank.
He razzed them (or bawled them out); he gave them hell.

Etwas ist in Bänken.
Something's up (or brewing).

Die Sache liegt schon lange unter der Bank.
The matter was shelved (or dropped) long ago.

Bann:
Sie wurde von der Gesellschaft in Acht und Bann getan.
Society gave her the cold shoulder; she was ostracized.

Er zwang die Hörer in seinen Bann.
He held the audience spellbound.

bannig:
Er hat bannig viel Geld.
He's lousy with (or made of) money.

Bannkreis:
  Sie geriet ganz in den Bannkreis seiner Persönlichkeit.

She fell completely under the spell of his personality.

bar:
  Er nimmt alles für bare Münze.

He takes everything literally (*or* at face value); he takes it all for Gospel truth.

Bär:
  Er schläft wie ein Bär.

He sleeps like a log (*or* top).

  Er ist ein ungeleckter Bär.

He's an unlicked cub; he's a rough-and-ready fellow.

  Wer hat Ihnen denn den Bären aufgebunden?

I wonder who told you that gag (*or* yarn)?

  Man soll das Fell nicht verkaufen, ehe man (nicht) den Bären hat.

First catch your hare!; don't count your chickens before they're hatched!

  Er versuchte, einen Bären anzubinden.

He tried to run up a bill.

Bärenhaut:
  Er liegt den ganzen Tag auf der Bärenhaut.

He loafs around all day long; he's taking life easy.

Bärenkälte:
  Es war eine Bärenkälte.

It was bitter cold.

barfuß:
  Er war barfuß bis an den Hals.

He was stark naked.

Barometer:
  Sein Barometer steht auf Sturm.

He's in a black (*or* vile) mood.

Bart:
  So ein Bart!

That story is old as the hills.

  Lassen Sie sich man keinen Bart darum wachsen!

Don't lose any sleep over it!; don't let it worry you!

  Man drehte ihm einen flachsenen Bart.

They pulled his whiskers (*or* leg); they played a joke on him.

  Er brummte seine Worte in den Bart.

He muttered the words between his teeth.

  Er lachte sich in den Bart hinein.

He laughed up his sleeve.

  Sie stritten sich um des Kaisers Bart.

They were splitting hairs; they argued over trifles.

  Sie ging ihm um den Bart und erhielt die Erlaubnis.

She wheedled (*or* cajoled) him into giving her permission.

Barthel:
  Der weiß, wo Barthel den Most holt.

He's on (*or* wise); he's been around; he knows his onions (*or* what's what).

Basel:
  Er sah aus wie der Tod von Basel.

He looked like a ghost; he was pale as death.

baß:
  Er war baß erstaunt.

He was completely nonplussed (*or* very much surprised).

basta:
  Und damit basta!

That's final!; let that be enough!

Batzen:
  Es kostete einen ganzen Batzen.

It cost a pile of money.

Bau:
  Er kommt nie aus seinem Bau heraus.

He's an old stay-at-home; he never comes out of his shell; he keeps to himself.

  Er ist einer vom Bau.

He knows the ropes; he knows his business.

Bauch:

Alles hielt sich den Bauch vor Lachen.	Everyone held his sides with laughter.
Er hat sich einen Bauch angefressen.	He's acquired a corporation (*or* bay window); he's grown fat.
Man liegt vor ihm auf dem Bauch.	Everybody licks his boots; they all eat out of his hand; everyone kowtows (*or* caters) to him.
Er fragte mir ein Loch in den Bauch.	He asked me a thousand and one questions.
Er lachte sich ein Loch in den Bauch.	He split his sides; he roared with laughter.

bauen:

Er läßt sich einen neuen Anzug bauen.	He's having a new suit made.
Wann wollen Sie Ihren Doktor bauen?	When are you getting your doctor's degree?

Bauer:

Ja, Bauer, das ist ganz was andres!	That's quite a different thing (*or* story), old man.
Was der Bauer nicht kennt, das ißt er nicht.	You can't teach an old dog new tricks.
Was versteht der Bauer vom Gurkensalat?	What does he know about it?; how can he be expected to appreciate that?
So ein Bauer!	What a hayseed (*or* yokel)!
Ein Bauer bleibt ein Bauer.	Once a farmer, always a farmer; what's bred in the bone will never come out of the flesh.
Die dümmsten Bauern haben die dicksten Kartoffeln.	Fools are born lucky.
So fragt man die Bauern aus.	Don't be so nosy (*or* inquisitive)!; stop pumping me!

Bauernjunge:

Er ist der reinste Bauernjunge.	He's a regular yokel (*or* rookie).
Es regnete Bauernjungen.	It rained cats and dogs.

Bauklötze(r):

Gelt, da staunst du Bauklötze!	That bowls you over (*or* knocks you flat), doesn't it?

Baum:

Auf einen Hieb fällt kein Baum.	Rome wasn't built in a day.
Es ist dafür gesorgt, daß die Bäume nicht in den Himmel wachsen.	We all have our limitations.
Der kann Bäume ausreißen.	He's strong as an ox.
Na, na, er wird schon keine Bäume ausreißen.	He won't set the world on fire; he'll never be a sensation.
Seine Frechheit steigt auf die Bäume.	His impertinence is becoming intolerable.

Baumöl:

Es ist um Baumöl zu schwitzen.	It gets my goat (*or* makes me angry); I could tear my hair.

Bausch:

Er verkaufte den Hof in Bausch und Bogen.	He sold out the entire ranch (*or* farm).

Baustein:

Er gab einen Baustein zur Errichtung der neuen Kirche.	He chipped in on (*or* contributed toward) the foundation of the new church.

bautz:

Bautz, da liegt er!	Bang (*or* Bingo), there he lies!

beackern:
Der Professor hat dieses Gebiet eingehend beackert. — The professor has made an exhaustive research in this field.

bebbern:
Er bebberte vor Kälte. — He shivered with cold.

bedecken:
Bitte, bedecken Sie sich doch! — Keep your hat on, please!

bedenken:
Er bedachte sich eines andern. — He changed his mind.

bedeppert:
Als er den Schaden sah, war er ganz bedeppert. — When he saw the damage, he was quite at a loss (*or* very much embarrassed).

bedeuten:
Das hat nichts zu bedeuten. — That's all right (*or* O.K.); never mind!; forget it!

Was soll denn das bedeuten? — What's the (big) idea?

bedienen:
Bitte, bedienen Sie sich! — Help yourself!

bedusselt:
Er ist immer bedusselt. — He's always lit up (*or* tight).

Beelzebub:
Er treibt den Teufel mit dem Beelzebub aus. — He's fighting the devil with fire (*or* his own weapons).

befehlen:
Was befehlen Sie? — What is your pleasure?
Er hat uns nichts zu befehlen. — We take no orders from him.

befinden:
Hier hat nur er zu befinden. — In this matter he alone will decide.

befleißigen:
Befleißigen Sie sich der Kürze! — Cut it short!; be brief!

befohlen:
Gott befohlen! — So long!; goodbye!

befreien:
Wollen Sie ihn davon befreien? — Will you take it off his hands?

befreunden:
Er kann sich damit nicht befreunden. — He doesn't approve of it; he can't warm up to (*or* get excited over) it.

befummeln:
Er wird das schon befummeln. — He'll fix that all right.

Begierde:
Er brennt vor Begierde, Sie kennen zu lernen. — He's itching (*or* dying) to meet you (*or* make your acquaintance).

begierig:
Ich bin begierig, wie er das anfängt. — I'm curious to see how he'll do that.

beginnen:
Erst besinn's, dann beginn's! — Look before you leap!
Was beginnen wir nun? — Where do we go from here?; now what do we do?

begoffen:
Er stand da wie ein begoffener Pudel.

He was completely nonplussed; he looked very sheepish.

begraben:
Du kannst dich damit begraben lassen!

That isn't worth a hoot in hell!; you ought to hide your face!

Begriff:
Sie verwechseln wohl die Begriffe!

Are you nuts (*or* crazy)?; you must be out of your right mind!

Er war eben im Begriff, ihr zu schreiben.

He was just going to write to her.

Er ist schwer von Begriff.

He's a little slow; he doesn't catch on easily.

behelfen:
Sie behelfen sich so kümmerlich.

They eke out a meager living; they barely make ends meet.

behüten:
Gott behüte!

Oh, no!; never!; God forbid!

bei:
Er ist schlecht bei Kasse.

He's short of money.

Es waren bei hundert Mann zugegen.

There were about a hundred men there.

Da ist doch nichts bei.

There's no harm in it; that's all right; it doesn't matter.

beibringen:
Dem werde ich's schon noch beibringen.

I'll teach (*or* show) him.

Es war schwer, ihr die böse Nachricht beizubringen.

It was not easy to break the bad news to her.

beigeben:
Er gab klein bei.

He came down a peg (*or* off his high horse); he gave in.

Beigeschmack:
Es ist ein Lob ohne Beigeschmack.

It's unqualified praise.

Beil:
Er warf das Beil zu weit.

He laid it on too thick; he lied like a trooper.

beileibe:
Tun Sie das beileibe nicht!

Don't you dare (do it)!

Bein:
Ist das wahr?—Ach, kein Bein!

Is that true?—Not a word of it!

Kein Bein war zu sehen.

Not a soul was there.

Es fror Stein und Bein.

It was freezing hard.

Er schwor Stein und Bein, daß es so war.

He swore on a stack of Bibles (*or* by all that is holy) that it was so.

Sie versuchten, ihm ein Bein zu stellen.

They tried to trip him up.

Reißen Sie sich man kein Bein aus!

Take it easy!

Alles, was Beine hatte, war da.

Everybody was there.

Dem werde ich aber Beine machen.

I'll step on that fellow; I'll make him hurry.

Sie standen sich die Beine in den Leib.

They were worn out from standing so long.

Lügen haben kurze Beine.

Cheaters never prosper; a bad penny always turns up; be sure your sins don't find you out!

Das hat noch lange Beine.

That's still a long way off; that can wait; there's no (need to) hurry.

Der Mensch ist ihnen ein Knüppel am Bein.	He's a drag (*or* ball and chain) on them; he's an awful nuisance.
Binden Sie es ans Bein!	Give it up (for lost)!; forget about it!; make the best of it!
Man wollte ihm etwas ans Bein hängen.	They wanted to put one over on him.
Er hat bei dem Geschäft eine Menge Geld ans Bein geschmiert.	He lost quite a bit of money in that deal.
Er ist den ganzen Tag auf den Beinen.	He's on the go all day long.
Sie ist gut auf den Beinen.	She's a good hiker.
Er war schnell wieder auf den Beinen.	He was up and around in no time; he pulled through (*or* recovered) very quickly.
Er steht auf festen Beinen.	He's got both feet on the ground; he knows what he's about.
Die Sache steht auf schwachen Beinen.	The affair is shaky (*or* on a weak footing).
Machen Sie sich auf die Beine!	You'd better be going (*or* on your way).
Er bemühte sich, ein Kabinett auf die Beine zu stellen.	He tried to form a cabinet.
Der Schreck ging ihm durch Mark und Bein.	His hair stood on end; he was scared to death.
Was man nicht im Kopf hat, muß man in den Beinen haben.	A good memory saves many a step; use your head to save your heels!
Bleiben Sie doch mit den Beinen auf der Erde!	Keep your feet on the ground!; don't lose yourself in speculation!
Er steht mit beiden Beinen in der Gegenwart.	He's very much up to date; he lives for the present.
Er kommt den ganzen Tag nicht von den Beinen.	He's on his feet all day.
Er warf ihnen einen Knüppel zwischen die Beine.	He threw a monkey wrench into the machinery; he queered (*or* spoiled) their plans.

Beinbruch:

Hals= und Beinbruch!	Good luck!
Das ist noch lange kein Beinbruch.	That cuts no ice; that's not even worth mentioning.

beisammen:

Er hat seine Gedanken nicht beisammen.	His thoughts are scattered (*or* miles away); he hasn't his wits about him.
Er ist heute nicht ganz beisammen.	He's under the weather (*or* ill) today; he's feeling seedy; he's not quite himself today.

beiseiteschaffen:

Man hat ihn beiseitegeschafft.	He was bumped off (*or* done away with).

beißen:

Sie haben nichts zu beißen.	Their cupboard is bare; they're hard up.

beitreten:

Er ist unsrer Auffassung beigetreten.	He adopted our views.

bejahend:

Er beantwortete die Einladung bejahend.	He accepted the invitation.

Bekanntschaft:

Sie hat eine Bekanntschaft.	She has a beau (*or* boy friend).
Er machte mit dem Boden Bekanntschaft.	He fell (*or* took a tumble).

befieken:

Das will ich mir erst mal befieken.	I want to take a good look at it first.

bekleiden:
Welches Amt bekleidet er? | What's his job?; what office does he hold?

bekneipen:
Er hatte sich schwer bekneipt. | He was thoroughly tight (*or* soused); he was dead-drunk.

bekommen:
Wohl bekomm's! | Here's to you!; your health!
Bekommen Sie schon? | Are you being served (*or* waited on)?
Ich glaube, wir bekommen Regen. | I think we shall have rain.
Wie ist Ihnen der gestrige Abend bekommen? | How did you like last night's party?
Das soll ihm schlecht bekommen. | He's going to get it in the neck; he'll be sorry.

bekümmern:
Bekümmern Sie sich um Ihre Sachen! | Hoe your own potatoes!; mind your own business!

belangen:
Er wird ihn gerichtlich belangen. | He'll take him to court; he'll sue him.

beleckt:
Er ist nicht von der Kultur beleckt. | He lacks polish; he's unsophisticated.

belegt:
Ich möchte ein belegtes Brot. | I'd like to have a sandwich.

belemmern:
Man hat sie belemmert. | They took her for an easy mark (*or* a sucker); she was taken in.

belemmert:
Das ist eine belemmerte Geschichte! | That's a tough break (*or* sorry fix)!; what a mess (*or* nuisance)!

belieben:
Wie beliebt? | Sir?; pardon?; what did you say?
Wie es Ihnen beliebt. | As you like (*or* please).

Belieben:
Wählen Sie nach Belieben! | Take your choice!

beliebig:
Anzug beliebig! | Go as you please!

bemänteln:
Er wollte seine Fehler bemänteln. | He wanted to hide (*or* cover up) his faults.

bemessen:
Er kann seine Ausgaben nicht nach den Einnahmen bemessen. | His income doesn't cover his expenses.

bemogeln:
Laß dich nicht bemogeln! | Don't take any wooden nickels!; don't let them fool you!

bemoost:
Er ist ein bemoostes Haupt. | He's been a student for ages; he's an old-timer.

bemühen:
Bemühen Sie sich nach oben! | Please walk (*or* come on) up!
Bemühen Sie sich nicht! | Don't bother!
Er bemüht sich sehr um sie. | He's paying her a lot of attention.

Bemühung:
  Er liquidierte zehn Mark für ärztliche Bemühungen. | The doctor charged ten marks for his services.

benebelt:
  Er war etwas benebelt. | He was a little befuddled (*or* hazy); he had been drinking.

benehmen:
  Er benahm ihr alle Hoffnung. | He gave her no hope.

Benehmen:
  Setzen Sie sich mit ihm ins Benehmen! | Contact him!; get in touch with him!

benommen:
  Er fühlte sich nach dem Sturz ganz benommen. | He was quite groggy (*or* dazed) after the fall.

bequem:
  Machen sie sich's bequem! | Make yourself at home!

berappen:
  Er mußte drei Mark berappen. | He had to fork out (*or* hand over) three marks.

berauben:
  Ich möchte Sie nicht Ihrer Zigaretten berauben! | Are you sure you can spare a cigarette?

berechtigen:
  Er berechtigt zu den besten Hoffnungen. | He'll go to town one of these days; he'll make a name for himself; he gives promise of future greatness.

beredt:
  Es war ein beredtes Schweigen. | There was no need for words.
  Er besitzt eine beredte Zunge. | He has the gift of gab (*or* a glib tongue); he can talk like a politician.

Bereich:
  Das liegt außerhalb seines Bereichs. | That's not up his alley (*or* in his province); that's not his line.

bereinigt:
  Das Verhältnis zwischen den beiden Ländern ist noch nicht bereinigt. | The relations between the two countries are still unsettled (*or* undetermined).

Berg:
  Bis dahin fließt noch viel Wasser den Berg hinab. | That's a long way off yet; it will be a long time before that happens; wait and see!
  Er verspricht goldne Berge. | He promises wonders (*or* the impossible).
  Da steht der Ochs am Berg! | That's where the shoe pinches; there's the rub (*or* difficulty).
  Er hielt damit nicht hinterm Berg. | He made no bones about it; he was very outspoken.
  Hinterm Berg wohnen auch Leute! | You're not the only pebble on the beach!; other people have brains too!
  Er ist über den Berg. | He's over the hump; the worst is behind him.
  Er ist über alle Berge. | He's off and away; he's gone.
  Er stand wie der Ochs vorm Berg. | He was up against a stone wall; he didn't know where to turn next.
  Die Haare standen ihm zu Berg, als er davon hörte. | His hair stood on end (*or* He was dumbfounded) when he heard about it.

bergehoch:
Die Arbeit türmt sich bergehoch.

Work is piling up (sky-high).

beriechen:
Die Mitglieder des Ausschusses berochen sich zunächst einander.

The members of the committee tried to establish rapport with one another.

beruflich:
Er muß beruflich verreisen.

He has to go away on business.

Berühmtes:
Das ist nichts Berühmtes.

That's not so hot; that's nothing to write home (or brag about).

berühren:
Das berührt sich mit meinen Gedanken.

That's just what I thought.

Berührungspunkt:
Es bestehen keinerlei Berührungspunkte zwischen ihnen.

They have nothing in common.

besabbern:
Besabber dich nicht!

Quit drooling!; don't talk foolishness!

besagen:
Das besagt gar nichts.

That doesn't mean a thing.

besaitet:
Sie hat ein fein besaitetes Gemüt.

She's a very sensitive soul.

beschaffen:
Wie ist es damit beschaffen?

How's that? how does the matter stand?

Bescheid:
Dem will ich aber gehörig Bescheid sagen.
Nun weiß ich Bescheid.
Er weiß in Hamburg gut Bescheid.

I'll tell him exactly where he gets off.
Now I see.
He knows his way about Hamburg.

bescheiden:
Sie wissen sich zu bescheiden.

They're modest (or unassuming) people.

Bescherung:
Das ist eine böse Bescherung!

What a mess!; that's a fine how-do-you-do (or pretty kettle of fish)!

Beschlag:
Seine Zeit ist ganz mit Beschlag belegt.

His time is all taken up.

beschlagen:
Er ist gut darin beschlagen.

He's well posted on (or versed in) the subject; he's thoroughly familiar with it.

beschließen:
Man beschloß mit allen gegen eine Stimme.

The resolution was passed with only one dissenting vote.

beschlossen:
Es war beschlossene Sache.

It was a foregone conclusion.

beschmuddeln:
Beschmuddel dich nicht!

Don't mess yourself up!; keep your hands clean!

beschnarchen:
Das will ich mir noch einmal beschnarchen.

I'll sleep on that again; let me think that over again.

beschneiden:
Man hat ihn in seiner Freiheit beschnitten.

His style is being cramped; his freedom of action (or expression) is being restrained.

beschnüffeln:
Das will ich mir erst mal in aller Ruhe beschnüffeln. — I want to mull it over (*or* ponder on it).

beschönigen:
Die Sache läßt sich nicht beschönigen. — There's no mincing matters; we must face the facts.

beschummeln:
Er wollte sie um eine Mark beschummeln. — He wanted to gyp (*or* cheat) her out of a mark.

beschupsen:
Er hat seinen eignen Freund beschupst. — He double-crossed (*or* deceived) his own friend.

beschwatzen:
Lassen Sie sich nicht beschwatzen! — Don't let yourself be taken in (*or* fooled)!; don't let them string you along!

beschwipst:
Er war beschwipst. — He was foggy (*or* soused).

Besen:
Der Besen hat das Zimmer noch nicht sauber gemacht. — The room has not yet been cleaned.
Wenn das nicht stimmt, dann fresse ich einen Besen. — I'll eat my hat if that's not so; I'll take an oath on it.
Er hat sie auf den Besen geladen. — He took them for a ride; he made fun of them.

Besenstiel:
Er geht, als hätte er einen Besenstiel verschluckt. — He's stiff as a poker; he's a perfect stick (*or* very straight-laced).

besetzt:
Ist alles besetzt? — Is every seat taken?
Der Zug ist sehr besetzt. — The train is very crowded.

Besetzung:
In welcher Besetzung wird das Stück gegeben? — Who's in the cast (of the play)?

besinnen:
Erst besinn's, dann beginn's! — Look before you leap!
Besinnen Sie sich mal! — Try to remember!; think back!
Er besann sich eines andern. — He changed his mind.

besorgen:
Dem werde ich's schon besorgen. — I'll fix him yet; he'll get what's coming to him.

besser:
Besser hab' ich, als hätt' ich. — A bird in hand is worth two in the bush.
Besser ist besser. — It's better to be on the safe side.
Das wäre noch besser! — That would take the cake (*or* beat everything)!

Bessere:
Das Bessere ist der Feind des Guten. — Let well enough alone!; don't tempt fortune!

Besserwisser:
Er ist ein unverbesserlicher Besserwisser. — He's an incorrigible smart-aleck (*or* know-it-all).

best:

Er hat sich aufs beste bewährt.	He proved entirely satisfactory.
Geben Sie eine Geschichte zum besten!	Tell us a story!
Man hatte ihn zum besten.	They were kidding (*or* making fun of) him.
Nehmen Sie den ersten besten Zug!	Take the first train that comes along.

Beste:

Es geschah zu seinem Besten.	It was for his own good.

bestechend:

Sein Wesen ist bestechend.	He has an engaging personality.

bestehen:

Er hat das Examen bestanden.	He passed the examination.
Sie können knapp dabei bestehen.	They can just squeeze by (*or* get along) on that.

bestellt:

Ist es so bestellt?	Is that the way matters stand?
Es ist schlecht mit ihnen bestellt.	They're hard up (*or* in a sad plight).

bestens:

Ich danke bestens.	Thanks a lot!

bestimmen:

Sie läßt sich zu sehr von ihren Gefühlen bestimmen.	She's too temperamental (*or* emotional).

bestimmt:

Er ist sehr bestimmt in seinem Auftreten.	He's cocksure of himself; he's very self-confident.

Bestreben:

Es ist sein heißes Bestreben, es gut zu machen.	He's set (*or* bent) on making a good job of it.

bestreiten:

Der Wettkampf wird von unserm Verein bestritten.	Our club is entering the meet (*or* contest).

betölpeln:

Er ist leicht zu betölpeln.	He's an easy mark; he's very gullible.

betraut:

Er ist mit der Führung des Geschäfts betraut.	He's in charge of the store (*or* business).

betreffen:

Was das betrifft.	As to that; as far as that goes.
Er wurde auf frischer Tat betroffen.	He was caught red-handed (*or* in the act).

Betreiben:

Er kam auf ihr Betreiben.	She urged him to come.

Betreten:

Das Betreten des Grundstückes ist verboten.	No trespassing!; keep off the premises!

betreuen:

Sie betreut rührend die Kinder.	She is very much concerned for the children's welfare.

Betrieb:

Jetzt geht der Betrieb los!	Here goes!; now the fun begins!
Die jungen Leute haben gestern mächtigen Betrieb gemacht.	The young folks made whoopee (*or* painted the town red) yesterday; they cut loose.
Die Fabrik ist außer Betrieb.	The plant has been closed (*or* shut down).

betrübt:
Er stand da wie ein betrübter Lohgerber, dem die Felle fortgeschwommen sind.

He looked as though he'd lost his best friend; he was down in the mouth (*or* very despondent).

Betschwester:
Der Mensch ist die reine Betschwester.

He's a regular goody-goody.

Bettel:
Er warf ihnen den ganzen Bettel vor die Füße.

He threw up (*or* turned down) the whole deal; he called the whole thing off.

bettelarm:
Er ist bettelarm.

He's poor as a church mouse (*or* Job's turkey).

Bettelmann:
Er hat's im Griff wie der Bettelmann die Laus.

He's a past master at it; he has it down pat; he has the knack of it.

betteln:
Die Kunst geht betteln.

Poverty is the mother of all arts.

Bettelsack:
Er fuhr sie an wie die Sau den Bettelsack.

He treated them like dirt; he snubbed them.

Bettelstab:
Er bringt sie noch an den Bettelstab.

He'll drive them to the poorhouse yet.

betten:
Wie man sich ·bettet, so schläft man.

One reaps what one has sown; do well and have well!

betulich:
Sie ist sehr betulich.

She's very considerate (*or* obliging).

betümpeln:
Er betümpelt sich dann und wann mal.

He goes on a spree every so often; he gets drunk now and then.

Beutel:
Der eine hat den Beutel, der andere das Geld.

Some folks have all the luck.

Es ging ihm an den Beutel.

He had to fork over (*or* come across with) the cash.

Er hat den Daumen auf dem Beutel.
Er hat die Schwindsucht im Beutel.

He's counting his pennies; he's thrifty.
He hasn't a nickel in his pocket (*or* to his name).

Beutelschneiderei:
Das ist üble Beutelschneiderei.

That's a regular holdup; that's highway robbery.

bewahren:
Bewahre!
Bewahren Sie uns ein gutes Andenken!

Nothing doing!; not on your life!
Don't forget us!

bewandert:
Er ist sehr darin bewandert.

He's very well informed; he knows it very well.

Bewandtnis:
Welche Bewandtnis hat es damit?

What's the nature of the case?; what are the facts?

Bewegung:
Sie sollten sich mehr Bewegung machen!

You ought to take more exercise!

beweihräuchern:
Er läßt sich gern beweihräuchern. — He eats (*or* laps) up praise; he thrives on flattery; he can't get enough of it.

Bewenden:
Dabei soll es sein Bewenden haben. — There the matter must rest.

bewirtschaftet:
Das Gasthaus ist nur im Sommer bewirtschaftet. — The hotel is open only in the summertime.

bewußt:
Die bewußte Sache ist erledigt. — The matter in question has been settled.

Bewußtlosigkeit:
Er langweilte sich zur Bewußtlosigkeit. — He was bored to tears (*or* death).

Bewußtsein:
Es kam ihm zum Bewußtsein, was er getan hatte. — He realized what he had done.

bezahlen:
Es ist nicht mit Geld zu bezahlen. — It's invaluable; you couldn't buy it (for love nor money).

biegen:
Sie bogen sich über seine Witze vor Lachen. — They doubled up (*or* howled) with laughter at his jokes.

Er wird kommen, mag es biegen oder brechen. — He'll come by hook or crook; he'll come if it kills him.

Bier:
Er bot sich an wie sauer Bier. — He was willing to work for a song (*or* practically nothing).

Biereifer:
Er schafft mit einem wahren Biereifer. — He works to beat the band (*or* with a vengeance).

Bieridee:
Das ist eine Bieridee. — That's a crazy idea.

Bierreise:
Wohin geht die Bierreise? — Where are you bound (*or* headed) for?

Biest:
Er ist ein großes Biest geworden. — He's become a big shot (*or* an important personage).

bieten:
Das dürfte ihm niemand bieten. — He wouldn't take (*or* stand for) that from anyone.

Bild:
Sie ist ein Bild von einem Mädel. — She's pretty as a picture; she's a peach (*or* knockout).

Machen Sie sich ein Bild davon! — Feature that!; just imagine!
Jetzt bin ich im Bilde. — Now I get you (*or* catch on); I begin to see what you're driving at.

Bildfläche:
Diese Streitfrage erscheint immer wieder auf der Bildfläche. — This argument recurs (*or* comes to the fore) time and again.

billig:
Was dem einen recht ist, ist dem andern billig. — What is sauce for the goose is sauce for the gander; what goes for one goes for all.
Das ist nicht mehr wie recht und billig. — It's only fair.

Bimbam:
  Heiliger Bimbam!

Great Caesar (*or* Scott)!; holy cow!; my word!

Binde:
  Da fiel ihm die Binde von den Augen.
  Lassen Sie uns einen hinter die Binde gießen!

Then it dawned on him; he saw the light.
Let's wet our whistles!; let's have a snifter (*or* drink)!

Bindfaden:
  Es regnete Bindfäden.

It rained cats and dogs.

Binse:
  Sein Vermögen ist in die Binsen gegangen.

His fortune has gone by the board; he has lost all his money.

Binsenwahrheit:
  Das ist eine Binsenwahrheit.

Everybody knows that.

Birne:
  Er hat eine weiche Birne.

He's not quite right in his upper story; his brain is soft (*or* weak); he's feeble-minded.

bis:
  Sie ist bis morgen abend zurück.
  Sie waren alle da bis auf einen.

She'll be back by tomorrow night.
They were all there but one.

Bischof:
  Er ist aus einem Bader ein Bischof geworden.

He has risen from corporal to field marshal.

Bissen:
  Sein Gewinn war ein fetter Bissen.

He broke the bank (*or* won the jackpot); he made a fat profit.

Bitte:
  Das ist einer aus der siebten Bitte.

He's a pain in the neck; I can't stand the sight of him.

bitten:
  Darf ich es tun?—Bitte!
  Darf ich um die Zeitung bitten?—Bitte schön!
  Haben Sie schönen Dank!—Bitte sehr!

  Nein, ich bitte Sie!
  Wenn ich bitten darf.
  Ich lasse Herrn M. bitten.
  Da muß ich doch sehr bitten!

May I?—Please, do!
Would you kindly hand me the paper?—Certainly!; of course!
Thanks a lot!—You're welcome; that's quite all right.
You don't say so!; come, now!
If you please.
Please show Mr. M. in.
I say!; be careful what you say!

bitter:
  Es ist ihm bitterer Ernst damit.

He's in dead earnest; he means it in all seriousness.

bitterböse:
  Er blamierte sich bitterböse.

He made a holy show (*or* an awful fool) of himself.

bittersüß:
  Sie lächelte bittersüß.

She made a wry face; she smiled sourly.

Blamage:
  Das wäre eine schöne Blamage!

That would be awful (*or* a shame).

blank:

Jetzt hab' ich's blank!	Now I see!; I've got it straight now!
Er ist wieder mal blank.	Once more he's broke (*or* penniless).
Sie stehen blank miteinander.	They're at swords' points (*or* in open enmity).

Blase:

Da ist die Blase schon wieder!	There's that gang (*or* bunch) back again!

blasen:

Was dich nicht brennt, das blase nicht!	What you don't know won't hurt you!; mind your own business!
Das läßt sich nicht nur so blasen.	That can't be done over night (*or* in a hurry); that needs time and care; it's no cinch.

Blasen:

Er hat keine Ahnung von Tuten und Blasen.	He doesn't know beans about it; he knows as much about it as the man in the moon.

blaß:

Er hat keinen blassen Dunst (*or* blasse Ahnung) davon.	He hasn't the faintest notion (*or* least idea).

Blatt:

Er ist ein unbeschriebenes Blatt.	He's an unknown quantity.
Er nahm kein Blatt vor den Mund.	He didn't mince matters; he was plain-spoken.
Das steht auf einem andern Blatt.	That's another story (*or* quite a different thing).
Sie spielte vom Blatt.	She played (the music) at sight.

Blättchen:

Das Blättchen hat sich gewendet.	The tables have turned.

blau:

Er macht heute blau.	He's loafing (*or* taking it easy) today; he's taking the day off.
Er ist blau.	He's stewed (*or* tight).
Ihm wurde blau vor den Augen.	Everything turned black before his eyes; he fainted.
Er kam mit einem blauen Auge davon.	He got off pretty easy; he escaped by the skin of his teeth.
Er erhielt den blauen Brief.	He got the pink slip; he was fired (*or* discharged).
Mach uns doch keinen blauen Dunst vor!	That's a lot of hooey (*or* hot air)!; stop blowing (*or* spoofing us)!
Er wird noch sein blaues Wunder erleben.	Will he be surprised one fine day!; he'll get the surprise of his life.

Blaue:

Er log das Blaue vom Himmel herunter.	He swore black was white; he swore by all that was holy; he lied shamelessly.
Er würde für sie das Blaue vom Himmel holen.	He'd give them the shirt off his back, he'd bring them the moon.
Er redete ins Blaue hinein.	He chewed the rag; he talked a blue streak (*or* on and on).

Blech:

Schwätz doch kein Blech!	That's the bunk!; don't talk rot (*or* rank nonsense)!

blechen:
    Er mußte zwei Mark dafür blechen.

He had to cough up (*or* come across with) two marks for it.

Blechschädel:
    Er hat einen gehörigen Blechschädel.

He has an awful hangover (*or* headache).

Blei:
    Es lag ihm wie Blei in den Gliedern.

He was dog-tired; his limbs were leaden.

Bleibe:
    Sie haben keine Bleibe.

They've no place to stay.

bleiben:
    Ich bleibe dabei.

I'll stick to that; I'll stand by what I've said.

    Es bleibt dabei.

That's final.

    Wo bleibt nur das liebe Geld?

Where does the money go to?

    Dabei wird es nicht bleiben.

Matters won't stop there; you haven't heard the last of it.

Bleiben:
    Hier ist seines Bleibens nicht.

He can't stay here; this is no place for him.

bleibenlassen:
    Laß (das) bleiben!

Don't (you) do it!; lay off (that)!

    Wenn Ihnen das nicht paßt, so können Sie es bleibenlassen.

Like it or lump it!; take it or leave it!

    Das sollte er wohl bleibenlassen.

I'd like to see (*or* Just let) him try that; he'd better not do that.

bleiern:
    Er schwimmt wie eine bleierne Ente.

He swims like a rock.

blendend:
    Blendend!

Hotsy-totsy!; swell!; excellent!

Blender:
    Der Kerl ist nichts andres als ein gemeiner Blender.

He's nothing but a fourflusher; he's just a big bluff.

blicken:
    Das läßt tief blicken.

That speaks volumes; there's a lot in that.

    Er läßt sich nicht mehr blicken.

He makes himself scarce.

blind:
    Blinder Eifer schadet nur.

Too much zeal spoils all; the more haste, the less speed.

    Ein blindes Huhn findet auch mal ein Körnchen.

Fortune favors a fool.

    Es war nur blinder Lärm.

It was just a false alarm.

    Ein blinder Passagier war an Bord.

There was a stowaway aboard.

    Sie ist ein blindes Werkzeug in seinen Händen.

She's a mere tool (*or* like putty) in his hands; he can do with her what he wants; she eats out of his hand.

Blinder:
    Er versteht sich darauf wie ein Blinder auf die Farben.

He knows as much about it as the man in the moon; he doesn't know the first thing about it.

Blitz:
    Potz Blitz!

Good heavens!; great Scott!

    Er war weg wie der Blitz.

He was off like a shot.

    Er war wie vom Blitz gerührt.

He was thunderstruck.

Blitzjunge:
Er ist ein Blitzjunge. — He's a whiz (*or* sharp as a whip).

blitzsauber:
Sie ist ein blitzsauberes Mädel. — She's neat as a pin; she keeps everything in apple-pie order.

Blocksberg:
Ich wünschte, der Kerl wäre auf dem Blocksberg! — To hell with that fellow!

blöde:
Ein blöder Hund wird selten fett. — Faint heart never won fair lady.

blödsinnig:
Er freute sich ganz blödsinnig, als er uns sah. — He was tickled to death (*or* awfully glad) to see us.

bloß:
Was machen Sie bloß für Dinge! — What in the world are you doing (*or* up to)?

Blöße:
Er wollte sich keine Blöße geben. — He didn't want to commit himself.

blubbern:
Blubber doch nicht so! — Quit jabbering (*or* chattering) so!

Blücher:
Er ging drauf wie Blücher. — He went at it with a vengeance.

Blume:
Ich komme Ihnen meine Blume! — Here's to you!; your health!
Er sagte es durch die Blume. — He spoke in metaphors (*or* figuratively); he dropped a hint.

blümerant:
Ihm wurde ganz blümerant. — He felt quite giddy (*or* dizzy).

Blut:
Nur ruhig Blut! — Don't boil over!; keep your temper!; take it easy!

Sie sieht aus wie Milch und Blut. — She looks like peaches and cream; she looks blooming (*or* very healthy).

Er ist ein junges Blut. — He's a young chap.
Es sind Menschen unsres Bluts. — They're people of our race; they're in our set; they're our own kind.

Er schwitzte Blut vor Angst. — He was in a blue funk (*or* cold sweat); he was scared to death.

Er verlor Gut und Blut. — He lost both life and property.
Er peinigte sie bis aufs Blut. — He tormented them almost to death.
Es liegt im Blut. — It's bred in the bone.
Der Gedanke ist ihm in Fleisch und Blut übergegangen. — The idea has become part and parcel of him; it's second nature to him.

blutarm:
Sie sind blutarm. — They're poor as church mice.

Blüte:
Er ist in der Blüte seiner Jahre. — He's in his prime.

blutend:
Er tat es blutenden Herzens. — He did it with a heavy heart; much as it hurt, he did it.

blutig:
Es ist ihm blutiger Ernst damit. — He's in dead earnest.

blutjung:
Er ist noch blutjung. — He's still a kid (*or* child).

blutsauer:
Er läßt sich die Arbeit blutsauer werden — He toils like a slave.

Bock:
Ihn stieß der Bock. — He moped; he blubbered (*or* bawled).

Er hat den Bock zum Gärtner gemacht. — He set a fox to mind the geese; it was like leading the lambs to slaughter.

Den Bock kann man nicht melken. — You can't make a silk purse out of a sow's ear; you can't get blood out of a turnip.

Er schoß einen gehörigen Bock. — He made an awful break (*or* blunder).

bockbeinig:
Sei doch nicht so bockbeinig! — Don't be such a mule!; don't be so stubborn!

bocksdämlich:
Der Kerl ist bocksdämlich. — He's a big ass.

Bockshorn:
Er jagte sie ins Bockshorn. — He scared them out of their wits.

Boden:
Die Sache hat weder Grund noch Boden. — There's no rhyme or reason in it.

Das schlägt dem Faß den Boden aus! — That's the finish (*or* last straw)!; that takes the cake!

Handwerk hat goldnen Boden. — Trade is the mother of money.

Sein Vorschlag gewinnt an Boden. — His suggestion is finding more and more support.

Er hat Korn auf dem Boden. — He's got money in the bank; he's well fixed.

Stellen Sie sich auf den Boden der Wirklichkeit! — Let's face the facts!

Er fuhr die Maschine in einem Jahr in Grund und Boden. — He completely ruined the car within a year.

Er machte mit dem Boden Bekanntschaft. — He fell (*or* took a tumble).

Er bringt sie noch unter den Boden. — He'll be the death of her (*or* get her down) yet.

Sie schlug die Augen zu Boden. — She cast down her eyes.

bodenlos:
Es war ein bodenloser Leichtsinn. — It was frightfully careless (*or* indiscreet).

Es ist eine bodenlose Schweinerei. — It's a crying shame.

Bodenlose:
Das geht ins Bodenlose. — That's going too far.

bodenständig:
Hier lebt ein bodenständiges Geschlecht. — These people are rooted to the soil.

Bogen:
Er hat den Bogen raus. — He has the knack of it; he's on to all the tricks; he knows how to do it.

Er überspannt den Bogen. — He goes too far; he forgets himself.

Er spuckt große Bogen. — He puts on airs (*or* the dog).

Er verkaufte den Hof in Bausch und Bogen. — He sold out the entire ranch (*or* farm).

Er flog in hohem Bogen aus seinem Geschäft. — His firm dropped him like a hot potato; he flew out on his ear.

böhmisch:
Das sind mir böhmische Dörfer. — That's all Greek to me; I don't know beans (*or* the first thing) about it.

Bohne:

Stimmt das?—Nicht die Bohne!

Is it correct?—Decidedly not!; not a word of it!

Das ist keine Bohne wert.

It isn't worth a straw.

Er hat Bohnen gegessen.

He's deaf as a post; he's stone-deaf.

Bohnenlied:

Das geht übers Bohnenlied.

That beats all; that takes the cake.

Bohnenstroh:

Sie ist dumm wie Bohnenstroh.

She's dumb as they come; she's a regular blockhead (or numskull).

Er war grob wie Bohnenstroh.

He was a regular boor; he was extremely rude (or coarse).

bohren:

Er bohrte so lange, bis sie nachgaben.

He hammered away (or persisted) until he had them; they gave in to get rid of him.

bolzen:

Bolz doch nicht so!

Don't be so crude!

Bolzen:

Er sauste davon wie ein Bolzen.

He was off like a shot (or in no time).

Bombenhitze:

Es war eine Bombenhitze.

It was hot as blazes.

Bombenkerl:

Er ist ein Bombenkerl.

He's a hefty (or husky) fellow; he's a regular prizefighter.

bombenmäßig:

Sie haben bombenmäßig viel Geld.

They're lousy with (or made of) money.

bombensicher:

Der Platz ist bombensicher.

The place is safe as Gibraltar.

Ich weiß das bombensicher.

I'll eat my hat on it; that's sure as death; I'm positive.

Bonze:

Der Bonze versuchte, uns was vorzumachen.

The darned fool tried to make us believe it.

borstig:

Er wurde ganz borstig.

He flew off the handle (or got angry); he bristled with anger.

Sie haben borstig viel Geld.

They're rolling in wealth.

böse:

Sie sind sehr böse auf ihn.

They're very angry with him.

Er machte gute Miene zum bösen Spiel.

He made the best of it; he played the game; he grinned and bore it.

Bosheit:

Er arbeitet mit konstanter Bosheit.

He's a glutton for punishment; he keeps his nose to the grindstone; he works with a vengeance.

Bote:

Der hinkende Bote kommt nach.

Bad news travels fast.

Brand:

Er hatte einen mächtigen Brand.

He was dry as a gourd; he was dying of thirst.

braten:

Daß dich der Teufel brate! — Go to hell (*or* the devil)!

Da bratet's und siedet's alle Tage. — Every day is feast day (*or* a holiday) there.

Braten:

Die Erbschaft war ein fetter Braten. — The inheritance was a windfall (*or* fat sum).

Da haben wir den Braten! — A fine mess!; that's a pretty kettle of fish!

Er roch den Braten. — He smelled a rat; he had a hunch; he got wind of it.

Bratwurst:

Er schickte den Hund nach der Bratwurst. — He set a fox to keep the geese; it was like leading the lambs to slaughter.

brauchen:

Er braucht nicht lange dazu. — It won't take him long.

Wozu ist er zu brauchen? — What can he do?; what's he fit for?

Braus:

Er lebt in Saus und Braus. — He's a high-stepper; he lives fast; he leads a gay life.

Braut:

Wer das Glück hat, führt die Braut heim. — Luck is everything; the lucky man wins.

Brautvater:

Der Onkel der Braut war Brautvater. — The bride was given away by her uncle.

brav:

Brav gemacht! — Good work!; well done!

brechen:

Er kommt, es mag biegen oder brechen. — He'll come by hook or crook; he'll come if it kills him.

Brechen:

Der Saal war zum Brechen voll. — The hall was jammed; it was full to capacity (*or* overflowing).

Brechmittel:

Er ist das reinste Brechmittel. — He gives me a pain; he gets on my nerves; I can't stand the sight of him.

Bredouille:

Er ist böse in der Bredouille. — He's in the soup for fair; he's in an awful jam (*or* fix).

Brei:

Der Brei wird nicht so heiß gegessen, wie er gekocht ist. — Things are never so bad as they seem.

Regnet's Brei, fehlt ihm der Löffel. — If it were raining five-dollar gold pieces, he'd be in jail; he's always out when opportunity knocks.

Viele Köche verderben den Brei. — Too many cooks spoil the broth.

Er gab seinen Brei dazu. — He put in his two cents; he had his say.

Er machte einen langen Brei darüber. — He made a big stew (*or* fuss) about it.

Er mischte sich in den Brei. — He joined the fray.

Gehen Sie doch nicht wie die Katze um den heißen Brei! — Don't beat about the bush!; talk turkey!; out with it!

breit:

Er schwatzte ein langes und breites. — He rang the changes (*or* chewed the rag); he talked at great length.

Er hat einen breiten Rücken. — He can take (*or* stand) it; he can put up with a great deal.

breitmachen:

Mach dich doch nicht so breit! | Quit shoving!; don't put on airs!

breitschlagen:

Es gelang ihm, sie dafür breitzuschlagen. | He finally got around them (*or* won them over).

breitspurig:

Er benahm sich breitspurig. | He acted as if he owned the world.

breittreten:

Treten Sie die Sache doch nicht so breit! | You're making a mountain out of a molehill; don't make so much of it!

bremsen:

Man muß bei ihm immer bremsen. | You always have to hold him in check; he needs to be toned down.

brennen:

Was dich nicht brennt, das blase nicht! | What you don't know won't hurt you!; mind your own business!

Wo brennt's denn? | Where's the fire?; what's the hurry?

Er brannte darauf, es zu erfahren. | He was dying (*or* most eager) to hear about it.

Er wollte sich rein brennen. | He tried to whitewash himself (*or* cover his guilt).

Brennpunkt:

Er steht im Brennpunkt des Interesses. | He's in the limelight; he's the center of attraction.

brenzlig:

Die Sache wird brenzlig. | The situation is growing serious; it's a tough proposition (*or* ticklish situation).

Brett:

Er bohrt auch lieber das Brett, wo es am dünnsten ist. | He follows the line of least resistance; he takes the easiest course.

Der Junge hat ein Brett vor dem Kopf. | The boy's a blockhead.

Er sitzt hoch am Brett. | He's sitting high up (*or* pretty); he's in with the authorities (*or* powers that be).

Er kommt noch ans schwarze Brett. | He'll find himself on the black list one fine day; he'll be branded (*or* in disrepute) yet.

Er bezahlte auf einem Brett. | He paid in a lump (sum).

Er kann durch zehn Bretter sehen. | He can see through a brick wall; he's smart as they come; he's very discerning.

Er hat bei ihr einen Stein im Brett. | He's in good with her; he's in her good graces.

Er wird bald in die Bretter gehen. | He'll soon go by the board; it'll soon be over with him.

Da ist die Welt mit Brettern vernagelt! | Now we're up against it!; we're stuck (*or* in a rut) for fair!

Brezelbacken:

Das geht ja wie's Brezelbacken! | That goes slick as a whistle!; that's as easy as rolling off a log!; it's a cinch!

Brief:

Darauf gebe ich Ihnen Brief und Siegel. | I'll take an oath on it; you can bank (*or* count) on that.

Er hat den blauen Brief bekommen. | He got the pink slip; he was fired (*or* discharged).

Er hat die ältesten Briefe dazu. | He has first claim (*or* right) to it.

Brille:

Er verfuchte, ihnen eine Brille aufzufetzen.	He tried to pull the wool over their eyes (*or* put one over on them).
Er fieht die Sache durch die Brille an.	He's prejudiced; he won't face the facts.
Lefen Sie ohne gelehrte Brille!	Use your head (*or* common sense)!

bringen:

Das bringt mich auf etwas.	That reminds me (of something).
Was bringt die Zeitung?	What's new?; what does the paper say?
Er bringt es noch weit.	He'll go places yet; he's bound to make good (*or* be a big success).
Er brachte es auf fiebzig.	He reached the age of seventy.
Er brachte fie zur Verzweiflung.	He drove her to despair.
Er wird fie fchon dazu bringen.	He'll make them do it.

brocken:

Wie man es brockt, muß man es effen.	As you've made your bed, so you must lie in it; you reap what you sow.

Brocken:

Das war ein harter Brocken.	That was a hard pill to swallow; that was a tough job.
Sie kennt nur ein paar Brocken Deutfch.	She knows but a few words of German.
Er fifchte die Brocken aus der Suppe.	He took the best for himself.
Er fchmiß feine Brocken in die Ecke.	He threw his duds (*or* things) into the corner.

Brot:

Dem ift fein Brot gebacken.	His goose (*or* hash) is cooked; he'll get what's coming to him; he's on his last legs; he's a goner.
Er ift das tägliche Brot bei ihnen.	He drops in to see them every day.
Wes Brot ich eß', des Lied ich fing'.	I know where my bread is buttered; I never quarrel with those that employ me; I sing my boss' praises.
Der kann mehr als Brot effen.	He's not slow; he's smart; he knows a trick or two.
Von dem nimmt kein Menfch ein Stück Brot mehr.	I wouldn't touch him with a ten-foot pole; no one will have a thing to do with him.
Er nahm ihm das Brot vor dem Munde weg.	He cooked his goose (*or* hash); he killed (*or* ruined) his chances.
Er fieht aus, als hätten ihm die Hühner das Brot vor dem Munde weggenommen.	He looks as if he'd lost his last friend; he looks down and out.
Sie will ihr eignes Brot effen.	She wants to paddle her own canoe (*or* be her own mistress).
Er hat's nötig wie's liebe Brot.	He needs it badly; he's hard up for it.
Er wird es ihm fchon aufs Brot geben.	He'll let him hear about it; he'll tell him a thing or two.
Das fchmiert man doch nicht jedem aufs Brot.	Why bother everyone with that?; that doesn't concern everyone.
Er fitzt bei Waffer und Brot.	He's on a diet of bread and water; he's in jail.
Die Kunft geht nach Brot.	Art goes begging.
Ihm fiel die Butter vom Brot.	His face fell; he was crestfallen; he was ready to give up.
Er läßt fich nicht die Butter vom Brot nehmen.	He knows how to look out for himself; he never runs short; no one can put anything over on him.

Brotkorb:
Man hat ihm den Brotkorb höher ge=
hängt. | He's on short rations; they've cut his al-
lowance.

brotlos:
Es ist eine brotlose Kunst. | It's a white-collar job; it's a pleasant but
unprofitable occupation.

Brotneid:
Er tat es aus Brotneid. | He did it out of professional (*or* commer-
cial) jealousy; it was cut-throat compe-
tition on his part.

Bruch:
Das ist Bruch. | That's rotten (*or* no good).
Der Flieger machte beim Landen Bruch. | The pilot crashed (*or* smashed up) as he
landed.
Sein Plan ging in die Brüche. | His scheme went flooey; his plan fell
through (*or* failed).

Bruder:
Er ist ein Bruder Leichtfuß. | He's a happy-go-lucky (*or* thoughtless)
fellow.
Er ist ein nasser Bruder. | He's a tippler (*or* drunkard).
Gleiche Brüder, gleiche Kappen. | Share and share alike.
Soviel ist es unter Brüdern wert. | That's a bargain (*or* reasonable price).

brüderlich:
Dies ist meine brüderliche Liebe. | That's my dear brother.

Brüderschaft:
Sie machten Brüderschaft. | They became pals (*or* friends).

Brühe:
Das ist eine schöne Brühe. | That's a nice mess (*or* pretty kettle of
fish); that's a nice pickle to be in.
Der eine hat die Mühe, der andre schöpft
die Brühe. | One man does all the work so the other
fellow can have all the fun.
Er bezahlte die ganze Brühe. | He paid for the whole works; he settled the
entire bill.
Er machte eine lange Brühe darüber. | He made a big stew (*or* fuss) about it.
Er ließ sie in der Brühe sitzen. | He left them in the lurch; he deserted them.

brühsiedendheiß:
Es war brühsiedendheiß. | It was dreadfully (*or* unbearably) hot.

brühwarm:
Die Nachricht ist noch brühwarm. | The news is hot off the griddle (*or* just out).

Brummbär:
Er ist ein alter Brummbär. | He's an old grouch.

brummen:
Er brummt schon wieder. | He's back in jail (*or* the pen); he's behind
the bars again.

Brummochse:
So ein Brummochse! | What an ass (*or* dolt)!

Brummschädel:
Er hatte einen mächtigen Brummschädel. | He had a bad hangover (*or* headache).

Brunnen:
Wenn das Kind in den Brunnen gefallen
ist, deckt man ihn zu. | The garage door is bolted after the car has
been stolen; precaution is taken when it
is too late.

Er trägt Wasser in den Brunnen.	He carries coals to Newcastle; he's wasting his time (*or* energy).
Brunnenvergiftung:	
Der Bericht stellt eine moralische Brunnenvergiftung dar.	The report deliberately misrepresents the facts; it has no foundation in fact and is nothing but a malicious invention.
Brust:	
Er ist eben schwach auf der Brust.	He's short of cash (*or* money) right now.
Er warf sich in die Brust.	He strutted; he put on airs.
Brustton:	
Er sprach im Brustton der tiefsten Überzeugung.	He spoke with great conviction (*or* fervor); he spoke from the heart.
Buch:	
Das ist mir ein Buch mit sieben Siegeln.	That's Greek to me; I can't make it out.
Er wälzt den ganzen Tag Bücher.	He's a bookworm; he reads all day long.
Er steht im schwarzen Buch.	Everybody is down on him; he's in general disrepute.
Stecken Sie die Nase ins Buch!	Learn something!; read a book for a change!
Büchse:	
Das ist aus einer Büchse geschmiert.	It's six of one and half a dozen of the other; it's all the same.
Buchstabe:	
Er sieht die Buchstaben doppelt.	He's seeing things; he's drunk.
Buckel:	
Rutschen Sie mir doch den Buckel runter!	Go to blazes!; go sit on a tack!
Er log ihnen den Buckel voll.	He told them a pack of lies.
Ich werde ihm den Buckel vollprügeln.	I'll break his neck.
Das macht der Katze keinen Buckel.	That won't change matters any; that doesn't alter the facts.
Er hat einen breiten Buckel.	He can take it; he can stand a lot.
Er hat manches Jahr auf dem Buckel.	He carries many years on his shoulders; he's an old man.
buck(e)lig:	
Er lachte sich bucklig.	He split his sides with laughter.
Bude:	
Sein Zimmer ist eine elende Bude.	His room is a miserable hang-out (*or* hole).
Die Firma hat die Bude zugemacht.	The firm closed down (*or* went out of business).
Dem werde ich schön auf die Bude steigen.	I'll give him hell (*or* what's coming to him).
Er brachte Leben in die Bude.	He was the life of the party; he pepped them up.
Es wird ihm eklig in die Bude regnen.	He'll get hell (*or* what he's not looking for).
Es hat ihm in die Bude geschneit.	Something has crossed his path (*or* gone wrong with him).
büffeln:	
Er büffelt schwer.	He's grinding (*or* plugging) away; he studies hard.
Bühne:	
Er ist von der politischen Bühne abgetreten.	He gave up politics (*or* his political career).

Bullenhitze:
Es war eine Bullenhitze.
It was hot as Hades.

Bummel:
Lassen Sie uns einen Bummel machen!
Let's go for a walk (*or* stroll)!

Bummelfritz:
Er ist ein alter Bummelfritz.
He's an old dawdler (*or* slowpoke); he's always late and unconcerned about it.

Bumslokal:
Er führte sie in ein Bumslokal.
He took them to a dive (*or* night club).

Bündel:
Er hat sein Bündel geschnürt.
He's picked up and left.

bündig:
Er lehnte es kurz und bündig ab.
He refused point-blank.

bunt:
Es ging bunt her.
There were gay goings-on; things were happening at a lively pace.

Das wird mir doch zu bunt.
That's going too far; that's a little more than I can stand.

Er ist bekannt wie ein bunter Hund.
You'd spot (*or* recognize) him in the dark; he's known everywhere.

Gelt, da staunst du bunte Leuchtkugeln!
It surely bowls you over (*or* knocks you flat), doesn't it?

Es wurde bunte Reihe gemacht.
They paired off.

Bürde:
Würde bringt Bürde.
Uneasy lies the head that wears the crown; honor involves responsibility.

bürgerlich:
Dort gibt es einen gut bürgerlichen Mittagstisch.
You can get a good plain meal there.

Burschikosität:
Sie verzichtet auf Burschikosität.
She's frail (*or* a clinging vine); she's very feminine (*or* a woman through and through).

Bürstenbinder:
Er trinkt wie ein Bürstenbinder.
He's a tank; he drinks like a fish.

Busch:
Dem will ich mal auf den Busch klopfen.
I'll pin him down; I'll get it out of him.

Er kam wie Zieten aus dem Busch.
He popped up from nowhere; he came like a bolt from the blue.

Er hielt damit hinterm Busch.
He beat about the bush; he evaded the issue.

Er schlug sich seitwärts in die Büsche.
He slipped away.

Busen:
Da haben Sie sich eine Schlange am Busen genährt.
You're cutting your own throat; you're digging your own grave.

Er hat einen Hasen im Busen.
He's chickenhearted; he's a timorous soul.

Butter:
Er ist weich wie Butter.
He's very soft-hearted.

Er stand da wie Butter an der Sonne.
He didn't know which way to turn; he was perfectly helpless (*or* hopelessly lost).

Ihm fiel die Butter vom Brot.	His face fell; he was crestfallen; he was ready to give up.
Er läßt sich nicht die Butter vom Brot nehmen.	He knows how to look out for himself; he never runs short; no one can put anything over on him.
Es ist alles in Butter.	Everything is in apple-pie order; it's smooth sailing; the works are well oiled.
Er sitzt dick in der Butter.	He's in the fat; he's on Easy Street; he's well fixed.
Hand von der Butter!	Hands off!

Butterbrot:

Das werde ich ihm aufs Butterbrot schmieren.	I'll throw that up to him (*or* in his face); I'll come back at him with that.
Er verkaufte es für ein Butterbrot.	He sold it for a mere song (*or* dirt-cheap).

Buttermilch:

Sie kamen wie die Fliegen in der Buttermilch gezogen.	They came in droves; there was no end to them.

buttern:

Das buttert!	Great stuff!; good work!; well done!

Chor:
    Seine Kinder sind ein gräßliches Chor.

His children are holy terrors (*or* a bunch of hoodlums).

Christ:
    Er ist und bleibt ein wunderlicher Christ.
    Er sah aus wie das Leiden Christi.

He'll always be a queer egg (*or* duck).
He looked as if he had one foot in the grave; he looked wretched (*or* very miserable).

Clou:
    Was war der Clou des Abends?

What was the high light (*or* feature) of the evening?

Cour:
    Er schneidet ihr die Cour.

He necks (*or* spoons) with her; he makes love to her.

da:

Da ist er!	Here he is!
Nichts da!	Nothing doing!
Ich traf ihn da und da.	I met him at such and such a place.
Er schreibt hie(r) und da.	He writes now and then.

dabei:

Dabei fällt mir ein.	That reminds me.
Es bleibt dabei.	Done!; settled!; it's final.
Ich bin dabei!	Count me in!
Was ist denn dabei?	What of it?; so what?

Dach:

Sie haben weder Dach noch Fach.	They've neither house nor home.
Ein Spatz in der Hand ist besser als eine Taube auf dem Dach.	A bird in hand is worth two in the bush.
Er sitzt ihnen auf dem Dach.	He keeps close tabs (*or* an eagle eye) on them.
Jemand hat ihm den roten Hahn aufs Dach gesetzt.	Someone set fire to his house.
Steigen Sie dem Kerl mal aufs Dach!	Take that fellow down a peg!; set him to rights!
Bei ihm ist gleich Feuer im Dach.	He flies off the handle (*or* gets hot and bothered) easily; he's very hot-headed (*or* quick-tempered).
Er kam gerade noch vor dem Regen unter Dach.	He got in out of the rain just in time.
Das Projekt ist unter Dach und Fach.	The project is completed.
Die Spatzen pfeifen es von allen Dächern.	It's the talk of the town; it's common knowledge.

Dachs:

Er schläft wie ein Dachs.	He sleeps like a log (*or* top).
Er ist ein frecher Dachs.	He's a fresh mug (*or* an impudent fellow); he's a wretch (*or* rascal).

dafür:

Dafür sei Gott!	God forbid!
Er ist arm, dafür aber tüchtig.	Though poor, he's a good fellow.
Was wird ihm dafür?	Where does he come in?; what will he get out of it?

dafürkönnen:

Wer kann dafür?	Whose fault is it?

dagegen:

Dagegen hilft nichts.	It can't be helped.
Er gab ihr ein Buch, sie gab ihm ein Bild dagegen.	He gave her a book and she gave him a picture in exchange.
Seine Arbeit ist gut, die Ihre nichts dagegen.	His work is good—yours doesn't begin to compare with it.

daheim:

Daheim ift daheim. — There's no place like home.

Sie find wohl nicht daheim! — Are you batty?; you must be out of your mind!

Daher:

Daher ift er nicht gegangen. — That's why he didn't go.

dahin:

Dahin ift es mit ihm gekommen. — Matters have come to such a pass (*or* gone that far) with him; he's come to that.

Seine Anficht geht dahin, daß er unfchuldig ift. — In his opinion, the man is not guilty.

Das gehört nicht dahin. — That has no bearing on the subject; that's beside the point (*or* irrelevant).

Er ift tot und dahin. — He's dead and gone.

dahingehen:

Die Zeit geht dahin. — Time flies.

Er ift dahingegangen. — He passed away (*or* died).

dahingeftellt:

Ich laffe es dahingeftellt, ob er recht oder unrecht hat. — I'm undecided (*or* I leave it to you) whether he's right or wrong.

dahinter:

Bei ihm ift nichts dahinter. — There's nothing to him; he's all froth (*or* very shallow).

dahinterher:

Er ift fehr dahinterher. — He's hard at it; he's getting after the matter in earnest.

dahinterkommen:

Er wird gewiß dahinterkommen. — He'll certainly find out.

dahinterfetzen:

Er hat fich endlich dahintergefetzt. — At last he's working hard; he's on the job at last.

dahinterftecken:

Er fteckt dahinter. — He's at the bottom of it all.

Es fteckt etwas dahinter. — There's some secret about it.

Dalles:

Sie haben wohl den Dalles! — Are you nuts (*or* crazy)?

Er hat den Dalles. — He's done for; he's on his last legs.

Er ift im Dalles. — He's flat broke.

dalli:

Dalli, dalli! — Make it snappy!; step on it!; speed it up!

Damaskus:

Er hat fein Damaskus gefunden. — He turned over a new leaf.

damit:

Er geht damit um auszuziehen. — He intends moving.

Es ift nichts damit. — That's out; it's out of the picture (*or* question); it won't do.

dämlich:

Halten Sie ihn denn für fo dämlich? — What do you take him for?; do you think he's a fool?

Damm:

Er ift wieder auf dem Damm. — He's back on his feet; he's all right again.

dämmernd:
   Er hat eine dämmernde Hoffnung.   He has faint hopes.

Dampf:
   Er ist ein Hans Dampf.   He's full of hot air; he's a windbag.
   Der Kerl hat aber Dampf vor Ihnen!   The fellow surely is afraid of you!

danach:
   Es ist auch danach!   Don't ask what it's like!; it's a fright!

Danaiden:
   Er schöpft ins Faß der Danaiden.   That's so much water over the falls; he's wasting his time (*or* energy).

danebenhauen:
   Er hat danebengehauen.   He put his foot into it; he made a break (*or faux pas*).

Dank:
   Es bedarf keines Dankes.   Don't mention it!; it's all right; forget it!
   Sie wissen ihm Dank.   They feel obliged to him.
   Man kann es ihm nie zu Dank machen.   It's impossible to please him.
   Er ist ihnen zu Dank verpflichtet.   He's indebted to them.

danken:
   Das danken Sie ihm.   You owe that to him.
   Nichts zu danken!   You're welcome; that's quite all right; never mind!

dann:
   Selbst dann, wenn es wahr wäre.   Even if it were true.
   Was dann?   What next?; now what?
   Er kommt dann und wann mal.   He comes now and then.

dannen:
   Er machte sich von dannen.   He took the air; he went away.

d(a)ran:
   Er denkt nicht daran, es zu tun.   He wouldn't dream of doing it.
   Daran erkenne ich ihn.   That's him all over.
   Er muß dran glauben.   He has to take his medicine (*or* pay the price).

   Es liegt daran, daß . . .   The reason is . . .
   Was liegt daran?   What of it?; what does it matter?
   Ihm liegt sehr daran.   It's very important to him; it means everything to him; his heart is set on it.

   Machen Sie sich dran!   On the job!; get busy (*or* going)!
   Einmal müssen wir alle dran.   We must all die some time.
   Du bist dran.   You're next; it's your turn; it's up to you.
   Er weiß nicht, wie er dran ist.   He doesn't know what to think of it.
   Er ist böse dran.   He's up against it.
   Es ist nichts dran.   There's nothing to it.
   Er tat gut daran.   He did well.
   Wenn es drauf und dran geht.   If it comes to a showdown; if things come to a head.

   Er war drauf und dran zu gehen.   He was on the point of leaving.

d(a)rankommen:
   Komm nicht dran!   Hands (*or* Keep) off!
   Wer kommt dran?   Whose turn is it?; who's next?

d(a)ranfriegen:
Den wollen wir schon drankriegen.   We'll put him in his place; we'll set him to
                                                      rights.

d(a)rannehmen:
Er hat sie tüchtig drangenommen.   He gave them the works; he bawled them
                                                      out soundly.

d(a)rauf:
Den Tag darauf kam er.   He came the next day.
Er läßt es drauf ankommen.   He takes a chance; he takes it as it comes.
Er wird nie drauf kommen.   He'll never guess.
Wenn es drauf und dran geht.   If it comes to a showdown; if things come
                                                      to a head.
Er war drauf und dran zu gehen.   He was on the point of leaving.

d(a)reinschicken:
Er kann sich nicht dreinschicken.   He can't tune (or fit himself) in; he can't
                                                      adjust himself to the situation.

darüber:
Darüber geht nichts.   This tops everything; that's unique.
Eine lange Zeit wird darüber hingehen.   It will take considerable time.

darum:
Darum eben!   That's just the reason!; that's precisely
                                                      why!
Es ist ihm darum zu tun.   That's his object.
Warum taten Sie's?—Darum!   Why did you do it?—Because!
Es sei darum!   Very well!; so be it!; done!
Er weiß darum.   He's in the know; he's on (or wise).

d(a)rumkommen:
Er ist drumgekommen.   He was gypped; he was done out of it.

d(a)runter:
Es ist kein Unterschied darunter.   There's no difference; it amounts to the
                                                      same thing.
Es steckt etwas darunter.   There's something at the bottom of it.
Er tut es nicht darunter.   He won't do it for less.
Was verstehen Sie darunter?   What do you understand by this?; what
                                                      does this mean to you?

das:
Er ist sehr zufrieden damit.   Das bin   He's very satisfied. So am I; same here.
ich auch.

dasein:
Es ist alles schon dagewesen.   There's nothing new under the sun.

daß:
Daß Gott erbarm!   Mercy!; heaven help us!
Daß Sie das ja nicht tun!   Don't you dare do it!
Es ist noch keine Minute her, daß ich ihn   I saw him but a moment ago.
sah.

dastehen:
Wie stehe ich nun da?   Is my face red?; didn't I do fine?

dastehend:
Es ist einzig dastehend.   It's unique; there's nothing like it.

Dauer:
Auf die Dauer wird er krank. | He's sure to get sick.
Das kann auf die Dauer nicht so bleiben. | It can't go on like that.
Es ist auf die Dauer gemacht. | It's made to last; it's durable.

dauern:
Es dauerte über eine Woche, bis er schrieb. | It was over a week before he wrote.

dauern:
Lassen Sie sich die Mühe nicht dauern! | Leave no stone unturned!; don't spare yourself!

Daumen:
Halten Sie mir den Daumen! | Hold your thumbs!; keep your fingers crossed!; wish me luck!

Er hat den Daumen auf dem Beutel. | He's saving every penny; he's a tightwad (*or* very thrifty).

Er setzte ihnen den Daumen aufs Auge. | He brought pressure to bear upon them; he kept a tight rein on them.

Er rührte keinen Daumen. | He didn't lift a finger; he made no move to help.

Er schätzte die Unkosten über den Daumen. | He gave a rough estimate of the expenses.

Daumenschraube:
Man legte ihm Daumenschrauben an. | They put the screws on him; they made him talk (*or* come across).

Daus:
Ei der Daus! | Gee whiz!; great Scott!

davon:
Was habe ich davon? | What good does it do me?
Das kommt davon. | That's what happens.
Mach dich auf und davon! | Beat it!; get away!

davor:
Davor sei Gott! | God forbid!

dazu:
Dazu gehört Zeit. | That requires time.
Er kommt nie dazu, ein Buch zu lesen. | He never finds time to read a book.

dazumal:
Es war anno dazumal. | It was way back (*or* ages ago).

dazwischen:
Er hat überall seine Finger dazwischen. | He has his finger in every pie; he's a busybody.

dazwischenplatzen:
Bitte, nicht immer dazwischenplatzen, wenn er redet! | Don't butt in while he's talking, please!

Decke:
Die Decke fiel ihm von den Augen. | The veil was lifted from his eyes; he suddenly saw the light.

Sie müssen sich nach der Decke strecken. | They have to make both ends meet.
Er kam unter der Decke der Freundschaft. | He came under the guise of friendship.
Die beiden stecken unter einer Decke. | The two are in cahoots; they're fellow conspirators.

Deckmantel:
Er kam unter dem Deckmantel der Freundschaft. | He came (*or* posed) as a friend.

deftig:

Sie sind deftig eingerichtet.

They're very comfortably fixed (*or* established).

Er ist ein deftiger Kerl.

He's a good scout (*or* fellow).

Degen:

Er ist ein alter Degen.

He's an old blade (*or* soldier).

deichseln:

Das wollen wir schon deichseln.

We'll fix that.

dein:

Er hat mein und dein verwechselt.

He stole.

Deixel:

Pfui Deixel!

Hol dich der Deixel!

Phew!

Go jump in the river (*or* bay)!; go to hell!

demütig:

Er bat de= und wehmütig um Verzeihung.

He ate humble pie; he begged forgiveness on all fours.

denken:

Daran ist nicht zu denken.

That's out of the question.

denn:

Was denn?

Ach woher denn!

What is it?; what do you mean?

I should say not!; not at all!

Depp:

So ein Depp!

What a sap (*or* fool)!

Deputat:

Der hat sein Deputat.

He got his (share); he got what was coming to him.

der:

Der Narr, der!

Sind Sie Herr A.?—Ja, der bin ich.

Fool that he is!

Are you Mr. A.?—That's me; the same; I am (he).

Es geschah zu der und der Stunde.

It happened at such and such an hour (*or* a time).

Da soll doch der und jener dreinfahren!

Dash it all!; the devil with it!; deuce take it!

Deubel:

Er fluchte auf Deubel komm (he)raus.

He cursed in fourteen languages; he swore like a trooper.

Deut:

Er kümmert sich keinen Deut darum.

He doesn't care a hoot (*or* whoop); he doesn't give a damn.

Deutlichkeit:

Seine Antwort ließ an Deutlichkeit nichts zu wünschen übrig.

He hit the nail on the head; his answer was very much to the point; he couldn't have made it plainer.

deutsch:

Das heißt auf gut deutsch.

Said in plain language; to put it straight from the shoulder.

Dezem:

Er hat seinen Dezem bekommen.

He got his (deserts); he got what was coming to him.

Dichten:
Sein Dichten und Trachten geht dahin. | His heart is set on it.

dichthalten:
Er kann nicht dichthalten. | He's a blab (*or* tattletale); he can't keep anything to himself.

dick:
Er hat es dick. | He's fed up with (*or* tired of) it.
Sie tut gern dick. | She likes to show off (*or* boast).
Er hat sich dick und voll gegessen. | He's stuffed himself; he's eaten his fill.
Die vorderste Linie bekam dicken Dunst. | The front was kept under heavy fire.
Das dicke Ende kommt nach. | The worst is yet to come.
Er saß mit einem dicken Kopf da. | He was down at the mouth; he was in the dumps.

Dicke Luft! | Danger ahead!; look out!
Er hat dicke Mäuse. | He's got plenty of lucre (*or* money).
Die Einladung ist eine dicke Sache. | We've been invited to a big affair.
Das ist so klar wie dicke Tinte. | That's clear as crystal; that's obvious (*or* self-evident).

Er markiert den dicken Wilhelm. | He puts on airs (*or* the dog); he's strutting (*or* showing off).

Dieb:
Gelegenheit macht Diebe. | An open door may tempt a saint.

diebisch:
Er hat sich diebisch gefreut. | He was tickled pink (*or* to death); he enjoyed himself immensely.

Diebstahl:
Er beging geistigen Diebstahl. | He was guilty of plagiarism.

dienen:
Ich werde ihm schon wieder darauf dienen. | I'll get even with him.
Es wird dazu dienen, ihn mißtrauisch zu machen. | It's likely to make him suspicious.
Womit kann ich Ihnen dienen? | What can I do for you?; may I help you?

Dienst:
Ein Dienst ist des andern wert. | One good turn deserves another.
Die Beine versagten ihm den Dienst. | His legs went back on him; he couldn't stand up.

Er hat heute keinen Dienst. | Today is his day off.
Ich will ihm auf den Dienst passen. | I'll keep my eagle eye on him; I'll watch him closely.

Er ist schon lange außer Diensten. | He's retired long ago.
Was steht zu Ihren Diensten? | What can I do for you?

dienstlich:
Er ist dienstlich verhindert. | Business prevents him from coming.

Dienstspritze:
Nur die Dienstspritze war da. | Only the maid was there.

dieser:
Hol mich dieser und jener! | The deuce!; confound it!

Ding:
Es ist ein Ding der Unmöglichkeit. | It's utterly impossible.
Gut Ding will Weile haben. | Haste makes waste.
Sei doch guter Dinge! | Cheer up!; snap out of it!

Er nennt gern die Dinge beim rechten Namen.	He likes to call a spade a spade; he always hits the nail on the head; he's very much to the point.
Es geht nicht mit rechten Dingen zu.	Something's rotten in Denmark; it smells fishy; there's something funny (*or* not right) about it.
Vor allen Dingen muß er schreiben.	First of all he must write.

Dingsda:

Geben Sie mir doch das Dingsda!	Please give me that doohinky (*or* what-do-you-call-it)!

Dingskirchen:

Wie heißt das Dingskirchen da drüben?	What's the name of that thing(umajig) over there?

dir:

Er kam mir nichts, dir nichts herein.	He dropped in cool as a cucumber (*or* quite nonchalantly).
Heute mir, morgen dir.	Every dog has his day; everyone in his turn; we must all die someday.
Wie du mir, so ich dir.	Tit for tat; an eye for an eye, a tooth for a tooth; I'll treat you to some of your own medicine.

doch:

Habe ich doch niemals solchen Unsinn gehört!	I never heard such nonsense in all my life!
Also doch!	Am I surprised!; you don't say so!
Kommen Sie nicht mit?—Ja doch!	Aren't you coming along?—Sure thing!; you bet I am; yes, indeed!
Sagen Sie es uns doch!—Nicht doch!	Tell us, won't you?—Nothing doing!; certainly not!

Doktorfrage:

Das ist eine Doktorfrage.	That's a poser (*or* sticker); that's a hard question.

doll:

Das ist ja doll!	It can't be; it's not possible!; that's a little too strong (*or* going too far); I can't believe it!

Donnerschlag:

Donnerschlag!	Good gravy!; gosh!; golly!

Donnerwetter:

Da soll doch gleich ein Donnerwetter dreinfahren!	Confound it!; to blazes with it!
Er fuhr wie ein heiliges Donnerwetter drein.	He raised the roof; he gave them hell.
Zum Donnerwetter noch mal!	Hang it all!

doof:

Er ist ein doofer Kerl.	He's a Caspar Milquetoast; he's a regular goof (*or* sap).

doppelt:

Doppelt genäht hält besser.	A stitch in time saves nine; better too much than not enough.
Er sieht die Buchstaben doppelt.	He's seeing things; he's drunk.

Dorf:

Das sind mir böhmische Dörfer.

That's all Greek to me; I don't know the first thing about it.

Er wohnt auf dem Dorf.

He lives in the country.

Er geht jetzt auf die Dörfer.

He has come down in the world.

Tragen Sie doch die Kirche nicht ums Dorf!

Get to the point!; cut it short!; be brief!

Er kommt vom Dorf.

He's a hayseed (or hick); he's a yokel.

Dorn:

Er ist ihnen ein Dorn im Auge.

He's an eyesore (or a pain in the neck) to them; he's a thorn in their side.

Sein Lebensweg ist voller Dornen.

His life is not all smooth sailing; he has his ups and downs.

dorthinaus:

Er wußte seine Sache bis dorthinaus.

He knew his lesson from A to Z (or perfectly).

dösig:

Sitz doch nicht so dösig da!

Don't sit there wool-gathering (or daydreaming)!; come down to earth!

Döz:

Er erhielt einen Schlag auf den Döz.

He got a blow on the bean (or head).

Drache(n):

Sie ist ein alter Drachen.

She's an old hell-cat (or battle-ax); she's a troublemaker.

Draht:

Der Draht zwischen ihnen ist gerissen.

They're not on speaking terms; they've broken with one another.

Er ist ohne Draht.

He's short of cash.

Dran:

Es kostet zehn Mark mit allem Drum und Dran.

With all the trappings (or extras) included, it costs ten marks; ten marks covers everything.

Drang:

Im Drang des Augenblicks verstand sie ihn nicht.

She didn't understand him just then (or at the moment).

Drasch:

Hat der aber Drasch!

He certainly is rushed (or swamped with work).

Draufgänger:

Er ist ein toller Draufgänger.

He's a fast worker (or go-getter); he's a regular dare-devil.

draufgehen:

Das Tier ging bald drauf.

The animal soon died.

Er läßt viel draufgehen.

He spends money like a drunken sailor; he's a regular spendthrift.

drauflosreden:

Er redete einfach drauflos.

He talked a blue streak; he rambled on; he spouted.

drauffetzen:

Lassen Sie uns noch einen drauffetzen!

Let's have a snifter (or drink) on it!

drechseln:

Er drechselte nichtssagende Phrasen.

He was phrase-mongering (*or* making conversation).

Dreck:

Was kostet der ganze Dreck?

How much is the whole shooting match (*or* business)?

Er hat Dreck am Stecken.

He has a guilty conscience.

Das geht Sie einen Dreck an!

You haven't any stake in this game!; it's none of your business!

Er macht sich einen Dreck draus.

He doesn't care a hoot (*or* whoop).

Er muß den Karren aus dem Dreck ziehen.

He has to pull them out of the rut; he has to help them over the rough spots.

Er ist aus dem größten Dreck heraus.

He's out of the woods; the worst is behind him.

Er geht mit ihnen durch Dreck und Speck.

He sticks to them through thick and thin; he stands by them in fair weather or foul.

Er ließ sie im Dreck sitzen.

He left them in the lurch.

Sie kümmert sich um jeden Dreck.

She's a busybody; she pokes her nose into everything.

dreckig:

Tun Sie das nicht, oder es geht Ihnen dreckig!

You'll get it in the neck if you do that!

Augenblicklich geht es seiner Familie dreckig.

At present his family is up against it (*or* badly off).

Dreh:

Er hat den Dreh weg.

He's an old hand (*or* a past master) at it; he knows how to do it.

Er machte den folgenden Dreh.

He played this trick.

drehen:

Darum dreht es sich gerade.

That's the crux (*or* point) of the whole matter; it hinges (*or* depends) on just this.

Er hat schon wieder ein Ding gedreht.

He pulled a new job (*or* committed another crime).

drei:

Bleiben Sie mir drei Schritte vom Leib weg!

Keep (*or* Hands) off!; keep your distance!

Dann gehen Sie doch in drei Teufels Namen!

Then go, for all I care!; for heaven's sake, go then!

Das läßt sich mit drei Worten sagen.

In a nutshell (*or* word); to put it briefly; to sum it up.

Dreier:

Er gab seinen Dreier dazu.

He threw in his two bits' (*or* cents') worth; he put in a word.

Dafür kriegen Sie keinen Dreier.

You won't get much for that.

Spare deine Dreier!

Save your pennies!

Dreikäsehoch:

Er ist nur ein Dreikäsehoch.

He's nothing but a half-pint (*or* shrimp); he's just a little runt (*or* shaver).

dreizehn:

Jetzt schlägt's aber dreizehn!

That's the limit!; that's going too far!

Dresche:

Er bezog schwere Dresche.

He got an awful wallop(ing).

dritt:
    Diese Redensart ist sein drittes Wort.

It's his middle name; it's a pet word (*or* expression) of his.

dröhnig:
    Er ist furchtbar dröhnig.

He creeps like a snail; he's an awful slow-poke.

drüben:
    Er ging in den achtziger Jahren nach drüben.

He went abroad in the eighties.

drüber:
    Alles ging drunter und drüber.

Everything was topsy-turvy; bedlam broke loose.

Druckposten:
    Er hat einen feinen Druckposten.

He has a soft job; his job is a snap.

druckfen:
    Er druckste eine Weile, bis er es zugab.

He hemmed and hawed a minute before he admitted it.

Drum:
    Es kostet zehn Mark mit allem Drum und Dran.

With all the trappings (*or* extras) included, it costs ten marks; ten marks covers everything.

drunter:
    Alles ging drunter und drüber.

Everything was topsy-turvy; bedlam broke loose.

du:
    Sie stehen miteinander auf du.

They're buddies (*or* pals); they're very thick; they're close friends.

    Bei ihm geht alles gleich per du.

It doesn't take him long to be on familiar terms with a person.

    Er tut, als ob er mit unserm Herrgott per du wäre.

He acts as if he were the Almighty Himself.

ducken:
    Den will ich schön ducken.

I'll take him down a peg; I'll put him in his place.

dufte:
    Es war eine dufte Sache.

It was a honey; it was the berries; it was a beaut(y).

dumm:
    Das ist nun doch zu dumm!
    Der Kerl ist dumm und gefräßig.
    Das ist eine dumme Geschichte!
    Dummes Zeug!

Darn the luck!; how stupid (*or* awkward)!
He's an arrogant ass; he's got some ego.
That's a messy business (*or* pretty fix)!
Bunk!; rats!; applesauce!; nonsense!

dummerhaftig:
    Ihm war ganz dummerhaftig zumute.

His head was in a whirl (*or* going round and round).

Dummerjan:
    So ein Dummerjan!

What a sap (*or* fool)!

Dummheit:
    Er kommt mit seiner Dummheit fort.

Fortune favors a fool.

Dummsdorf:
    Ich bin doch nicht von Dummsdorf!

I'm from Missouri!; I wasn't born yester-day!; I'm not altogether dumb!

dun:
Er war ziemlich dun. — He was pretty well soused (*or* drunk).

dunkel:
Er redete so dunkel. — He spoke in riddles (*or* very mysteriously).
Er ist ein dunkler Ehrenmann. — He's a fly-by-night; he's a shady (*or* doubtful) character.

In jeder Familie gibt es einen dunklen Punkt. — There's a skeleton in every closet; every family has its ugly duckling.

dünn:
Mach dich dünn! — Scram!; beat it!; off with you!; make yourself scarce.

Dunnerlittchen:
Dunnerlittchen, ist das eine Kälte! — Boy, but it's cold!

Dunst:
Er hat keinen blassen Dunst davon. — He hasn't the faintest notion (*or* least idea).
Er machte ihnen blauen Dunst vor. — He gave them a line; he strung them along; he pulled the wool over their eyes.

Die vorderste Linie erhielt dicken Dunst. — The front was kept under heavy fire.

durch:
Der Anzug ist durch. — The suit is on the fritz (*or* worn out).
Es ist drei durch. — It's past three.
Es regnete den ganzen Tag durch. — It rained all day long.

durchackern:
Er muß das Buch noch durchackern. — He has to wade through (*or* finish) the book.

durchaus:
Werden Sie's tun?—Durchaus nicht! — Will you do it?—Not on a bet!; I should say not!
Er handelte durchaus gegen die Vorschriften. — He acted in direct opposition to the regulations.
Sie will es so durchaus. — She insists on it.

durchbeißen:
Er wird sich schon durchbeißen. — He'll clear the hurdle; he'll make the grade (*or* succeed).

durchbrennen:
Sie brannte mit ihm durch. — She eloped (*or* ran off) with him.

durchbringen:
Er hat das große Vermögen durchgebracht. — He squandered the huge fortune.

durchdringen:
Ich glaube nicht, daß er damit durchdringt. — I doubt that he'll get away with that.

durchdrungen:
Er ist von der Idee durchdrungen. — He's sold on the idea; it went over big with him.

durchfallen:
Der Vorschlag fiel durch. — The motion was defeated.

durchfliegen:
Er flog in der Prüfung durch. — He flunked out; he failed the test.
Er hat das Buch nur durchflogen. — He just skimmed over (*or* glanced through) the book.

durchfüttern:
  Er läßt ſich von ſeinen Verwandten durch= | He sponges (*or* imposes) on his relatives; his
füttern. | folks support him.

Durchgänger:
  Sie iſt ein kleiner Durchgänger. | She's a little high-stepper; she's a little go-
| getter (*or* fast worker).

durchgeben:
  Die Nachricht wurde im Rundfunk durch= | The news was broadcast over the radio.
gegeben. |

durchgedreht:
  Er iſt völlig durchgedreht. | He's all fagged (*or* worn out); he's com-
| pletely screwy.

durchgehen:
  Der Antrag ging durch. | The motion was carried.
  Die Mutter läßt ihr alles durchgehen. | Her mother lets her have her own way.
  Sollen wir das Gepäck durchgehen laſſen? | Shall we check over the baggage?
  Er muß ſeine Aufgabe noch durchgehen. | He must first finish his lesson.

durchhecheln:
  Sie hechelten die lieben Verwandten durch. | They razzed (*or* criticized) their relatives.

durchhelfen:
  Sie helfen ſich ſo durch. | They barely get along (on what they earn);
| they eke out a meager existence.

durchkommen:
  Er kommt mit ſeiner Einnahme ſo eben | He can just make both ends meet; he just
durch. | manages to squeeze (*or* pull) through (on
| what he earns).
  Ich verſtehe nicht, wie er damit durchkam. | I don't see how he got away with it (*or* put
| it across).

durchmachen:
  Sie haben viel durchgemacht. | They've been through (*or* put up with) a
| great deal; they've had a lot of trouble.

durchnäßt:
  Er war völlig durchnäßt. | He was drenched (*or* soaked) to the skin.

durchnehmen:
  Er nahm das Kapitel noch einmal durch. | He went over (*or* reviewed) the chapter
| once more.

durchplumpſen:
  Er iſt in der Prüfung durchgeplumpſt. | He flunked out; he failed the test.

durchringen:
  Ein neuer Gedanke ringt ſich mehr und | A new thought is emerging (*or* coming to
mehr durch. | the fore).

durchſchlagen:
  Die Abmachung gilt, ſchlag durch! | O.K. (*or* That's a go) — shake (hands) on it!
  Er ſchlägt ſich ſo durch. | He lives on a shoestring; he barely makes a
| go of it.

durchſchlagend:
  Seine Rede hatte einen durchſchlagenden | His speech went over with a bang; it was a
Erfolg. | sensation (*or* big success).

durchſehen:
  Ich ſehe in der Sache nicht durch. | I don't see my way clear in the matter; I'm
| in the dark about it.

durchsetzt:

Das Volk ist durchsetzt mit diesen Ideen.

The people are imbued (*or* obsessed) with such ideas.

Durchstecherei:

Sie begingen Durchstechereien.

They played into each other's hand; they plotted (*or* conspired) together.

durchtrieben:

Er ist ein durchtriebener Kunde.

He's a sly fox (*or* crafty fellow).

durchwichsen:

Er hat den Jungen durchgewichst.

He spanked the boy.

durchwutschen:

Er ist der Polizei durchgewutscht.

He gave the police the slip; he got away from them.

Durchzieher:

Er hatte einen mächtigen Durchzieher im Gesicht.

He had a big scar on his face.

Durchzug:

Machen Sie doch ein wenig Durchzug im Zimmer!

Air out the room, please!

dürfen:

Darf ich bitten?
Das darf und soll nicht sein.
Sie dürfen mir's glauben.
Sie dürfen es nur sagen.

If you please!
That must not be; it's out of the question.
All kidding (*or* fooling) aside!; believe me!
You need only say the word.

Dusche:

Ihr Brief gab ihm eine kalte Dusche.

Her letter threw cold water on him (*or* dampened his enthusiasm); it brought him down to earth.

Dusel:

Da haben Sie aber Dusel gehabt!

That was a real break (*or* stroke of luck)!; you were really lucky!

Er ist fast immer im Dusel.

Most of the time he's lit (*or* soused).

Dussel:

So ein Dussel!

What a sap (*or* fool)!

Duzfuß:

Sie stehen miteinander auf dem Duzfuß.

They're buddies (*or* chums); they're thick; they're close friends.

Ebbe:

In seinem Geldbeutel ist Ebbe.	His funds are low; he's broke.

eben:

Eben darum!	That's just why!
Den eben suche ich.	He's the very man I'm looking for.
Er ist eben krank.	Remember that he's sick.
Das nun eben nicht!	Rather the contrary!
Ja eben!	You said it; precisely!

Ebene:

Arbeitslosigkeit brachte ihn auf die schiefe Ebene.	Unemployment put him on the downgrade.

Eber:

Er ist wütend wie ein angeschossener Eber.	He's mad as hops (or a wet hen).

Eckart:

Hindenburg war ein getreuer Eckart seines Volkes.	Hindenburg was a warm friend and an impartial adviser to his people.

Ecke:

Lassen Sie uns noch eine kleine Ecke bummeln!	Let's walk another block!; let's stroll along a little farther!
An allen Ecken und Kanten sah man Menschen.	People were seen everywhere.
Es ging bunt über Eck her.	There were wild goings-on; things were happening right and left.
Er ist letzten Sommer um die Ecke gegangen.	He cashed in (or died) last summer.
Ich traue ihm nicht um die Ecke.	I wouldn't trust him to the door (or out of my sight).
Sie kamen von allen Ecken und Enden der Welt.	They came from all parts of the world.

eckig:

Er lachte sich eckig.	He doubled up with laughter; he laughed himself sick.

effeff:

Die Ware ist effeff.	The article is A number one (or first-rate).

Effeff:

Er versteht seine Sache aus dem Effeff.	He knows his onions (or stuff); he knows his business.

Effet:

Geben Sie dem (Billard) Ball etwas Effet!	Put some English on the ball!

egal:

Er setzt sich egal auf ihren Platz.	He takes her seat time and again.

egalweg:

Er redete egalweg.

He rattled (*or* raved) on and on; he talked interminably.

eher:

Alles eher als das.

Anything but that.

Das läßt sich eher hören.

That sounds better; that's more like it.

Ehre:

Geben Sie der Wahrheit die Ehre!

Speak the truth!

Damit kann er keine Ehre einlegen.

That does him no credit.

Ihr Wort in Ehren.

With all deference to you.

Ehrenmann:

Er ist ein dunkler Ehrenmann.

He's a fly-by-night; he's a shady (*or* doubtful) character.

Ehrensache:

Kann ich mich darauf verlassen?—Ehrensache!

Can I rely on it?—Honor bright!; you can bank (*or* count) on me!

ehrlich:

Es geht nicht ehrlich damit zu.

There's foul play abroad; it's not aboveboard.

Er freut sich ehrlichen Herzens darüber.

He's genuinely pleased about it.

ei:

Ei freilich!

Why, yes (*or* of course)!; indeed!; surely!

Ei:

Das Ei des Kolumbus!

Elementary, my dear Watson!; that's simple!

Will das Ei klüger sein als die Henne?

Wise guy, eh?; telling me?; so you think you know it all?; children should be seen and not heard.

Sie gleichen sich wie ein Ei dem andern.

They're alike as two peas in a pod.

Er muß wie ein rohes Ei behandelt werden.

He must be handled with kid gloves (*or* very gently); he's very touchy (*or* sensitive).

Er wollte sein Ei dazwischen legen.

He wanted to put in his two cents (*or* have his say.)

Er muß das Ei unterm Huhn verkaufen.

He needs money badly.

Auch ein gescheites Huhn legt die Eier neben das Nest.

It's a good horse that never stumbles; everyone makes mistakes.

Das hat seine Eier.

That's not so easy as it looks.

Er ist kaum aus dem Ei gekrochen.

He's not yet dry behind his ears; he's only half-baked.

Er sieht aus wie aus dem Ei gepellt.

He looks spick and span; he looks as if he had just stepped out of a bandbox.

Kümmern Sie sich nicht um ungelegte Eier!

Don't count your chickens before they're hatched!; don't cross your bridges before you come to them!

Eiche:

Es fällt keine Eiche vom ersten Streich.

Rome wasn't built in a day; that takes time.

Eichel:

Er ist gesund wie eine Eichel.

He's fit as a fiddle.

Eichhörnchen:

Sie ist flink wie ein Eichhörnchen.

She's quick as a flash.

Eiertanz:
   Er mußte einen regelrechten Eiertanz aufführen. — He had to handle the matter with kid gloves (*or* very tactfully).

eigen:
   Machen Sie sich das zu eigen! — Get that down pat!; keep that in mind!
   Das ist doch eigen. — That's odd (*or* strange).
   Es ist ein eigner Ausdruck. — It's an idiom (*or* colloquialism); it's a slang expression.
   Er weiß es aus eigner Erfahrung. — He knows it from personal experience.
   Eigner Herd ist Goldes wert. — Be it ever so humble, there's no place like home.
   Er kam in eigner Person. — He came in person; he himself came.

Eigennutz:
   Gemeinnutz geht vor Eigennutz. — Public welfare (*or* good) comes before private profit.

eigens:
   Man lud ihn eigens dazu ein. — They made it a point to invite him.

Eigensinn:
   Sie ist ein kleiner Eigensinn. — She's a stubborn little mule; she's headstrong (*or* has a mind of her own).

Eilbote:
   Durch Eilboten zu bestellen! — Special delivery!

Eile:
   Die Sache hat keine Eile. — Take it easy!; no (need to) hurry!; the matter is not urgent.

eilen:
   Eile mit Weile! — Haste makes waste.
   Eilt! (auf Briefen) — Urgent! (*referring to letters*).

eilig:
   Warum so eilig? — What's the hurry?

Eimer:
   Jetzt kann er in den Eimer gucken. — Now he may go (and) whistle for it; let him try and get it.

ein:
   Er fragte in einem fort. — He put one question after another.
   Es geht in einem hin. — It's killing two birds with one stone.

ein:
   Er weiß weder ein noch aus. — He doesn't know where to turn next.
   Er geht bei ihnen ein und aus. — He's a frequent guest at their home.

einbringen:
   Er möchte die verlorne Zeit wieder einbringen. — He would like to make up for lost time.

einbrocken:
   Was man sich eingebrockt hat, muß man auch ausessen. — One must reap what one has sown; you have to pay the piper; you have to suffer the consequences.
   Er hat was einzubrocken. — He's well fixed; he's well-to-do.

einbürgern:
   Viele Fremdwörter haben sich eingebürgert. — Many foreign words have been adopted.

eindecken:
   Sie haben sich für den Winter gut mit Kohlen eingedeckt. — They got in a good(ly) supply of coal for the winter.

eindeutig:
Seine Antwort ist völlig eindeutig.

His answer leaves no doubt; his answer is perfectly clear.

eindrillen:
Er drillt sie für das Examen ein.

He's tutoring them for the exam.

Eindruck:
Er hat Eindruck geschunden.

He went over big; he made a hit (*or* good impression).

eind(r)useln:
Er ist gerade etwas eingedruselt.

He's just taking a little nap (*or* snooze).

eine:
Sie sind aber eine!
Schwuppdich, hatte er eine weg.

You're a case!; you're a riot (*or* panic)!
Bingo (*or* Before he knew it), he got one in the face.

einer:
Das ist einer!
Unser einer darf das nicht tun.

What a man!
People like us don't dare do that.

einfach:
Nach Berlin, dritter Klasse, einfach!

A one-way ticket to Berlin, third class.

Einfachheit:
Er kam der Einfachheit halber selbst.

To save trouble, he came himself.

einfädeln:
Er hat die Sache geschickt eingefädelt.

He did that very neatly (*or* cleverly).

Einfall:
Er hat Einfälle wie ein altes Haus.

He gets crazy notions.

einfallen:
Halt, da fällt mir ein!

Hold on (*or* Just a minute), I've got an idea!; by the way.

Das fällt mir im Traum nicht ein.
Lassen Sie sich das nicht einfallen!
Das sollte mir einfallen!

I wouldn't dream of it.
Don't you dare!; just you try it!
What do you take me for?; do I look that dumb?

Einfalt:
Sie ist eine kleine Einfalt.

She's a little dumbbell.

einfinden:
Hoffentlich findet er sich bald ein.

I hope he'll turn up soon.

einflechten:
Er flocht viele Zitate in seine Rede ein.

He quoted freely in his speech.

einflößen:
Ein Telegramm flößt ihr immer Furcht ein.

A telegram always terrifies her.

einfuchsen:
Er wird darauf eingefuchst.

He's being coached (*or* trained) for it.

eingefleischt:
Er ist ein eingefleischter Junggeselle.

He's a confirmed (*or* born) bachelor.

eingefressen:
Er hegt einen tief eingefressenen Haß gegen sie.

He hates them like poison.

eingehakt:
Sie gingen eingehakt davon.

They left arm in arm.

eingehen:
Es geht ihm schwer ein.
It sinks in slowly with him; he's slow to catch on.

Die Zeitschrift ging ein.
The periodical was discontinued.

eingehenkelt:
Sie kamen eingehenkelt.
They came arm in arm.

eingeimpft:
Die Gewohnheit ist ihm sozusagen eingeimpft.
It has become second nature to him.

eingekeilt:
In der Menschenmenge waren sie völlig eingekeilt.
They were lost in the crowd.

eingelocht:
Er ist schon wieder eingelocht.
He's back in jail (or the pen); he's behind the bars again.

eingenommen:
Er ist sehr dafür eingenommen.
He's very keen (or enthusiastic) about it; he's all for it.

Er ist sehr von sich eingenommen.
He's too big for his boots; he has an excellent opinion of himself.

Er hatte einen eingenommenen Kopf.
He had a hangover (or headache).

eingeregnet:
Sie waren volle drei Tage eingeregnet.
The rain kept them in for three whole days.

eingerichtet:
Die Wohnung ist nett eingerichtet.
The apartment is beautifully furnished.

eingeseift:
Er kam schwer eingeseift heim.
He came home all lit up (or dead-drunk).

eingespielt:
Die Mannschaft war glänzend aufeinander eingespielt.
It was perfect teamwork.

eingestellt:
Er ist gegen sie eingestellt.
He's on the outs with them; he has it in for them.

Sie sind pazifistisch eingestellt.
They have pacifist leanings (or sympathies).

eingeweicht:
Er kam gründlich eingeweicht zurück.
He came back drenched to the skin (or soaking wet).

einhacken:
Alle hackten auf ihn ein.
Everyone picked on him; they all had it in for him.

einhauen:
Er haute tüchtig ein.
He pitched in with gusto; he ate heartily.

einheimsen:
Er heimst stets die Vorteile ein.
He gets all the breaks; luck is always with him.

einheizen:
Er hat tüchtig eingeheizt.
He's been drinking heavily.
Dem sollten Sie mal einheizen.
You should make it hot (or disagreeable) for him.

einholen:
Er kann das Pensum kaum einholen.
He can hardly make up the lesson (or work).

einig:
Er ist mit sich selbst nicht einig, was er tun soll. | He himself doesn't know what he'll do.

einiggehen:
Er geht mit uns darin einig. | It's all right with him; it suits him.

Einkehr:
Halten Sie einmal Einkehr bei sich selbst! | You'd better go into a huddle (with yourself)!; take stock of yourself!

einkommen:
Er ist um seine Entlassung eingekommen. | He sent in his resignation.

einkratzen:
Er versteht es, sich bei seinem Chef einzukratzen. | He knows how to get next to (*or* in good with) his boss.

einlassen:
Laß dich nicht darauf ein! | Have nothing to do with it!; don't go in on it!

einlaufen:
Er läuft uns fast das Haus ein. | He wouldn't take "no" for an answer; he's been bothering the life out of us.

einlegen:
Er wird große Ehre damit einlegen. | He'll gain great honor by that; it will boost his reputation considerably.

einlenken:
Er lenkte sofort wieder ein. | He came round at once; he immediately changed his tone of voice; he became very affable.

einleuchten:
Das leuchtet mir ein. | I get the idea; I (begin to) see.

(ein)mal:
Er wiederholte es einmal ums andere. | He repeated it over and over again.
Das soll mal einer nachmachen! | Can you beat that?; I'd like to see somebody else do that!
Wenn er nur erst mal hier wäre! | If only he were here!
Er hörte es nicht einmal. | He didn't even hear it.
Er bricht sich noch einmal den Hals. | He'll break his neck one of these days.
Er ist noch einmal so alt. | He's twice as old as that.
Es ist nun mal so. | That's how it is, and nothing can be done about it.
Es war nun mal ihre Freude nicht. | She simply didn't enjoy it.

einnicken:
Er wollte gerade ein wenig einnicken. | He was just on the point of taking a nap (*or* snooze).

einpacken:
Pack ein mit diesen Scherzen! | Cut out the wisecracks!; don't be funny!
Das haben Sie so fein gemacht, daß ich einpacken kann. | There's nothing left for me to teach you; you know it all.

einpökeln:
Sie können sich einpökeln lassen! | You ought to hide your face!; shame on you!

einreden:
Das lasse ich mir nicht einreden! | I'm from Missouri!; I've got to be shown!; prove it!

einreißen:
Die Unsitte reißt immer weiter ein. | The bad habit is growing worse all the time.

einrenken:
Er versuchte, die Sache einzurenken. | He tried to straighten out the matter.

einrichten:
Er richtet sich auf einen längeren Aufenthalt ein. | He's planning on a longer stay.
Sie wissen sich einzurichten. | They know how to balance their budget.

einrühren:
Da haben Sie sich was Schönes eingerührt! | You surely got yourself into deep water!; a nice mess you got yourself into!

eins:
Eins ins andere gerechnet. | Altogether; taken all in all.
Verflucht noch eins! | Heck!; drat it!; damn it all!
Mir ist das eins. | It makes no difference to me; I don't care.
Sie sind eins. | They're in agreement.
Er mengte eins ins andere. | He got everything balled (*or* mixed) up; he got it wrong.
Wenn man eins zum andern nimmt. | If you put two and two together.
Mit eins sprang er auf. | Suddenly he jumped up.

einsalzen:
Das werde ich ihm aber einsalzen. | I'll make him pay for that; I'll fix him.

einsargen:
Er mußte alle Hoffnungen einsargen. | He had to bury his hopes; he gave up all hope.

Einsatz:
Das Amt verlangt vollen Einsatz seiner Persönlichkeit. | The position demands his best.

einschenken:
Schenken Sie sich ein! | Help yourself!; fill up (your glass)!

einschlafen:
Die Sache ist eingeschlafen. | The matter has been shelved (*or* postponed).

Einschlag:
Er sprach von dem germanischen Einschlag in den verschiedenen Völkern. | He spoke about the Germanic strain (*or* blood) in the various nationalities.

einschlagen:
Schlagen Sie ein! | Shake (hands) on it!
Der Junge schlägt nicht gut ein. | The boy isn't making the grade; he's not doing so well.
Das schlägt nicht in sein Fach ein. | That's not up his alley; it's out of his line.
Die Ware schlägt nicht ein. | The article doesn't sell; it's a lemon (*or* flop).
Er schlug alle möglichen Wege ein. | He tried every which (*or* possible) way.
Er hat den kürzeren Weg eingeschlagen. | He took the short cut.

einschlägig:
Benutzen Sie die einschlägigen Werke. | Consult the literature on the subject!

einschmeicheln:
Er versucht, sich bei ihnen einzuschmeicheln. | He soft-soaps them; he tries to worm his way into their good graces.

einschnappen:
Er schnappt auf jede Kleinigkeit gleich ein. — He's quick to get sore; he takes offense easily.

einschneidend:
Die Sache ist von einschneidender Bedeutung. — The matter is of the first (*or* greatest) importance.

einschränken:
Sie wird sich einschränken müssen. — She'll have to cut down expenses.

einschulen:
Er wird Sie einschulen. — He'll show you the ropes; he'll break you in; he'll train you.

einsehen:
Er sah das früh genug ein. — He realized that in time.

Einsehen:
Das Wetter hatte ein Einsehen mit ihnen. — The weatherman favored them; they had fair weather.

einseifen:
Er hat sie gehörig eingeseift. — He hoodwinked (*or* deceived) them shamelessly.

einsetzen:
Er setzte sich für sie ein. — He put in a good word for them.

Einsicht:
Haben Sie doch Einsicht! — Use some sense!; use your head!

einspannen:
Spannen Sie den Kerl fester ein! — Clamp down (*or* Sit) on him harder!; give him less leeway!

Einspänner:
Er ist ein Einspänner. — He's a lone wolf (*or* an individualist); he shuns people.

einspinnen:
Man hat ihn gestern eingesponnen. — He was arrested yesterday.

einspringen:
Bei welcher Verbindung sprang er ein? — What fraternity did he make (*or* join)?
Als er verwundet wurde, sprang ein anderer Spieler für ihn ein. — When he was injured, another player took his place.

einstecken:
Vergiß nicht, etwas Geld einzustecken! — Don't forget to take some money along!
Er mußte viel einstecken. — He had to put up with many things.

einstehen:
Jeder muß für sich selbst einstehen. — Every man for himself!

einsteigen:
Alles einsteigen! — All aboard!

Einstellung:
Was ist seine Einstellung dazu? — What stand does he take?; what's his opinion?

einstreichen:
Er strich bei dem Geschäft tausend Mark ein. — He cleaned up (*or* made) a thousand marks on the deal.

Eintrag:
Meinungsverschiedenheiten dann und wann tun ihrer Freundschaft keinen Eintrag. — An occasional disagreement in no wise affects (*or* endangers) their friendship.

einträuken:
Das wird er ihnen schon eintränken. — He'll make them suffer for that.

eintreffen:
Seine Erwartungen sind nicht einge-troffen. — His hopes failed to materialize.

eintrichtern:
Er hatte es ihm noch eingetrichtert, was er sagen sollte. — He had even coached him in what he was to say.

Einvernehmen:
Setzen Sie sich mit ihm ins Einver-nehmen! — Try to come to terms with him!

einverstanden:
Einverstanden! — O.K.!; agreed!
Die Provision einverstanden. — Commission included.

einwickeln:
Lassen Sie sich nicht von ihm einwickeln! — Don't let him pull the wool over your eyes!; don't be taken in by him!

einzeln:
Er erörterte einzelnes. — He discussed several things.
Er ging nicht ins einzelne ein. — He didn't go into detail.

Eis:
Zu Pfingsten auf dem Eis! — Never!; not a chance!
Man führte ihn aufs Eis. — He was duped (*or* taken in).
Wenn dem Esel zu wohl ist, geht er aufs Eis. — Pride goeth before a fall; too much luck makes a man foolhardy.

Eisen:
Not bricht Eisen. — Necessity knows no law.
Man muß das Eisen schmieden, solange es warm ist. — Make hay while the sun shines!; make the most of your opportunities.
Man hat ihn zum alten Eisen geworfen. — They threw him on the scrap heap; he was given the gate; he was discarded (*or* discharged).

Eisenbahn:
Mach schnell, es ist die höchste Eisenbahn! — Hurry up, it's high time (you got started)!

eitel:
Sie schwamm in eitel Wonne. — She was in seventh heaven; she was ecstatically (*or* blissfully) happy.

Elefant:
Er ist so ungeschickt wie ein Elefant im Porzellanladen. — He's clumsy as a bull in a china shop; he falls all over himself.
Er macht aus einer Mücke einen Ele-fanten. — He makes a mountain out of a molehill; he makes much ado about nothing.

elend:
Er wußte seine Sache elend gut. — He had his subject down pat; he knew it inside out.

Elend:
Er hat das graue Elend. — He has a hangover (*or* headache).

elft:
Halte dich ans elfte Gebot! — Watch your step!; don't let them put one over on you (*or* take you in)!

Ellbogenfreiheit:
Er hat Ellbogenfreiheit.

He has elbow room (*or* free play); he can do as he pleases.

Elle:
Er geht, als hätte er eine Elle verschluckt.

He's stiff as a poker (*or* board).

Elster:
Er bindet gern etwas der Elster auf den Schwanz.

He's an old magpie; he likes to spread the dirt (*or* carry tales); he loves to gossip.

Eltern:
Dieser Wein ist nicht von schlechten Eltern.

This wine isn't half bad; it comes of good stock (*or* vintage).

Emmchen:
Er bat sie um drei Emmchen (= Mark).

He touched (*or* begged) them for three marks.

empfehlen:
Empfehlen Sie mich ihm!
Ich empfehle mich.
Er empfahl sich auf französisch.

Remember me to him!
So long!; good-bye!
He took French leave; he beat it.

Endchen:
Kommen Sie noch ein Endchen mit!

Come along a little way!; walk a block with me!

Ende:
So was zu behaupten, das ist doch das Ende von weg!

I call that laying it on a bit thick; that's putting it strong; that's going a little too far.

Das dicke Ende kommt nach.
Es ist noch ein gutes Ende bis dahin.
Letzten Endes ist es egal.

The worst is yet to come.
It's a long way off yet.
When you get right down to it (*or* In the last analysis), it really makes no difference.

Die Arbeit geht ihrem Ende entgegen.
Hoffentlich nimmt alles ein gutes Ende.
Am Ende kommt er doch noch.
Sie kamen von allen Ecken und Enden der Welt.
Es geht mit ihm zu Ende.
Es ist zu Ende.

The work is nearing completion.
I hope everything will turn out for the best.
He may come after all.
They came from all parts of the world.
He's on his last legs; he's done for.
It's all over.

eng:
Sitzen Sie denn nicht zu eng hier?

Aren't you too crowded here?; are you sure you have enough room to sit comfortably?

Ihm wurde zu eng.

He felt ill at ease.

Enge:
Er hat sie in die Enge getrieben.

He has placed them in an awkward position; he has driven them into a corner.

Engel:
Plötzlich flog ein Engel durchs Zimmer.

Suddenly a dead calm descended on the room.

Dein guter Engel gab dir das ein.

Your fairy godmother must have been there; luck was with you.

entblöden:
Er entblödete sich nicht wiederzukommen.

He had the nerve (*or* crust) to come back.

Ente:
Die Nachricht erwies ſich als eine Ente. | It was a bum steer (*or* false rumor).
Er ſchwimmt wie eine bleierne Ente. | He swims like a rock.
Laſſen Sie uns eine kalte Ente trinken! | Let's have a soft drink!

entfallen:
Das Wort iſt mir entfallen. | The word has slipped my mind.

entfernteſt:
Er denkt nicht im entfernteſten daran, es zu tun. | He wouldn't dream of doing it.

entgeiſtert:
Er ſah ſie entgeiſtert an. | He looked at her flabbergasted.

entgleiſen:
Der Redner entgleiſte einige Male. | The speaker slipped a few times; he made some mistakes.

entheben:
Entheben Sie ihn der Unannehmlichkeit! | Spare him the embarrassment!

entkräften:
Er vermochte nicht, den Verdacht zu entkräften. | He couldn't defend himself (against the suspicion).

entlang:
Hier entlang, bitte! | This way, please!

entnehmen:
Woraus entnehmen Sie das? | What makes you think so?; what gives you that idea?

entpuppen:
Die Sache entpuppte ſich als grober Schwindel. | The matter turned out to be a big fraud (*or* swindle).

entrücken:
Der Tod hat ihn allen Sorgen entrückt. | Death put an end to his sorrows.

entrümpelt:
Der Boden in ihrem Haus iſt bereits entrümpelt. | All the junk has been cleared out of their attic.

entſchieden:
Er beſtreitet das entſchieden. | He disagrees emphatically.

entſcheidend:
Er legt entſcheidendes Gewicht darauf. | He makes it a point; he stresses it.

entſchlagen:
Entſchlagen Sie ſich des Gedankens! | Drop (*or* Give up) the idea!

entſchloſſen:
Kurz entſchloſſen entfernte er ſich. | He departed abruptly.

entſchlummern:
Er entſchlummerte gegen zwei Uhr. | He passed away in his sleep at about two o'clock.

entſchuldigen:
Er entſchuldigte ſich mit Kurzſichtigkeit. | He pleaded shortsightedness.

Entſpannung:
Eine Entſpannung der politiſchen Lage trat ein. | The political tension let (*or* eased) up a bit.

entsprechen:
Das entspricht nicht seinen Erwartungen. — That falls short of (*or* doesn't come up to) his expectations.

entwenden:
Jemand wollte ihm den Mantel entwenden. — Someone tried to steal his overcoat.

entziehen:
Das entzieht sich meiner Kenntnis. — I don't know that; I'm not informed on that point.

Epistel:
Er hat ihnen ordentlich die Epistel gelesen. — He talked to them like a Dutch uncle; he lectured them good and proper.

erbarmen:
Er singt, daß sich Gott erbarm. — He sings like a screech owl; he has the most God-awful voice.

erbaulich:
Das ist ja recht erbaulich! — That's a fine how-do-you-do (*or* state of affairs)!

erbaut:
Er ist von dem Vorschlag wenig erbaut. — He isn't overly keen (*or* enthusiastic) about the proposition; he can't warm up to (*or* get excited about) it.

erben:
Hier gibt's nichts zu erben. — There's nothing for us here.

Erbpacht:
Er tut, als hätte er die Weisheit in Erbpacht. — He's playing the wise guy (*or* know-it-all).

Erde:
Alle Schuld rächt sich auf Erden. — A bad penny always turns up; we must all pay the piper.

Erfahrung:
Man kann nur aus Erfahrung urteilen. — The proof of the pudding is in the eating; time will tell.

Er wird das schon in Erfahrung bringen. — He's sure to find it out.

erfinderisch:
Die Liebe macht erfinderisch. — Love finds a way.

Erfüllung:
Sein Traum ging in Erfüllung. — His dream materialized (*or* came true).

ergattern:
Es gelang ihm noch, zwei Karten zu ergattern. — He was lucky enough to get two tickets.

ergeben:
Ihr ergebener . . . . — Yours sincerely . . . .

ergehen:
Er erging sich in Lobeserhebungen über sie. — He praised her to the skies.

Wie ist es Ihnen ergangen, seit ich das Vergnügen hatte, Sie zu sehen? — How have you been since I last saw you?

Er läßt alles über sich ergehen. — He eats humble pie; he submits to everything.

erhalten:
Erhalten Sie uns Ihre Freundschaft! — Don't forget us!

erhärten:
   Er kann das eidlich erhärten. — He can swear to it; he'll vouch for it.

erkennen:
   In der Not erkennt man den Freund. — A friend in need is a friend indeed.
   Er gab ſich zu erkennen. — He revealed his identity.

erkenntlich:
   Er wird ſich dafür erkenntlich zeigen. — He won't forget the favor; he won't be ungrateful.

erklären:
   Er kann es ſich nicht erklären. — He cannot account for it.

erlauben:
   Er kann ſich das erlauben. — He can blow (*or* treat) himself to that; he can afford it.

erleben:
   Hat man je ſo was erlebt? — Did you ever see the like of it?
   Wer das tut, der kann was erleben! — It will get you into trouble!

erledigt:
   Erledigt! — That's that!; that's settled (*or* out of the way)!
   Er iſt bei ſeinem Chef erledigt. — He's in the doghouse; his boss is through with him.
   Er war ganz erledigt. — He was all in (*or* exhausted).

Erliegen:
   Die Grube iſt zum Erliegen gekommen. — The mine is closed (*or* shut) down.

erlogen:
   Das iſt erlogen und erſtunken. — That's a filthy lie.

erlöſt:
   Er iſt erlöſt. — He's dead.

Ernſt:
   Er machte ſich mit allem Ernſt daran. — He went at it tooth and nail (*or* in all seriousness).

Ernte:
   Was hat Ihnen denn die Ernte verhagelt? — Why are you so low (*or* down in the mouth)?; what's troubling you?

erpicht:
   Er iſt ganz aufs Geld erpicht. — He's money-crazy.

Erſcheinung:
   Sie iſt eine blendende Erſcheinung. — She's a stunner (*or* looker); she's a dazzling creature.

erſchlagen:
   Sie fühlt ſich wie erſchlagen. — She's dead tired.
   Er war wie erſchlagen, als er davon hörte. — You could have knocked him down with a feather when he heard of it; he was dumbfounded at the news.

erſt:
   Nun erſt ſprach er. — Not till then did he talk.
   Er kommt erſt in zwei Stunden. — He won't come for two hours yet.
   Wäre er nur erſt hier! — If only he were here!
   Das macht es erſt recht ſchlimm. — That makes it even worse.
   Jetzt tut er's erſt recht nicht. — Now he won't do it at all; he's sure not to do it now.

Fürs erste genügt das.	That will do for the present.
Erste:	
Er zählt zu den Ersten der Stadt.	He's one of the four hundred; he belongs to the élite.
Ersticken:	
Der Saal war zum Ersticken voll.	The hall was packed (*or* jammed) to the rafters.
erstunken:	
Das ist erlogen und erstunken.	That's a filthy lie.
erträglich:	
Es geht ihm erträglich.	He's pretty fair; he's quite well.
erübrigen:	
Es erübrigt sich jedes weitere Wort.	There's nothing more to be said; there will be no further discussion; that's my last word.
erwachsen:	
Es erwachsen keine weiteren Kosten daraus.	There will be no additional expenses.
erweisen:	
Es erwies sich anders, als er erwartete.	It fell short of (*or* didn't come up to) his expectations.
es:	
Es ist jemand da.	Somebody is at the door.
Er hat es gut.	He's well off; he's lucky.
Sind Sie der Arzt?—Ich bin es.	Are you the doctor?—I am.
Esel:	
Er paßt dazu wie der Esel zum Lautenschlagen.	He's like a square peg in a round hole; he isn't suited to it at all.
Ein Esel schimpft den andern Langohr.	The pot calls the kettle black; one crook accuses another.
Er läutete dem Esel zu Grab.	He dangled his fee on the ground.
Wenn's dem Esel zu wohl ist, geht er aufs Eis.	Pride goeth before a fall; too much luck makes a man foolhardy.
Er schlägt den Sack und meint den Esel.	He says one thing and means another.
Wenn man den Esel nennt, kommt er gerennt.	Speak of the devil, and he appears.
Er ist vom Pferd auf den Esel gekommen.	He's come down in the world; his luck has gone back on him.
Er sitzt auf dem Esel und sieht ihn nicht.	He doesn't see the forest for the trees.
Eselsbrücke:	
Er benutzte eine Eselsbrücke.	He used a pony (*or* translation).
Esse:	
Er ist in seinem Esse.	He's in his element; he's very much at home.
Das Geld können Sie in die Esse schreiben.	You can kiss that money good-bye; that money is gone for good.
essen:	
Man ißt dort sehr gut.	The food is very good there.
Es wird nichts so heiß gegessen, wie es gekocht wird.	Nothing is so bad as it is painted; things are always better than they seem.
Selber essen macht fett.	Look out for number one (*or* yourself) first!

Wie man es brockt, muß man es essen.

As you've made your bed, so you must lie in it; you reap what you sow.

Wer nicht arbeitet, soll nicht essen.

No mill, no meal!; earn your keep!

Essig:

Damit ist es Essig.

That's out (of the question).

etepetete:

Sie ist sehr etepetete.

She's so keep-off-the-grass-ish; she's very finicky (or fussy); she's too particular.

etwa:

Ist es Ihnen etwa heute recht?

Will today suit you?

Denken Sie nicht etwa, daß er lügt!

Don't think for a moment that he's lying!

Sahen Sie ihn etwa?

Did you happen to see him?

Eule:

Er ist Eule unter den Krähen.

He's a swan among the geese.

Er trägt Eulen nach Athen.

He carries coals to Newcastle; he's wasting his time (or energy).

ewig:

Ich habe ihn ewig nicht gesehen.

It's ages since I saw him.

Das ist ewig schade.

That's really too bad.

Er ist schon ein ewiger Jude.

He's a wandering Jew; he can't stay put; he's a restless fellow.

Ewigkeit:

Es ist eine Ewigkeit her, daß ich Sie sah.

I haven't seen you for ages.

Sie redete eine ganze Ewigkeit.

She talked endlessly (or on and on).

Exbummel:

Sie machen heute einen Exbummel.

They're making whoopee today; they're on a spree today.

exemplarisch:

Man hat ihn ganz exemplarisch bestraft.

He was severely punished.

Existenz:

Seine Existenz ist gefährdet.

His career is in danger.

Er ist eine dunkle Existenz.

He's a fly-by-night; he's a mysterious character.

Der Orkan vernichtete tausende von Existenzen.

The hurricane took thousands of lives.

extra:

Er hat extra danach gefragt.

He asked expressly about it.

Extrawurst:

Er will immer eine Extrawurst gebraten haben.

He always wants something special; he always wants to be toadied (or catered) to.

F:

Bei ihm geht alles nach Schema F. — He's a regular rubber stamp (*or* automaton); he does everything by rote (*or* in a routine manner).

fabelhaft:

Einfach fabelhaft! — Hot dog (*or* stuff)!; wonderful!; it's amazing (*or* incredible)!

Seine Erzählung klingt fabelhaft. — His story sounds fishy.

Der Hut steht ihr fabelhaft. — The hat is perfectly ducky; it suits her to perfection.

Das ist fabelhaft billig. — That's dirt-cheap.

Er ist ein fabelhafter Kerl. — He's a crackerjack (*or* an amazing fellow); he's a brick (*or* fine fellow).

Fach:

Sie haben weder Dach noch Fach. — They've neither house nor home.

Das schlägt nicht in sein Fach. — That's not in his line (*or* field).

Das Projekt ist unter Dach und Fach. — The project is completed.

Er ist einer vom Fach. — He's an old hand; he knows the ropes (*or* his business).

Kommen Sie damit zu Fach? — Can you make (*or* fix) it?

Fachmann:

Da staunt der Laie, der Fachmann aber wundert sich. — There's nothing to it if you know how.

fachsimpeln:

Sie fachsimpelten den ganzen Abend. — They talked shop (*or* business) all evening long.

fackeln:

Er fackelte nicht lange, sondern kaufte es. — He lost no time in buying it.

Faden:

Ihm riß der Faden der Geduld. — He lost his temper (*or* self-control).

Der Gedanke zieht sich wie ein roter Faden durch das Buch. — The idea forms the central theme of the book.

Da beißt keine Maus den Faden ab. — That's dead sure (*or* final)!

Er nahm den Faden des Gesprächs wieder auf. — He took up the conversation where he had left off.

Er ließ keinen guten Faden an ihr. — He tore her to shreds; he didn't have a good word for her.

Sie spinnen keinen guten Faden miteinander. — They don't get along together.

Er hat alle Fäden in der Hand. — He's pulling wires; he has pull (*or* influence).

Er machte sie nach Strich und Faden herunter. — He raked them over the coals; he gave them hell; he bawled them out soundly.

fadenſcheinig:
  Seine Gründe ſind fadenſcheinig. | His arguments don't hold water; they have no basis in fact.

fahl:
  Er wurde auf einem fahlen Pferd geſehen. | He was caught red-handed (*or* in the act).

fahren:
  Fahren Sie rechts! | Keep to the right!
  Wer gut ſchmeert (=ſchmiert), der gut fährt. | Grease well, and you'll go fast!; a little soft soap (*or* graft) will get you far.
  Er fährt immer gut. | He never runs short; he always comes off well.

fahrend:
  Er vermachte ihnen seine fahrende Habe. | He bequeathed them his personal property.

fahrig:
  Der Junge iſt fahrig. | The boy is a scatterbrain.

Fahrt:
  Er nahm die Kehre in voller Fahrt. | He took (*or* drove around) the corner on two wheels (*or* at top speed).

Fahrwaſſer:
  Dort iſt er in seinem Fahrwaſſer. | That's right up his alley; he's in his element there; he's very much at home on that subject.
  Die Debatte geriet ins politiſche Fahr=waſſer. | The debate drifted into politics.

Fall:
  Das iſt ganz mein Fall. | That suits me fine.
  Er wurde Knall und Fall entlaſſen. | He was bounced (*or* fired) without a moment's notice.
  Nehmen wir den Fall an. | Let's suppose.
  Tun Sie das auf jeden Fall! | By all means, do it!
  Er iſt auf alle Fälle gefaßt. | He's prepared for the worst.
  Nehmen Sie für alle Fälle Ihren Regen=mantel mit! | Be on the safe side and take your raincoat along!
  Er tut es im äußerſten Fall. | He'll do it in a pinch (*or* if he has to).

Falle:
  Er iſt bereits in die Falle gegangen. | He's hit the hay (*or* slats); he's turned in (*or* gone to bed).

fallen:
  Es fällt ihm leicht. | It's easy for him.
  Das Barometer fällt. | The barometer is going down.

fällen:
  Wann wird das Urteil gefällt werden? | When will the verdict be delivered?

Fallſtrick:
  Man legte ihm Fallſtricke. | He was framed; a trap was set for him.

falſch:
  Sie faſſen das falſch auf. | You misunderstand; you've got the wrong idea (*or* impression).
  Er sang falſch. | He was singing off key (*or* out of tune).
  Plötzlich wurde sie falſch. | Suddenly she blew up (*or* got angry).
  Sie iſt ein falſcher Fuffzger. | She's a cheap fraud (*or* imitation); she's an old phoney; she's faking (*or* bluffing).

Er ist ein falscher Kerl.	He's not a square shooter; he's not on the level (*or* aboveboard).
Er trieb falsches Spiel mit ihnen.	He did them dirt; he double-crossed them.

Falte:

Wer kennt die geheimsten Falten des menschlichen Herzens?	Who knows (*or* can probe) the innermost recesses of the human heart?
Er zog die Stirn mißbilligend in Falten.	He frowned disapprovingly.

famos:

Famos, daß ich Sie treffe!	My, but it's good to see you!
Famose Sache!	Hot dog!; great stuff!; swell!

Fang:

Er gab dem Hirsch den Fang.	He finished the deer with his knife.

Farbe:

Er muß Farbe bekennen.	He has to show his cards; he must take sides.
Das gibt der Sache eine gute Farbe.	That puts the matter in a favorable light; that makes a good impression.
Er trägt die Farben zu dick auf.	He puts it on too thick; he exaggerates grossly.
Er versteht sich darauf wie ein Blinder auf die Farben.	He knows as much about it as the man in the moon; he doesn't know the first thing about it.
Heraus mit der Farbe!	Spit it out!; out with it!; say it!

faseln:

Sie faseln wohl?	Are you talking through your hat?; what foolishness is that?

Faß:

Das schlägt dem Faß den Boden aus!	That's the finish (*or* last straw)!; that takes the cake!
Er schöpft ins Faß der Danaiden.	That's so much water over the falls; he's wasting his time (*or* energy).

fassen:

Faß dich!	Keep your shirt on!; compose yourself!; calm down!
Fassen Sie sich kurz!	Be brief!; make it snappy (*or* short and sweet)!

Fassung:

Er brachte sie ganz außer Fassung.	He got her all hot and bothered; he fluttered (*or* bewildered) her completely.

fatal:

Wie fatal!	What a tough break!; it's too bad!; that's a shame!

Fatzke:

Er ist ein großer Fatzke.	He's an awful snob; he's a conceited ass.

faul:

Er, nicht faul, griff nach der Pistole.	He was not slow to draw his pistol.
Seine Sache steht faul.	The odds are against him.
Das sind faule Fische.	Those are lame excuses.
Er liegt auf der faulen Haut.	He's loafing (*or* idling); he's taking it easy.
Machen Sie keine faulen Scherze!	Oh, go on!; you don't say so!; you wouldn't kid me?

Das ist fauler Zauber.	That's all humbug (*or* bosh); that's tommy-rot.
Faulpelz:	
Er ist ein großer Faulpelz.	He's a big hooligan (*or* lazy lubber).
Faust:	
Das paßt wie die Faust aufs Auge.	That's a lot of hooey; that's preposterous (*or* ridiculous); it doesn't make sense.
Er machte eine Faust im Sack.	He gritted his teeth; he steeled himself to it.
Er tut es auf eigne Faust.	He's doing it on his own (initiative *or* responsibility); he's free-lancing.
Er schrieb von der Faust weg.	He wrote offhand (*or* extemporaneously).
Fäustchen:	
Er lachte sich ins Fäustchen.	He laughed up his sleeve.
faustdick:	
Er hat es faustdick hinter den Ohren.	He's a slicker (*or* sharper); he's a clever scoundrel.
Das ist faustdick gelogen.	That's an eighteen-carat lie; that's a whopper (*or* whale of a lie).
Es kommt immer gleich faustdick.	It never rains but it pours.
Faxe:	
Mach keine Faxen!	Cut the comedy!; don't try to crawl out of it!
Er hat den Kopf voller Faxen.	He's got monkey business on the brain; he's up to something.
fechten:	
Er geht jetzt fechten.	He's panhandling now; he goes begging.
Fechtbruder:	
Ein Fechtbruder stand vor der Tür.	A tramp was at the door.
Feder:	
Er mußte Federn lassen.	He had his wings clipped; he got scratched; he lost out.
Er ist gerade aus den Federn gekrochen.	He just got up out of bed.
Er schmückte sich mit fremden Federn.	He plagiarized.
Er ist von der Feder aufs Stroh gekommen.	He lost his fortune; he's hard up.
Er ist zu Federn gekommen.	He's well fixed (*or* well-to-do).
Federlesen:	
Er machte nicht viel Federlesens damit.	He put the kibosh (*or* finish) on it; he made short work of it.
fehlen:	
Was fehlt Ihnen?	What's the matter with you?
Bei Ihnen fehlt's wohl!	Are you nutty?; wake up!; you must be out of your mind!
Er fehlt ihnen sehr.	They miss him a lot.
Das fehlte noch!	It never rains but it pours; and now that had to happen!; what next?
Es fehlte nicht viel, so wäre er gestorben.	He was at death's door; he nearly died.
Es kann ihm nicht fehlen.	He's sure to succeed.
Sie läßt es an nichts fehlen.	She spares herself no pains.
An uns soll es nicht fehlen.	We'll do our part.
Fehler:	
Es war ein Fehler wider die Zeitrechnung.	It was an anachronism.

fehlgeschossen:
　Fehlgeschossen! — Wrong!; missed!

fehlschlagen:
　Das Geschäft schlug fehl. — The business turned out to be a flop (*or* failure).

Feierabend:
　Lassen Sie uns Feierabend machen! — Let's knock off!; let's call it a day!

feiern:
　Jetzt heißt es nicht feiern! — This is no time to play!; get down to work!

Feige:
　Er wies ihnen die Feige. — He told them to go to hell; he thumbed his nose (*or* snapped his fingers) at them.

Feile:
　Er legte die letzte Feile an seine Arbeit. — He put the finishing touches on his work.

fein:
　Sie fühlt sehr fein. — She's very sensitive.
　Das ist aber fein! — That's great (*or* swell)!
　Das war nicht fein von ihm. — That wasn't nice of him.
　Sei fein artig! — Be good!
　Er ist fein heraus. — He got a break; he's a lucky fellow.

Feines:
　Da haben Sie was Feines angestiftet! — A fine mess you made of things!; now you've started something!

Feind:
　Das Bessere ist der Feind des Guten. — Let well enough alone!; don't tempt fortune!
　Er wütete gegen Freund und Feind. — He took it out on (*or* had it in for) everybody; he was down on the world in general.

Feindschaft:
　Darum keine Feindschaft nicht! — No hard feelings!

Feld:
　Er behauptete das Feld. — He stuck to his guns; he stood his ground.
　Er räumte das Feld. — He took a back seat; he gave in.
　Er hat freies Feld. — He has plenty of elbow room; he has the run of the place; he can do as he pleases.
　Er schlug seine Gegner aus dem Feld. — He won the day (from the other contestants); he eliminated his opponents.
　Das liegt noch in weitem Feld. — That's still a long way off.
　Er führte viele Gründe ins Feld. — He advanced many arguments.

Feld-, Wald- und Wiesensoldat:
　Er war im Krieg ein ganz gewöhnlicher Feld-, Wald- und Wiesensoldat. — He was just an ordinary front-line soldier during the war.

Fell:
　Ihn juckt das Fell. — He's itching (*or* looking) for trouble; he's in a quarrelsome (*or* fighting) mood.
　Er stand da wie ein betrübter Lohgerber, dem die Felle fortgeschwommen sind. — He was down in the mouth; he looked very despondent (*or* dejected).
　Man soll das Fell nicht verkaufen, ehe man (nicht) den Bären hat. — First catch your hare!; don't count your chickens before they're hatched!
　Er hat ihm das Fell versohlt. — He tanned his hide; he beat him up.

Er zog ihnen das Fell über die Ohren.	He fleeced (*or* defrauded) them.
Er iſt ihm aufs Fell geſtiegen.	He raked him over the coals; he called him on the carpet (*or* gave him hell).

felſenfeſt:

Er iſt felſenfeſt davon überzeugt.	He's dead-sure (*or* absolutely convinced) of it.

Fenſter:

Das ſchmeißt Ihnen kein Fenſter ein.	That won't do you any harm.
Er ſitzt hinter vergitterten Fenſtern.	He's in the pen; he's behind the (prison) bars.
Er warf ſein Geld zum Fenſter hinaus.	He squandered his money.
Er möchte die Stube zum Fenſter hinaus= werfen.	He'd like to cut up (*or* let loose); he feels like kicking over the traces; he's itching for trouble.

Ferne:

Das liegt noch in weiter Ferne.	That's still a long way off.

Ferngeſpräch:

Melden Sie das Ferngeſpräch an!	Call long distance!

fernliegen:

Es lag ihm fern, ſie zu verletzen.	He never meant to hurt their feelings.

fernmündlich:

Er iſt fernmündlich zu erreichen.	You can reach him by phone.

fernſtehen:

Er ſteht ihnen fern.	They don't know him.

Ferſe:

Er wollte Ihnen nicht auf die Ferſen treten.	He didn't mean to step on your toes (*or* hurt your feelings).

Ferſengeld:

Er gab Ferſengeld.	He took to his heels (*or* made a hasty exit); he ran away.

fertig:

Mit dem bin ich fertig.	He and I are quits; I'm through with him.
Er hatte alles fix und fertig.	He had everything cut and dried (*or* in order).
Er iſt fix und fertig.	He's raring to go; he's all set.
Er war ganz fertig.	He was all washed (*or* played) out.
Mag er ſehen, wie er fertig wird.	Let him see how he can manage!; let him look out for himself!
Er kann mit ſeinen Leuten nicht fertig werden.	He can't handle (*or* manage) his men.

fertigkriegen:

Er kriegt das fertig.	He's got what it takes; he'll put it across; he'll do it.

fertigmachen:

Er hat ſeinen Gegner fertig gemacht.	He knocked out (*or* beat) his opponent.

feſch:

Sie iſt ein feſches Mädel.	She's a fashion plate; she's very smart-looking.

feſſeln:

Seine Erzählung feſſelte uns.	His story thrilled us; we got a big kick (*or* thrill) out of it.

feſt:

Immer feſte druff! — Let him have it!; give it to him!; keep it up, boy!; more power to you!

Er verſicherte es ſteif und feſt. — He stuck to his point; he maintained it obstinately.

Er ſteht auf feſten Beinen. — He's got both feet on the ground; he knows what he's about.

Sie haben feſten Fuß gefaßt. — They've gained a footing; they're making headway (*or* progress).

Feſt:

Es war mir ein Feſt! — It was a real pleasure; I enjoyed doing it.

Man muß die Feſte feiern, wie ſie fallen. — Christmas comes but once a year; enjoy life while you may!

feſtfahren:

Er hat ſich feſtgefahren. — He ran into a snag; he got into a jam (*or* tight spot).

feſtlegen:

Er mochte ſich nicht darauf feſtlegen. — He didn't like to commit himself.

feſtnageln:

Ich werde ihn auf ſeine Bemerkung feſtnageln. — I'll pin him down; I'll hold him to his word.

feſtſitzen:

Er ſitzt feſt. — He's stuck (*or* in a rut) for fair; he's in an awful fix (*or* predicament).

feſtſtehen:

Soviel ſteht feſt. — One thing is certain.

Feſtung:

Mit Gold iſt jede Feſtung zu erobern. — Money talks.

fett:

Selber eſſen macht fett. — Look out for number one (*or* yourself) first!

Er iſt wieder mal fett. — He's stewed (*or* tight) again; he's drunk once more.

Vom Lecken wird keiner fett. — That's a mere drop in the bucket; that won't get you very far.

Ein blöder Hund wird ſelten fett. — Faint heart never won fair lady.

Fett:

Er ſchöpft immer das Fett ab. — He always gets the cream of the crop; he always wins (*or* comes out on top).

Da haben Sie Ihr Fett weg! — Serves you right!; now you've got what's coming to you!

Fettnäpfchen:

Er iſt bei ihr ins Fettnäpfchen getreten. — He cooked his goose there; he lost out (*or* spoiled his chances) with her.

Fetzen:

Hau ihn, daß die Fetzen fliegen! — Let him have it!; knock the stuffing out of him!

Feuer:

Bei ihm iſt gleich Feuer im Dach. — He flies right off the handle; he's very hot-headed; he gets hot and bothered right away.

Er iſt Feuer und Flamme dafür. — He's all het up (*or* very enthusiastic) about

	it; he's sold on it; he's all (*or* heart and soul) for it.
Das Feuer brennt ihm unter den Füßen.	The place is getting too hot for him; he's got the fidgets (*or* jitters); he's ill at ease (*or* hard-pressed).
Er wird schon Feuer dahinter machen.	He'll put some steam behind (*or* life into) it; he'll make things hum.
Er spie Feuer und Flamme.	He fretted and fumed.
Er kocht sich gern sein Süppchen am Feuer anderer.	He's an old moocher (*or* sponger); he's always taking advantage of the other fellow's good nature (*or* hospitality).
Je mehr er sprach, desto mehr geriet er ins Feuer.	The more he talked, the more he warmed up to his subject.
Ich lege die Hand dafür ins Feuer.	I'd give my right arm; I'll vouch for it.
Darf ich Sie um Feuer bitten?	Can you spare a light?; have you a match, please?
Er kam zwischen zwei Feuer.	He was between the devil and the deep blue sea.
Feuerprobe:	
Er bestand die Feuerprobe.	He took it standing up; he stood the gaff (*or* test).
feuerrot:	
Er wurde feuerrot.	He grew red as a beet.
Fiduz:	
Ich habe kein Fiduz in seine Worte.	I put no stock (*or* faith) in what he says; I'm not convinced.
Fiedel:	
Sie mußten ihm die Fiedel entzwei schlagen.	They had to cut him short.
Fimmel:	
Er hat einen richtigen Fimmel für Fußball.	He's a real football fan; he's crazy about football.
finden:	
Ich finde nichts dabei.	I see nothing in it.
Finden Sie nicht?	Don't you think so?
Wie fanden Sie das Essen gestern abend?	How did you enjoy the dinner last night?
Er hat sich selbst gefunden.	He's back to normal; he's himself again.
Was sollen wir hier tun?—Das wird sich schon finden.	What are we supposed to do here?—You'll see (*or* soon find out).
Sie weiß sich in alles zu finden.	She knows how to adapt herself to circumstances.
Finger:	
Mein kleiner Finger sagte mir das.	A little bird told me.
Er legte den Finger auf den Mund.	He motioned for silence.
Er legte den Finger an die Nase.	He began to think.
Er wich keinen Finger davon ab.	He wouldn't budge an inch (*or* retract a word); he stood pat; he stood his ground.
Lassen Sie die Finger davon!	Hands (*or* Keep) off!
Verbrenn dir nicht die Finger dabei!	Don't get yourself into hot water (*or* trouble)!
Er macht krumme Finger.	He's light-fingered; he's a pickpocket.
Er leckt alle zehn Finger danach.	He's itching (*or* dying) to get it; he can't keep his hands off it.

Er hat Pech an den Fingern.	He's a blundering idiot; he spoils everything he touches.
Das kann man sich leicht an den fünf Fingern abzählen.	That's plain as day (*or* the nose on your face).
Sehen Sie ihm mehr auf die Finger!	Keep closer tabs on him!; watch him more closely!
Das Gerücht ist nicht aus den Fingern gesogen.	That's no lie; it's true (*or* a fact).
Er hat ihnen lange genug durch die Finger gesehen.	He's let them get away with murder long enough; he's always closed one eye (*or* made allowances) for them.
Da haben Sie sich aber in den Finger geschnitten.	You figured wrong there; that's where you made a mistake.
Er griff mit allen fünf Fingern zu.	He made a beeline for it; he jumped at it.

fingern:

Er wird die Sache schon fingern.	He'll fix that; he'll manage somehow.

Fingerspitzengefühl:

Die Erledigung dieser heiklen Sache erfordert ein gewisses Fingerspitzengefühl.	This is a ticklish matter calling for a great deal of tact.

finster:

Die Sache sieht finster aus.	The prospects aren't any too bright; things look bad (*or* serious).

Finsternis:

Es herrschte eine ägyptische Finsternis.	It was pitch-dark.

Firnis:

Ihre Bildung ist lediglich Firnis.	Her culture is all on the surface.

Fisch:

Das ist weder Fisch noch Fleisch.	That's neither fish nor fowl; what in the world is this?
Er ist so gesund wie ein Fisch im Wasser.	He's fit as a fiddle; he's in the best of health.
Er wurde stumm wie ein Fisch.	He shut up like a clam.
Das sind faule Fische.	These are lame excuses.

fischen:

Es ist nichts dabei zu fischen.	There's nothing (*or* no money) in it.

Fisimatenten:

Machen Sie keine Fisimatenten!	Don't try to crawl out of it!; stop making excuses!

fitschenmadennaß:

Er war fitschenmadennaß.	He looked like a drowned cat; he was soaked (*or* drenched) to the skin.

Fittich:

Er kriegte ihn beim Fittich.	He seized him by the scruff of the neck; he called him on the carpet; he bawled him out.

fitzen:

Er fitzt leicht.	He does sketchy (*or* superficial) work.

fix:

Fix, hol das Buch!	Get the book, and make it snappy!
Er ist darin nicht so fix.	That's not his strong point; he's not so good at that.

Er hatte alles fix und fertig.	He had everything cut and dried (*or* in order).
Er ist fix und fertig.	He's raring to go; he's all set.
Er ist ein fixer Junge.	He's a smart fellow.
flach:	
Das liegt auf der flachen Hand.	That's clear as day; everybody knows that.
flachſen:	
Sie drehten ihm einen flachſenen Bart.	They pulled his whiskers (*or* leg); they played a joke on him.
Flagge:	
Er ſegelt unter falſcher Flagge.	He flies under false colors; he goes under an assumed name; he's making false pretenses.
Flamme:	
Er ist Feuer und Flamme dafür.	He's all het up (*or* very enthusiastic) about it; he's sold on it; he's all (*or* heart and soul) for it.
Er ſpie Feuer und Flamme.	He fretted and fumed.
Flandern:	
Er ist von Flandern.	He's fickle (*or* undependable).
Flanke:	
Er quatſchte ſie von der Flanke an.	He horned (*or* butted) in; he intruded upon them.
Flaſche:	
So eine Flaſche!	What a blundering idiot (*or* lummox)!
Man ſoll die Begeiſterung nicht auf Flaſchen ziehen.	Make hay while the sun shines!; don't step on (*or* repress) your enthusiasm—let it work for you (*or* capitalize on it)!; one shouldn't kill enthusiasm.
flau:	
Mit ſeiner Zahlungsfähigkeit ſteht es flau.	His business may not be solvent.
Ihm war ganz flau zumute.	He felt limp as a rag; he was all washed (*or* worn) out; he felt faint.
Flaumachen:	
Flaumachen gilt nicht!	Don't be a wet blanket (*or* kill-joy)!
Flauſen:	
Das ſind alles Flauſen.	That's a lot of hot air; that's nothing but talk; there's nothing to (*or* behind) it.
Flaute:	
In Effekten herrſcht Flaute.	The market is holding its own (*or* marking time); stocks and bonds are quiet.
fläzen:	
Er fläzte ſich aufs Sofa.	He plumped himself on (*or* sprawled all over) the sofa.
Fleck:	
Er ſetzte den Fleck neben das Loch.	He fell short of the mark; he did a poor job.
Mach dir nur keinen Fleck!	Don't be afraid!; don't put on the dog!
Er traf den rechten Fleck.	He struck home; he hit the nail on the head.
Er hat das Maul auf dem rechten Fleck.	He always has a snappy comeback (*or* ready answer); he's quick at repartee.

Seine Arbeit kommt nicht vom Fleck.

> He has struck a snag; he's not making any headway (*or* progress) with his work.

Er antwortete vom Fleck weg.

> He answered right off the bat; he had a ready comeback (*or* answer).

flecken:
Das fleckt!

> Hot dog!; good work!; swell!

Flegeljahr:
Er ist noch in den Flegeljahren.

> He's still in his teens and full of the devil.

Fleisch:
Das ist weder Fisch noch Fleisch.

> That's neither fish nor fowl; what in the world is this?

Besser eine Laus im Kohl als gar kein Fleisch.

> Anything is better than nothing.

Er trägt faules Fleisch.

> He's a lazybones.

Diese Sache ist ihm ein Pfahl im Fleisch.

> That's his weak spot; it's a thorn in his flesh; it's a source of great worry to him.

Der Gedanke ist ihm in Fleisch und Blut übergegangen.

> The idea has become part and parcel of him; it's second nature to him.

Schneiden Sie sich nicht ins eigne Fleisch!

> Don't cut off your own nose to spite your face!; don't be a fool!

Fleischer:
Bei dem guckt der Fleischer heraus.

> He has a hole in his suit.

Fleischergang:
Er tat einen Fleischergang.

> He went on a wild-goose chase; it got him nowhere.

Fleiß:
Er tat das nicht mit Fleiß.

> He didn't mean (to do) that; he didn't do that intentionally (*or* on purpose).

Ohne Fleiß kein Preis.

> No pains, no gains; earn your keep!

Fliege:
Ihn ärgert die Fliege an der Wand.

> His nerves are all on edge; everything gets (*or* grates) on his nerves.

Sie kamen wie die Fliegen in der Buttermilch gezogen.

> They came in droves; there was no end to them.

In der Not frißt der Teufel Fliegen.

> Anything is better than nothing.

Er schlug zwei Fliegen mit einer Klappe.

> He killed two birds with one stone.

fliegen:
Wer nicht pariert, der fliegt!

> Fall in line (*or* Toe the mark) or out you go!

fliegend:
In dieser Stadt gibt es keine fliegenden Händler.

> No street vendors (*or* peddlers) allowed in this town.

Er kam in fliegender Hast.

> He came flying (*or* in hot haste).

Flinte:
Werfen Sie nicht die Flinte ins Korn!

> Don't throw up the sponge!; don't give up (the game)!

Himmel, hast du keine Flinte!

> Good night!; drat it all!

flirren:
Es flirrte ihr vor den Augen.

> Everything was dancing before her eyes.

Flitterwoche:
Nach den Flitterwochen kommen die Zitterwochen.

> Life is not all roses (*or* one sweet song); even lovers must come down to earth again.

Floh:

Lieber Flöhe hüten als das! — I'd rather be shot than do that!

Er hört die Flöhe husten. — He hears the grass grow; he thinks he knows it all.

Flosse:

Reich mir die Flosse! — Put it here!; shake (hands)!·

Nimm deine Flossen weg! — Pull in your gunboats (or big feet)!

Flöte:

Da schweigen alle Flöten! — Out of luck!; stuck!; (it's) hopeless!

Sie ist nicht zufrieden, wenn sie nicht die erste Flöte spielt. — She wants to be the whole show; she isn't happy unless she can play first fiddle.

flötengehen:

Sein ganzes Vermögen ging flöten. — His whole fortune went to the winds; he lost everything he had.

Flötenton:

Dem werde ich schon die Flötentöne beibringen. — I'll teach him manners (or how to behave).

flott:

Das Geschäft geht flott. — Business is very good.

Er lebt flott. — He's a high-stepper (or gay bird); he lives fast.

Er ist wieder flott. — He's flush (or in the money) again.

Er ist ein flotter Junge. — He's a dashing fellow.

Flucht:

Er trat die Flucht in die Öffentlichkeit an. — He broke into print; he took refuge in literary expression.

Er bestellte eine Flucht von Zimmern. — He reserved a suite of rooms.

Er ist sehr in der Flucht vor ihr. — He's very much afraid of her.

Er suchte sein Heil in der Flucht. — He ran for dear life (or all he was worth).

Sie schlugen den Feind in die Flucht. — They put the enemy to rout.

flüchtig:

Er machte ihnen einen flüchtigen Besuch. — He dropped in to see them.

Flug:

Die Zeit vergeht wie im Flug. — Time flies.

Flügel:

Plötzlich bekam er Flügel. — He suddenly plucked up courage; he gained confidence in himself.

Er läßt die Flügel hängen. — He's down in the mouth; he's dejected.

Verbrennen Sie sich nicht die Flügel! — Don't burn your fingers!; don't get yourself into trouble!

Nehmen Sie ihn mal beim Flügel! — Tell him where he gets off!; give it to him!

Flunder:

Da werden sich die Flundern wundern! — He'll get the surprise of his life!; will he be surprised!

flunkern:

Er flunkerte schrecklich. — He peddled cock-and-bull (or fish) stories; he told terrible yarns.

Flunsch:

Sie zog einen Flunsch. — She pouted.

Fluß:

Die Verhandlungen kamen langsam in Fluß. — Negotiations were gradually resumed.

flüstern:
Dem werde ich was flüstern. — I'll give him a piece of my mind; I'll tell him a thing or two.

flutschen:
Das flutscht besser! — That's the stuff!; attaboy!; that's more like it!

Folge:
In der Folge wird das anders. — Things will be different in the future.

Folio:
Er ist ein Narr in Folio. — He's a darned fool.

Folter:
Spannen Sie ihn doch nicht auf die Folter! — Don't give him the third degree!; don't be so hard on him!

Format:
Der Kerl hat Format. — He's a regular guy; he is somebody.

förmlich:
Er mußte sie förmlich dazu zwingen. — He practically had to force them to do it.
Es besteht eine förmliche Feindschaft zwischen ihnen. — They're evidently at swords' points; they're avowed enemies.

Forsche:
Das ist seine Forsche. — That's his strong point; he knows all about that.

fortmüssen:
Er hat schon früh fortgemußt. — He died young.

fortreißen:
Seine Beredtsamkeit riß die Zuhörer fort. — His eloquence swept the audience off its feet.

fortwursteln:
Er wurstelt immer so fort. — He's in the same old rut; he's still plodding away at the same old job.

Frack:
Er lachte sich einen Frack. — He howled with laughter; he laughed himself sick.
Er erschien zum Essen in Frack und Lack. — He came to the dinner in tails (*or* full dress).

Frage:
Es ist noch sehr die Frage. — It's not at all certain.
Das ist ja eben die Frage. — That's just the point.
Das ist eine andere Frage. — That's another matter.
Das ist gar keine Frage. — There's no doubt about that.
Soweit er in Frage kommt. — As far as he's concerned.

fragen:
Ich frage mich, ob das stimmt. — I wonder whether that's correct.
Er fragt nichts danach. — He doesn't care.
Es fragt sich. — It's a question.
Wenn ich fragen darf. — If you please.

Fragezeichen:
Hinter seine Behauptung muß ich ein großes Fragezeichen setzen. — I'll take his word with a grain of salt; I can't quite swallow (*or* believe) it.

Fraktur:
Reden Sie einmal Fraktur mit ihm! — Tell him in plain English!

franko:
Man wende sich schriftlich und franko an Herrn M.

Write to Mr. M. and enclose a stamped envelope.

Frankreich:
Er lebt wie der Herrgott in Frankreich.

He's leading the life of Riley; he's living like a king (*or* in grand style).

frappant:
Er hat eine frappante Ähnlichkeit mit seinem Bruder.

There's a striking resemblance between the two brothers.

Fratz:
Sie ist ein niedlicher Fratz.

She's a cute little trick (*or* number).

Fräulein:
Das Fräulein vom Amt hat eine Nachricht für Sie hinterlassen.

The (telephone) operator left a message for you.

Frechdachs:
So ein Frechdachs!

What a fresh mug!; such a scalawag!

frei:
Bahn frei!

Gangway!; clear the track!

Er hat heute frei.

Today is his day off.

Haben Sie einige Minuten für mich frei?

Can you spare me a few minutes?

Wollen Sie nicht Platz nehmen?—Ich bin so frei!

Won't you sit down?—Don't mind if I do!

Sie benahm sich sehr frei.

She was anything but reserved.

Er sprach vollkommen frei.

He spoke without notes.

Bei der Firma ist eine Stelle frei.

The firm has an opening (*or* a vacancy).

Die Tagung ist unter freiem Himmel.

The meeting is in the open (*or* out of doors).

Er läßt den Dingen freien Lauf.

He lets things slide.

freibleibend:
Die Preise verstehen sich netto und freibleibend.

Prices are net and without option.

Freibrief:
Er betrachtete ihre Freundschaft als Freibrief für seine Ansprüche.

He took advantage of their hospitality; he used them.

Freiersfüße:
Er geht auf Freiersfüßen.

He's on the lookout (*or* in the market) for a wife.

freihalten:
Er hielt sie frei.

He paid all their expenses.

freimachen:
Machen Sie den Brief frei!

Stamp the letter!

fremd:
Er ist hier fremd.

He's a stranger here; he doesn't know this place.

Das kommt mir sehr fremd vor.

That strikes me as very fishy (*or* queer).

Er soll fremde Gelder angegriffen haben.

He's said to have embezzled money entrusted to him.

Das Haus ist in fremde Hände übergegangen.

The house has changed hands; strangers have taken it over.

Aus fremdem Leder ist gut Riemen schneiden.

It's easy when you make the other fellow pay.

Er reist unter fremdem Namen.	He travels incognito (*or* under an assumed name).
Fremde:	
Er ging in die Fremde.	He went abroad.
Fresse:	
Meine Fresse!	My word!; gosh!; golly!
Halt die Fresse!	Dry (*or* Shut) up!; keep quiet!
fressen:	
Friß, Vogel, oder stirb!	Do or die!
Friß mich nur nicht!	Don't bite my head off!; don't take it out on me!
Den habe ich aber gefressen!	I can't stomach (*or* stand) that man.
Jetzt hat er's gefressen.	Now he's got the hang of it; now he's caught on.
Fressen:	
Es war ein elendes Fressen.	The food (*or* meal) was terrible.
Das ist ein gefundenes Fressen für die Presse.	It's a scoop (*or* story) for the press; it's front-page news.
Freßsack:	
Er ist ein kleiner Freßsack.	He's a little pig; he's a regular little glutton.
Freßsage:	
Der Kerl hat eine unangenehme Freßsage.	The fellow has an awful mug (*or* face); he's homely as hell.
Freude:	
Er lebt herrlich und in Freuden.	He's in clover; he's on Easy Street; he's living off the fat of the land (*or* in peace and plenty).
Er nahm den Vorschlag mit Freuden an.	He jumped at the chance.
freudig:	
Sie sieht einem freudigen Ereignis entgegen.	She's expecting a blessed event.
Freund:	
Freund Hein hat ihn geholt.	The grim reaper (*or* Death) took him away.
Er wütete gegen Freund und Feind.	He took it out on (*or* had it in for) everybody; he was down on the world in general.
freundlich:	
Bitte, recht freundlich!	Smile!; look pleasant!
Freundschaft:	
Die ganze Freundschaft nahm an der Hochzeit teil.	The whole clan (*or* family) attended the wedding.
Friede(n):	
Ich traue dem Frieden nicht.	I smell a rat; I have my suspicions; I don't like the looks of things.
friedlich:	
Sie haben sich schiedlich, friedlich geeinigt.	They've come to terms amicably.
frieren:	
Friert Sie?	Are you cold?
frisch:	
Frisch drauflos!	Let's go!; get down to work!
Frisch gestrichen!	Wet paint!

Frisch gewagt ist halb gewonnen.	A good beginning is half the battle; fortune favors the brave.
Es ist frisch draußen.	It's pretty snappy (*or* cold) outside.
Er ist frisch und gesund.	He's hale and hearty.
Er sprach frisch von der Leber weg.	He didn't mince matters; he talked turkey; he spoke his mind frankly.
Er ging mit frischen Kräften an die Arbeit.	He went to work with renewed energy.
Er wurde auf frischer Tat ertappt.	He was caught red-handed (*or* in the act).
Frische:	
Er kam in alter Frische.	He was as peppy (*or* alert) as ever.
frisieren:	
Er hatte die Bilanz frisiert.	He had doctored up (*or* falsified) the account; he had faked a balance.
Frist:	
Er wird in kürzester Frist hier sein.	He'll be here any moment now; he'll come in a trice (*or* before long).
Fritz:	
Das ist für den Alten Fritz.	That's labor lost; that's a waste of time.
froh:	
Er wird seines Lebens nicht froh.	He has no end of trouble.
fromm:	
Er ist fromm wie ein Lamm.	He's meek as a lamb; he's got the patience of Job (*or* a saint).
Fromme:	
Es ist zu seinem Nutz und Frommen.	It's for his own good.
Front:	
Machen Sie Front dagegen!	Defend yourself!; fight back!
Frosch:	
Er war kühl wie ein Frosch.	He was cool as a cucumber.
Sei kein Frosch!	Come on now!; snap out of it!; don't be a fool!
Er stand da wie ein geprellter Frosch.	He was up a tree; he was completely mystified (*or* at sea).
frotzeln:	
Er frotzelt gar zu gern.	He's a great kidder; he's a big tease.
Früchtchen:	
Er ist ein sauberes Früchtchen geworden.	He went completely to seed; he went wrong (*or* to the dogs).
Frühe:	
Er wird in aller Frühe hier sein.	He'll be here the first thing in the morning.
Frühling:	
Die Wirtschaft geht einem neuen Frühling entgegen.	Business is picking up.
Fuchs:	
Er ist erst Fuchs.	He's just a freshman (in college).
Er kommt von einem Ort, wo Fuchs und Hase sich gute Nacht sagen.	He comes from Hickville (*or* the sticks); he's from the country.
Das hat der Fuchs gemessen.	That's some long mile.
Er macht es wie der Fuchs mit den Trauben.	It's a case of sour grapes with him; he sticks up his nose at it.

Er ist darüber her wie der Fuchs über den Hühnern.

He's making short work of it; he's going at it with a vengeance.

Die Füchse brauen.

The mist is rising.

fuchsen:

Die Sache fuchst ihn mächtig.

He's very sore (or peeved) about it; it's got his goat.

fuchsteufelswild:

Er wurde fuchsteufelswild.

He got hot under the collar; he became rip-roaring mad.

Fuchtel:

Nehmen Sie ihn unter Ihre Fuchtel!

Hold on to him!; don't let him go!

fuchtig:

Er wurde ganz fuchtig.

He got his dander up; he became very angry (or annoyed).

fuffzehn:

Er machte kurze fuffzehn damit.

He made short work of it; he put a stop to it.

Fuffzger:

Sie ist ein falscher Fuffzger.

She's a cheap fraud (or imitation); she's an old phoney; she's faking (or bluffing).

Fug:

Er tat das mit Fug und Recht.

He had good reason to do so; he was justified in doing it.

Fuge:

Der Wagen ging aus den Fugen.

The car went to pieces; it fell apart.

fühlen:

Sie fühlt sehr fein.

She's very sensitive.

führen:

Sie führt eine gewählte Sprache.

She uses choice language.

Der Junge führt sich gut.

The boy behaves well; he's on his best behavior.

Fuhrmann:

Er ist ein alter Fuhrmann.

He's an old hand; he knows his onions (or stuff).

Fülle:

Sie haben alles in Hülle und Fülle.

They've got plenty and to spare; they have more than enough of everything.

fünf:

Lassen Sie auch mal fünf gerade sein!

Let well enough alone!; let it pass!; don't be so particular!

Es ist fünf Minuten vor zwölf.

It's high time.

Nehmen Sie Ihre fünf Sinne zusammen!

Pay attention!; put your mind to it!

funkelnagelneu:

Der Hut ist funkelnagelneu.

It's a brand-new hat.

für:

Er kam Abend für Abend.

He came evening after evening.

Sie findet das für gut.

She considers it right (or fitting).

Das hat viel für sich.

There's a lot in that; there's a lot to be said for it.

Er lebt ganz für sich.

He keeps aloof (or to himself).

Er ist eine Nummer für sich; man weiß nie, was er als nächstes tut.	He's a funny bird—one never knows what he'll do next.
Der Gedanke ist an und für sich nicht schlecht.	The idea in itself is a good one.

fürlieb:

Er nimmt mit allem fürlieb.	He's easily pleased; he hasn't been spoiled.
Wollen Sie bei uns fürliebnehmen?	Will you take potluck (or have a bite) with us?

Fürsorge:

Sie sind in Fürsorge.	They're on relief; they're public charges.

fürstlich:

Sie hatten ein fürstliches Mahl.	They ate like kings (or in grand style).

Fuß:

Er kam stehenden Fußes.	He came at once.
Das hat Hand und Fuß.	You've got something there; that's a good idea; that's very much to the point.
Er setzte ihm den Fuß in den Nacken.	He put him in his place; he made him toe the mark; he stepped on him.
Sie haben festen Fuß gefaßt.	They've gained a footing; they're making headway (or progress).
Machen Sie ihm mal Füße!	Step on him!; speed him up!; make him hurry!
Er steckt gern seine Füße unter andrer Leute Tisch.	He's a moocher (or sponger); he imposes on other people's hospitality.
Lassen Sie uns etwas die Füße vertreten!	Let's stretch our legs a bit!; let's go for a walk!
Er folgte ihr auf dem Fuß.	He followed at her heels.
Er ist wieder auf freiem Fuß.	He was acquitted (or set free); his case was dismissed.
Sie stehen auf gespanntem Fuß.	They're on the outs; they're not on speaking terms.
Sie führen das Geschäft auf großem Fuß.	They do business on a large scale.
Er lebt auf großem Fuß.	He's a high-stepper; he lives fast.
Das Unternehmen steht auf schwachen Füßen.	The undertaking has no sound basis; it lacks a solid foundation.
Jemand trat ihm auf die Füße.	Somebody stepped on his toes (or corns); someone insulted him.
Er versprach es mit Hand und Fuß.	He swore on a stack of Bibles; he took a solemn oath.
Sie sind wohl mit dem linken Fuß zuerst aufgestanden!	You must have got up on the wrong side of the bed this morning!
Er sträubte sich mit Händen und Füßen dagegen.	He fought tooth and nail; he put up a stiff fight.
Der Boden brennt ihm unter den Füßen.	The place is getting too hot (or uncomfortable) for him; he has to leave.
Sie haben etwas unter den Füßen.	They're well fixed (or off); they're on Easy Street.
Der Boden wankt ihm unter den Füßen.	He's losing ground; he's weakening.
Er warf ihm den ganzen Bettel vor die Füße.	He threw up (or turned down) the whole deal; he called the whole thing off.
Sollen wir zu Fuß gehen oder fahren?	Shall we walk or ride?
Sie ist gut zu Fuß.	She's a good hiker.

Fußangel:
Man hat ihm Fußangeln gelegt.   He was framed; they set a trap for him.

Fußbreit:
Er geht keinen Fußbreit davon ab.   He doesn't budge an inch; he stands pat; he holds his ground (*or* point).

fusselig:
Er redete sich den Mund fusselig.   He was talking his ear off; he talked himself deaf, dumb, and blind.

fußen:
Worauf fußt er seine Hoffnungen?   What is he banking on?; on what does he base his hopes?

futsch:
Die Einlage ist futsch.   The investment is lost.

Der neue Laden ist schon wieder futsch.   The new store has gone out of business again.

Als sie das Meer zum ersten Mal sah, war sie ganz futsch.   When she saw the ocean for the first time, she was swept off her feet (*or* in ecstasies over it).

futtern:
Futter nicht so!   Behave yourself!; keep a civil tongue in your head!

Gardine:
Er sitzt hinter schwedischen Gardinen. | He's in the pen; he's behind the (prison) bars.

Garn:
Er wollte sie ins Garn locken. | He wanted to rope them in; he tried to catch them.

Gärtner:
Er hat den Bock zum Gärtner gemacht. | He set a fox to mind the geese; it was like leading the lambs to slaughter.

Gas:
Junge, gib Gas! | Snap into it, boy!; step on it!
Man hat ihm das Gas abgedreht. | He was bumped off (or murdered).

Gashahn:
Sie drehten den Gashahn auf. | They turned on the gas; they committed suicide.

Gasse:
Man hört davon auf allen Gassen. | It's common parlance (or knowledge); it's the talk of the town.

Er ist Hans in allen Gassen. | He's a jack-of-all-trades and master of none.

Verkauft der Wirt offnes Bier auch über die Gasse? | Does the innkeeper sell beer on draft (or tap) over the counter (for home consumption)?

Gassendreck:
Der Kerl ist frech wie Gassendreck. | The fellow is fresh as they make them (or as they come); he's a fresh guy.

Gassenhauer:
Er pfiff einen Gassenhauer. | He whistled a popular air.

gastfrei:
Sie haben ein gastfreies Haus. | They keep open house; their house is full of guests.

Gastrolle:
Früher kam er fast täglich, aber jetzt gibt er nur noch Gastrollen. | He used to come nearly every day, but now we seldom see him.

Gaul:
Er zäumte den Gaul beim Schwanz auf. | He put the cart before the horse; he began at the wrong end; he reversed the procedure.

Das bringt einen Gaul um. | No one can stand that; that's (expecting) too much.

Mach mir nicht die Gäule scheu! | Don't spoil the whole works!

Gaumen:
Die Zunge klebte ihm am Gaumen. | He could spit cotton; he was dry as a gourd.

Gazelle:
Sie ist flink wie eine Gazelle. | She's quick as a flash.

geartet:
Er ist anders geartet. | He's cast in a different mold; he's made (or inclined) differently.

Der Junge ist gut geartet. | The boy is well behaved; he's been well brought up.

gebannt:

Er blieb wie gebannt stehen. | He stood rooted to the spot.

Gebein:

War jemand da?—Kein Gebein! | Was anybody there?—Not a soul!!

geben:

Was gibst du, was hast du? | What'll you give for it?; what have you to offer?

Er gibt es ihnen zu fühlen. | He rubs it in; he makes them feel it.

Er gibt nichts drauf. | He doesn't care for it; he pays no attention to it.

Wie gibt man das auf deutsch? | How would you say that in German?

Wer abhebt, gibt nicht. | Whoever cuts doesn't deal; you can't have your cake and eat it too.

Er gibt sich, wie er ist. | He's no hypocrite; he's (true to) himself.

Er gibt sich damit zufrieden. | He puts up with it; he makes the best of it.

Es gibt gleich was! | You'll get it in a minute!; you're in for it now.

Es gibt heute noch was. | The storm will break (*or* it'll rain *or* snow) before the day is over.

Das gibt sich auch wieder. | It'll all come out in the wash; it'll come out all right eventually.

Was gibt's? | What's up (*or* happening)?; what's the matter?

Daß es so was gibt! | To think that such things happen!

Das gibt's nicht! | Nothing doing!; none of that!

Was wird heute abend gegeben? | What's being shown (*or* played) tonight (in the theater)?

Gebet:

Man nahm ihn scharf ins Gebet. | He was grilled (*or* quizzed); they cross-questioned him closely.

gebildet:

Er ist ein gebildeter Mann. | He's a gentleman.

geboren:

Er ist nicht zum Lehrer geboren. | He wasn't cut out for (*or* meant to be) a teacher.

Sie ist eine geborene Knopf. | Her maiden name was Knopf.

Frau Koch, geborene Müller. | Mrs. Koch, *née* Müller.

Gebot:

Halte dich ans elfte Gebot! | Watch your step!; don't let them put one over on you!; don't let them take you in!

geboten:

Rücksicht scheint hier geboten. | This calls for consideration.

Gebratenes:

Da gibt's Gesottenes und Gebratenes. | They're having a grand feast.

gebrauchen:

Er gebraucht viel Zeit dazu. | It takes him a long time.

Er ist zu nichts zu gebrauchen. | He's a good-for-nothing (*or* rolling stone).

gebrechen:

Es gebricht ihm an Zeit. | He's short of time.

gebügelt:

Er geht immer geschniegelt und gebügelt. | He always looks spick-and-span (*or* as if he had just stepped out of a bandbox); he's always immaculately groomed.

Gebühr:
Man feierte ihn über Gebühr. — He got more than was coming to him; they praised him beyond his merits.

gebürstet:
Kurzes Haar ist bald gebürstet. — A poor man's table is soon spread.

geck:
Sie sind wohl geck! — You must be nuts (*or* crazy)!

Gedanke(n):
Stimmt's?—Kein Gedanke! — Is that correct?—I'll say it isn't!; far from it!

Warum (soll man) sich darüber Gedanken machen? — Why worry about that?; let George (*or* the other fellow) do it!

Er kann sich nicht in den Gedanken finden. — He can't realize the fact; he can't make it out.

Er tat es in Gedanken. — He did it absent-mindedly.

Er trägt sich schon lange mit dem Gedanken. — He's had it on his mind for a long time.

gedeckt:
Mein Bedarf ist reichlich gedeckt. — That will do me royally; that's ample for me.

Gedeih:
Sie sind auf Gedeih und Verderb miteinander verbunden. — They'll stick to each other through thick and thin; they're pledged to each other for life.

gedeihen:
Die Verhandlungen sind schon recht weit gediehen. — The negotiations are well under way.

gedenken:
Er wird es ihnen schon gedenken. — He'll get even with them yet; he'll fix them.

gediegen:
Sie sind aber gediegen! — You're a queer duck (*or* sort)!

gedruckt:
Er lügt wie gedruckt. — He's a shameless liar.

Geduld:
Mit Geduld und Spucke fängt man eine Mucke. — Everything comes to him who waits; patience is crowned with success; keep up the good work—you'll get there yet!

geduldig:
Papier ist geduldig. — Anything goes!; you can print almost anything.

Geduldsfaden:
Ihm riß der Geduldsfaden. — He lost his temper (*or* patience).

geehrt:
Sehr geehrter Herr! — Dear Sir!

geeicht:
Er ist darauf geeicht. — He has the hang (*or* knack) of it.

Gefahr:
Sie laufen Gefahr, sich zu erkälten. — You're likely to catch cold.

Wer sich in Gefahr begibt, kommt leicht darin um.

Those who play with fire will get their fingers burned.

gefährlich:
Tun Sie man nicht so gefährlich!

Don't paint the picture so black!; don't make it worse than it is!

Gefälle:
Der hat aber ein gutes Gefälle!

He's a regular tank; he can drink like a fish.

gefallen:
Das lasse ich mir gefallen!

Attaboy!; that's the stuff!; that's how I like it!

Er läßt sich das nicht gefallen.

He won't put up with that.

gefällig:
Was gefällig?

Sir?; pardon?; what did you say?

Hier ist was gefällig.

There's something doing (or going on) here; here's where they soak you (or hold you up); the prices here are exorbitant.

Etwas Zucker gefällig?

Do you take sugar?

Er verfügt über ein gefälliges Äußeres.

He's a good-looking man; he puts up a good front.

gefälligst:
Nehmen Sie gefälligst Platz!

Won't you be seated?; have a seat.

gefaßt:
Sein Entschluß ist gefaßt.

His mind is made up.

Er ist auf alles gefaßt.

He's prepared for the worst.

Er kann sich auf was Schönes gefaßt machen.

He sure(ly) is in for it.

gefehlt:
Weit gefehlt!

You're way off (or all wrong)!; you've missed the point entirely!

gefeiert:
Besser geleiert als gefeiert.

Anything is better than nothing; better to do little than nothing at all.

Gefitze:
Da gibt's kein Gefitze!

No funny business!; don't pull any tricks now!

gefräßig:
Der Kerl ist dumm und gefräßig.

He's an arrogant ass; he has an inflated ego.

gefreit:
Jung gefreit hat noch niemand gereut.

Happy's the wooing that's not long in the doing.

Gefühl:
Sie läßt sich gern von ihren Gefühlen bestimmen.

She's too temperamental (or emotional).

gefunden:
Das ist geradezu gefunden.

That's a bargain; that's a downright find.

gegeben:
Gut gegeben!

A fine comeback!; that was an excellent bit of repartee!

Unter den gegebenen Umständen.

Under the circumstances.

gegen:
  Es ist nichts gegen das, was er tut.   That's nothing compared to what he can do.
  Nur gegen Kasse!   No credit allowed.

Gegenliebe:
  Mit seinem Vorschlag fand er keine Gegenliebe.   His suggestion didn't meet with favor (or support); his idea failed to go over.

Gegenseitigkeit:
  Das beruht auf Gegenseitigkeit.   Same here; it's mutual.

Gegenstand:
  Er ist Gegenstand allgemeiner Verehrung.   Everyone respects him.

gegenüber:
  Ihr gegenüber ist er nett.   He's kind to her.

Gegenüber:
  Er hatte ein nettes Gegenüber.   He had an attractive *vis-à-vis* (or partner).

Gegenwart:
  Dieser Arzt steht mit beiden Beinen in der Gegenwart.   This doctor is very up to date; he uses the very latest methods.

gegenwärtig:
  Halten Sie sich die Lage gegenwärtig!   Keep the situation in mind!; get an idea of it!

gehaben:
  Gehab dich wohl!   Farewell!; so long!; God bless you!

Gehalt:
  Der Gehalt macht's.   Quality is what counts.

gehalten:
  Er will es so gehalten wissen.   He wants it that way.

geharnischt:
  Er erhob einen geharnischten Protest.   He entered a vigorous protest; he protested strenuously.

gehauen:
  Das ist weder gehauen noch gestochen.   That's neither one thing nor the other; that doesn't say (or mean) a thing!

Gehege:
  Kommen Sie mir nicht ins Gehege!   You keep out of here!; leave me alone!

gehen:
  Das geht.   That's O.K. (or all right); that works (or will do).

  Es geht so.   So so; pretty fair.
  Es geht mir auch so.   Same here; me too; that's how I feel.
  Es geht nun mal nicht anders.   It can't be helped.
  Darüber geht nichts.   There's nothing like it; this tops everything; this takes the cake.

  Was geht hier vor sich?   What's up?; what's going on here?
  Worum geht's hier?   What's the issue (or point)?; what's it all about?

  Es gehe, wie es will!   Let come what will!
  Er kam so, wie er ging und stand.   He came just as he was.
  Wenn es nach ihm ginge.   If he had his way.
  Wie wird es noch mit uns gehen?   Where do we come off?; what's to become of us?

  Er läßt sich niemals gehen.   He never slips (or loses control of himself).

Sie sollten einmal in sich gehen.	You should go into a huddle with yourself!; give yourself the once-over!; check up on yourself sometime!
Er half, wo es nur gehen wollte.	He did what he could to help.

gehetzt:

Er ist mit allen Hunden gehetzt.	He's a sly fox; he's up to all sorts of tricks.
Er kam sich vor wie ein gehetztes Wild.	He felt like a fox in the chase; he was being hounded (*or* persecuted).

geheuer:

Das kommt mir nicht geheuer vor.	That looks phoney (*or* fishy) to me.

gehext:

Das geht wie gehext!	That works like magic!

gehoben:

Er war in gehobener Stimmung.	He was in high spirits.

Gehör:

Er schenkte ihr kein Gehör.	He didn't listen to her.

gehören:

Er gehört gehängt.	He ought to be hanged.
Er gehört mit dazu.	He's one of them; he's a member of that gang (*or* crowd).
Es gehört nicht viel dazu.	It doesn't take much.
So gehört es sich.	That's as it should be.
Es gehört sich nicht.	It's (in) bad taste; it's all wrong.

gehörig:

Es regnete gehörig.	It was raining hard; it was pouring.

gehüpft:

Das ist gehüpft wie gesprungen.	There's not much choice; it's six of one and half a dozen of the other; it's pretty much the same either way.

Geier:

Hol's der Geier!	Confound (*or* Drat) it!

Geige:

Er tanzt nach ihrer Geige.	He dances to her tune; she has him trained (*or* on a leash).
Glauben Sie wirklich, in Amerika hänge der Himmel voller Geigen?	Do you really believe that America is the land of golden opportunity (*or* peace and plenty)?

geigen:

Dem wird er aber die Wahrheit geigen.	He'll tell him what's what; he'll give him a piece of his mind.

Geist:

Das hat ihm ein guter Geist eingegeben.	Luck was with him; he had an inspiration.
Die Geister platzten aufeinander.	There was a clash (*or* difference) of opinion.
Ich weiß, wes Geistes Kind er ist.	I've got his number; I know him.
Sind Sie denn von allen guten Geistern verlassen?	Are you crazy (*or* out of your mind)?; have you lost your senses?

Geistesgröße:

Er ist keine solche Geistesgröße.	He's no mental giant; he's not so outstanding.

geistig:

Er beging geistigen Diebstahl.	He was guilty of plagiarism.

Er hat seine Arbeit ohne eigne geistige Unkosten geschrieben.	He wrote his paper without using his thinking cap (*or* gray matter); he never gave it a thought.
geizen:	
Er geizt mit der Zeit.	He counts every minute; he budgets (*or* makes the most of) his time.
Geizkragen:	
Er ist ein Geizkragen im kleinen und ein Verschwender im großen.	He's penny-wise and pound-foolish.
gekleckert:	
Da kommt der Kerl schon wieder gekleckert!	Here comes that nuisance (*or* pest) again!
geknickt:	
Sie stand da wie eine geknickte Lilie.	She looked like the last rose of summer; she was down in the dumps; she looked very forlorn (*or* dejected).
gekränkt:	
Er markiert die gekränkte Leberwurst.	He's putting on his hurt act; he's pretending to be angry (*or* highly insulted).
gelacht:	
Das wäre gelacht!	That's absurd (*or* ridiculous)!
Gelackmeierte:	
Er war der Gelackmeierte bei der Geschichte.	He was left holding the bag; he was the dupe (*or* sucker) in the affair.
geladen:	
Er ist schwer auf sie geladen.	He has it in for them; he's furious with them.
gelb:	
Er war gelb und grün vor Neid.	He was green with envy.
Gelbschnabel:	
Er ist noch ein Gelbschnabel.	He's not yet dry behind his ears; he's still green (*or* young and inexperienced).
Geld:	
Der eine hat den Beutel, der andere das Geld.	Some folks have all the luck.
Das Haus wächst ins Geld.	The value of the house is increasing.
Es ist nicht mit Geld zu bezahlen.	It's invaluable; money couldn't buy it.
Geldsache:	
In Geldsachen hört die Gemütlichkeit auf.	Business is business; you can't take it easy when there's business to be done.
Geldschneiderei:	
Das ist eine üble Geldschneiderei.	That's a regular swindle (*or* holdup); that's blackmail.
Geldstrafe:	
Er wurde in eine Geldstrafe von zehn Mark genommen.	He was fined ten marks.
geleckt:	
Die Wohnung sah wie geleckt aus.	The home was neat as a pin.
gelegen:	
Komme ich Ihnen morgen gelegen?	Will it be convenient for you if I come tomorrow?

Das kommt mir sehr gelegen.	That comes in very handy.
Was ist daran gelegen?	What of it?; what difference does it make?
Es ist ihm sehr daran gelegen, die Stelle zu bekommen.	He's very anxious to get the job.
Er kam zu gelegener Zeit.	He came in the nick of time.

Gelegenheit:

Gelegenheit macht Diebe.	An open door may tempt a saint.
Er nahm die Gelegenheit beim Schopfe.	He made hay while the sun shone; he took time by the forelock; he made the most of the opportunity.

Gelegenheitsarbeit:

Er verrichtet so kleine Gelegenheitsarbeiten.	He does odd jobs; he's doing some chores; he's puttering around.

gelegentlich:

Gelegentlich seines Hierseins erfuhren sie davon.	They heard of it when he was here.
Er wird das gelegentlich besorgen.	He'll get around to that sometime.

gelehrt:

Lesen Sie ohne gelehrte Brille!	Use your head (*or* common sense)!
Hören Sie doch endlich auf mit dem gelehrten Kram!	Can that highbrow stuff!; stop talking like a book!; stop being so superior!

Gelehrte:

Gelehrten ist gut predigen.	A word to the wise is sufficient.

geleiert:

Besser geleiert als gefeiert.	Anything is better than nothing; better to do little than nothing at all.

Geleimte:

Nun ist er der Geleimte.	Now he's the sucker; now the joke's on him.

G(e)leis(e):

Die Verhandlungen sind auf ein totes Gleis geraten.	The negotiations have reached a deadlock (*or* are stymied).
Es geht alles im alten Gleise fort.	Everything is going on as usual.
Das läßt sich schon wieder ins richtige Gleis bringen.	That can be fixed all right.

Gelichter:

Es sind alles Leute eines Gelichters.	They're birds of a feather; they're all of the same stamp (*or* kind).

geliefert:

Er ist geliefert.	He's done for; he's on his last legs.

gelitten:

Sie ist wohl gelitten.	She has a way with her; she's well liked.

gelt:

Gelt, Sie machen mit?	You'll go with us, won't you?

gelten:

Das gilt!	It's a go!; O.K.!; agreed!
Das gilt Ihnen.	That means you.
Das gilt ihm gleich.	It's all the same to him.
Das gilt von ihm.	That's true of him; that applies to him.
Das gilt nicht.	That's not fair; that doesn't count; that's not allowed.

Es gilt sein Leben.	His life is at stake.
Jetzt gilt's, oder wir kommen zu spät.	Let's go, or we'll be late.
Was gilt's, er kommt doch noch?	What will you bet that he'll still come?
Für ihn gilt nur eins.	Only one thing matters to him.
Er gilt hier viel.	He's a big shot around here; they make much of him here.
Das lasse ich gelten.	There's something in (or to) that; I'll let that pass.

geltend:

Sein Einfluß macht sich geltend.	His influence is felt; he makes effective use of his power.
Das ist gegen das geltende Recht.	That's against the law.

Geltung:

Das Kleid bringt ihre Schönheit zur Geltung.	The dress brings out (or sets off) her beauty.

gelungen:

Das ist aber gelungen!	That's funny!

gemacht:

Gemacht!	It's a go!; O.K.!; agreed!
Er ist ein gemachter Mann.	He's well off (or well-to-do).
Sie trug eine gemachte Ruhe zur Schau.	She assumed an air of calm.

gemalt:

Das ist wie gemalt.	It's pretty as a picture.

Gemeinnutz:

Gemeinnutz geht vor Eigennutz.	Public welfare (or good) goes before private profit.

gemeinsam:

Sie beschlossen, gemeinsame Kasse zu führen.	They decided to pool expenses; they all chipped in.

gemischt:

Es ging recht gemischt zu.	Things were happening right and left; there were all sorts of goings-on.

Gemse:

Sie ist scheu wie eine Gemse.	She's very shy.

gemünzt:

Das ist auf ihn gemünzt.	That dig is (meant) for him; that crack (or remark) is aimed at him.

Gemüse:

Es war nur junges Gemüse bei der Veranstaltung.	There were only youngsters at the affair.

Gemüt:

Sie hat ein fein besaitetes Gemüt.	She's very sensitive.
Er führte sich eine Pulle Wein zu Gemüt.	He drank a bottle of wine.

gemütlich:

Nur immer gemütlich!	Take it easy!; don't get excited (or angry)!; keep your shirt on!
Er ist ein gemütlicher Mann.	He's a genial man.
Er hat ein gemütliches Zimmer.	He has a cozy room.

Gemütlichkeit:

Da hört doch die Gemütlichkeit auf!	That takes the cake!; that's the limit!
In Geldsachen hört die Gemütlichkeit auf.	Business is business; you can't take it easy when there's business to be done.

Gemütsmenſch:
　Donnerwetter!　Der iſt aber ein Ge=
　mütsmenſch!

That fellow has his crust (*or* nerve)!

Gemütsruhe:
　Da ſaß er in aller Gemütsruhe.

There he sat as calm and complacent as you please.

Genagelten:
　Er zog die Genagelten an.

He put on his hiking (*or* spiked) boots.

genäht:
　Doppelt genäht hält beſſer.

A stitch in time saves nine; better too much than not enough.

genau:
　Das iſt genau ſo viel.
　Nehmen Sie es nicht ſo genau!

That's just as much.
Don't take it literally!; don't be so particular!

　Er entkam mit genauer Not.

He had a close shave (*or* narrow escape); he got away by the skin of his teeth.

Genaues:
　Das ſcheint mir nichts Genaues.

That doesn't strike me as very convincing (*or* definite).

genehmigen:
　Genehmigen Sie den Ausdruck meiner
　vorzüglichen Hochachtung.

Respectfully (*or* Very truly) yours.

geneigt:
　Der geneigte Leſer.

The gentle reader.

Geneſung:
　Sie ſieht ihrer Geneſung entgegen.

She's on the mend; she's getting better (*or* recuperating).

genieren:
　Genieren Sie ſich nicht!

Make yourself at home!; don't stand on ceremony!

　Das geniert ihn nicht.

He doesn't mind; that doesn't bother him.

genießen:
　Er hat eine gute Erziehung genoſſen.

He's been well educated; he's had a good education.

genommen:
　Genau genommen.
　Im ganzen genommen.

Strictly speaking.
On the whole; all in all.

genudelt:
　Er war wie genudelt.

He felt like a stuffed pig; he was fed up; he'd had his fill.

Genüge:
　Den kennen wir zur Genüge.

We know him well enough.

geölt:
　Das geht wie geölt.

That goes like clockwork; that works **perfectly** (*or* like a charm).

geordnet:
　Sie leben in geordneten Verhältniſſen.

They're pretty well off; they live in comfortable circumstances.

gepellt:
　Er ſieht aus wie aus dem Ei gepellt.

He looks spick-and-span; he looks as if he had just stepped out of a bandbox.

gepfeffert:
Das ist aber eine gepfefferte Rechnung! | Isn't that bill rather steep (*or* exorbitant)?

gepfiffen:
Gott sei's getrommelt und gepfiffen! | Hot dog!; hurrah!; hallelujah!

gepflegt:
Er setzte ihnen einen gepflegten Wein vor. | He gave them a wine mellowed with age.

gepfropft:
Das Zimmer war gepfropft voll. | The room was chock-full; the room was packed.

geprellt:
Er stand da wie ein geprellter Frosch. | He was up a tree; he was completely mystified (*or* at sea).

gerade:
So siehst du gerade aus! | You would!; says you!; not on your life!; nothing doing!

Das ist mir gerade recht. | That's the very thing I want.
Er kam gerade zur rechten Zeit. | He came just in the nick of time.
Nun tut er es gerade recht. | Now he does it all the more.
Lassen Sie auch mal fünf gerade sein! | Don't be so particular!; let well enough alone!; let it pass!

Er steht für sie gerade. | He'll vouch for them.

gerädert:
Er war wie gerädert. | He was all washed out (*or* utterly exhausted).

geradezu:
Das ist geradezu Unsinn. | That's sheer nonsense.
Er schrie geradezu. | He fairly screamed.
Er ist sehr geradezu. | He's very outspoken.

gerammelt:
Das Zimmer war gerammelt voll. | The room was packed.

geraten:
Ihm gerät nichts. | He fails in everything.
Sie gerieten aneinander. | They were at loggerheads; they quarreled (*or* came to blows).

Er ist ganz nach seinem Vater geraten. | He's a chip off the old block; he's just like his father.

geraten:
Damit ist ihm nicht geraten. | That won't do him much good.

Geratenste:
Das Geratenste für ihn wäre, wenn. . . . | The best thing for him to do would be to. . . .

Geratewohl:
Er versuchte es aufs Geratewohl. | He took a chance.

gerechnet:
Hoch gerechnet sind es fünf Mark. | At the top (*or* most), it's five marks.

gerecht:
Er wird der Sache nicht gerecht. | He can't put it across; he can't make it; he's no match for it.

Er ist in allen Sätteln gerecht. | He can turn his hand to anything; he fits in anywhere.

Gerechter Gott! | Good gracious!; heavens!

Gericht:

Die Sache ist beim Gericht anhängig. | The trial is pending.

Man ging mit ihm hart ins Gericht. | They raked him over the coals; he was severely reprimanded.

gerieben:

Er ist ein geriebener Kunde. | He's a sharper (*or* slicker); he's a smart (*or* shrewd) fellow.

gering:

Vornehm und gering war da. | Rich and poor alike were there.

Geriß:

Sie steht im Geriß. | She's very popular; she's much in demand (with the boys).

gerissen:

Er ist ein gerissener Geschäftsmann. | He's a smart (*or* keen) businessman.

gern:

Bitte, gern geschehen! | That's quite all right!; you're welcome!; don't mention it!

Er kann mich gern haben! | He can go hang!; I don't give a damn about him.

Er hat's nicht gern getan. | He didn't mean to do it; he didn't do it on purpose.

Das glaube ich gern. | I dare say; I can readily believe that.

Dafür kann man auch gut und gern was ausgeben. | It's worth your money.

Gernegroß:

Er ist ein kleiner Gernegroß. | The little man likes to play big.

Gerneklug:

Er ist ein Gerneklug. | He's a smart-aleck (*or* know-it-all).

Geruch:

Er steht in üblem Geruch. | He has a bad rep(utation).

gerufen:

Er kam wie gerufen. | He came just in (the nick of) time.

Gerüst:

Fallen Sie nicht vom Gerüst! | Hold your hat(s)!

gerüttelt:

Nun ist das Maß seiner Verfehlungen aber gerüttelt voll. | Now he's reached the end of his rope; he's gone the limit.

gesagt:

Unter uns gesagt. | Between you and me and the lamp post; confidentially.

gesalbt:

Red doch nicht so gesalbt! | Can the highbrow stuff!; stop talking like a book!; quit using such big words!

gesalzen:

Donnerwetter ja! Die Rechnung ist aber gesalzen! | Boy, is this bill steep!; this is some bill!

Sein Chef hielt ihm eine gesalzene Philippika. | His boss gave him a good roasting (*or* panning); he bawled him out good and proper.

Das war ein gesalzener Witz. | That was a dirty crack (*or* joke).

Gesang:
Den Vogel erkennt man am Gesang. — Actions speak louder than words.

gesät:
Die Äpfel lagen auf der Erde wie gesät. — The ground was strewn with apples.
Solche Leute sind dünn gesät. — Such people are scarce (*or* few and far between).

gesattelt:
Ich bin gesattelt. — I'm raring to go; I'm all set.

geschaffen:
Er ist dazu wie geschaffen. — He's got what it takes; he's just the man for it; he's cut out for the job.

geschäftlich:
Er ist eben geschäftlich tätig. — He's in conference; he's engaged (*or* busy) at the moment.

geschehen:
Das geschieht ihm recht. — It serves him right.
Er wußte nicht, wie ihm geschah. — He didn't know what to make of it.
Bitte, gern geschehen! — That's quite all right!; you're welcome!; don't mention it!
Es ist um ihn geschehen. — He's done for; it's all over with him.

geschehen (*adj*):
Geschehene Dinge leiden keinen Rat. — It's no use crying over spilt milk; what's done is done.

gescheit:
Sei doch gescheit! — Don't be a fool!
Er wurde nicht recht gescheit daraus. — He couldn't make head or tail out of it; it didn't make sense to him.
Auch ein gescheites Huhn legt die Eier neben das Nest. — It's a good horse that never stumbles; we all make mistakes.

gescheitert:
Er ist eine gescheiterte Existenz. — He's a total wreck; his life is ruined.

Gescheites:
Er sagte nichts recht Gescheites. — He said nothing important (*or* worth repeating).

geschenkt:
Für den Preis ist es halb geschenkt. — It's practically a gift at this price.
Es soll ihm noch einmal geschenkt sein. — I'll let him off this once.

Geschichte:
Die Geschichte fiel unter den Tisch. — The matter (*or* subject) was dropped.
Gestern passierte mir eine dumme Geschichte. — A funny thing happened to me yesterday.
Das sind ja schöne Geschichten! — That's a fine mess to be in!; a pretty state of affairs, indeed!
Mach keine Geschichten! — Don't be a fool!; don't start something!

Geschick:
Er hat ein feines Geschick dafür. — With him, it's a gift; he has the knack of it.
Er wird die Sache wieder ins Geschick bringen. — He'll straighten it out (*or* fix it up); he'll make it right again.

geschieden:
Wir sind geschiedene Leute. — We're through (*or* quits); it's all over between us; we're no longer friends.

Geſchirr:

Wie der Herr, ſo's Geſcherr (= Geſchirr).	Jack is as good as his master.
Er legte ſich tüchtig ins Geſchirr.	He got down to brass tacks; he snapped into it; he went to work with a will.

geſchlagen:

Er iſt ein geſchlagener Mann.	He's ruined.
Er behelligte ſie eine geſchlagene Stunde.	He pestered (*or* bothered) them for one solid hour.

geſchloſſen:

Die Verſammlung ſtimmte geſchloſſen dafür.	The assembly voted for it unanimously.
Er iſt eine in ſich geſchloſſene Perſönlichkeit.	He has a well-rounded personality.

Geſchmack:

Er kann der Sache keinen Geſchmack abgewinnen.	It doesn't go over big with him; he isn't impressed by it.
Über den Geſchmack läßt ſich ſtreiten.	Tastes differ; there's no accounting for tastes.

Geſchmackloſigkeit:

Das iſt eine Geſchmackloſigkeit.	That's in bad taste.

geſchmeichelt:

Sein Bild iſt geſchmeichelt.	The picture flatters him.

geſchmiert:

Das geht wie geſchmiert.	That goes like clockwork; it works perfectly (*or* like a charm).

geſchminkt:

Die Nachricht iſt geſchminkt.	The news is colored (*or* biased).

geſchneit:

Er kam ihnen plötzlich ins Haus geſchneit.	He suddenly blew in on them; he surprised them with a visit.

geſchniegelt:

Er geht immer geſchniegelt und gebügelt.	He always looks spick-and-span (*or* as if he had just stepped out of a bandbox); he's always immaculately groomed.

geſchoben:

Der Sieg war geſchoben.	The fight (*or* game) was fixed (*or* predetermined); the decision was in the bag (*or* a foregone conclusion) before the fight began.

geſchraubt:

Sie drückt ſich ſehr geſchraubt aus.	She speaks in a very stilted manner; her speech is very affected.

Geſchrei:

Viel Geſchrei und wenig Wolle.	Much ado about nothing; that's all ballyhoo; it's nothing but empty talk.

geſchürzt:

Die leicht geſchürzte Muſe beherrſchte das Programm.	The program consisted mainly of vaudeville.

Geſchütz:

Er fuhr grobes Geſchütz gegen ſie auf.	He turned his heavy guns on them; he gave them rough treatment.

geschwärzt:
Er verkauft geschwärzte Ware. | He's a bootlegger; he sells goods illegally; his commodity is on the black list.

geschweige (denn):
Er hat sie nicht gesehen, geschweige denn gesprochen. | He hasn't seen them, much less spoken to them.

geschweigen:
Anderer Umstände ganz zu geschweigen. | Not to mention the other circumstances.

Geschwindigkeit:
Geschwindigkeit ist keine Hexerei. | Sleight of hand is no witchcraft; there's no trick to it.

geschwollen:
Red nicht so geschwollen! | Don't talk so highfalutin (or big)!

Geseire:
Machen Sie kein Geseires! | Cut that out!; don't talk tommyrot (or foolishness)!

gesellen:
Zu diesem Punkt gesellt sich noch ein zweiter. | This question brings up (or leads to) still another.

Gesellschaft:
Das ist mir eine schöne Gesellschaft! | That's a nice gang (or outfit)!

gesetzt:
Gesetzt, es wäre so. | Supposing it were so; assuming it to be the case.

Er ist in gesetztem Alter. | He's of mature age.

Gesicht:
Das gibt der Sache ein andres Gesicht. | That's a horse of another color; that's an entirely different story; that throws a different light upon the matter.

Er ist seinem Vater wie aus dem Gesicht geschnitten. | He's a chip off the old block; he's the image of his father.
Wir verloren ihn aus dem Gesicht. | We lost sight (or track) of him.
Er lief uns gerade ins Gesicht. | He bumped (or ran) right into us.
Das schlägt der Tatsache ins Gesicht. | That belies (or is contrary to) the facts.
Er steckte sich eine Zigarre ins Gesicht. | He took (or lit) a cigar.
Er kam mit zufriedenem Gesicht zurück. | He came back looking well pleased (or satisfied).
Er feixte übers ganze Gesicht. | He grinned from ear to ear.
Sie lachte übers ganze Gesicht. | She beamed with joy.
Kommen Sie mir nicht mehr vors Gesicht! | Don't ever let me see you again!
Er bekam die Sache bald zu Gesicht. | He soon caught sight of it.
Das steht ihr gut zu Gesicht. | That's just her style; that's very becoming to her.

Gesinnung:
Gesinnung ist Trumpf. | It's the principle that counts.
Er legte eine niedrige Gesinnung an den Tag. | He revealed a base mind.
Er zeigte seine wahre Gesinnung. | He showed his true colors (or self).

gesonnen:
Er ist nicht gesonnen nachzugeben. | He'll not give in; he has no intentions of giving in.

gesotten:

Du kommst mir wie gesotten! — You're the very man I'm looking for!

Gesottenes:

Da gibt's Gesottenes und Gebratenes. — They're having a grand feast.

gespannt:

Ich bin gespannt, was noch wird. — I wonder how that will end.

Sie stehen auf gespanntem Fuß. — They're on the outs; they're not on speaking terms.

Er hörte mit gespanntem Ohr zu. — He listened attentively.

Gespenst:

Das rote Gespenst droht. — There's a danger of a Red (*or* Communist) revolution; the Reds are a constant menace.

gespickt:

Er hat immer eine gespickte Börse. — He always has ready cash on hand.

gespornt:

Als wir ankamen, war er bereits gestiefelt und gespornt. — When we arrived he was all set (*or* ready) to go.

gespritzt:

Er kam zu uns gespritzt. — He sprinted (*or* ran) over to us.

gesprungen:

Das ist gehüpft wie gesprungen. — There's not much choice; it's six of one and half a dozen of the other; it's pretty much the same either way.

Gestalt:

Er zeigte sich in seiner wahren Gestalt. — He revealed his true character; he appeared as he really is.

Er sah aus wie der Ritter von der traurigen Gestalt. — He looked like Don Quixote himself; he looked very mournful (*or* woebegone).

Gesteck:

Sie ist das reinste Gesteck. — She's thin as a rail; she's painfully thin.

gestellt:

Er ist hoch gestellt. — He's in the upper brackets; he holds a high position.

Sie sind schlecht gestellt. — They're hard up.

Er ist ganz auf sich gestellt. — He's on his own; he has to shift for himself.

Das ist in sein Belieben gestellt. — That's up to him; that's for him to decide.

gestiefelt:

Als wir ankamen, war er bereits gestiefelt und gespornt. — When we arrived he was all set (*or* ready) to go.

gestimmt:

Sie ist nicht zum Schreiben gestimmt. — She doesn't feel like writing.

gestochen:

Sie schreibt wie gestochen. — She writes a beautiful hand; her handwriting is exquisite.

Das ist weder gehauen noch gestochen. — That's neither one thing nor the other; that doesn't say (*or* mean) a thing.

gestohlen:

Er kann mir gestohlen bleiben. — He can go to hell, for all I care.

gestopft:

Der Saal war gestopft voll. — The hall was jammed (*or* packed).

gestrandet:

Es ist ein Heim für gestrandete Mädchen. | It's a home for homeless (*or* unfortunate) girls.

gestrichen:

Frisch gestrichen! | Wet paint!

Das Glas war gestrichen voll. | The glass was brimful; it was full to overflowing.

Er hat die Hosen gestrichen voll. | He's in a blue funk; he's scared to death.

Sein Sündenmaß ist gestrichen voll. | He's gone the limit; he's done his worst; he's broken all ten commandments.

gestrig:

Sie suchen wohl den gestrigen Tag? | Are you dreaming?

gesucht:

Der Vergleich ist gesucht. | That's a forced comparison.

Er ist ein gesuchter Anwalt. | He has a large (legal) practice; he has many clients.

gesund:

Durch den günstigen Verkauf des Hauses konnte er sich gesund machen. | The profitable sale of the house put him on his feet again.

Das ist ihm sehr gesund. | It serves him right.

Er hat einen gesunden Menschenverstand. | He has good common sense; he's a practical person.

Gesundheit:

(Zur) Gesundheit! (beim Niesen) | God bless you! (*after someone has sneezed*).

getan:

Jung gewohnt, alt getan. | The child is father to the man; habits learned in childhood persist throughout life.

Es ist um ihn getan. | He's done for; he's a goner (*or* hopeless case).

Selber tun ist bald getan. | If you want a thing done (well), do it yourself!

Damit ist es nicht getan. | That won't do it; that doesn't settle the matter.

Das will getan sein. | That needs time and care.

getarnt:

Der Klub besteht getarnt unter falschem Namen weiter. | The club goes on under an assumed name.

geteilt:

Darüber kann man geteilter Ansicht sein. | That's a matter of opinion.

Sie las den Brief mit geteilten Gefühlen. | She read the letter with mixed emotions.

getrennt:

Lassen Sie uns getrennte Kassen führen! | Let's go Dutch (*or* fifty-fifty); let each pay his own check.

Getriebe:

Er kam gerade ins größte Getriebe. | He came just at the rush hour; traffic was at its heaviest when he came.

getroffen:

Getroffen! | Right!; exactly!; you've hit the nail on the head!

Sie sind glänzend getroffen! | That's just like you!; you couldn't have done it any better!

getrommelt:
Gott sei's getrommelt und gepfiffen! — Hot dog!; hurrah!; hallelujah!

getrost:
Sie sind wohl nicht recht getrost? — Are you crazy?; you must be out of your head (*or* mind)!

Tun Sie das getrost! — Go right ahead!; you're perfectly safe in doing that!

Getue:
Laß doch das alberne Getue! — Cut out the monkey business!; stop being funny!

Gevatter:
Seine Uhr steht Gevatter. — His watch is in hock (*or* pawn).
Er stand bei dem Unternehmen Gevatter. — He backed the business (financially).
Er verkehrt nur mit Gevatter Schuster und Schneider. — He's slumming; his friends are all butchers and bakers and candlestick makers.

gewachsen:
Er ist der Sache nicht gewachsen. — He's not equal to the task; he's no match for it; he can't make the grade.

gewagt:
Frisch gewagt ist halb gewonnen. — A good beginning is half the battle; fortune favors the brave.

Er machte einen gewagten Witz. — He told a shady (*or* an off-color) joke.

gewähren:
Laß ihn nur gewähren! — Let him have his way!

Gewalt:
Er tat der Auslegung des Zitats Gewalt an. — He read more into the quotation than it warranted.
Er tat sich Gewalt an, ruhig zu bleiben. — He forced himself to keep quiet.
Er hat sich Gewalt angetan. — He took his own life; he committed suicide.
Sie hatte sich in der Gewalt. — She had herself under control.
Er will mit Gewalt weg. — He wants to go regardless (*or* in spite of everything).

Gewandtheit:
Seine fabelhafte Gewandtheit in politischen Machenschaften führte ihn zum Ziel. — His astounding political acumen achieved the desired end.

gewaschen:
Er ist mit allen Wassern gewaschen. — He's an old hand; he's been through every type of situation.

geweift:
Das hat seine geweiften Schubsäcke. — That's not so simple as it looks (*or* sounds); there are good reasons for it.

gewichst:
Er ist ein gewichster Junge. — He's a slick (*or* smart) boy.

Gewicht:
Er legt entscheidendes Gewicht darauf. — He makes it a point; he stresses it.
Das fällt bei ihr nicht ins Gewicht. — That carries no weight with her.

gewickelt:
Da sind Sie aber schief gewickelt! — That's where you're all wet (*or* wrong)!; there you're making a great mistake.

gewieft:
Er ist ein gewiefter Bursche. — He's a smart fellow (*or* clever lad).

gewiegt:
Er ist ein gewiegter Anwalt. | He's an experienced lawyer.

gewinnen:
Er kann es nicht über sich gewinnen, es zu tun. | He can't bring himself to do it.

gewiß:
In gewissem Sinne stimmt das. | In a sense, that's right.

Gewissen:
Er machte sich kein Gewissen daraus, sie hereinzulegen. | He thought nothing of cheating them; he had no scruples when it came to cheating them.

Den haben Sie auf dem Gewissen. | He blames you for that.

Können Sie das mit gutem Gewissen vertreten? | Are you positive?; would you swear to that?

Er handelte nach Pflicht und Gewissen. | He did his best; he used his best judgment.

Gewissensbiß:
Machen Sie sich deswegen keine Gewissensbisse! | Don't lose any sleep over that!; don't let it cause you any qualms!; don't worry about it!

Gewißheit:
Er hat keine Gewißheit darüber. | He's not at all sure of that.

gewitzigt:
Er ist ein gewitzigter Junge. | He's a shrewd fellow.

gewogen:
Er kann mir gewogen bleiben! | He can go hang (*or* to the devil)!

gewohnt:
Jung gewohnt, alt getan. | The child is father to the man; habits learned in childhood persist throughout life.

gewonnen:
Wie gewonnen, so zerronnen. | Easy come, easy go.

Er hatte gewonnenes Spiel. | He held the whip (*or* upper) hand; he won the day.

gewünscht:
Das kommt mir wie gewünscht. | That suits me fine (*or* to a T).

gezinkt:
Er spielte mit gezinkten Karten. | He played with marked cards.

Gicht:
Ich wünsche ihm die Gicht an den Hals. | I hope he breaks his neck; to hell with him!

gicks:
Er weiß weder gicks noch gacks. | He can't tell A from B; he's a numbskull (*or* nitwit).

Gießkanne:
Es regnete wie mit Gießkannen. | The rain came down in buckets.

Gift:
Er war Gift und Galle. | He was mad as hops; he was ready to chew nails.

Da können Sie Gift drauf nehmen! | You can bet your life (*or* last dollar) on that!

giftig:

Er sah sie giftig an.	He looked daggers at them; he gave them a dirty look.
Er wird leicht giftig in seinen Bemerkungen.	He gets catty (*or* spiteful) very easily; he's quick to give offense.
Er fand einen giftigen Stachel darin.	He discovered a fly in the ointment; he ran into unpleasantness (*or* difficulties).

Gimpelfang:

Er geht auf den Gimpelfang aus.	He's on the lookout for suckers (*or* dupes).

Gipfelleistung:

Er vollbrachte eine Gipfelleistung.	He broke the record.

Gips:

Hat Sie das nicht eine Menge Gips gekostet?	Didn't that set you back a lot?; didn't it cost a pile of dough (*or* money)?

Glanz:

Er bestand das Examen mit Glanz.	He passed the exam(ination) with flying colors; he made a very high grade.
Er flog mit Glanz aus der Firma.	He was thrown out on his ear; he was fired (*or* discharged) then and there (*or* on the spot).

Glas:

Ich bringe Ihnen mein Glas!	Here's to you!; I drink (to) your health!
Er hat zu tief ins Glas geguckt.	He took a drop too much; he drank more than he could hold.

glatt:

Er bezahlte den teuren Wagen glatt aus der Westentasche.	He paid spot cash for the expensive car.
Es geht nicht immer alles glatt.	It isn't all smooth sailing.
Er vergaß es glatt.	He clean forgot it; it slipped his mind completely.
Der Hund tötete ein glattes Dutzend Schafe.	The dog killed a round dozen of sheep.
Das ist eine glatte Lüge.	That's a downright lie.

Glatteis:

Er führte sie aufs Glatteis.	He tricked (*or* deceived) them; he got them into a dilemma (*or* scrape).

glattmachen:

Er hat die Sache glattgemacht.	He settled it; he fixed it up.

glattweg:

Er lehnte es glattweg ab.	He refused (it) point-blank.

glauben:

Ich glaube gar!	Well, I never!
Das glaube ich gern.	I dare say; I can readily believe that.
Er mußte daran glauben.	He had to pay the price (*or* suffer the consequences).

Glauben:

Der Vertrag ist auf Treu und Glauben abgestellt.	It's a gentlemen's agreement.

gleich:

Gleich und gleich gesellt sich gern.	Birds of a feather flock together.
Das habe ich mir gleich gedacht.	That's just what I thought.

Es geht uns diesmal allen gleich.	We're all in the same boat this time.
Das ist gleich geschehen.	That's easily done; it will only take a minute.
Das ist gleich ganz anders.	You see that's quite different; that changes the whole face of things.
Wo wohnen Sie doch gleich?	Where do you live?
Ich komme schon, gleich, gleich!	Coming, coming!; I'm on my way!; I'll be there in a minute!

Gleiches:

Er vergalt ihnen Gleiches mit Gleichem.	He gave them tit for tat (or a dose of their own medicine); he repaid them in kind.

gleichgültig:

Es ist ihm gleichgültig.	He doesn't care; it's all the same to him.

Glied:

Es zuckte ihr durch alle Glieder.	It thrilled her to the core (or through and through).

Glimmstengel:

Haben Sie noch einen Glimmstengel übrig?	Have you a stogie (weed or cigar) left?; can you spare an el ropo?

glimpflich:

Sie kamen noch glimpflich davon.	They got away none the worse (or unhurt).

Glocke:

Ich werde ihm schon sagen, was die Glocke geschlagen hat.	I'll tell him what the score is (or where he gets off); I'll set him to rights.
Er hat die Glocken läuten hören, weiß aber nicht wo.	He's all at sea about it; he can't quite make it out.
Hängen Sie es nicht an die große Glocke!	Don't shout it from the housetops!; don't let the whole town hear about it!

Glosse:

Er macht seine Glossen darüber.	He makes dirty cracks (or remarks) about it.

Glück:

Das Glück hat ihm schon in der Wiege gelächelt.	He was born with a silver spoon in his mouth; he was born rich.
Bei allem Unglück ist immer noch ein Glück.	Every cloud has its silver lining; everything has its good side.
Jeder ist seines Glückes Schmied.	Man is master of his own destiny.
Ich wünsche Ihnen Glück zur Beförderung.	Congratulations on your promotion!
Wer das Glück hat, führt die Braut heim.	Luck is everything; the lucky man wins.
Er kam auf gut Glück in der Hoffnung, sie anzutreffen.	He came on the chance of finding them.
Er kann auch von Glück sagen.	He was lucky; he may thank his lucky star.

glücken:

Es glückt nicht immer.	It doesn't come out right every time; it doesn't always work.

glücklich:

Alles lief glücklich ab.	Everything went off well (or smoothly).
Er kam glücklich an.	He arrived safely.
Nun hat er sich glücklich auch noch seine Stelle verscherzt.	On top of all that, he lost his job.

Glückspilz:
  Er ist ein Glückspilz   He's a lucky dog.

Glückwunsch:
  Viele herzliche Glückwünsche zum Geburtstag!   Many happy returns of the day!; happy birthday!

glühend:
  Er saß wie auf glühenden Kohlen.   He was on pins and needles; he was all on edge; he felt very nervous (*or* scared).

Gnade:
  Er ließ Gnade für Recht ergehen.   He showed mercy; he was compassionate.
  Er mußte sich auf Gnade und Ungnade ergeben.   He had to make an unconditional surrender.
  Der Kerl muß ohne Gnaden weg.   That man must go, and no mistake about it (*or* there's no help for it).

Gnadenstoß:
  Die neue Bewegung gab mancher faulen Einrichtung den Gnadenstoß.   The new movement spelt the doom of (*or* did away with) many a decadent institution.

gnädig:
  Er kam noch gnädig davon.   He got off easy.

Gold:
  Er ist treu wie Gold.   He's true as steel (*or* good as gold); he's true-blue.
  Eigner Herd ist Goldes wert.   Be it ever so humble, there's no place like home.
  Morgenstunde hat Gold im Munde.   The early bird catches the worm.
  Mit Gold kommt man überall durch.   Money talks.

golden:
  Er verspricht golden Berge.   He promises wonders (*or* the impossible).
  Handwerk hat goldenen Boden.   Trade is the mother of money.

Goldfisch:
  Er hat sich einen Goldfisch geangelt.   He married (a woman with) money.

goldig:
  Das ist aber goldig!   That's perfect (*or* priceless)!; that's as good as a show!; swell!

Goldwaage:
  Sie müssen nicht jedes seiner Worte auf die Goldwaage legen.   Take him with a grain of salt!; don't believe everything he says!

Gosche:
  Halt die Gosche!   Shut up!; keep quiet!

Gosse:
  Er zog sie durch die Gosse.   He threw mud on them; he slandered them.

Gott:
  Gott bewahre!   Nothing doing!; heaven forbid!
  Er singt, daß sich Gott erbarm.   He sings like a screech owl; he has the most God-awful voice.
  Grüß (dich) Gott!   Hello!; good-bye!
  Gott strafe mich!   Strike me pink (*or* dead)!; so help me God!
  Das walte Gott!   Amen!; so be it!
  Gerechter Gott!   Good gracious!; heaven above!
  Wahrhaftiger Gott!   Upon my word!; you bet!; heavens!; good Lord!

Er lebt wie der liebe Gott in Frankreich.	He lives the life of Riley; he lives like a king.
Das weiß der liebe Gott!	Heaven only knows!
Leider Gottes kann er nicht kommen.	Sad to say (*or* Unfortunately) he can't come.
Gott befohlen!	So long!; farewell!; good-bye!
Er schuldet Gott und aller Welt.	He's head over heels in debt.
Gott sei's getrommelt und gepfiffen!	Hot dog!; hurrah!; hallelujah!
Er läßt Gott einen guten Mann sein.	He lets things slide (*or* take care of themselves); he doesn't worry about anything.
Der Mensch versuche die Götter nicht!	Man should never tempt providence!
Es ist ein Schauspiel für die Götter.	It's a wonderful spectacle.
Er ist mit Gott und der Welt zerfallen.	He's down on the world; he's soured (*or* embittered).
Sie sind wohl ganz von Gott verlassen!	Are you nuts (*or* crazy)?
Gottchen:	
Ach Gottchen!	Gosh!; golly!
Gotteslohn:	
Er arbeitet um Gotteslohn.	His is a labor of love; he's working for nothing.
göttlich:	
Seine Derbheit ist göttlich.	His frankness is rare (*or* refreshing).
gottsjämmerlich:	
Sie weinte gottsjämmerlich.	She wept pitifully (*or* disconsolately).
gottvoll:	
Sie sind ja gottvoll!	Well, I'll be darned!; you surely take the cake (*or* prize)!; you're a riot (*or* scream)!
Grab:	
Er läutete dem Esel zu Grab.	He dangled his feet on the ground.
Graben:	
Er ist noch nicht über den Graben.	He's not yet over the hump; the worst is still to come.
gram:	
Man kann ihm nicht gram sein.	How can anyone be angry at him?
grämen:	
Das sollte Sie nicht grämen!	Don't let that bother you!
grapschen:	
Er hat meinen Bleistift gegrapscht.	He swiped (*or* snatched) my pencil.
Gras:	
Darüber ist längst Gras gewachsen.	That has long been forgotten; that's dead and buried long ago.
Wo der hinhaut, da wächst kein Gras mehr.	What a horse (*or* lumbering jackass)!; what a clodhopper (*or* clumsy fellow)!
Er hat schon lange ins Gras gebissen.	He dropped off long ago; he's long since dead.
gratulieren:	
Er kann sich gratulieren, wenn ich ihn erwische.	He'll catch hell when I get hold of him.
grau:	
Er malte die Sache grau in grau.	He painted a dark (*or* dismal) picture.
Er hat das graue Elend.	He has a hangover (*or* headache).

graulich:

Mach uns doch nicht graulich! — Don't give us the creeps!; don't scare us out of our wits!

Graupe:

Er hat Graupen im Kopf. — He's full of big ideas.

greifbar:

Die Vorzüge dieses Wagens sind greifbar. — The advantages of this car are obvious (or self-evident).

greifen:

Die Krankheit greift immer weiter um sich. — The disease is spreading more and more.

greis:

Er schüttelte sein greises Haupt. — He shook his learned head.

Grete:

Jeder Hans findet seine Grete. — Every Jack has his Jill; there's a girl for every boy.

Greuel:

Der Kerl ist mir ein Greuel. — The fellow gives me a pain; I can't stand the sight of him; he annoys me to death.

Griff:

Sie tun damit einen falschen Griff. — You're making a mistake there; that's a false move.

Er hat die Sache im Griff. — He has it down pat; he has the knack (or hang) of it.

Griffel:

Das ist mit ehernem Griffel in das Buch der Geschichte eingetragen. — That's gone down in history; it's on the records.

Grille:

Er fängt Grillen. — He's got something in (or on his) mind.

Setz doch dem Jungen keine Grillen in den Kopf! — Don't turn the boy's head!; don't put any notions into his head!

Grind:

Hier sitzen wir wie die Laus im Grind. — Here we are, snug as bugs in a rug (or cozy as can be).

Die Laus ist ihm über den Grind gelaufen. — Something's got under his skin; he's peeved (or vexed); he's out of sorts.

Grips:

Der Junge hat Grips im Kopf. — That boy has brains.

Er packte ihn beim Grips. — He took him by the scruff of the neck.

grob:

Er beging einen groben Fehler. — He pulled a boner; he made a bad break (or mistake).

Er fuhr grobes Geschütz gegen sie auf. — He turned his heavy guns on them; he gave them rough treatment.

Auf einen groben Klotz gehört ein grober Keil. — Tit for tat!; pay him in his own coin!

Das ist grober Schwindel. — That's an awful racket; that's a big gyp (or swindle).

Gröbste:

Er ist aus dem Gröbsten heraus. — He's out of the woods; he's over the worst.

Groschen:

Sie sind wohl nicht recht bei Groschen! — Are you nuts (*or* crazy)?

groß:

Er sah sie groß an. — He looked at her wide-eyed with wonder; he looked at her in amazement.

Bei denen geht's groß her. — They live in class (*or* high style).

Er kümmert sich nicht groß darum. — He cares little for it; it doesn't bother him much.

Im großen und ganzen hat er recht. — On the whole, he's right.

Sie machte große Augen. — Her eyes popped (with surprise); she stared in astonishment.

Wo verbringen Sie die Großen Ferien? — Where will you spend your summer vacation?

Hängen Sie es nicht an die große Glocke! — Don't shout it from the housetops!; don't let the whole town hear about it!

Alle erschienen in großer Toilette. — All appeared in regalia (*or* war paint); all were in full dress.

Wenn es keine allzu großen Umstände macht. — If it won't put you out any; if it's not too much trouble.

Großbetrieb:

Heute herrschte Großbetrieb im Geschäft. — Today we had a big day at the store (*or* shop); business was good.

größenwahnsinnig:

Sind Sie größenwahnsinnig geworden? — What gave you a swelled head?; who do you think you are anyway?; are you suffering from delusions of grandeur?

Großmutter:

Erzählen Sie das Ihrer Großmutter! — Tell that to Sweeney (*or* the marines)!; I don't believe a word of it!

Grube:

Wer andern eine Grube gräbt, fällt selbst hinein. — Watch out, lest you fall into your own trap!

Er ist in die Grube gefahren. — He cashed in (*or* passed away); he kicked the bucket; he died.

Grummet:

Sie machten das Grummet vor dem Heu. — They put the cart before the horse; they began at the wrong end; they had a child before they were married.

grün:

Er ist ihnen nicht grün. — He has it in for them; he bears them a grudge.

Das ist dasselbe in grün. — That's practically the same thing.

Es ist nur eine grüne Bekanntschaft. — It's just a casual (*or* recent) acquaintance.

Der Grüne Heinrich holte die Gefangenen ab. — The prisoners were rushed off in the Black Maria (*or* police wagon).

Man lobt ihn über den grünen Klee. — They praise him to the skies.

Ach, du grüne Neune! — Whew!; for Pete's sake!; I'll be darned!; will you look at that!

Der eine ißt gern Schwartenwurst, der andre grüne Seife. — It's all a matter of taste; tastes differ.

Sie sitzen an seiner grünen Seite. — They're in good (*or* on good terms) with him.

Diese Anordnung kommt vom grünen Tisch.	That's a swivel-chair order; it comes from the inner office (*or* big boss).
Er kommt nie auf einen grünen Zweig.	He'll never get ahead in the world.

Grün:

Sie schliefen bei Mutter Grün.	They slept out of doors (*or* in the open).

Grund:

Die Sache hat weder Grund noch Boden.	There's neither rhyme nor reason to it.
Er setzte ihr die Gründe auseinander.	He argued with her.
Er fuhr die Maschine in einem Jahr in Grund und Boden.	He completely ruined the car within a year.

grundlegend:

Er machte grundlegende Ausführungen dazu.	He made basic (*or* important) disclosures with reference to it.

grundstürzend:

Er plant grundstürzende Veränderungen.	He plans radical (*or* fundamental) changes.

Gruß:

Er ging ohne Gruß davon.	He went away without saying good-bye.

grüßen:

Grüßen Sie Ihre Eltern herzlichst!	Remember me to the folks!; give my love (*or* best regards) to your parents!

Grütze:

Er hat weder Grütz noch Witz.	He has neither brains nor wit; he's utterly stupid.

Guck:

Er kam bloß auf einen Guck.	He dropped in for just a moment; he just wanted to say "hello."

Guckindiewelt:

Er ist nur ein Guckindiewelt.	He's a mere babe in arms (*or* stripling).

Gunst:

Er sonnt sich in der Gunst seiner Vorgesetzten.	He's in good (*or* on good terms) with his superiors.

günstiger:

Die Sache stellt sich günstiger dar, als ich dachte.	Matters aren't really half so bad as I thought.

günstigst:

Im günstigsten Fall bleibt er noch eine Woche.	At best (*or* the most), he'll stay another week.

Gurgel:

Er jagt all sein Geld durch die Gurgel.	He spends all his money on drink.

Gurke:

Das ist aber eine komische Gurke!	Isn't he a funny egg?; what a queer duck (*or* person)!
Der hat aber eine Gurke!	What a long beak (*or* nose) he has!
Was hat der Mensch für Gurken an!	Look at that fellow's old boats (*or* shoes)!

Gurkensalat:

Was versteht der Bauer vom Gurkensalat?	What does he know about it?; how can he be expected to appreciate that?

gut:

Er hat's gut.	He's lucky; he's well off.
Er ist gut bei Kasse.	He's flush (*or* in the money).
Sie ist ihm gut.	She's sweet on (*or* in love with) him.

Was dem einen gut ist, ist dem andern schädlich.	What is one man's meat is another man's poison.
Das kann ganz gut sein.	That may easily be; it's very likely.
Lassen Sie's gut sein!	Never mind!; forget it!
Er steht für sie gut.	He'll vouch for them.
Das tut nicht gut.	That won't do.
Er wird schnell wieder gut.	His good humor is easily restored; his anger soon blows over.
Heute ist gut arbeiten.	This is a fine day to work.
Sie haben gut reden!	Talk is cheap!
Kurz und gut, er reiste ab.	To cut a long story short, he left.
Dafür kann man auch gut und gern was ausgeben.	It's worth your money.
Ich sage Ihnen das in gutem!	I tell you that in all sincerity (*or* friendliness).
Gute Besserung!	A speedy recovery!
Das heißt auf gut deutsch.	Said in plain language; to put it straight from the shoulder.
Gut Ding will Weile haben.	Haste makes waste.
Es ist noch ein gutes Ende bis dahin.	It's still a long way off; we have a long way to go.
Sind Sie denn von allen guten Geistern verlassen?	Are you crazy (*or* out of your senses)?; have you lost your mind?
Sie ist guter Hoffnung.	She's with child (*or* pregnant).
Er schlug bei Tisch eine gute Klinge.	He did justice to the meal; he ate heartily.
Er ist ein guter Lateiner.	He's an authority on Latin.
Er läßt den Herrgott einen guten Mann sein.	He lets things drift (*or* slide); he doesn't worry about anything.
Er machte gute Miene zum bösen Spiel.	He made the best of it; he played the game; he grinned and bore it.
Da ist guter Rat teuer!	It's hard to advise in a case like that; that's a ticklish (*or* very difficult) situation to be in.
Damit hat es noch gute Wege.	That's still a long way off.
Es ist nicht gut Wetter bei ihm.	He's in a vile mood; he's very ill-tempered.
Er bat um gut Wetter.	He apologized; he pleaded for a friendly reception.
Er tat es für Geld und gute Worte.	He did it for money and flattery.

Gut:

Er verlor Gut und Blut.	He lost both life and property.
Er verspielte sein ganzes Hab' und Gut.	He gambled away everything he had.

Gütchen:

Er tat sich ein Gütchen am Wein, als wir eintraten.	He was sitting contentedly over a glass of wine when we entered.

Gutdünken:

Handeln Sie ganz nach Gutdünken!	Use your own discretion!; do as you think best!

Gute:

Es ist manches Gute daran.	It has its good points; there's much to be said in its favor.
Nichts Gutes hat ihn hergeführt.	The devil brought him here; he's here for no good.

Das Bessere ist der Feind des Guten. | Let well enough alone!; don't tempt fortune!

Er hat des Guten zuviel getan. | That was too much of a good thing for him; he took a drop too much; he overdid it.

Ich wünsche Ihnen alles Gute. | Good luck to you!

Güte:

Eine Güte ist der andern wert. | One good turn deserves another.

Versuchen Sie es in aller Güte! | Try being friendly for a change!

gütigst:

Machen Sie gütigst Gebrauch davon! | Please use it!; won't you please help yourself whenever you need it?

gütlich:

Sie taten sich an der Mahlzeit gütlich. | They enjoyed their meal.

H

Haar:

Es gilt Haut und Haar.
It's a matter of life and death.

Kurzes Haar ist bald gebürstet.
A poor man's table is soon spread.

Er fand ein Haar in der Sache.
He discovered a fly in the ointment; he found something wrong with it.

Man ließ kein gutes Haar an ihr.
They tore her character all to pieces; they didn't leave her a shred.

Sie hat Haare auf den Zähnen.
She's a tough customer; she's a little spitfire; she's not to be trifled with.

Er ließ Haare dabei.
He got scratched; he lost out.

Es ist, um sich die Haare auszuraufen.
It's enough to make one despair.

Lassen Sie sich deswegen keine Haare ausfallen!
Don't let it get you down!; don't worry about it!

Sein Leben hängt an einem Haar.
His life is hanging by a thread; his life is in jeopardy (or danger).

Er wußte es aufs Haar.
He knew it letter-perfect; he had it down pat (or to a T).

Der Beweis ist bei den Haaren herbeigezogen.
The argument is far-fetched; it's exaggerated.

Sie liegen sich in den Haaren.
They're at loggerheads (or each other's throats); they have it in for one another.

Er verschlang die Mahlzeit mit Haut und Haar.
He cleaned the plate; he licked the platter clean.

Um ein Haar wäre er getötet worden.
He had a close shave (or narrow escape); he came within an ace of being killed.

Das ist um kein Haar besser.
That's not a bit better; that's just as bad as before.

haarig:

Es ging haarig dabei zu.
Everything was (or Queer things were) happening; it was a bad state of affairs.

haarklein:

Er erzählte es haarklein.
He told the long and the short of it; he went into great detail.

haarscharf:

Er bewies es haarscharf.
He proved it with mathematical precision.

Der Wagen fuhr haarscharf an uns vorüber.
The car missed us by an inch; we narrowly escaped being run over.

haarsträubend:

Seine Bummelei ist haarsträubend.
It's scandalous the way he loafs.

Habchen:

Er verlor sein ganzes Habchen und Babchen.
He lost the shirt off his back; he lost everything he owned.

Habe:

Er verspielte sein ganzes Hab' und Gut.
He gambled away everything he had.

139

haben:

Hab' dich nur nicht so!	Don't be silly!; don't make such a fuss!; don't carry on so!
Besser hab' ich, als hätt' ich.	A bird in the hand is worth two in the bush.
Da hast du's!	There you are!; I told you so!
Was hast du?	What's wrong (or the matter) with you?
Was gibst du, was hast du?	What'll you give for it?; what have you to offer?
Wer nicht will, der hat schon!	Like it or lump it!; take it or leave it!; all right, do without it then!
Er hat das so an sich.	That's just his way.
Was hat er davon?	What good is that to him?
Er hat's ja.	He can afford it.
Er hat's gut.	He's lucky; he's well off.
Wie schlecht er sich dabei hat!	What a bungler he is!
Er hat viel von seinem Vater.	He's like his father in many ways.
Hat sich was!	Nothing doing!; no sale!; that's where you're wrong!
Es hat nichts auf sich.	It's O.K. (or all right); it doesn't really matter; never mind!
Die Aufgabe hat es in sich.	That's a tough job; it's a difficult assignment.
Die beiden haben es miteinander.	They're sweet on each other; they're in love.
Die haben sich aber böse gehabt.	They must have been down on (or sore at) each other.
Dafür bin ich nicht zu haben.	Not me!; count me out!
Sie ist noch zu haben.	She's still single (or unmarried).
Er hat es so haben wollen.	That's his own fault; he has only himself to thank for it.

Habenichts:

Er ist ein Habenichts.	He's a have-not (or poor devil); he's hard up.

Hacke:

Er wird schon der Hacke einen Stiel finden.	He'll find a peg to fit the hole; he'll manage (or fix) that.

Hacken:

Machen Sie sich auf die Hacken!	Take to your heels!; get a move on!; beat it!

Hafen:

Er ist in den letzten Hafen eingelaufen.	He made his last trip; he died.

Hafer:

Ihn sticht der Hafer.	He feels his oats; he's feeling frisky; he's looking for trouble.

Hahn:

Er ist Hahn im Korb.	He's cock of the walk; he's a ladies' man.
Kein Hahn kräht danach.	Nobody cares (or gives a hoot) about it.
Jemand hat ihm den roten Hahn aufs Dach gesetzt.	Someone set fire to his house.

Häkchen:

Früh krümmt sich, was ein Häkchen werden will.	As the twig is bent the tree is inclined; what's bred in the bone will out in the flesh.
Sie hat ein Häkchen auf ihn.	She has something on (or against) him.

häkeln:
    Er häkelt sich gern mit den Leuten.
    He's a great spoofer (*or* joker); he likes to kid (*or* jolly) folks along.

Haken:
    Hier ist der Haken.
    Here's the rub (*or* hitch); here's where the difficulty comes in.

halb:
    Halb so wild, junger Mann!
    Hold your horses, young fellow!; not so fast there, son!

    Für diesen Preis ist es halb geschenkt.
    It's practically a gift at this price.

    Sie hörte ihm mit halbem Ohr zu.
    She lent him a deaf ear; she listened inattentively.

Hälfte:
    Es waren ihrer um die Hälfte zuviel.
    There were twice as many as necessary.

    Lassen Sie mich die Rechnung zur Hälfte tragen!
    Let's go Dutch (*or* fifty-fifty)!; let's split the bill!

Hallo:
    Er machte ein großes Hallo darum.
    He made a big fuss (*or* much ado) about it.

Halm:
    Er mußte sein Getreide auf dem Halm verkaufen.
    He had to sell his green corn.

Hals:
    Er lief Hals über Kopf davon.
    He ran away helter-skelter (*or* pell-mell).

    Das dürfte ihm den Hals abdrehen.
    That may cook his hash (*or* finish him).

    Lassen Sie uns einer Flasche den Hals brechen!
    Let's crack (drink, *or* kill) a bottle!

    Er kann den Hals nicht voll genug kriegen.
    He's such a pig; he never gets enough.

    Sie stopften ihm den Hals zu.
    They shut him up.

    Da kann man sich die Schwindsucht an den Hals ärgern!
    It gets my goat; it makes me sick.

    Es geht ihm an den Hals.
    It's a matter of life or death.

    Er schwatzte es ihr an den Hals.
    He stuck her with it; he palmed it off on her; he talked her into taking it.

    Ich wünsche ihm die Gicht an den Hals.
    To hell with him!; I hope he breaks his neck.

    Er liegt ihnen den ganzen Tag auf dem Hals.
    He hangs around all day.

    Er lud sich viele Feinde auf den Hals.
    He made many enemies.

    Er lachte aus vollem Hals.
    He laughed out loud.

    Er schrie aus vollem Hals.
    He yelled for dear life; he shouted at the top of his lungs.

    Das Wasser geht ihm bis an den Hals.
    He's up to his neck in debt (*or* trouble); he's in deep (*or* hot) water; he's in straitened circumstances.

    Er ist bis an den Hals in Schulden.
    He's up to his ears in debt.

    Er war barfuß bis an den Hals.
    He was stark-naked.

    Ihm steht die Sache bis an den Hals.
    He's fed up with it; he's sick and tired of it.

    Das Herz schlug ihr bis zum Hals, als sie ihn sah.
    Her heart was in her mouth (*or* beat wildly) when she saw him.

    Er redet sich noch um den Hals.
    His tongue will get him into trouble yet; he talks too much for his own good.

    Halten Sie mir den Menschen vom Hals!
    Don't let that fellow get in my way!; don't let him cross my path!

Die Zunge hing ihm zum Hals heraus.	He could have spit cotton; he was dry as a gourd.
Die Geschichte wächst uns zum Hals heraus.	We're fed up with the matter; we're sick and tired of it.

Halsbruch:

Hals- und Beinbruch!	Good luck!

halt:

Das ist halt so und nicht anders.	That's about the size of it; that's how matters stand.

halten:

Ich halte es so.	That's how I feel about it; that's my way of doing (or thinking).
Wofür hälst du ihn?	What do you take him for?
Sie hält ihn sehr gut.	She looks after him very well.
Er hält sehr auf sich.	He's very fastidious; he's very particular about his appearance.
Man hält ihn für einen andern.	He's mistaken for another.
Er hält es mit ihnen.	He sides with them.
Er hält nichts davon.	He thinks nothing of it; he has no use for it.
Er hält sich an sie.	He relies upon her.
Er hält sich gut.	He's doing well.
Er hält sich kaum noch.	He can barely restrain himself.
Es hält schwer.	It's hard (or difficult).
Er kann es halten, wie er will.	He can do as he likes.
Er kann sich nicht länger halten.	He can't hang on (or keep going) any longer.
Er muß sich sehr halten.	He must watch himself very carefully.
Das läßt sich halten.	That's fair.

Haltung:

Er nimmt eine abwartende Haltung ein.	He steers a neutral course; he lays low; he bides his time.

Hammel:

Um auf den besagten Hammel zurückzukommen.	To return to the subject.

Hammelbein:

Den will ich schon beim Hammelbein kriegen.	I'll wring his neck; I'll set him to rights.

Hammer:

Du mußt Hammer oder Amboß sein.	You must be either master or servant.
Er ist zwischen Hammer und Amboß.	He's between the devil and the deep blue sea; he's in a tight spot (or an embarrassing situation).

Hand:

Hand aufs Herz!	Cross your heart!; honor bright!; take an oath on it!
Hand von der Butter!	Hands (or Keep) off!
Eine Hand wäscht die andere.	If you scratch my back, I'll scratch yours; one good turn deserves another.
Er lebt von seiner Hände Arbeit.	He lives by the sweat of his brow.
Sie gehen Hand in Hand darin.	They're in agreement.
Er legte Hand an sich.	He committed suicide.
Das hat Hand und Fuß.	You've got something there; that's a good idea; that's very much to the point.

Er gab ihr die Hand.	He shook hands with her.
Er hat die Hand im Spiel.	He has his finger in the pie; he's mixed up in the deal.
Er legt die Hand dafür ins Feuer.	He'd give his right arm; he'll vouch for it.
Er legte die Hand ans Werk.	He put his shoulder to the wheel; he buckled (*or* got) down to work.
Er legte die letzte Hand an.	He put the finishing touches to it.
Er hat eine lange Hand.	He has pull (*or* influence); his influence is far-reaching.
Er hat eine sichere Hand.	He's a dead (*or* sure) shot; he always hits the mark.
Es hat keinen Zweck, jetzt die Hände in den Schoß zu legen.	There's no sense in giving up (the ghost) now; you can't lie down on the job now.
Verbrennen Sie sich nicht die Hände daran!	Don't get your fingers burnt!; don't get yourself into hot water (*or* trouble)!
Er versuchte, ihm die Hände zu versilbern.	He tried to bribe him.
Sie schlug die Hände überm Kopf zusammen.	She threw up her hands in amazement; she was completely taken aback (*or* off her feet); she was dumbfounded (*or* very much surprised).
Ich wasche meine Hände in Unschuld.	I wash my hands of it; I'm not responsible.
Es gelang ihm an der Hand seines Vaters.	He succeeded with the help of his father.
Er gab ihm die Mittel dazu an die Hand.	He backed him (financially); he furnished him with the funds.
Das liegt auf der flachen Hand.	That's clear as day; it's obvious (*or* self-evident).
Er tut es auf eigne Hand.	He does it on his own hook (*or* at his own expense).
Er trägt sie auf Händen.	He does everything he can for her; he's very kind to her.
Sehen Sie ihm auf die Hände!	Keep tabs (*or* your eagle eye) on him!; watch him!
Er gab seinen Anspruch aus der Hand.	He waived his right.
Er tat es aus freier Hand.	He did it of his own accord (*or* free will).
Er hat immer eine Ausrede bei der Hand.	He always has a ready alibi (*or* excuse).
Er ist in allem schnell bei der Hand.	He's quick on the trigger; he's quick to act.
Er hat alle Fäden in der Hand.	He's pulling wires; he has pull (*or* influence).
Sie hat das Heft in der Hand.	She wears the pants in that house; she rules the roost (*or* household); she's in charge.
Mit dem Hut in der Hand kommt man durchs ganze Land.	It pays to be courteous.
Das liegt ganz in seiner Hand.	That rests entirely with him; that's entirely up to him.
Nicht in die Hand!	Not on your life!; nothing doing!
Nimm deine Beine in die Hand!	Pick up your feet!; make it snappy!; put your best foot forward!
Er gab seinem Gegner Waffen in die Hände.	He laid himself open to attack; he furnished his opponent with arguments.
Jungs, laßt uns in die Hände spucken!	Let's go, boys!; here goes, fellows!; let's get going!
Er versprach es mit Hand und Fuß.	He swore on a stack of Bibles; he took a solemn oath.
Sie ist mit Herz und Hand dafür.	She's for it, heart and soul.
Er nahm die Stadt mit bewaffneter Hand.	He captured the town by force of arms.

Das ist mit leichter Hand getan.	That's a snap (*or* cinch); there's nothing to it; that's easily done.
Er sträubte sich mit Händen und Füßen.	He fought tooth and nail; he put up a stiff fight.
Das läßt sich mit beiden Händen greifen.	That's plain as day (*or* the nose on your face).
Er griff mit beiden Händen zu.	He jumped at the opportunity.
Er gab sein Geld mit vollen Händen aus.	He spent his money liberally (*or* without giving it a thought).
Die Arbeit geht ihm flink von der Hand.	He makes things hum; he's a fast worker.
Er wies das Angebot von der Hand.	He turned down the offer.
Das läßt sich nicht von der Hand weisen.	That can't be denied.
Es war von langer Hand vorbereitet.	The affair was premeditated (*or* prearranged); it was a foregone conclusion.
Er geht einem gern zur Hand.	He likes to be helpful (*or* of service).
Er hatte die Beweise zur Hand.	He could quote chapter and verse; he could prove his case (in black and white); he had the (documentary) evidence in his possession.

handeln:
Worum handelt es sich? — What's the issue?; what's it all about?

händeringend:
Er lehnte händeringend ab. — He wouldn't do it for the world.

handfest:
Es war eine handfeste Lüge. — It was an atrocious (*or* a downright) lie. *

Handgelenk:
Er hat ein lockeres Handgelenk. — He swings a wicked left; he has a hard punch.

Das läßt sich nicht so aus dem Handgelenk machen. — You can't pull that out of your hat; that's not easy to do.

Handkuß:
Er nahm die Einladung mit Handkuß an. — He accepted the invitation with alacrity.

Handschrift:
Er schreibt eine kräftige Handschrift. — He has a hard punch.

Handtuch:
Das paßt wie der Igel zum Handtuch. — That's like a square peg in a round hole; they don't fit (*or* go together) at all.

Handumdrehen:
Er tat es im Handumdrehen. — He did it in a jiffy (*or* the twinkling of an eye); it took him no time at all.

Handwerk:
Ihm wurde endlich das Handwerk gelegt. — He was finally squelched (*or* put down).
Er versteht sein Handwerk. — He knows the ropes (*or* his business).
Pfuschen Sie mir nicht ins Handwerk! — You keep out of here!; mind your own business!

Klappern gehört zum Handwerk. — Publicity is part of the game.

hanebüchen:
Das ist wirklich hanebüchen! — That takes the cake!; that beats all!; why, it's awful!

Hanf:
Er kann sich nicht aus dem Hanf finden. — He can't see the point.

Er sitzt wie der Vogel im Hanf.	He's in clover, he's sitting pretty; he's well off.
Hangen:	
Es war eine Zeit des Hangens und Bangens.	It was an anxious (*or* harrowing) time.
hängen:	
Hier hängt er!	Here I am!
Er hängt bei mir.	He has it coming to him from me; he's due (*or* ripe) for punishment.
Woran hängt es?	Where's the hitch?; what seems to be the difficulty?
Die Sache hängt noch.	The matter is still hanging fire; it's pending.
Alles, was drum und dran hängt.	Everything connected with it.
Hängen:	
Mit Hängen und Würgen bestand er die Prüfung.	He passed the test by the skin of his teeth; he just skimmed by; he barely made (*or* passed) it.
hängenbleiben:	
Er blieb in der Schule hängen.	He flunked out of school; he was left behind.
Hans:	
Was Hänschen nicht lernt, lernt Hans nimmermehr.	You can't teach an old dog new tricks.
Hans und Kunz wissen das.	Tom, Dick, and Harry know that; any- (*or* everybody) knows that.
Jeder Hans findet seine Grete.	Every Jack has his Jill; there's a girl for every boy.
Er ist ein Hans Dampf.	He lets off steam (*or* hot air); he's a windbag (*or* blusterer).
Er ist ein Hans Huckebein.	He gets all the tough breaks; he always has hard luck.
hänseln:	
Er hänselt gern.	He likes to kid (*or* rib); he's a big tease.
hapern:	
Woran hapert es?	Where is the rub (*or* catch)?
Es hapert ihm am Geld.	He's short of money.
Happen:	
Es war ein fetter Happen, den die Polizei mit seiner Festnahme machte.	The police made a big haul when they arrested him.
Er will sich den Happen nicht entgehen lassen.	He won't let this opportunity slip through his fingers.
happig:	
Seien Sie nicht so happig!	Don't be such a hog!
Der Preis ist ein bißchen happig.	The price is pretty steep (*or* high).
Harke:	
Ich werde ihm schon zeigen, was eine Harke ist!	I'll show him what's what!; I'll give him a good piece of my mind!
Harnisch:	
Er geriet in Harnisch.	He got his dander up; he lost his temper.
hart:	
Es ging hart auf hart in der Verhandlung.	They gave tit for tat (*or* blow for blow) at the conference.

Er bohrt nicht gern hartes Holz.	He follows the line of least resistance; he doesn't like to exert himself (*or* put himself out).
Haſcherl:	
Sie iſt ein armes Haſcherl.	She's a poor little thing.
Haſe:	
Er kommt von einem Ort, wo Fuchs und Haſe ſich gute Nacht ſagen.	He comes from Hickville (*or* the sticks); he's from the country.
Mein Name iſt Haſe, ich weiß von nichts.	Ask me another!; don't ask me, I'm dumb!
Er weiß, wie der Haſe läuft.	He knows which way the wind blows; he knows what's up (*or* going on).
Er lebt wie der Haſe im Klee.	He's in clover; he's got it soft (*or* easy).
Da liegt der Haſe im Pfeffer!	That's where the shoe pinches!; there's the rub!; there's where the trouble lies!
Ihm iſt ein Haſe über den Weg gelaufen.	A black cat ran across his path; he had a foreboding of hard luck.
Er iſt doch auch kein heuriger Haſe mehr.	He wasn't born yesterday; he's no longer a child.
Schulden ſind keine Haſen.	Debts never run away; no one will pay your debts for you.
Viele Hunde ſind des Haſen Tod.	There's no use fighting against great odds.
Sie werden doch einem alten Haſen nicht das Laufen beibringen wollen?	You don't think you can take in an old-timer with a tale like that?
Er hat einen Haſen im Buſen.	He's chicken-hearted; he's a timorous soul.
Haſenbalg:	
Sie zankten ſich um den Haſenbalg.	They quarreled over nothing.
Haſenfuß:	
Er iſt ein rechter Haſenfuß.	He's timid as a hare; he's a regular fraidcat; he's afraid of his own shadow.
Haſenjagd:	
Das iſt doch keine Haſenjagd.	There's no (need to) hurry; take your time.
Haſenpanier:	
Er ergriff das Haſenpanier.	He took to his heels; he ran for dear life (*or* all he was worth).
Haſt:	
Nur keine jüdiſche Haſt!	Where's the fire?; what's all the rush about?; take it easy!
haſte:	
Haſte nich(t) geſehn ſtand er da.	Presto, there he was!; suddenly he stood there.
Er lief haſte was kannſte weg.	He ran away as fast as he could.
Haube:	
Der Chef iſt ihm auf der Haube.	His boss keeps an eye (*or* close watch) on him.
Sie iſt unter die Haube gekommen.	She got married.
Hauch:	
Er iſt nur noch ein Hauch.	He's nothing but a shadow of his former self; he's a walking skeleton.
hauen:	
Das haut!	Hot dog!; great stuff!; capital!

Häufchen:

Er saß da wie ein Häufchen Unglück.

He sat there looking as if he had lost his last friend; he looked woebegone (*or* miserably unhappy).

Haufen:

Viele Körner machen einen Haufen.

Great oaks from small acorns grow; look after the pennies and the dollars will look after themselves.

Er schoß ihn über den Haufen.

He shot (*or* brought) him down.

Er warf alle Bedenken über den Haufen.

He threw caution to the winds; he cast aside all scruples.

haufenweise:

Haben Sie genug Geld bei sich?—Ja, haufenweise!

Have you money enough with you?—Sure, oodles (*or* piles) of it!

Haupt:

Er ist ein bemoostes Haupt.

He has been a student for ages; he's an old-timer.

Sie schlugen den Feind aufs Haupt.

They put the enemy to rout.

Hauptkerl:

Du bist auch ein Hauptkerl!

What a man!; there's an ace (*or* a real fellow) for you!

Hauptrolle:

Sie möchte die Hauptrolle spielen.

She wants to play first fiddle; she wants to run things.

Hauptspaß:

Es machte ihm einen Hauptspaß, ihnen zuzusehen.

He got a big kick out of watching them; it did his heart good to watch them.

Haus:

Hallo, altes Haus!

Hello there, old-timer!; how's the old boy?

Er hat Einfälle wie ein altes Haus.

He gets crazy notions.

Er ist ein fideles Haus.

He's a jolly good fellow.

Man nahm ihm Haus und Hof.

They cleaned him out; they took every last thing he owned.

Er läuft ihr fast das Haus ein.

He won't take "no" for an answer; he's been bothering the life out of her.

Der Sterbende konnte noch sein Haus bestellen.

The dying man was still able to draw up his will.

Sie machen ein großes Haus.

They live in grand style.

Auf ihn kann man Häuser bauen.

You may put your faith in (*or* rely on) him.

Er ist wie Kind im Haus.

He's like one of the family.

Er fiel mit der Tür ins Haus.

He blurted out the news.

Er hat von Haus aus Geld.

He has means of his own; he has a private income.

Er ist Zimmermann von Haus aus.

He's a carpenter by trade.

Er ist schon von Haus aus schwächlich.

He's been a weakling since birth.

Bleiben Sie mir mit ihren Einwendungen zu Hause!

Mind your own business!; keep your opinions to yourself!

Bei uns zu Hause ist das anders.

In our country it's different.

Wo sind Sie zu Hause?

Where do you hail (*or* come) from?; where's your home town?

Wie steht's zu Hause?

How are the folks?

hausbacken:

Er ist tüchtig, aber sehr hausbacken.	He's a good fellow, but very provincial (*or* unsophisticated).

Häuschen:

Er geriet ganz aus dem Häuschen, als er davon hörte.	He was quite upset (*or* nearly beside himself) when he heard about it.

hausen:

Der Sturm hat im Walde arg gehaust.	The hurricane played havoc with the forest.

häuslich:

Er ließ sich häuslich bei ihnen nieder.	He took over (*or* possession of) their place.

Haut:

Es gilt Haut und Haar.	It's a matter of life and death.
Er ist eine ehrliche Haut.	He's a square-shooter (*or* an honest fellow).
Wehren Sie sich Ihrer Haut!	Defend yourself!; fight back!
Jeder muß seine Haut zu Markte tragen.	Every man (must look out) for himself!; no one can fight your battles for you.
Er liegt auf der faulen Haut.	He's loafing (*or* idling); he's taking it easy.
Es kann keiner aus seiner Haut heraus.	A leopard can't change his spots; we can't help being what we are.
Ich möchte nicht in seiner Haut stecken.	I wouldn't like to be in his boots (*or* place); I don't envy him.
Er steckt in keiner guten Haut.	He's in bad health; he's sickly.
Er verschlang die Mahlzeit mit Haut und Haar.	He cleaned the plate; he licked the platter clean.
Er kam mit heiler Haut davon.	He saved the bacon; he got off scot-free; he came away unhurt.

Hebel:

Er setzte alle Hebel in Bewegung.	He left no stone unturned; he did everything in his power.

heben:

Heb dich weg!	Scram!; beat it!; go chase yourself!
Er hebt gern einen.	He's addicted to the bottle; he likes his little drink.

Hechel:

Sie zogen ihn durch die Hechel.	They razzed (*or* ridiculed) him unmercifully.

Hecht:

Er ist der Hecht im Karpfenteich.	He's a big frog in a little puddle; he's the whole cheese (*or* show); he's the trouble-shooter.
Er ist ein feiner Hecht.	He's a regular guy; he's a good scout (*or* fine fellow).
In dem Zimmer war ein unglaublicher Hecht.	The air in the room was thick (*or* dense) with tobacco smoke.

Hechtsuppe:

Es zieht wie Hechtsuppe.	There's a gale blowing in the room; there's a terrible draft.

Heft:

Er ist ein verrücktes Heft.	He's a crazy loon; he's madder than a March hare.
Sie hat das Heft in der Hand.	She wears the pants in that house; she rules the roost (*or* household); she's in charge.

Der Vorschlag ist ein Messer ohne Heft und Klinge.	The suggestion doesn't hold water; it's impractical (*or* useless).
Heftelmachen: Das geht ja wie's Heftelmachen!	That goes slick as a whistle!; that's easy as pie!
Heftelmacher: Er paßt auf wie ein Heftelmacher.	He's watching like a hawk; he's paying the closest attention.
Hehl: Er macht aus seiner wahren Gesinnung keinen Hehl.	He makes no bones about (*or* secret of) his true feelings in the matter.
Heidenangst: Er hat eine Heidenangst.	He's in a blue funk; he's scared to death.
Heidenlärm: Er machte einen Heidenlärm, als er davon hörte.	He raised a great hue and cry (*or* made an awful commotion) when he heard about it.
heidenmäßig: Er hat heidenmäßig dabei verdient.	He cleaned up (*or* made a fortune) on that deal.
heidi: Sein Geld ist heidi.	His money is gone (*or* lost).
heikel: Er ist sehr heikel in Bezug auf Essen.	He's very finicky (*or* fussy) about food; he's very particular about what he eats.
Heil: Er suchte sein Heil in der Flucht. Lassen Sie ihn sein Heil versuchen!	He ran for dear life (*or* all he was worth). Let him try his luck!
heilig: Er fuhr drein wie ein heiliges Donnerwetter. Es ist mein heiliger Ernst.	He raised the roof; he gave them hell; he bawled them out. I'm in dead earnest; in all seriousness; I absolutely mean it.
Heilige: Ist die Gefahr vorbei, wird der Heilige ausgelacht. Er ist ein wunderlicher Heiliger.	No sooner is the danger past than God is forgotten. He's an old codger; he's a queer egg (*or* sort).
heiligen: Der Zweck heiligt die Mittel.	Anything goes; the end justifies the means.
heimgehen: Er ist heimgegangen.	He has gone to his last resting place; he died.
heimgeigen: Damit können Sie sich heimgeigen lassen!	Try and cash in on that!; that wouldn't even get you carfare home!; that's not worth a darn!
heimleuchten: Er hat ihnen schwer heimgeleuchtet.	He sent them packing; he sent them about their business.

heimzahlen:

Er wird ihnen das heimzahlen.	He'll pay them off; he'll get even with them.

Hein:

Freund Hein hat ihn geholt.	The grim reaper (*or* Death) took him away.

Heinrich:

Der Grüne Heinrich holte die Gefangenen ab.	The prisoners were rushed off in the Black Maria (*or* police wagon).

heiß:

Es wird nichts so heiß gegessen, wie es gekocht wird.	Nothing is so bad as it is painted; things are always better than they seem.
Was ich nicht weiß, macht mich nicht heiß.	What I don't know won't hurt me.
Es überrieselte ihn heiß und kalt.	It gave him the creeps; it sent the shivers up and down his spine.
Es ist sein heißes Bestreben, es gut zu machen.	He has his heart set on making a good job of it.
Gehen Sie doch nicht wie die Katze um den heißen Brei!	Don't beat about the bush!; talk turkey!; out with it!
Heißen Dank!	Thanks a lot!

heißen:

Jetzt heißt's aber geeilt!	Now we must step on it!; let's make it snappy!
Was soll das heißen?	What's the big idea?; what do you mean by that?
Das soll so etwas heißen.	He wants to play big; he's trying to show off.
Das will schon etwas heißen.	That's something.

heiter:

Das kann ja heiter werden!	That's only the beginning!; that promises to be exciting!

Hekuba:

Das ist ihm Hekuba.	He doesn't care a fig; he doesn't give a damn (*or* hoot).

Held:

Er ist kein Held im Lernen.	He's not much of a student; he's no mental giant.
Sie sind mir ein schöner Held!	You're a fine one (to deal with)!; what a flop (*or* disappointment) you turned out to be!

helfen:

Dem werde ich schwer helfen.	I'll tell that man a thing or two; I'll give it to him.
Er weiß sich zu helfen.	He's able to take care of himself.
Er weiß sich nicht mehr zu raten noch zu helfen.	He's up against it; he doesn't know which way to turn; he's at his wits' end.

hell(e):

Mensch, sei helle!	Watch your step!; keep your head (*or* wits) about you!; steady there!
Sie kamen in hellen Haufen.	They came in throngs (*or* crowds).
Der helle Neid schaute ihm aus den Augen.	He was green with envy.
Es geschah am hellen Tag.	It happened in broad daylight.

Die hellen Tränen standen ihr in den Augen.
Her eyes were filled with tears.

Das wäre heller Wahnsinn.
That would be sheer madness.

Heller:
Er bezahlte auf Heller und Pfennig.
He paid up to the last cent.

hellhörig:
Er ist hellhörig.
His ear is never far from the ground; he has sharp ears.

hellicht:
Es geschah am hellichten Tag.
It happened in broad daylight.

hellichterloh:
Das Haus brannte hellichterloh.
The house was all ablaze.

Hemd:
Das Hemd ist mir näher als der Rock.
Blood is thicker than water; charity begins at home.

Er wechselt seine Gesinnung wie das Hemd.
He's as changeable as the weather.

Er hat kein reines Hemd an.
His hands aren't clean; he is not innocent.

Man zog ihn bis aufs Hemd aus.
He was fleeced (or badly taken in); he took an awful beating.

Henker:
Er schert sich den Henker darum.
He doesn't give a damn (or hoot).

Es müßte mit dem Henker zugehen, könnte ich das nicht schaffen.
It would be funny (or one on me) if I couldn't do that.

Zum Henker!
Jumping Jupiter!; drat it all!; the devil with it!

Henkersmahlzeit:
Wann steigt Ihre Henkersmahlzeit?
When does your farewell dinner come off?

Henne:
Will das Ei klüger sein als die Henne?
Wise guy, eh?; are you telling me?; so you think you know it all?; children should be seen and not heard.

her:
Her damit!
Come across (with it)!; give it to me!

Mit seinem Wissen ist es nicht weit her.
He's no shining light (or great student); he knows blessed little.

Er weiß nicht wo hin noch her.
He doesn't know which way to turn; he's in a quandary.

Er überlegte hin und her.
He considered the pros and cons.

Das ist hin wie her.
That's six of one and half a dozen of the other; it's all the same.

herab:
Sie behandelte ihn von oben herab.
She high-hatted him; she treated him like a servant.

heranmachen:
Machen Sie sich an die Sache heran!
Get down to brass tacks (or business).

heranschlängeln:
Er schlängelte sich leise heran.
He sidled up stealthily.

heraus:
Jetzt hat er's heraus.
Now he's got it; he's on to it; he's found out.

Er hat die Sache heraus.
He has the hang (or knack) of it; he knows how to do it.

Er möchte ein Zimmer nach vornen heraus.	He wants a room in the front.
Er ist fein heraus.	He made out (*or* came off) well; he was lucky.
herausbeißen:	
Er beißt zu sehr den Vorgesetzten heraus.	He's too bossy (*or* superior).
herausekeln:	
Man hat ihn aus der Partei herausgeekelt.	He was frozen (*or* put) out of the party.
herausgeben:	
Können Sie mir auf fünf Mark herausgeben?	Can you change a five-mark piece?
herausgehen:	
Er geht nicht aus sich heraus.	He's very reserved; he keeps to himself.
heraushängen:	
Man hat ihn auf einen Monat aus der Verbindung herausgehängt.	He was suspended from the fraternity for a month.
herausholen:	
Er holte das Letzte aus sich heraus.	He put all he had into it; he did his best.
herauskehren:	
Er kehrt zu sehr den Vorgesetzten heraus.	He's too bossy (*or* superior).
herauskommen:	
Es kommt alles auf eins heraus.	It's all the same in the end.
Dabei kommt doch nichts heraus.	This doesn't lead anywhere; it won't get you anywhere.
Man kam aus dem Staunen nicht heraus.	One thrill followed another; it was a round of surprises.
herausmachen:	
Er hat sich nach seiner Krankheit wieder gut herausgemacht.	He pulled through (*or* came around) very nicely after his illness.
herausnehmen:	
Er nimmt sich zuviel heraus.	He's too fresh (*or* forward).
herausöden:	
Er wurde aus seiner Firma herausgeödet.	The firm made it so hot (*or* disagreeable) for him that he had to leave.
herausrücken:	
Rücken Sie doch endlich mit der Sprache heraus!	Come across!; talk turkey!; out with it!
herausschauen:	
Dabei schaut nichts heraus.	There's nothing to be gained by it.
herausstecken:	
Was hat der Junge nun wieder herausgesteckt?	Now what has the boy been up to?
herausstreichen:	
Er strich sein Vaterland heraus.	He cracked up his own country; he sang its praises.
herauswimmeln:	
Man hat ihn aus seiner Stellung herausgewimmelt.	They forced (*or* pushed) him out of his job.
Herd:	
Eigner Herd ist Goldes wert.	Be it ever so humble, there's no place like home.

Herdenmensch:
Er ist der richtige Herdenmensch.

He follows the band wagon; he goes with the crowd.

hereinhängen:
Er hängt sich in alles herein.

He sticks his nose into everything; he's a busybody.

hereinlotsen:
Er lotste uns auf seine Bude herein.

He enticed (*or* tricked) us in.

hereinrasseln:
Er rasselte bei dem Geschäft schwer herein.

He was snowed under (*or* lost heavily) in that deal.

hereinreiten:
Er hat sich tüchtig hereingeritten.

He got himself into hot water (*or* difficulties).

hereinsegeln:
Da sind Sie aber ordentlich hereingesegelt!

That was a bad spill (*or* encounter) for you!; you surely took a tumble that time!

herfallen:
Die Presse fiel gewaltig über ihn her.

The papers rode roughshod over him; the press roasted (*or* panned) him unmercifully.

hergehen:
Es ging hoch her.

It was a gay party; everybody was in high spirits.

Es ging über ihn her.

They dragged him in the mud; they slandered him.

herhalten:
Er muß stets bei ihnen herhalten.

They always have it in for him.

Er mußte schwer herhalten.

He had to fork out (*or* come across with) a lot of money.

Hering:
So ein Hering!

What a beanpole (*or* skinny ninny)!

Sie saßen wie die Heringe.

They were packed into their seats like sardines.

Man hat ihm einen Hering erteilt.

He was given a calling-down; he was severely reprimanded.

Herkules:
Beim Herkules!

By George!

herleiern:
Sie leierte das Gedicht nur so her.

She just rattled off the poem.

hermachen:
Er machte sich über sein Essen her.

He pitched in (*or* fell to); he tackled his meal.

Herr:
Herr du meines Lebens!

Leaping lizards!; holy cow!; jumping Jupiter!

Wer ist hier Herr?

Who's boss (*or* in charge) here?

Er kann der Sache nicht Herr werden.

He can't do (*or* manage) it.

Wie der Herr, so's Gescherr (= Geschirr).

Jack is as good as his master.

Den Seinen gibt's der Herr im Schlafe.

Good fortune comes over night.

Er ist „Alter Herr."

He's a grad(uate); he's an alum(nus).

Sein alter Herr war daheim.	His old man (*or* father) was at home.
Meine Herren!	Good night!; gosh!
Sie kamen aus aller Herren Länder.	They came from all over the world.
Sie haben einen möblierten Herrn.	They have a star boarder (*or* roomer).
Er fand seinen Herrn.	He met his match.
Mit großen Herren ist nicht gut Kirschen essen.	Small fry don't stand a chance with the big shots; the weak always go to the wall; they get the shorter end (*or* come off worst).
Er ist ein großer Klugschnacker vor dem Herrn.	He's a smart-aleck (*or* wise guy); he thinks he knows it all.

Herrgott:

Er lebt wie der Herrgott in Frankreich.	He's leading the life of Riley; he's living like a king (*or* in grand style).
Er stiehlt dem Herrgott die Tage.	He's killing time; he's loafing (*or* idling).
Er läßt den Herrgott einen guten Mann sein.	He lets matters drift (*or* slide); he lets things take their course.
Er tut, als ob er mit unserm Herrgott per du wäre.	He acts as if he were the Almighty Himself.

Herrgottsfrühe:

Er kam in aller Herrgottsfrühe.	He came early in the morning.

herrje(mine):

Herrjemine!	Gemini crickets!; whew!

herrlich:

Er lebt herrlich und in Freuden.	He's in clover; he's on Easy Street; he's living off the fat of the land (*or* in peace and plenty).

Herrlichkeit:

Ist das die ganze Herrlichkeit?	Is that all there is to it?; is that the whole show?

Herrschaft:

Herrschaft noch mal!	My word!; golly!

herrschend:

Die herrschende Stimmung im Volk ist dagegen.	The majority of the people are against it.

herscheren:

Scher dich her!	Come here at once!

herumbummeln:

Er ist den ganzen Tag in der Stadt herumgebummelt.	He's been puttering (*or* bumming) around town all day.

herumdrücken:

Wo er sich nur wieder herumdrückt?	Where does he hang out (*or* keep himself) these days?
Er kann sich nicht länger um die Sache herumdrücken.	He can't get out of it (*or* put it off) any longer.

herumdrucksen:

Er druckst schon über eine Woche an der Arbeit herum.	He's been stalling around (*or* working over) on this job for over a week.

herumfummeln:

Woran fummelt er nun herum?	Now what is he doing (*or* up to)?

herumkriegen:
Den wollen wir schon herumkriegen. — We can win him over.

herummimen:
Wo er nur herummimt? — I wonder where he's hanging out (*or* keeping himself)?

herumreiten:
Er reitet immer auf der Sache herum. — He keeps harping on it; he keeps bringing it up.

herumstehen:
Hier darf niemand herumstehen! — No parking (*or* loitering) here!

herumstöbern:
Er stöberte in meinen Büchern herum. — He was browsing among my books.

herumtreiben:
Er hat sich drei Jahre in den Staaten herumgetrieben. — He's been knocking about (*or* traveling in) the States for three years.

herunterkullern:
Tränen kullerten ihr die Backen herunter. — Tears rolled down her cheeks.

herunterlangen:
Er langte ihm eine herunter. — He handed him one; he slapped him.

herunterleiern:
Er leierte seinen Vortrag herunter. — He rattled (*or* spieled) off his lecture.

herunterputzen:
Er hat sie heruntergeputzt. — He called them on the carpet; he bawled them out.

herunterwirtschaften:
Er hat das Geschäft ganz heruntergewirtschaftet. — He let the business go all to seed (*or* pot); he let it run down.

hervorrufen:
Der Schauspieler wurde wiederholt hervorgerufen, ehe der Beifall sich legte. — The actor had to take many curtain calls before the applause died down.

Herz:
Was die Augen sehen, glaubt das Herz. — Seeing is believing.

Das Herz lachte ihm im Leib. — He was tickled pink (*or* to death); he was delighted.

Sie sind ein Herz und eine Seele. — They're hand and glove; they're fast friends.

Sein Herz hängt am Geld. — He's out to make money.

Er freut sich ehrlichen Herzens darüber. — He's genuinely pleased about it.

Er machte seinem Herzen Luft. — He relieved (*or* took a load off) his mind.

Er trägt das Herz auf der Zunge. — He wears his heart on his sleeve; he's very outspoken.

Er schüttete uns sein Herz aus. — He made a clean breast of it; he told us everything.

Sie legte ihm die Angelegenheit ans Herz. — She brought the matter to his attention.

Der Junge ist ihnen ans Herz gewachsen. — The boy is very dear to them; they've grown very fond of him.

Was haben Sie auf dem Herzen? — What's on your mind?; what's troubling you?

Er prüfte sie auf Herz und Nieren. — He gave them the works; he put them to the acid test; he cross-examined them very closely.

Hand aufs Herz!	Cross your heart!; honor bright!; take an oath on it!
Er sprach uns aus dem Herzen.	He took the words out of our mouths; he said exactly what we were thinking.
Er macht aus seinem Herzen keine Mördergrube.	He makes no bones about it; he's very outspoken.
Er blieb kühl bis ans Herz hinan.	He remained cool as a cucumber; he preserved his equanimity (or composure).
Es ging ihr durchs Herz.	It thrilled her to the core.
Es gab ihr einen Stich ins Herz.	It touched her to the quick.
Sie haben den Jungen ins Herz geschlossen.	They've grown very fond of the boy.
Er ist mit Herz und Hand dafür.	He's for it, heart and soul.
Wenn er es nur übers Herz bringen könnte!	If only he could prevail upon himself!
Ihm war so froh ums Herz.	He felt so happy (or light-hearted).
Sie trägt ein Kind unterm Herzen.	She's with child (or pregnant).
Ihr fiel ein Stein vom Herzen.	A weight was lifted from her mind.
Er tut es von Herzen gern.	He gets a tremendous kick (or thrill) out of it; he loves to do it.
Es geht ihr sehr zu Herzen.	It affects her very deeply; she's very much touched by it.

Herzdrücken:

Er stirbt nicht an Herzdrücken.	He's no shrinking violet; he's not afraid to speak up.

herzhaft:

Er tat einen herzhaften Schluck.	He took a long, deep drink.

herziehen:

Sie zogen über ihn her.	They ran him down; they spoke disparagingly of him.

herzig:

Sie haben zwei herzige Kinder.	They've two sweet (or lovely) children.

herzlich:

Er weiß herzlich wenig.	He knows mighty (or precious) little.
Viele herzliche Glückwünsche zum Geburtstag!	Many happy returns of the day!; happy birthday!
In dem Lager herrschte ein rauher, aber herzlicher Ton.	They spoke the rough, frank language of the camp.

herzlichst:

Grüßen Sie Ihre Eltern herzlichst!	Give my love (or best regards) to your parents (or folks).

Hetzjagd:

Es war die reine Hetzjagd.	It was a mad scramble (or rush).

Heu:

Er hat Geld wie Heu.	He has money to burn; he's rolling in wealth.
Er hat sein Heu herein.	He's made his (profit).
Er hat sein Heu im trocknen.	He pulled up his stakes in time; his money is safe.
Sie machten das Grummet vor dem Heu.	They put the cart before the horse; they began at the wrong end; they had a child before they were married.

Heuochse:
So ein Heuochse!

What a blockhead (*or* sap)!

Heupferd:
Sie Heupferd!

You big louse (*or* bum)!

heurig:
Er ist doch auch kein heuriger Hase mehr.

He wasn't born yesterday; he's no longer a child.

heute:
Heute mir, morgen dir.

Every dog has his day; everyone in his turn; we must all die some day.

Es ist mir noch wie heute.

It seems like yesterday to me.

Er ist auch nicht von heute.

He wasn't born yesterday; he's not so dumb (*or* green) as he looks.

Das läßt sich nicht von heute auf morgen tun.

Rome wasn't built in a day; that takes time.

hexen:
Ich kann doch nicht hexen.

I'm no magician; I can't do the impossible.

hie:
Er schreibt hie und da.

He writes now and then.

Hieb:
Der Hieb galt ihm.

That was a dig at him; that was meant for (*or* aimed at) him.

Der Hieb sitzt.

That strikes home; that hits the nail on the head; that makes its mark.

Du hast wohl einen Hieb!

Are you crazy?; you must be drunk!

Auf einen Hieb fällt kein Baum.

Rome wasn't built in a day; that takes time.

hier:
Hier ist nicht zu scherzen.

This is no joking matter.

Es steht mir bis hier.

I'm fed up with it; I'm sick and tired of it.

Sie sind wohl nicht von hier!

Are you crazy?

Er schreibt hier und da.

He writes now and then.

hierher:
Bis hierher und nicht weiter!

Let that be enough!

Himmel:
Himmel, hast du keine Flinte!

Good night!; drat it all!

Wenn der Himmel einfällt, sind die Spatzen alle gefangen.

We're all in the same boat (*or* predicament).

Glauben Sie wirklich, in Amerika hänge der Himmel voller Geigen?

Do you really believe that America is the land of golden opportunity (*or* peace and plenty)?

Du lieber Himmel!

Gee whiz!; leaping lizards!

Er war wie aus allen Himmeln gefallen.

He was stunned; he was badly let down (*or* disappointed).

Man erhebt ihn in den Himmel.

They praise him to the skies.

Es ist dafür gesorgt, daß die Bäume nicht in den Himmel wachsen.

We all have our limitations.

Er hat seine Rechnung mit dem Himmel gemacht.

He's squared up his account with God and man; he's made his peace with the world; he's prepared to die.

Die Tagung ist unter freiem Himmel.

The meeting is being held in the open.

Es iſt noch kein Meiſter vom Himmel ge= fallen.	Masters are made, not born; no man is born a master of his craft.
Er log das Blaue vom Himmel herunter.	He swore black was white; he swore by all that was holy; he lied shamelessly.
Er würde für ſie das Blaue vom Himmel holen.	He would get them the moon if he could; he'd give them the shirt off his back.
Das ſchreit zum Himmel.	That's atrocious; it's a crying shame; it's an abomination.

himmelangſt:
Ihr war himmelangſt.	She was petrified (*or* scared to death).

Himmelhund:
So ein Himmelhund!	That son of a gun!; the wretch!

Himmelreich:
Des Menſchen Wille iſt ſein Himmelreich.	My mind to me a kingdom is.

himmelſchreiend:
Dieſer Blödſinn iſt himmelſchreiend.	That's the height of absurdity; that's sheer nonsense.

himmelviel:
Welch himmelviele Arbeit ſteckt darin!	What a hell of a lot (*or* terrific amount) of work this must have been (*or* called for)!

himmelweit:
Es iſt ein himmelweiter Unterſchied.	It makes a tremendous (*or* whale of a) differ- ence.

himmliſch:
Iſt das nicht himmliſch?	Isn't that the berries?; isn't it swell (*or* perfect)?
Dazu gehört eine wahrhaft himmliſche Geduld.	That calls for the patience of Job.

hin:
Rechts hin!	To the right!
Er iſt ſchon lange hin.	He died long ago.
Sein Geld iſt hin.	His money is lost (*or* gone).
Wie weit iſt es noch hin?	How far is it from here?
Sie war nach dem langen Marſch ganz hin.	She was all fagged out after the long hike.
Er weiß nicht wo hin noch her.	He doesn't know which way to turn; he's in a quandary.
Er überlegte hin und her.	He considered the pros and cons.
Das iſt hin wie her.	That's six of one and half a dozen of the other; it's all the same.
Er kommt hin und wieder.	He comes now and then.
Er nahm eine Fahrkarte hin und zurück.	He took a round-trip ticket.

hinaus:
Er weiß nicht wo hinaus.	He doesn't know which way to turn (*or* what to do); he's in a quandary.
Er iſt längſt darüber hinaus.	He's long past that stage; he's been ad- vanced.
Wo ſoll das noch hinaus?	I wonder what the upshot will be; where will it all lead to, I wonder?

hinausbeißen:
Man hat ihn hinausgebiſſen.	They froze him out; he was ousted.

hinausgehen:
Die Tür geht auf den Garten hinaus. | The door opens on the garden.

hinauspfeffern:
Er wurde hinausgepfeffert. | He was bounced (*or* fired); he was discharged.

hinauslaufen:
Das läuft auf eins hinaus. | That amounts to the same thing.

hinauspilgern:
Wir haben vor, morgen zu Ihnen hinauszupilgern. | We plan to go all the way to your place tomorrow.

hinauswollen:
Er wollte zu hoch hinaus. | He bit off more than he could chew; he aimed too high.

Ich wußte nicht, wo er hinauswollte. | I didn't know what he was driving at.

hinbringen:
Wie bringen Sie Ihre Zeit hin? | How do you spend your time?

hinein:
Er blieb bis in die Nacht hinein. | He stayed far into the night.

hineinfallen:
Er ist dabei hineingefallen. | He was taken in by it.

hineinknien:
Knien Sie sich in die Sache hinein! | Dig (*or* Pitch) in!; get down to business!

hineinlegen:
Er hat sie hineingelegt. | He took (*or* roped) them in; he put one over on them.

hineinreden:
Sie haben hier nichts mit hineinzureden! | You keep out of this!; you have nothing to say here!

hineinreiten:
Er hat sich tüchtig hineingeritten. | He got himself into an awful jam (*or* fix).

hingegossen:
Er lag auf dem Sofa wie hingegossen. | He lay on the couch in solid comfort; he'd made himself thoroughly at home on the sofa.

hingehen:
Es geht in einem hin. | It's like killing two birds with one stone.

hingenommen:
Sie war von der Musik ganz hingenommen. | She was thrilled (*or* carried away) by the music.

hinhalten:
Er hielt sie hin. | He put them off; he jollied them along; he kept them in suspense.

hinhängen:
Er läßt die Sache hinhängen. | He lets the matter ride (*or* drift).

hinhauen:
Hau hin! | Make it snappy!; hurry up!
Da haut's einen lang hin! | Well, what do you know about that!; now isn't that something!; you could have knocked me over with a feather!

Er haute sich einen Augenblick hin. | He lay down for a while.

hinken:
Er hinkt nach beiden Seiten.

He won't take sides; he's straddling the fence; he's hedging.

Der Vergleich hinkt.

That's a poor comparison.

hinkend:
Der hinkende Bote kommt nach.

Bad news travels fast.

hinmachen:
Machen Sie hin!

Hurry up!

Wo machen Sie hin?

Where are you going (*or* headed for)?

hinnen:
Er ist von hinnen gegangen.

He departed this life.

hinreden:
Er hat nur so hingeredet.

He was just making conversation.

hinreißend:
Sie fanden ihn hinreißend.

He thrilled them; they thought him simply marvelous.

hinschlagen:
Da schlag doch einer lang hin!

Jumping Jupiter!; great Scott!; wouldn't that bowl (*or* knock) you over!

Hinsicht:
In der Hinsicht hat er recht.

He's right on that point.

hinten:
Da heißt es dauernd: lieber Karl hinten und lieber Karl vorn.

It's always Charlie here, Charlie there, and Charlie everywhere.

Er half ihnen hinten herum.

He slipped them some money on the q.t. (*or* sly).

hinterbringen:
Er hinterbrachte es ihnen.

He let them in on the secret; he told them confidentially.

Hintergedanke:
Er trägt sich nicht mit Hintergedanken.

He has no ax of his own to grind; he's perfectly honest.

hintergehen:
Er hinterging sie lange.

He fooled them for a long time.

Hinterhalt:
Sie hat einen starken Hinterhalt an ihm.

She has a powerful backer in him; he's a real friend in need to her.

hinterher:
Hinterher ist gut reden.

It's easy to say: "I told you so!"; talk is cheap when it's too late.

hinterlassen:
Er hinterließ, daß er in einer Stunde zurück wäre.

He left word that he would be back within an hour.

Hintertreffen:
Er gerät immer mehr ins Hintertreffen.

He's losing ground more and more.

hintertreiben:
Er hintertrieb ihre Pläne.

He queered (*or* foiled) their plans.

Hintertür:
Halten Sie sich diese Hintertür offen!

Save your ace!; keep that trump in hand!; keep that bridge (*or* avenue of escape) clear (*or* open)!

hinüber:
Der Mantel ist hinüber. | The topcoat is on the blink (*or* worn out).
Er ist längst hinüber. | He's long since dead and gone.

hinweggehen:
Er kann über diese Beschwerde nicht hinweggehen. | He can't dodge (*or* disregard) this complaint.

Hinz:
In diesem Lokal verkehren nur Hinz und Kunz. | Only the hoi polloi (*or* rabble) patronize this place; every Tom, Dick, and Harry goes there.

hirnverbrannt:
So hirnverbrannt wird er hoffentlich nicht sein. | I hope he won't be that foolish (*or* dumb).

Hitze:
In der ersten Hitze wollte er weglaufen. | His first impulse was to run away.

Hobel:
Blas mir den Hobel aus! | Go to hell!

hoch:
Hoch gerechnet sind es drei Mark. | At the top (*or* most), it comes to three marks.

Es ging hoch her. | It was a gay party; everybody was in high spirits.

Kopf hoch! | Chin up!; cheer up!; keep smiling!
Der Alte ist heute hoch. | The boss is hot under the collar (*or* on a rampage) today; he's in a dangerous mood today.

Das ist mir zu hoch. | That's beyond me; I don't get (*or* understand) that.

Er ist hoch in den Fünfzigern. | He's well along in the fifties.
Er versicherte hoch und teuer. | He swore on a stack of Bibles; he took a solemn oath.

Er flog in hohem Bogen aus seiner Firma. | His firm dropped him like a hot potato; they threw him out on his ear.

Das ist allerhand bei seinen hohen Jahren. | That's quite a stunt (*or* feat) at his age (*or* for an old man).

Er hat sich etwas auf die hohe Kante gelegt. | He has a nest egg; he put something aside for a rainy day; he saved (*or* laid by) a tidy little sum.

Er sang ein hohes Lied zu ihrem Preis. | He sang her praises; he lauded her to the skies.

Hoch:
Sie brachten ein Hoch auf ihn aus. | They gave him three cheers.

Hochachtung:
Allerhand Hochachtung! | Swell!; capital!; congratulations!

Hochbetrieb:
Es herrschte Hochbetrieb im Laden. | There was a mad scramble (*or* rush) at the store; business was booming; customers were crowding the store.

hochgehen:
Auf diese Bemerkung ging er hoch. | He blew up (*or* lost his temper) at this remark.

hochleben:
Er lebe hoch! — Here's to him!; more power to him!; three cheers (*or* hurrah) for him!

hochnehmen:
Er nahm sie in der Prüfung tüchtig hoch. — He gave them the works; he gave them an acid test; he made the test very stiff (*or* difficult).

Man hat sie in dem vornehmen Lokal schwer hochgenommen. — They soaked the life out of them in that swanky joint (*or* restaurant); they were soundly bled (*or* mulcted) there.

hochoffiziell:
Sei doch nicht so hochoffiziell! — Don't be so stiff (*or* formal)!; don't be so businesslike (*or* officious)!

hochrot:
Er hatte einen hochroten Kopf. — His face was very red.

höchst:
Die Spannung stieg aufs höchste. — Interest rose to a high pitch.
Die Polizei ist in höchster Alarmbereitschaft. — The police are ready (*or* prepared) to act at a moment's notice.
Es ist die höchste Zeit. — It's high time.

Hof:
Er verlor Haus und Hof. — He was cleaned out; he lost everything he owned.

Er macht ihr den Hof. — He courts her; he makes love to her.

Hoffnung:
Sie ist guter Hoffnung. — She's with child (*or* pregnant).

Höflichkeit:
Darüber schweigt des Sängers Höflichkeit! — Don't let's talk about it!; better say no more about it!

Höhe:
Das ist doch die Höhe! — That's going some!; that's the limit!; that's the height of nerve!

Der Boxer ist auf der Höhe. — The boxer is in top form.

höher:
Höher hinauf geht's nicht mehr! — That's the limit!; that beats all!
Sein Herz schlug höher. — His heart skipped a beat; it began to beat faster.

Sie schwebt immer in höheren Regionen. — She's always living in the clouds; she's forever daydreaming.

hohl:
Das ist nur für den hohlen Zahn. — That's a mere drop in the bucket; that's precious little.

Hohn:
Das ist der reine Spott und Hohn. — That's out-and-out mockery; that's sheer spite.

Holle:
Frau Holle schüttelt ihr Bett aus. — It's snowing.

Hölle:
Machen Sie ihm mal die Hölle heiß! — Make it hot for him!; get after him!

höllisch:
Er ist höllisch gescheit. — He's keen (*or* smart) as a whip; he's devilishly clever.

Er hatte höllisches Pech.	He had the world's worst breaks (*or* luck); he ran into a heap of trouble.
Holz:	
Er läßt Holz auf sich hacken.	He puts up with everything.
Er bohrt nicht gern hartes Holz.	He takes the path of least resistance; he doesn't like to exert himself (*or* put himself out).
Sie sind aus demselben Holz geschnitzt.	They're made on the same last; they're birds of a feather (*or* two of a kind).
Er ist aus gutem Holz.	He's of good stock; he comes of a good family.
holzen:	
Nach der Tanzerei wurde tüchtig geholzt.	A regular scrimmage (*or* fight) followed the dance.
Holzhammer:	
Er hat offenbar eins mit dem Holzhammer abgekriegt.	He seems to be cracked (in his upper story); he's plumb nerts (*or* crazy).
Holzweg:	
Da sind Sie aber schwer auf dem Holzweg!	That's where you're wrong!; you're on the wrong track there!
Man hat ihn auf den Holzweg geschickt.	He was sent on a wild goose chase (*or* fool's errand).
Honig:	
Er schmierte ihnen Honig ums Maul.	He soft-soaped them; he wheedled them.
Hopfen:	
An ihm ist Hopfen und Malz verloren.	He's a hopeless case; he's beyond help.
Hopfenstange:	
Sie ist die reine Hopfenstange.	She's thin as a rail; she's a regular bean pole.
hopps:	
Die Sache ist hopps gegangen.	The thing went fluey (*or* up in smoke); it came to nothing.
hören:	
Er hört nicht auf dem linken Ohr.	He's deaf in the left ear.
Das läßt sich eher hören.	That sounds better; that's more like it.
Hören:	
Ihm verging Hören und Sehen.	He was stunned (*or* stupefied); he was struck dumb.
Horn:	
Er hat sich noch nicht die Hörner abgelaufen.	He's still sowing his wild oats; he's still too young to settle down.
Zeigen Sie ihm mal die Hörner!	Show him your teeth!; make him sit up and take notice!; assert yourself!
Nehmen Sie die Sache auf Ihre Hörner!	Take the responsibility upon yourself!
Er bläst immer in ihr Horn.	He always chimes in (*or* agrees) with them.
Es gelang ihnen, ihm das Seil über die Hörner zu werfen.	They finally roped him in; they outwitted him after all.
Hornberger:	
Die Angelegenheit ging aus wie's Hornberger Schießen.	The whole thing went up in smoke; nothing came of it.

Hose:

Das ist Jacke wie Hose.

That's six of one and half a dozen of the other; it's all the same.

Ziehen Sie ihm mal die Hosen an!
Er hat die Hosen gestrichen voll.
Er hat Pech an den Hosen.

Spank the seat of his pants!
He's in a blue funk; he's scared to death.
He's like a sticking plaster; you can't budge him; he doesn't know when to go home.

Er sollte sich mehr auf die Hosen setzen.

He should work harder; he should keep his mind more on his work.

Das Herz fiel ihm in die Hosen.

His heart was in his mouth; he lost his nerve (*or* courage).

hübsch:

Lassen Sie das hübsch bleiben!
Nun sitz hübsch still!

Lay off that!; hands (*or* keep) off!
Now be good and sit still!

Hucke:

Er log ihnen die Hucke voll.

He handed them a terrible line; he lied shamelessly (*or* like a trooper).

Huckebein:

Er ist ein Hans Huckebein.

The world treats him like a stepchild; he always has hard luck.

hufen:

Er hufte einen Augenblick, ehe er antwortete.

He hesitated a moment before answering.

Huhn:

Ein blindes Huhn findet auch mal ein Körnchen.

Fortune favors a fool.

Auch ein gescheites Huhn legt die Eier neben das Nest.

It's a good horse that never stumbles; we all make mistakes.

So ein verrücktes Huhn!
Da lachen ja die Hühner!
Er sieht aus, als hätten ihm die Hühner das Brot weggenommen.

What a crazy loon!
That's ridiculous (*or* absurd)!
He looks as if he'd lost his last friend; he looks down and out.

Er ist darüber her wie der Fuchs über den Hühnern.

He's making short work of it; he's going at it with a vengeance.

Er muß das Ei unterm Huhn verkaufen.

He has to raise money by hook or crook.

Hühnchen:

Ich habe noch ein Hühnchen mit ihm zu pflücken.

I've got a bone to pick with him; we still have an account to settle.

hui:

Oben hui, unten pfui!

Fine feathers don't make a fine bird; appearances are deceiving.

Hui:

Die Arbeit ist im Hui gemacht.

The work has been dashed off; it's been turned out (*or* done) in a hurry.

Hülle:

Seine sterbliche Hülle wurde beigesetzt.
Er hat alles in Hülle und Fülle.

His remains were laid to rest.
He has plenty and to spare; he has more than enough of everything.

Hummel:

Sie ist eine wilde Hummel.
Er hat Hummeln im Kopf.

She's a regular tomboy.
He's got something in (*or* on his) mind.

Hund:
Da liegt der Hund begraben.

That's where the shoe pinches (*or* trouble lies); there's the rub (*or* hitch).

Das hält kein Hund aus.
Kein Hund würde ein Stück Brot von ihm nehmen.

That's too much; no one can stand that.
I wouldn't touch that man with a ten-foot pole; no one will have a thing to do with him.

Das ist kein Hund.
Ein blöder Hund wird selten fett.
Er ist bekannt wie ein bunter Hund.

That's not to be sneezed at; it's no trifle.
Faint heart never won fair lady.
You'd spot (*or* recognize) him in the dark; he's known everywhere.

Er ist ein großer Hund geworden.

He's become a big shot (*or* an important personage); he is somebody now.

Er fror wie ein junger Hund.

He was a frozen turnip; he shivered with cold.

Ein toter Hund beißt nicht.
Den letzten beißen die Hunde.

Dead men tell no tales.
The last one out must foot (*or* pay) the bill; the tail end always gets left.

Viele Hunde sind des Hasen Tod.
Er schickte den Hund nach den Brat=
würsten.
Es kann einen Hund jammern.

There's no use fighting against great odds.
He set the fox to keep the geese; it was like leading the lambs to slaughter.
It's a dirty shame; it's an awful state of affairs.

Damit kann man keinen Hund hinterm Ofen hervorlocken.
Es ist, um junge Hunde zu kriegen.

That won't do the trick; that won't get you anywhere.
Confound it!; it's enough to drive you wild!

Er ist mit seinen Nerven auf dem Hund.

His nerves are shot (*or* on edge); he's a nervous wreck.

Da liegt der Knüppel beim Hund.

Do or die; take it or leave it; there's no way out.

Er ist mit allen Hunden gehetzt.

He's a son of a gun; he's up to all sorts of tricks.

Kommt man über den Hund, so kommt man auch über den Schwanz.

When the main part is done, the rest follows of itself; once the worst is over, the rest is easy going.

Die Arbeit ist unter allem Hund.
Er ist vor die Hunde gegangen.

That's a hellish (*or* rotten) job.
He's gone to the dogs; he's down and out.

Hundeangst:
Er hat eine Hundeangst.

He's scared to death.

Hundearbeit:
Es war eine Hundearbeit.

It was a nasty (*or* tough) job.

Hundehütte:
Er sucht Speck in der Hundehütte.

He's barking up the wrong tree; he's in the wrong pew; he won't get anything from that source.

Hundekälte:
Es war eine Hundekälte.

It was bitter cold.

hundert:
Freunde in der Not gehen hundert auf ein Lot.

A friend in need is a friend indeed; when good cheer is lacking, our friends will be packing.

Hundertſte:
Er kam vom Hundertſten ins Tauſendſte.   He couldn't stick to the subject; he talked on and on.

Hundeſchnauze:
Er iſt kalt wie eine Hundeſchnauze.   He's cold as ice; he's frozen stiff.

Hundewetter:
Es war ein Hundewetter.   It was rotten weather.

hundsgemein:
Sie behandelten ihn hundsgemein.   They treated him like dirt (*or* a dog).

hundsmiſerabel:
Sein Vortrag war hundsmiſerabel.   He gave a bum (*or* very poor) lecture.

Hungerpfote:
Er ſaugt an den Hungerpfoten.   He's living on a shoestring; he's starving.

Hungertuch:
Sie nagen am Hungertuch.   Their cupboard is bare; they're on the verge of starvation.

Hurra:
Die Arbeit iſt im Hurra gemacht.   The work was dashed off in a hurry.

huſch:
Huſch, huſch!   Hurry up!; be quick!
Er macht das alles huſch huſch.   He does a slipshod job; he's a sloppy (*or* careless) worker.

Huſch:
Er war nur auf einen Huſch da.   He just stopped in to say hello.

huſten:
Dem werde ich was huſten.   He can go to hell; I'll see him damned first.

Hut:
Man hat ihm eins auf den Hut gegeben.   He got a dressing-down; he was severely reprimanded.

Mit dem Hut in der Hand kommt man durchs ganze Land.   It pays to be courteous.

Es fehlt ihm unterm Hut.   He's a bit cracked; he's not quite right in the upper story; he's not all there.

Sie ſtecken miteinander unter einem Hut.   They're in cahoots; they've got a secret understanding with one another.

Es iſt ſchwer, ſo viele Köpfe unter einen Hut zu bringen.   It's difficult to reconcile so many conflicting ideas (*or* opinions).

hüten:
Ich werde mich ſchwer hüten, das zu tun.   Catch me doing that!; I'll take jolly good care not to do that.

Er muß das Zimmer hüten.   He's confined to his room.

Hutſchnur:
Das geht denn doch über die Hutſchnur!   That takes the cake!; that's going too far!; I don't believe it!

J

i:

J der Tausend! — Great guns!; good gracious!

Stimmt das?—J wo! — Is that correct?—Says you!; like fun it is!; I should say not.

J:

Das sitzt wie das Tüpfelchen auf dem J. — That fits perfectly; it's a perfect fit.

Er übersieht nicht das Tüpfelchen auf dem J. — He dots his i's and crosses his t's; he's very exacting.

Ich:

Er ist nur noch der Schatten von seinem früheren Ich. — He's a mere shadow of his former self.

Idee:

Noch etwas Sahne gefällig?—Eine Idee, bitte! — Will you have a little more cream?—Just a drop, if you please!

Ist das wahr?—Keine Idee! — Is that true?—Not by a long shot!; you're ice cold (*or* way off)!; far from it!

Igel:

Das paßt dazu wie der Igel zum Handtuch. — That's like a square peg in a round hole; they don't fit (*or* go together) at all.

So ein Igel! — That man's as stubborn as a mule; he's terribly pig-headed.

Ihre:

Tun Sie das Ihre! — Do your part!

Wie geht's den Ihren? — How are the folks?

immer:

Immer mit der Ruhe! — Keep your shirt on!; take it easy!; don't get excited!

Er las es immer wieder durch. — He read it over and over again.

Er kommt doch nicht mehr; wir wollen immer anfangen. — He's sure not to come now—we might just as well start.

Wie klug er auch immer sein mag. — Clever as he may be.

Er ist doch immer unser Freund. — After all, he's our friend.

Er ist immer noch hier. — He's still here.

Er zog sich für immer von der Öffentlichkeit zurück. — He's retired for good.

in:

Die Aufgabe hat es in sich. — That's a sticker (*or* tough problem).

inne:

Er wurde dessen bald inne. — He soon became conscious of it; he began to understand.

innehalten:

Er hält niemals die Zeit inne. — He's never punctual (*or* on time).

Sie hielt plötzlich im Reden inne. — All of a sudden she stopped talking.

inner:

Es fiel ihm schwer, den inneren Schweine=
hund zu überwinden.

It was hard for him to overcome his baser instincts (*or* lower nature).

Er hat kein inneres Verhältnis zu seiner
Arbeit.

His heart isn't in his work.

Innere:

Im Innern gab sie ihm recht.

At heart (*or* Secretly), she agreed with him.

Innung:

Blamieren Sie doch nicht die ganze In=
nung!

Don't let us down!

in petto:

Er hat was andres in petto.

He has something else in mind (*or* up his sleeve).

intus:

Er hatte seine Lektion nicht intus.

He hadn't learned his lesson; he didn't know it.

J=Punkt:

Er führte den Befehl bis auf den letzten
J=Punkt aus.

He carried out instructions to a T (*or* the letter).

irre:

Sie wurden an ihm irre.

They couldn't figure him out; they didn't know what to make of him.

irremachen:

Er ließ sich nicht irremachen.

He wouldn't be dissuaded (*or* disturbed).

Irrtum:

Da sind Sie aber schwer im Irrtum!

That's where you're wrong!; you're quite mistaken!

Irrwisch:

Sie ist ein rechter Irrwisch.

She's a fickle (*or* flighty) wench; she's changeable as the wind (*or* weather).

is nich:

Können Sie mir drei Mark pumpen?—
Nee, is nich (= Nein, is nicht)!

Could you let me have three marks?— Nothing doing!

J

ja:

Ja du lieber Himmel! — Good gracious!

Ja, was ich noch sagen wollte. — And as I was going to say.

Ja so, das ist was andres. — Of course, that's different.

Du bist ja dumm. — How stupid you are!

Das ist ja nicht schwer. — That's not at all difficult.

Tun Sie das ja nicht! — Don't you (dare) do it!

Er wurde verletzt, ja sogar schwer. — He was injured—seriously, in fact.

Sie besuchen uns also, ja? — You'll call on us, won't you?

Ich denke, ja. — I rather think so.

Gehen Sie ja! — By all means, go!

Da ist er ja! — Why, there he is!; that's he!

Kommen Sie doch mit!—Na ja! — Please, come along!—O.K.!; all right then!; very well!

Jacke:

Das ist Jacke wie Hose. — That's six of one and half a dozen of the other; that's all the same.

Das ist eine alte Jacke. — That's the way it goes; it's the same old story.

Er kriegte die Jacke voll. — He got a beating.

Er log ihnen die Jacke voll. — He handed them an awful line; he lied to them shamelessly.

Jagd:

Ist' das eine Jagd! — What a mad scramble (*or* hectic rush)!

jagen:

Damit können Sie mich jagen! — How I hate that!

Jahr:

Das ist allerhand bei seinen hohen Jahren. — That's quite a stunt (*or* feat) at his age (*or* for an old man).

Er ist in den besten Jahren. — He's in the prime of life.

Nach Jahr und Tag kam er wieder. — He came back a full year later.

Hoffentlich sehen wir uns übers Jahr wieder! — I hope we'll meet again next year.

Er starb vor seinen Jahren. — He died before his time; he died young.

Er ist zu seinen Jahren gekommen. — He has aged.

Jahrgang:

Der Jahrgang 1917 wurde zu den Waffen gerufen. — Men of the class of 1917 were called to the colors.

Er hat einen guten Jahrgang im Keller. — He has some fine (old) wine in his cellar.

Jakob:

Sie sind mir der wahre Jakob! — You're the very man I'm looking for!; you're a fine fellow (to deal with)!

Jammer:
Das ist der alte Jammer.

That's the way it goes; it's the same old story.

jammerschade:
Das ist jammerschade.

That's a crying shame; that's too bad.

japsen:
Er konnte kaum noch japsen.

He was all out of breath.

Jawort:
Er erhielt ihr Jawort.

She said yes; she accepted him.

je:
Je nachdem.
Je acht unter zehn Studenten.
Haben Sie je so was gehört?
Er gab ihnen je einen Apfel.

That all depends.
Eight out of every ten students.
Did you ever hear the like?
He gave them each an apple.

jedenfalls:
Jedenfalls ist er schon da.

He'll very likely be there; you'll probably find him there.

jeher:
Es war von jeher so.

It has always been that way.

jener:
Hol mich dieser und jener!

The deuce!; blankety blank!; damn it all!

Jenseits:
Er wurde ins Jenseits abberufen.

He answered the call; he checked out (*or* died).

Joch:
Er ist wieder im Joch.

He's back on the job; he's in harness again.

Jubeljahr:
Das kommt höchstens alle Jubeljahre einmal vor.

That happens but once in a dog's age (*or* lifetime); that's a seven-day wonder (*or* very rare occurrence).

jucken:
Wen es juckt, der kratze sich!

If the shoe fits, wear it (*or* put it on)!; take advantage of your opportunities!

Jude:
Er ist schon ein ewiger Jude.

He's a wandering Jew; he can't stay put; he's a restless fellow.

Haust du meinen Juden, hau' ich deinen Juden.

Tit for tat; an eye for an eye, a tooth for a tooth; you get what you give.

Judenschule:
Es ging zu wie in einer Judenschule.

Bedlam broke loose; it was like a madhouse.

jüdisch:
Nur keine jüdische Hast!

Where's the fire?; what's the rush?; take it easy!

Jugend:
Jugend hat keine Tugend.

Boys will be boys.

jung:
Jung gefreit hat noch niemand gereut.
Jung gewohnt, alt getan.

Happy's the wooing that's not long in doing.
The child is father to the man; habits learned in childhood persist throughout life.

Junge:

Wie die Alten sungen, so zwitschern die Jungen.

The young pigs grunt like the old sow; like father, like son; it runs in the family.

Die Polizei faßte einen schweren Jungen.

The police caught a bad egg (*or* dangerous criminal).

kabbeln:
Die beiden kabbeln sich andauernd.

The two scrap (*or* squabble) all the time.

Kadett:
Ihr seid mir schöne Kadetten!

A fine bunch of yokels (*or* boobs) you are!

Kadi:
Damit läuft man doch nicht gleich zum Kadi!

Why take it to court?; what's there to get excited about?

Käfer:
Sie ist ein netter, kleiner Käfer.

She's a cute little trick (*or* number).

Er hat einen Käfer.

He's bugs (*or* nutty); he's had a drop too much.

Kaff:
Das ist alles Kaff.

What tripe!; that's all rubbish (*or* nonsense).

Dieser Ort ist ein elendes Kaff.

What a godforsaken place!; what a dump (*or* hole) this is!

Kaffeeschwester:
Er ist eine alte Kaffeeschwester.

He's an old gossip; he carries tales like an old woman.

Kaffer:
So ein Kaffer!

What an ass (*or* fool)!

Kahn:
Er sitzt im Kahn.

He's in the coop (*or* pen); he's in jail.

Er ist bereits in den Kahn gestiegen.

He's hit the hay; he's turned in (*or* gone to bed).

Kaiser:
Wo nichts ist, hat selbst der Kaiser sein Recht verloren.

You can't get blood out of a turnip (*or* water out of a stone); nothing ever came of nothing.

Sie stritten sich um des Kaisers Bart.

They were splitting hairs; they argued over trifles.

Kakao:
Er zog sie durch den Kakao.

He razzed (*or* ridiculed) them; he made fun of them.

Er hat sich in den Kakao gesetzt.

He got himself into a jam (*or* fix).

Kalb:
Sie ist noch ein rechtes Kalb.

She's still a chicken (*or* very young).

Er nahm das Kalb beim Schwanz.

He put the cart before the horse; he began at the wrong end; he reversed the procedure.

Er schlug das Kalb ins Auge.

He made a bad break (*or faux pas*); he was tactless.

Kälbchen:
Er treibt das Kälbchen aus.

He's sowing his wild oats; he's having a good time.

Kalbfleisch:
  Er hat noch viel Kalbfleisch an sich. | He's just half-baked; he's still pretty young.

Kalender:
  Er macht Kalender. | He's got something in (or on his) mind.
  Das steht nicht in meinem Kalender. | I know nothing about that.

kalt:
  Es überrieselte ihn heiß und kalt. | It gave him the creeps; it sent the shivers up and down his spine.

  Lassen Sie uns eine kalte Ente trinken! | Let's have a soft drink.
  Er wärmt sich am kalten Ofen. | He's barking up the wrong tree; he's got the wrong number; he won't get anything from that source.

Kälte:
  Sie hatten drei Grad Kälte. | It was three (degrees) below (zero).

kaltmachen:
  Sie haben ihn kaltgemacht. | They bumped him off; they killed him.

kaltschnäuzig:
  Er drehte ihnen kaltschnäuzig den Rücken. | He gave them the cold shoulder; he turned his back on them.

kaltstellen:
  Man hat ihn kaltgestellt. | He was sidetracked (or shelved).

Kamelle:
  Das sind olle Kamellen. | Those are chestnuts (or old stories); that's old stuff.

Kamin:
  Das Geld können Sie in den Kamin schreiben. | You can whistle for that money; you might just as well forget about it.

Kamm:
  Bei ihren Worten schwoll ihm der Kamm. | Her words made him boil (or furious).
  Ihm ist der Kamm geschwollen. | He struts like a cock; he puts on airs.
  Man hat ihm den Kamm gestutzt. | They took the starch (or fight) out of him; they put him in his place.

  Man hat ihm auf den Kamm getreten. | They stepped on him; they took him down a peg.

  Sie sind alle über einen Kamm geschoren. | They're all tarred with the same brush; they're all alike.

kämmen:
  Man hat ihm ordentlich gekämmt. | They tore him to pieces; they didn't leave him a shred.

Kanal:
  Er hat den Kanal voll. | He's fed up with it; he's had enough of it.

Kandare:
  Nehmen Sie ihn an die Kandare! | Put the kibosh on him!; step on him!

Kanne:
  Er hat zu tief in die Kanne geguckt. | He's down with the fish; he drank too much.
  Es goß mit Kannen. | The rain came down in buckets.

kannegießern:
  Er kannegießert gern. | He likes to talk politics.

kannibalisch:
  Es ist eine kannibalische Kälte. | It's bitter cold.

Kanone:

Er ist voll wie eine Kanone.	He's tight as a drum; he's intoxicated.
Er ist eine große Kanone auf dem Gebiet.	He's a big shot (*or* an authority) in that field.
Er schießt mit Kanonen nach Spatzen.	He's chasing up blind alleys; he's not getting anywhere; he's making no headway.
Sein Vortrag war unter aller Kanone.	He gave a punk (*or* terrible) lecture.

Kante:

Man lobt ihn nach allen Kanten.	They praise him to the skies.
Er hat sich was auf die hohe Kante gelegt.	He has a nest egg; he put something aside for a rainy day; he saved (*or* laid by) a tidy little sum.
An allen Ecken und Kanten sah man Menschen.	There were people to be seen everywhere.

Kanthaken:

Nehmen Sie ihn mal beim Kanthaken!	Take him by the scruff of the neck!; tell him what's what!

Kantonist:

Er ist ein unsicherer Kantonist.	He's slippery as an eel; you can't pin him down; he's a shifty fellow; he's not dependable.

Kapee:

Er ist schwer von Kapee.	He doesn't catch on easily; his mind works slowly.

Kapitel:

Das ist ein Kapitel für sich.	That's a story in itself.
Lesen Sie ihm die Kapitel!	Give him a lecture!; lay down the law to him!

kapitelfest:

Er ist noch nicht kapitelfest.	He still feels weak; he's not quite well yet.

kapores:

Der Motor ist kapores gegangen.	The engine went haywire (*or* broke down).

Kappe:

Jedem Narren gefällt seine Kappe.	Tastes differ; everyone has his eccentricities.
Gleiche Brüder, gleiche Kappen.	Share, and share alike.
Er gab ihnen eins auf die Kappe.	He gave it to them; he gave them a calling-down.
Er nahm die ganze Verantwortung auf seine Kappe.	He shouldered the whole responsibility.

kaputt:

Er arbeitet sich noch kaputt.	He works his head off; he'll kill himself yet.
Er schlug ihm die Knochen im Leib kaputt.	He beat him to a pulp.
Die Firma ist kaputt.	The firm went broke (*or* out of business).
Er war nach dem Spiel ganz kaputt.	He was all shot (*or* fagged out) after the game.

Karnickel:

Er muß immer das Karnickel machen.	He's always the scapegoat; he always has to shoulder the blame (*or* do the dirty work).

Karpfenteich:

Er ist der Hecht im Karpfenteich.	He's a big frog in a little puddle; he's the whole cheese (*or* show); he's the trouble-shooter.

Karre(n):

Die Karre ist vollständig verfahren.

The whole works are stalled (*or* tied up); everything is in a jam (*or* muddle).

Er läßt den Karren einfach laufen.

He simply lets matters ride (*or* drift); he lets things take their own course.

Er muß den Karren aus dem Dreck ziehen.

He has to do the dirty work; he has to pull them out of the hole (*or* rut); he has to help them out (of trouble).

Er ist unter den Karren gekommen.

He's gone to the dogs; he's down and out.

Kartause:

Er nahm ihn bei der Kartause.

He took him by the scruff of the neck; he told him a thing or two.

Karte:

Ober, bitte die Karte!

Waiter, please hand me the menu!

Man muß nicht alles auf eine Karte setzen.

Don't put all your eggs in one basket!; there's safety in numbers.

Er läßt sich nicht in die Karten sehen.

He doesn't show his hand; he keeps his business to himself.

Er spielt mit verdeckten Karten.

He doesn't put his cards on the table; he hides his intentions.

Kartoffel:

Der hat aber eine Kartoffel!

What a schnozzle (*or* beak)!; that's some nose he's got!

Er hat eine Kartoffel im Strumpf.

He has a hole in his sock.

Die dümmsten Bauern haben die dicksten Kartoffeln.

Fools are born lucky.

Rin in die Kartoffeln, raus aus den Kartoffeln!

You don't know whether he's hoeing beans or hoeing corn; turn and turn about!

Käse:

Er lebt wie die Made im Käse.

He's in clover; he's got it soft (*or* easy).

Käseblatt:

Er gibt irgendwo auf dem Lande ein kleines Käseblatt heraus.

He edits the local newspaper in some one-horse (*or* hick) town.

Kasse:

Lassen Sie uns Kasse machen!

Let's square up (*or* settle this account)!

Sie beschlossen, gemeinsame Kasse zu führen.

They decided to pool expenses.

Sie führen getrennte Kassen.

They go Dutch (*or* fifty-fifty); each pays for himself.

Er ist gut bei Kasse.

He's flush (*or* in the money).

Nur gegen Kasse!

We give no credit; we sell for cash only.

Kassel:

Ab nach Kassel!

Scram!; beat it!; be off!

Kasten:

Er erhielt drei Tage Kasten.

He was sentenced to three days in jail (*or* the coop).

Haben Sie meinen Brief in den Kasten geworfen?

Did you mail my letter?

Kater:

Er hat einen fürchterlichen Kater.

He has a terrible hangover (*or* headache).

katzbalgen:

Die Kinder katzbalgen sich schon wieder.	The children are scuffling (*or* romping). again.

Katze:

Die Vögel, die so früh singen, frißt die Katze.	Early ripe, early rotten; don't count your chickens before they're hatched!
Gehen Sie doch nicht wie die Katze um den heißen Brei!	Don't beat about the bush!; talk turkey!; out with it!
Die Katze läßt das Mausen nicht.	What's bred in the bone will out in the flesh; you can't change human nature.
Das macht der Katze keinen Buckel.	That won't change matters any; that doesn't alter the facts.
Er kauft nicht die Katze im Sack.	He doesn't buy a pig in a poke; he looks before he leaps; he's got his eyes open.
Das ist für die Katze.	That's of no use; that's good for nothing.

Katzenjammer:

Er hat einen üblen Katzenjammer.	He has a bad hangover (*or* headache); he feels seedy.

Katzensprung:

Er wohnt nur einen Katzensprung von hier.	It's only two whoops and a holler (*or* a stone's throw) to his place.

Kauderwelsch:

Er redete ein schreckliches Kauderwelsch.	He talked gibberish (*or* jargon).

kauen:

Er wird noch lange daran zu kauen haben.	He'll be a long time getting over that; he won't forget that for a long time to come.

Kauf:

Er kam leichten Kaufes davon.	He got off easy.
Das muß man mit in Kauf nehmen.	You have to put up with that; that all goes with (*or* belongs to) it; that's part of the game.

kaufen:

Was ich mir dafür koofe (=kaufe)!	That doesn't impress me at all.
Er hat sich einen gekauft.	He got pickled (*or* stewed); he's tight (*or* dead-drunk).
Den wird er sich schon noch kaufen.	He'll get even with him yet; he'll give him a piece of his mind.

Kauz:

Es muß auch solche Käuze geben.	It takes all kinds of people to make a world; we can't all be alike.

Kegel:

Er kam mit Kind und Kegel.	He came with bag and baggage; he brought the whole family along.

Kehle:

Er hat eine ausgepichte Kehle.	He can drink enough to float a battleship; he's a regular tank (*or* sponge).
Das Messer sitzt ihm an der Kehle.	He's got a rope around his neck; he's in a bad way (*or* fix).
Er lachte aus voller Kehle.	He laughed heartily.
Er schrie aus voller Kehle.	He shouted at the top of his voice.
Er jagte sein ganzes Vermögen durch die Kehle.	He squandered (*or* spent) his whole fortune on drink.

Kehraus:

Die Musik spielt den Kehraus. | The band is playing "Home, Sweet Home" (*or* the last dance).

Keil:

Ein Keil treibt den andern. | One nail drives out another; one thing leads to another.

Auf einen groben Klotz gehört ein grober Keil. | Tit for tat; pay him in his own coin!

Er bezog gehörig Keile. | He was soundly walloped (*or* beaten up).

keilen:

Die Studenten keilten ihn für ihre Verbindung. | He was rushed; the students were eager to have him join their fraternity.

Keilerei:

Es kam schließlich zu einer allgemeinen Keilerei. | It ended in a brawl (*or* free-for-all).

keinmal:

Einmal ist keinmal. | Once doesn't count.

Kerbe:

Er haut in dieselbe Kerbe wie sie. | He does as she does; he's supporting her.

Kerbholz:

Der Verbrecher hat viel auf dem Kerbholz. | The criminal has a long pedigree; he's got a record a mile long.

Kern:

Das also war des Pudels Kern! | So that was the gist (*or* crux) of the matter!; so that's how it was meant.

Verlieren Sie nicht über dem Schatten den Kern! | Don't get off the track!; don't lose sight of the main issue!

keß:

Sie ist ein kesses kleines Mädel. | She's a cute little trick.

Kieker:

Er hat sie auf dem Kieker. | He's got his eagle eye on them; he's watching them like a hawk.

Kien:

Reden Sie doch keinen Kien! | Don't talk bosh (*or* tommyrot)!

Kies:

Sie haben mächtig Kies. | They've got money to burn.

Kind:

Er ist wie Kind im Hause. | He's like one of the family.

Wes Geistes Kind ist er? | What sort of a fellow is he?

Wenn das Kind in den Brunnen gefallen ist, deckt man ihn zu. | The garage door is bolted after the car has been stolen; precaution is taken when it is too late.

Er ist ein Kind des Todes. | He's a dead man; he's as good as dead.

Er ist so unschuldig wie ein Kind im Mutterleib. | He's innocent as a lamb (*or* babe in arms).

Sie ist ein Frankfurter Kind. | She's a native of Frankfurt.

Der Plan war von Anfang an ein totgeborenes Kind. | It was an abortive plan from the start; the plan was predestined to failure.

Er schüttete das Kind mit dem Bade aus. | He threw good money after bad; he rejected both the good and the bad; he acted without discretion.

Er nannte das Kind beim Namen.
He called a spade a spade; he spoke the plain truth.

Er wird das Kind schon schaukeln.
He'll fix that; he'll do it yet.

Das macht mir kein Kind.
I should worry; that doesn't bother me any.

Er versuchte, sich lieb Kind zu machen.
He was bootlicking; he tried to curry favor.

Der Reiche hat die Rinder, der Arme die Kinder.
Rich men feed and poor men breed.

Aus Kindern werden Leute.
The youth of today are the men of tomorrow.

Er kam mit Kind und Kegel.
He came with bag and baggage; he brought the whole family along.

Kinderkrankheit:
Die junge Republik macht ihre Kinderkrankheiten durch.
The young republic is experiencing its growing pains.

kinderleicht:
Das ist doch kinderleicht.
That's as easy as rolling off a log; that's child's play.

Kinderschuh:
Sie ist kaum den Kinderschuhen entwachsen.
She's just out of rompers; she's scarcely more than a child.

Die Bewegung steckt noch in den Kinderschuhen.
The movement is still in its infancy.

Kinderstube:
Er hat eine gute Kinderstube gehabt.
He's well bred; he's had a good bringing up.

Kindesbeine:
Sie kennen ihn von Kindesbeinen an.
They've known him ever since he was knee-high to a grasshopper; they knew him as a little shaver (or fellow).

Kinkerlitzchen:
Mach doch keine Kinkerlitzchen!
Don't be an old fuss-budget!; don't quibble!

Kippe:
Gib Kippe!
Let me have the butt (of your cigarette).

Mit ihm steht's auf der Kippe.
He's on the brink of a precipice; he's in a dangerous position.

kippen:
Lassen Sie uns einen kippen!
Let's have a drink!

Kirche:
Tragen Sie doch die Kirche nicht ums Dorf!
Get to the point!; cut it short!; be brief!

Das kommt so bestimmt wie das Amen in der Kirche.
That's as sure as death and taxes.

Kirchenbuch:
Das stimmt wie's Kirchenbuch.
That's right as rain; that's dead certain.

Kirchenlicht:
Er ist kein großes Kirchenlicht.
He's no shining light; he's not very bright.

Kirchenstille:
Es herrschte eine Kirchenstille.
A deathlike silence reigned; it was quiet as the grave.

kirre:
Er wird ihn schon kirre kriegen.
He'll make him eat humble pie; he'll bring him to his knees.

Kirsche:
Mit großen Herren ist nicht gut Kirschen essen.

Small fry don't stand a chance with the big shots; the weak always go to the wall; they always get the shorter end (*or* come off worst).

Kiste:
Er wird die Kiste schon schmeißen.

He'll fix that; he'll put it over.

Kitsch:
Das ist Kitsch in Reinkultur.

That's pure tripe (*or* unadulterated trash).

Kitt:
Da haben Sie den ganzen Kitt!

Take the whole caboodle (*or* business); here, you have it all.

Kittchen:
Er sitzt im Kittchen.

He's in the hoosegow; he's in jail (*or* behind the bars).

Klabberadatsch:
Da haben wir den Klabberadatsch!

What a fine how-do-you-do!; what a mess!; now you've got it!

Klamauk:
Mach doch keinen solchen Klamauk!

Don't raise such a rumpus!; don't make such a fuss!

Klamotten:
Er packte seine Klamotten und ging.
Nimm doch deine Klamotten weg!

He packed his duds (*or* things) and left.
Draw in your dogs!; get your big feet out of the way!

Klang:
Sein Name hat keinen guten Klang.

He has a bad name (*or* reputation).

klanglos:
Er verschwand sang= und klanglos.

He took French leave; he disappeared without a word; he slunk away.

Klappe:
Halt die Klappe!
Er schwingt wieder mal die große Klappe.

Shut up!; keep your trap (*or* mouth) shut!
He's blowing his own horn again; he's bragging again.

Er ist schon in die Klappe gegangen.

He's hit the hay; he's turned in (*or* gone to bed).

Er schlug zwei Fliegen mit einer Klappe.

He killed two birds with one stone.

klappen:
Die Sache klappt nicht.

It doesn't click (*or* tally); it won't work; there's a hitch (*or* something wrong) somewhere.

Klappen:
Endlich kam es zum Klappen.

The matter finally came to a showdown (*or* head).

klapperdürr:
Sie ist klapperdürr.

She's nothing but a bag of bones; she's thin as a rail.

Klappern:
Klappern gehört zum Handwerk.

Publicity is part of the game.

Klaps:
Sie haben wohl einen Klaps!

You must be cracked (*or* crazy)!

klar:
Es ist ganz klipp und klar. | It's plain as day.

klatsch(e)naß:
Er war klatschnaß. | He was drenched (*or* dripping wet).

klauen:
Wo hat er das geklaut? | Where did he swipe (*or* steal) that?

Klaviatur:
Er beherrscht die Klaviatur. | He knows the ropes; he has the knack (*or* hang) of it.

kleben:
Er klebt zu sehr am Äußerlichen. | He stands too much on ceremony; he's too formal.

Er hat schon zwanzig Jahre geklebt. | He paid up twenty years on his insurance policy.

Ich werde dir gleich eine kleben. | I'll soon sock (*or* land) you one; I'll strike you.

Es bleibt bei ihm nichts kleben. | Nothing ever sinks in (*or* sticks) with him; he's very forgetful.

kleckern:
Wie geht das Geschäft?—Es kleckert. | How's business?—So so!; not so hot!; pretty slow!

Kledage:
Lassen Sie mal Ihre Kledage aufbügeln! | Have your suit pressed!

Klee:
Man lobt ihn bis über den grünen Klee. | They praise him to the skies.

Kleeblatt:
Das ist ein sauberes Kleeblatt. | They're a bad lot; they're tough customers; they're a bunch of crooks.

Kleid:
Kleider machen Leute. | Fine feathers make fine birds.
Ein Stich zur Zeit erhält das Kleid. | A stitch in time saves nine.

klein:
Er gab klein bei. | He came down a peg (*or* off his high horse); he gave in.

Er kann es nicht klein kriegen. | It doesn't sink in with him; he can't understand (*or* see) it.
Er schlug alles kurz und klein. | He smashed everything to bits.
Das ist ihm ein kleines. | That's a mere trifle (*or* nothing at all) to him.

Er ging ins kleine. | He went into detail.
Wir sehen Sie über ein kleines. | We'll see you in a little while.
Um ein kleines war er verloren. | He had a close shave (*or* narrow escape).

Kleine:
Er ging mit seiner Kleinen zum Tanz. | He took his girl (friend) to a dance.

Kleingeld:
Es fehlt ihm am nötigen Kleingeld. | He's short of cash (*or* money); he can't afford it.

Kleinigkeitskrämer:
Er ist ein Kleinigkeitskrämer. | He's a regular fuss-budget; he's a stickler for detail (*or* form).

kleinkriegen:
Den haben Sie schön kleingekriegt!

You certainly took the starch (*or* fight) out of him!; you surely made him eat humble pie (*or* grovel in the dirt)!

kleinst:
Der Anzug paßt ihm bis ins kleinste.

The suit fits him to a T; it's a perfect fit.

Klemme:
Er ist böse in der Klemme.

He's in a tight spot; he's in a bad fix (*or* jam).

klemmen:
Jemand hat ihm den Hut geklemmt.

Somebody swiped (*or* stole) his hat.

Klette:
Sie hängt an ihm wie eine Klette.

She's a clinging vine; she sticks to him like putty.

Klimbim:
Das Fest wurde mit großem Klimbim gefeiert.

The holiday was celebrated with much noise and merriment.

Klinge:
Er schlug beim Essen eine gute Klinge.

He did justice to the meal; he made short work of it.

Bleiben Sie doch bei der Klinge!

Stick to the point (*or* subject)!

Der Vorschlag ist ein Messer ohne Heft und Klinge.

The suggestion doesn't hold water; it's impractical (*or* useless).

Sie ließen ihn über die Klinge springen.

They bumped him off; they killed him.

Er forderte sie vor die Klinge.

He challenged them.

Klingel:
Er geht Klingeln putzen.

He goes panhandling (*or* begging).

klingen:
Die Ohren müssen Ihnen geklungen haben, soviel sprachen wir von Ihnen.

We talked about you so much that your ears must have been burning.

klingend:
Er läßt sich sein Können in klingende Münze umsetzen.

He capitalizes (*or* cashes in) on his talent; he exploits it.

Das Regiment rückte mit klingendem Spiel in die Stadt ein.

The regiment marched into town with drums beating.

klipp:
Die Sache liegt klipp und klar.

The case is plain as day.

Klippe:
Hier ist die Klippe, woran er scheitern wird.

Here's where he'll take a tumble (*or* come to grief).

Klippschule:
Der Kerl gehört noch in die Klippschule.

This fellow is green as grass; he's a rank amateur.

Klitsche:
Er verkaufte seine Klitsche.

He sold his ranch (*or* farm).

klitsch(e)naß:
Er war klitschnaß.

He was soaked to the skin.

Kloßbrühe:
Das ist doch klar wie Kloßbrühe.

That's clear as crystal; that's obvious (*or* self-evident).

Klotz:

Sein Gebrechen ist ihm ein Klotz am Bein. | His defect is a handicap to him.

Er ist ein grober Klotz. | He lacks polish; he's an oaf (*or* a crude fellow).

Auf einen groben Klotz gehört ein grober Keil. | Tit for tat; pay him in his own coin!

klotzig:

Sie haben klotzig viel Geld. | They're made of (*or* lousy with) money.

Kluft:

Er warf sich in seine gute Kluft. | He donned his glad rags (*or* best clothes).

klug:

Nun ist er so klug wie zuvor. | Now he knows as much as he did before.

Sie sind wohl nicht klug! | Don't be a fool!

Er wurde nicht klug daraus. | He couldn't make head or tail of it; it didn't make sense to him.

Er wird nie klug werden. | He'll never learn.

Klügere:

Der Klügere gibt nach. | The wiser head gives in.

Klugschnacker:

Er ist ein großer Klugschnacker. | He's a smart-aleck (*or* wise guy).

Klügste:

Auch der Klügste kann es versehen. | It's a good horse that never stumbles; to err is human; no one is perfect.

Klumpen:

Er wollte alles in Klumpen hauen. | He wanted to throw everything by the board; he wanted to wreck everything.

knabbern:

Sie haben nichts zu knabbern. | They live on a shoestring; they're hard up.

Knabe:

Er ist gar kein übler Knabe. | He's a good egg; he's not a bad sort.

knacken:

An dem knackt aber auch alles. | He's a regular fashion plate; he looks as if he'd just stepped out of a bandbox; he's a dapper dresser.

Knacker:

Er ist ein alter Knacker. | He's a funny old geezer (*or* bozo).

Knacks:

Er ist ein alter Knacks. | He's an old fogey; he's had his day.

Seine Gesundheit hat im Krieg einen Knacks abgekriegt. | His health was permanently injured in the war.

Knall:

Er wurde Knall und Fall entlassen. | He was bounced (*or* fired) without a moment's notice.

Er hat 'nen Knall. | He's cracked (*or* gone nutty); he's out of his mind.

Knalleffekt:

Das ist ja gerade der Knalleffekt bei dieser Geschichte. | That's just the point (*or* funny part of it).

knallen:

Sie hat ihm eine ins Gesicht geknallt. | She slapped him in the face.

knallrot:

   Er trug einen knallroten Schlips. | He wore a loud (*or* brilliant) red tie.

knapp:

   Nehmen Sie mein Angebot an?—Aber nicht zu knapp! | Do you accept my offer?—Sure thing!; you bet I do.

   Das Geschäft ist zurückgegangen, und zwar nicht zu knapp. | Business has fallen off, and how!

   Bei denen geht's knapp zu. | They just manage to get along (*or* make ends meet).

knappemang:

   Er kam knappemang davon. | He had a close shave (*or* narrow escape).

knausern:

   Sie müssen bei dem kleinen Einkommen sehr knausern. | They have to skimp on such a small income.

kneifen:

   Er hat elend gekniffen. | He wriggled (*or* backed) out of it.

Knie:

   Lieber lasse ich mir ein Loch ins Knie bohren, als daß ich das tue. | I'd rather be hung than do that.

   Brechen Sie die Sache nicht übers Knie! | Don't be rash (*or* reckless)!

Kniff:

   Er hat den Kniff raus. | He's an old hand (*or* past master) at it; he knows the ropes.

Knigge:

   Er hat Knigges „Umgang mit Menschen" nicht gelesen. | He's never read Emily Post; he has no manners (*or* breeding).

knipsen:

   Er ließ sich knipsen. | He had a snapshot taken.

Knochen:

   So ein elender Knochen! | Such a miserable wretch!

   Er blamierte sich bis auf die Knochen. | He made an ass (*or* awful fool) of himself.

   Er war naß bis auf die Knochen. | He was drenched to the skin.

   Er hat keinen Mumm in den Knochen. | He's a softy; he has no guts (*or* spunk).

   Die Nachricht fuhr ihm in die Knochen. | The news cut him to the quick; it upset him badly.

Knopf:

   Er ist ein fauler Knopf. | He's a lazybones.

Knopfloch:

   Er lehnte mit einer Träne im Knopfloch ab. | He refused politely (*or* apologetically).

Knöppchen:

   Er ist auch nur ein Knöppchen. | He's just a runt (*or* half-pint).

knorke:

   Das ist knorke. | That's the berries; that's swell (*or* grand).

Knote(n):

   So ein Knoten! | What a roughneck (*or* boor)!

Knoten:

   Der Knoten schürzt sich. | The plot thickens.

   Die Sache hat einen Knoten. | There's a hitch in the matter; there's a catch to it.

   Machen Sie sich einen Knoten in die Nase! | Tie a string around your finger; take it to heart; be sure to remember that.

knuffig:

Es war knuffig kalt. | It was beastly (*or* bitter) cold.

Knüppel:

Da liegt der Knüppel beim Hund. | Do or die; take it or leave it; there's no way out.

Er ist ihnen ein Knüppel am Bein. | He's a drag (*or* ball and chain) on them; he's an awful nuisance.

Er warf ihnen einen Knüppel zwischen die Beine. | He threw a monkey wrench into the machinery; he queered (*or* spoiled) their plans.

knüppeldick:

Er hat es knüppeldick. | He's fed up with it; he's sick and tired of it.
Es kommt immer gleich knüppeldick. | It never rains but it pours.

knurren:

Er hat immer was zu knurren. | He's always kicking (*or* complaining) about something.

knutschen:

Sie knutscht gern. | She's a snuggler; she likes to neck (*or* pet).

Koch:

Hunger ist der beste Koch. | Hunger is the best sauce.

kochen:

Es wird nichts so heiß gegessen, wie es gekocht wird. | Nothing is so bad as it is painted; things are always better than they seem.

kodd(e)rig:

Ihm war ganz koddrig zumute. | He felt very seedy; he was feeling generally miserable.

Er hat ein koddrige Schnauze. | He's a fresh mug (*or* guy).

Kohl:

Das ist alles Kohl. | That's all hooey (*or* tommyrot).
Schöne Worte machen den Kohl nicht fett. | You can't live on promises.
Wozu den alten Kohl wieder aufwärmen? | Why keep harping on that?; why bring that up all the time?

Besser eine Laus im Kohl als gar kein Fleisch. | Anything is better than nothing.

Kohldampf:

Er schob Kohldampf. | He was hungry (*or* starving).

Kohle:

Er saß wie auf Kohlen. | He was on pins and needles; he was all on edge; he felt very nervous (*or* scared).

kohlen:

Kohlen Sie nicht so! | Cut out that tommyrot!; stop the nonsense!

kohlpechrabenschwarz:

Es war in dem Zimmer kohlpechrabenschwarz. | It was pitch-dark in the room.

Koks:

So ein Koks! | Banana oil!; boloney!; nonsense!
Er hat viel Koks. | He's got lots of jack (*or* money).
Er handelt heimlich mit Koks. | He's in the dope (*or* narcotic) ring.

Kolbe:

Er wird ihm schon die Kolbe lausen. | He'll tell him where he gets off; he'll show him his place.

Kolleg:
   Ist heute Kolleg? | Are there any classes being held today?

Koller:
   Er bekam einen Koller. | He flew into a fit of rage.

Kollett:
   Er stieg ihm aufs Kollett. | He raked him over the coals; he gave him a piece of his mind.

Kolonne:
   Das ist dir eine Kolonne! | What a gang!

kolossal:
   Das freut mich ganz kolossal. | I'm tickled pink (*or* to death); I'm extremely pleased.

Kolumbus:
   Das Ei des Kolumbus! | Elementary, my dear Watson!; that's simple.

komisch:
   Das ist wirklich komisch. | That's funny (*or* queer); that's very peculiar.

kommen:
   Komme ich hier recht nach der Universität? | Is this the campus (*or* university)?
   Kommen Sir mir nicht mit dem alten Schwindel! | Don't pull that old gag on me!; you can't fool me!
   Nun kommt es an Sie. | Now it's your turn; you're next.
   Wie hoch kommt das? | How much is that?; what does that make (*or* amount to)?
   Wie kam er dazu? | How did he happen to do that?
   So darf er mir nicht kommen. | He can't talk to me like that and get away with it.
   Er kann nicht darauf kommen. | He can't think of it.

Komment:
   Er hat keinen Komment. | He has no breeding; he lacks polish.

Komödiant:
   Er ist ein großer Komödiant. | He's a big bluff (*or* fourflusher).

Konjunkturritter:
   Er ist der typische Konjunkturritter. | He's the typical opportunist (*or* profiteer).

können:
   Er kann was. | He's a capable fellow.
   Er kann auch anders. | He can be different if he wants to; he's not always like that.
   Uns kann keiner! | We're in a class by ourselves!

Konsorte:
   Das sind vielleicht Konsorten! | What men!

konstant:
   Er arbeitet mit konstanter Bosheit. | He's a glutton for punishment; he keeps his nose to the grindstone; he works with a vengeance.

Konto:
   Er hat schon viel auf dem Konto. | He has a bad record.

Kontor:
   Es war ein Schlag ins Kontor. | It was a blow from the rear; it was an unpleasant surprise.

Konzept:

Sein Besuch verdarb ihnen das Konzept.	His visit queered (*or* spoiled) their plans.
Der Redner kam aus dem Konzept.	The speaker got lost in a maze; he wandered from his subject.

Kopf:

Kopf hoch!	Chin up!; keep smiling!; cheer up!
Er wußte nicht, wo ihm der Kopf stand.	He didn't know what to do (*or* which way to turn).
Er ist ein fähiger Kopf.	He's a clever (*or* capable) fellow.
Soviel Köpfe, soviel Sinne.	Many men, many minds; every man is entitled to his own opinion.
Er folgt immer seinem eignen Kopf.	He always goes his own sweet way; he suits himself.
Er hat den Kopf nicht bei der Sache.	He's in a fog (*or* daze); he's absent-minded.
Er läßt den Kopf hängen.	He's down in the mouth; he's despondent.
Verlieren Sie nicht den Kopf!	Keep your wits about you!
Er hat den Kopf voll.	His mind is preoccupied.
Machen Sie ihm mal den Kopf warm!	Give him a little scare!
Sie wusch ihm gehörig den Kopf.	She raked him over the coals; she bawled him out soundly.
Er zerbrach sich den Kopf darüber.	He racked his brains over it.
Ich wette meinen Kopf darauf, daß er kommt.	I'll bet you anything he'll come.
Er muß stets seinen Kopf durchsetzen.	He wants everything his own way.
Nun soll er auch seinen Kopf hinhalten.	Let him face the music!; let him take his punishment!
Er setzt dabei seinen Kopf aufs Spiel.	He's taking the bull by the horns; he's risking his neck.
Sie bekam einen roten Kopf.	She blushed; she got red in the face.
Es geht an Kopf und Kragen.	It's a matter of life or death.
Er warf ihnen einige Liebenswürdigkeiten an den Kopf.	He razzed (*or* ridiculed) them; he bawled them out.
Alles steht auf dem Kopf.	Everything is topsy-turvy (*or* in disorder); things are in a terrible state of confusion.
Er ist nicht auf den Kopf gefallen.	He's no dumb bunny; he's plenty smart.
Er läßt sich nicht auf den Kopf spucken.	You can't ride roughshod over (*or* put anything over on) him.
Stellen Sie es auf den Kopf!	Turn it upside down!
Die Studenten beschlossen, das Nest auf den Kopf zu stellen.	The students decided to go out and paint the town red (*or* make whoopee).
Er geht, und wenn Sie sich auf den Kopf stellen.	He'll go no matter what you do; you can't stop him from going.
Das stimmt auf den Kopf.	That's absolutely correct.
Man sagte es ihm auf den Kopf zu.	They threw it in his face; they put it up to him.
Er besteht auf seinen Kopf.	He's pig-headed; he insists on it.
Sie sagte das Gedicht aus dem Kopf auf.	She recited the poem from memory.
Schlagen Sie sich das aus dem Kopf!	Give up the idea!; get it out of your mind!; forget about it!
Sie weinte sich die Augen aus dem Kopf.	She cried her eyes out.
Sie kriegten sich bei den Köpfen.	They had quite an argument (*or* fight); they came to blows.
Er steckt bis über den Kopf in Schulden.	He's head over heels in debt.
Der Gedanke fuhr ihm durch den Kopf.	The thought flashed through his mind.

Laſſen Sie ſich's mal durch den Kopf gehen!	Sleep on the idea!; think it over!
Er hat nichts weiter im Kopf.	He's got it on his brain (*or* mind); he thinks of nothing else.
Was man nicht im Kopf hat, muß man in den Beinen haben.	A good memory saves many a step; use your head to save your heels!
Er hat eine Ratte im Kopf.	He has bats in his belfry; he's not all there; he's a little touched (*or* crazy).
Sie hat große Roſinen im Kopf.	She entertains high-flown (*or* big) ideas; she has fancy notions.
Ihm gehen ganz andere Sachen im Kopf herum.	He has other fish to fry; he has other concerns (*or* interests).
Er hat einen Schwarm im Kopf.	He's got a bug; he's eccentric.
Er hat Stroh im Kopf.	He's a nitwit (*or* numskull).
Sie hat Tauben im Kopf.	She has crazy notions.
Sie hat Zwirn im Kopf.	She's got brains; she's no fool.
Sie hat ihm Raupen in den Kopf geſetzt.	She put a bee in his bonnet; she put crazy notions (*or* wild ideas) into his head.
Es will nicht in ſeinen Kopf hinein, daß er unrecht hat.	He can't see (*or* won't admit) that he's wrong.
Er will immer gleich mit dem Kopf durch die Wand.	He's a pig-headed (*or* an obstinate) cuss; he's always wanting to do the impossible.
Er ſaß mit einem dicken Kopf da.	He was down in the mouth; he was in the dumps; he was feeling blue (*or* dejected).
Alles muß nach ſeinem Kopf gehen.	He has everything his own way.
Er lief Hals über Kopf davon.	He ran away helter-skelter (*or* pell-mell).
Sie ſchlug die Hände überm Kopf zuſammen.	She threw up her hands in amazement; she was dumbfounded (*or* very much surprised).
Der Junge iſt ihr über den Kopf gewachſen.	The kid has become unmanageable (*or* too much for her); she can no longer handle him.
Er hat ein Brett vor dem Kopf.	He's a blockhead (*or* dunce).
Er ſtand da wie vor den Kopf geſchlagen.	He was flabbergasted; he was speechless with surprise.
Sein rauhes Weſen ſtößt alle vor den Kopf.	He shocks (*or* offends) everybody by his uncouth ways.
Kopfnuß:	
Er gab ihm eine Kopfnuß.	He gave him a sock (*or* box) on the ear.
kopfſcheu:	
Machen Sie den Jungen doch nicht kopfſcheu!	Don't scare the boy!; don't shy him off!
kopfſtehen:	
Auf dieſe gute Nachricht ſtand er kopf.	He was wild (*or* beside himself) over the good news he had received.
Korb:	
Sie gab ihm einen Korb.	She gave him the air; she turned him down.
Er iſt Hahn im Korb.	He's cock of the walk; he's a ladies' man.
Es geht über alle Körbe.	It's going too far; it's overstepping the bounds; it's getting out of control.
Korinther:	
Er geht drauflos wie Paulus auf die Korinther.	He's a real go-getter; he's very aggressive (*or* ambitious).

korksen:
Er hat gekorkst.

He pulled a boner; he made a blunder (*or* mistake).

Korkserei:
Es ist eine höhere Korkserei.

It's a beautiful mess; it's a mess and a half; it's a hopeless mixup.

Korn:
Viele Körner machen einen Haufen.

Great oaks from small acorns grow; look after the pennies and the dollars will look after themselves.

Er hat Korn auf dem Boden.
He's got money in the bank; he's well fixed.

Er nimmt sie scharf aufs Korn.
He's got his eagle eye on them; he's watching them like a hawk.

Wirf die Flinte nicht ins Korn!
Don't throw up the sponge!; don't give up (the game)!

Er ist ein Mann von altem Schrot und Korn.
He's a man of the good old stamp; he's true-blue; there's a real man for you.

Körnchen:
Ein blindes Huhn findet auch mal ein Körnchen.
Fortune favors a fool.

koscher:
Die Sache ist nicht ganz koscher.

There's a nigger in the wood pile; there's something not quite right about it.

Ihm war nicht ganz koscher.
He didn't feel up to snuff; he wasn't feeling very well.

Kost:
Man hat ihn auf schmale Kost gesetzt.

He's been put on short rations; his allowance has been cut.

köstlich:
Das ist ja köstlich!

That's precious (*or* perfect)!; that's ducky (*or* capital)!

Kostverächter:
Darf ich Ihnen eine gute Zigarre anbieten?—Nun, ich bin kein Kostverächter.

May I offer you a good cigar?—Well, I'm not proud!; I'll take anything you give me!

Kotzen:
Es ist zum Kotzen!

Confound it!; it's enough to make you sick!

Krabbe:
Sie ist eine kleine, muntere Krabbe.

She's a lively little brat (*or* youngster).

Krach:
In dem Verband herrscht Krach.

There's a rumpus (*or* row) going on in the organization.

Mach doch keinen solchen Krach!
Pipe down!; don't make so much noise!; keep quiet!

Er bestand die Prüfung mit Ach und Krach.
He passed the exam(ination) by the skin of his teeth (*or* with great difficulty).

krachen:
Die beiden krachen sich andauernd.

They're on the outs (*or* at odds) with each other all the time; they're always squabbling.

Kraft:

Er sucht für sein Geschäft eine erstklassige Kraft. — He's looking for a right-hand man (*or* first-class assistant) in his business.

Sie schrie aus Kräften. — She bawled (*or* yelled) at the top of her lungs; she cried with all her might.

Die Verordnung ist außer Kraft. — The ordinance is invalid; it has expired.

Das Gesetz tritt am 1. Januar in Kraft. — The law will take effect on January 1.

Er ging mit frischen Kräften an die Arbeit. — He went to work with renewed energy.

Er tat es nach besten Kräften. — He did the best that he could; he did it to the best of his ability.

Er ist ein Mensch ohne Saft und Kraft. — He's wishy-washy; he's a softy (*or* spineless creature).

Er kommt wieder zu Kräften. — He's gaining back his strength.

kräftig:

Er schreibt eine kräftige Handschrift. — He swings a wicked left; he has a hard punch.

Kraftmeierei:

Er erging sich in Kraftmeierei. — He was showing off.

Kragen:

Das hätte ihm den Kragen kosten können. — He had a close call (*or* shave); he had a narrow escape.

Es geht ihm an Kopf und Kragen. — It's a matter of life or death.

Nehmen Sie ihn mal beim Kragen! — Call him on the carpet!; take him to account!

Krähe:

Eine Krähe hackt der andern die Augen nicht aus. — There's honor among thieves.

Er ist Eule unter den Krähen. — He's a swan among the geese.

Krähwinkel:

Er kommt von Krähwinkel. — He comes from Podunk (*or* Hickville); he's from the sticks (*or* backwoods).

krakeelen:

Er krakeelt andauernd. — He keeps kicking (*or* complaining); he's always raising a howl about something.

Kram:

Was kostet der ganze Kram? — How much for the whole shooting match (*or* business)?

Machen Sie doch keinen Kram! — Come on now!; don't start something!

Das paßt ganz in meinen Kram. — That fills the bill exactly; that suits my purpose to a T.

Hören Sie doch endlich auf mit dem gelehrten Kram! — Can that highbrow stuff!; stop talking like a book!; stop being so superior!

Krämer:

Jeder Krämer lobt seine Ware. — Every cook praises his own dish.

Krampf:

Sie haben gestern nacht einen schönen Krampf gemacht. — They threw (*or* had) a wild party last night; they made whoopee (*or* cut loose).

Der Kerl geht auf Krampf aus. — He's up to some monkey business (*or* mischief).

Er nahm Urlaub auf Krampf. — He played hookey (from school); he sneaked out; he was absent without leave.

krampfhaft:
Er arbeitet krampfhaft daran. — He's working feverishly at it.
Sie sah krampfhaft geradeaus. — She stared straight ahead.

Kränke:
Da kann man die Kränke kriegen! — Confound it!; it's enough to make you sick!

kränken:
Er hat sie um drei Mark gekränkt. — He stuck her for three marks; he borrowed three marks of her.

krankhaft:
Es ist krankhaft bei ihr, sich über Kleinigkeiten aufzuregen. — She has a habit of getting worked up (or excited) about little things.

kraß:
Er ist erst krasser Fuchs. — He's just a (college) freshman.

Kratzbürste:
Sie ist eine kleine Kratzbürste. — She's an old crosspatch (or grouch).

kratzen:
Wen es juckt, der kratze sich! — Make hay while the sun shines!; if the shoe fits, wear it (or put it on)!; take advantage of your opportunities!
Ihr Lob hat ihn mächtig gekratzt. — Her praise tickled (or delighted) him.

Kraut:
Seine Kleider lagen herum wie Kraut und Rüben. — His clothes were dumped (or scattered) pell-mell all over the place.
Gegen den Tod ist kein Kraut gewachsen. — There's no cure for death; we all must die.
Das macht das Kraut nicht fett. — That won't help matters any.

krebsen:
Er hat tüchtig zu krebsen. — He's up against it (or badly off).
Er geht mit seinen Beziehungen krebsen. — He's cashing in (or capitalizing) on his pull; he's making use (or the most) of his connections.

Krebsgang:
Das Geschäft geht den Krebsgang. — Business is terribly slow; it's falling off.

Kreide:
Er steht bei ihnen in der Kreide. — He's in the red with them; he owes them some money.
Er schreibt mit doppelter Kreide. — He's a double-crosser (or cheat).

kreideweiß:
Er wurde kreideweiß. — He turned white as a sheet.

Kreis:
Das liegt außerhalb seines Kreises. — That's not up his alley; that's out of his line.

kreisen:
Lassen Sie, bitte, den Wein kreisen! — Please pass the bottle!

Krempel:
Der ganze Krempel kostet drei Mark. — The whole caboodle (or business) costs three marks.

Krethi:
Er will nichts mit Krethi und Plethi zu tun haben. — He has no use for the rabble (or hoi polloi); he'll have nothing to do with Tom, Dick, and Harry.

Kreuz:
Es ist ein Kreuz mit dem Jungen. — The boy is a real problem; he's a problem child.

Er muß erst zu Kreuze kriechen. — He'll have to eat humble pie; he must first repent (*or* apologize).

Kreuzdonnerwetter:
Kreuzdonnerwetter! — Hell and blazes!; damnation!

kreuzfidel:
Er war kreuzfidel. — He was merry as a lark.

kribbelig:
Sei doch nicht so kribbelig! — Don't be so perverse (*or* irritable)!

kriegen:
Ihn kriegt heute niemand aus dem Haus. — Nobody can get him (to go) out today.

Krippe:
Er kann gut lachen, er sitzt an der Krippe. — He can afford to be gay—he's sitting pretty (*or* he's on Easy Street).

Kritik:
Die Arbeit ist unter aller Kritik. — It's a hell of a job; the work is beneath contempt.

Krone:
Er ist die Krone der Zuvorkommenheit. — He's a perfect gentleman; he's the height of perfection.

Dem Verdienste seine Krone. — You reap as you sow; honor to whom honor is due.

Das setzt allem die Krone auf! — That's the last straw!

Es wird Ihnen keine Perle aus der Krone fallen. — You can't lose; you won't lose anything by it.

Er hat einen in der Krone. — He's stewed (*or* drunk).

Was ist ihm denn in die Krone gefahren? — What's biting (*or* eating) him?; what's come over (*or* gotten into) him?

Kroppzeug:
Laß doch das Kroppzeug im Garten spielen! — Let the kids (*or* youngsters) play in the garden!

Kröte:
Sie ist eine giftige Kröte. — She's a venomous cat (*or* spiteful person).

Er gab seine letzten Kröten aus. — He spent his last cent.

Krücke:
Schwing die Krücken! — Get a move on!; take to your legs!; beat it!

Kruke:
Er ist eine seltsame Kruke. — He's a queer duck (*or* bird).

krumm:
Er sah sie ganz krumm an. — He eyed her suspiciously.

Sie wollten sich krumm lachen. — They doubled up with laughter.

Nun müssen sie krumm liegen. — Now they've got to skimp (*or* economize).

Er braucht keinen Finger krumm zu machen. — He doesn't have to turn a finger.

Er macht krumme Finger. — He's light-fingered; he's a pickpocket.

Er schimpfte ihn einen krummen Hund. — He called him a crook (*or* rat).

krummnehmen:
Nehmen Sie mir's nicht krumm, wenn ich Sie darauf aufmerksam mache! — Don't mind my calling your attention to it!; don't take it amiss if I mention it to you.

Kruzitürken:
Kruzitürken! | Leaping lizards!; holy smoke!

Kübel:
Es goß wie mit Kübeln. | It rained cats and dogs; it came down in buckets.

Küche:
Sie boten ihm kalte Küche an. | They offered him a cold meal; they gave him the leftovers.

Da sind Sie in des Teufels Küche geraten! | You surely got yourself into a devil of a scrape!

Kuchen:
Ich hatte angenommen, er schickte mir das Buch zurück, ja Kuchen! | I had assumed he'd send me back the book, but like fun he did!

Er hat alle Rosinen aus dem Kuchen gepickt. | He kept all the plums (*or* cream) for himself; he took the best for himself and left them holding the bag.

Küchenmeister:
Bei ihnen ist Schmalhans Küchenmeister. | They're on short rations; they're on a diet.

Kuckuck:
Da klebt der Kuckuck dran. | The sheriff's notice of foreclosure is up; the place will be auctioned off.

Ich will des Kuckucks sein, wenn ich das tue. | I'll be hanged (*or* damned) if I do that.

Der hört den Kuckuck nicht mehr rufen. | He won't live to see another spring.

Scheren Sie sich zum Kuckuck! | Go jump in the lake!; go to hell!

Kuckucksei:
Da hat er sich ein schönes Kuckucksei ins Nest gelegt. | He certainly got himself into a fine scrape.

Kuddelmuddel:
Auf der Börse herrschte ein großer Kuddelmuddel. | The Stock Exchange was in perfect pandemonium; everything was topsy-turvy.

Kugeln:
Es war zum Kugeln. | It was a scream (*or* riot); I nearly died laughing.

Kuh:
Er stand da wie die Kuh vorm neuen Tor. | He stood there like a dumb bunny; he didn't know where to turn; he was at his wits' end.

Er versteht davon soviel wie die Kuh vom Sonntag. | He knows as much about it as the man in the moon; he hasn't the remotest idea of it.

Er benutzt die Stellung als milchende Kuh. | He regards the job as the goose that laid the golden egg; his job is a gold mine.

Kuhhandel:
Um die Vergebung von Pöstchen wurde der reine Kuhhandel getrieben. | There was plenty of logrolling (*or* bargaining) over the jobs that were being given out.

Kuhhaut:
Das geht auf keine Kuhhaut. | That takes the cake; it can't be beat; that oversteps all bounds.

Kulisse:
Das ist doch nur Kulisse. | That's only bluff; that's just being done for effect.

Kultur:
Dieser Mann ist nicht von der Kultur beleckt. | This man lacks polish; he's unsophisticated.

Kümmel:
Reiben Sie ihm den Kümmel! | Rub it into him!; tell him what's what!

Kümmeltürke:
Gehen Sie weg, Sie alter Kümmeltürke! | Scram (*or* Beat it), you old souse!

Kunst:
Was macht die Kunst? | How's tricks?; how are you making out (*or* getting along)?

Das ist keine Kunst. | There's no trick to that; that's easy enough.
Er besiegte ihn nach allen Regeln der Kunst. | He scored on every point; he defeated him in great style.
Er versteht die Passauer Kunst. | There's a tough bird (*or* hard-boiled) egg for you!; he's thick-skinned (*or* immune to everything).

Er ist mit seiner Kunst zu Ende. | He's played his last trump; he's at the end of his rope; he's on his last legs.

künstlich:
Regen Sie sich nicht künstlich auf! | Keep your shirt on!; take it easy; don't get excited!

Kunststück:
Der Sieg war kein Kunststück. | That was a walk-away (push-over *or* an easy victory); there was nothing to it.

Kunz:
Hans und Kunz wissen das. | Every Tom, Dick, and Harry knows that; any-(*or* every)body knows that.

In diesem Lokal verkehren Hinz und Kunz. | The rabble (*or* hoi polloi) patronize this place; every Tom, Dick, and Harry goes there.

Kupferstecher:
Lieber Freund und Kupferstecher! | My good fellow!; my pal!

Kuppelpelz:
Sie hat sich einen Kuppelpelz verdient. | She deserved a commission for making the match.

Kur:
Nehmen Sie ihn mal in die Kur! | Give him the works!; tell him what's what!

Kurve:
Er hat die Kurve weg. | He knows his stuff (*or* onions); he has the hang (*or* knack) of it.

kurz:
Kurz entschlossen entfernte er sich. | He departed abruptly.
Kurz und gut, er ist tot. | To cut a long story short, he's dead.
Er war kurz angebunden. | He was blunt (*or* to the point).
Ich sah ihn kurz vorher. | I saw him a little while ago.
Er lehnte es kurz und bündig ab. | He refused it point-blank.
Er schlug alles kurz und klein. | He smashed everything to bits.
Er kam zu kurz. | He got the shorter end; he was the loser.

Er hofft, sie binnen kurzem zu sehen.	He hopes to see her before long.
Über kurz oder lang tut er es doch.	Sooner or later he'll do it anyway.
Vor kurzem war er noch hier.	He was here only a short time ago.

Kürze:

In Kürze wird er hier sein.	He'll be here before long.
In der Kürze liegt die Würze.	Brevity is the soul of wit.

Kürzere:

Er zog den Kürzeren.	He got the worst of it.

kurzerhand:

Er tat es kurzerhand.	He did it without a word (*or* more ado).

kurzum:

Kurzum, er verlor seine Stelle.	To cut a long story short, he was fired.

Kußhand:

Er nahm den Vorschlag mit Kußhand an.	He jumped at the suggestion; he was very much interested in it.

Kutscher:

Das kann Lehmanns Kutscher auch.	That's as easy as falling off a log; anyone can do that.

L

Laban:	
Er ist ein langer Laban.	He's a daddy-long-legs.
labb(e)rig:	
Er ist ein labbriger Geselle.	He's wishy-washy (*or* soft); he's a spineless (*or* insipid) fellow.
lachen:	
Sie wollen das getan haben? Daß ich nicht lache!	You claim you did that? Tell it to Sweeney!; don't make me laugh!; I don't believe it.
Lachen:	
Am vielen Lachen erkennt man den Narren.	A fool will laugh when he's drowning.
Auf Lachen folgt Weinen.	Those who sing before breakfast will cry before night.
Würden Sie mir drei Mark leihen?—Erst können vor Lachen!	Could you lend me three marks?—Don't make me laugh!; where would I get it from?
Es ist zum Lachen.	It's a scream (*or* riot); it's a big joke; it's too funny for words.
Lächerliche:	
Er zieht alles ins Lächerliche.	He makes fun of everything.
Lachkrampf:	
Er bekam einen förmlichen Lachkrampf.	He nearly had fits; he nearly died laughing.
Lack:	
Fertig ist der Lack!	There you are!; that's that!; the job is finished!
Der Lack der Bildung ist sehr dünn bei ihr.	She has but a thin veneer of culture; her culture amounts to pseudo-sophistication.
Er erschien zum Essen in Frack und Lack.	He came to the dinner in tails (*or* full dress).
Lackel:	
So ein frecher Lackel!	The impudent fellow!; what a rascal!
Lackierte:	
Jetzt ist er der Lackierte.	Now he's the dupe (*or* sucker); the joke is on him.
laden:	
Er hat schief geladen.	He's in a drunken stupor; he's had more than his share (of drink).
Laden:	
Der Laden klappt!	Hot dog!; great stuff!; good work!
Wer schmeißt den Laden hier?	Who's the boss around here?; who's running this place?
Wenn das noch einmal vorkommt, dann können Sie Ihren Laden zumachen!	If that happens once more, you're through (*or* fired)!
Der macht aber einen langen Laden auf!	He's certainly ringing the changes (*or* chewing the rag)!; he's talking on and on!

Ladenhüter:

Er versucht, seine Ladenhüter abzusetzen. | He's trying to sell leftovers (*or* seconds); he's trying to get rid of his old stock.

Ladestock:

Er geht, als hätte er einen Ladestock verschluckt. | He's as stiff as a poker; he's very strait-laced.

Lage:

Er gab eine Lage Bier aus. | He paid for a round of beer.

Nach Lage der Dinge konnte er nicht anders handeln. | As matters stood (*or* Under the circumstances), he couldn't do otherwise.

lagern:

Der Wein hat noch nicht lange genug gelagert. | The wine hasn't aged long enough.

Laie:

Da staunt der Laie, der Fachmann aber wundert sich. | There's nothing to it if you know how.

Lamm:

Er ist fromm wie ein Lamm. | He's meek as a lamb; he has the patience of Job (*or* a saint).

Lämmerschwänzchen:

Sein Herz ging wie ein Lämmerschwänzchen. | His heart went pit-a-pat; he was all thrills and heart throbs.

Lampe:

Lassen Sie uns einen auf die Lampe gießen! | Let's wet the whistle!; let's have a drink!

Seine Arbeit riecht nach der Lampe. | He burned the midnight oil; he stayed up until all hours of the night.

Lamprete:

Lampreten können wir Ihnen leider nicht vorsetzen. | Unfortunately we have nothing much to offer you in the way of food.

Land:

Er hat Land und Leute gesehen. | He's been places (*or* around); he's seen the world.

Sie kamen aus aller Herrn Länder. | They came from all over the world.

Mit dem Hut in der Hand kommt man durchs ganze Land. | It pays to be courteous.

Bleib im Land und nähr dich redlich! | Seek an honest living at home!

Seitdem ist manches Jahr ins Land gegangen. | Many years have elapsed since then.

Sie ist die Unschuld vom Lande. | She's innocence personified; she's straight from the country; she's a simple country lass.

Verwandte Seelen finden sich zu Wasser und zu Lande. | Birds of a feather flock together.

landab, landauf:

Einen solchen Mann findet man landab, landauf nicht wieder. | It'll be a long time before you'll find another man like him.

landaus, landein:

Die Reise führt sie landaus, landein. | The trip takes them far and wide.

landen:

Bei dem können Sie nicht landen. | You don't cut any ice with him; you're no match for him.

Landfrieden:
    Ich traue dem Landfrieden nicht.

There's a nigger in the wood pile; I have my suspicions; I don't trust the looks of things.

ländlich:
    Ländlich, sittlich.

Every country has its own customs.

Landpomeranze:
    Sie sah aus wie eine Landpomeranze.

She looked like a hayseed (*or* farmer's daughter).

Landsknecht:
    Er flucht wie ein Landsknecht.

He swears like a trooper.

lang(e):
    Wer lang hat, läßt lang hängen.

He who has fine feathers likes to show them; those who can afford it like to splurge (*or* put on a big show).

Wer wird erst lange fragen?	What's the good of asking?
Er lag lang auf dem Boden.	He lay stretched out to his full length.
Er ist lange nicht so stark.	He isn't nearly that strong.
Er ist noch lang kein Held.	He's far from being a hero.
Er ist schon lange nicht mehr hier gewesen.	It's now a long time since he was here.
Das ist für ihn lange gut.	That's good enough for him.
Was lange währt, wird gut.	Good work takes time.
Da können Sie lange warten.	You'll never see the like of it again!; you're out of luck!; you've got a good wait coming!

Was besinnen Sie sich so lange?	Why do you hesitate?
Was macht der Mensch lange!	How slow he is!
Was macht er so lange?	What's he doing all this time?
Er war ein ganzes Jahr lang da.	He was there for a whole year.
Die Zeit wurde ihr lang.	Time hung heavy on her hands; she was bored.

Über kurz oder lang tut er es doch.	Sooner or later he'll do it anyway.
Er ließ sich des langen und breiten darüber aus.	He rang the changes (*or* chewed the rag); he talked at great length.
Er schiebt es auf die lange Bank.	He keeps putting it off.
Das hat noch lange Beine.	That can wait; there's no (need to) hurry; that's still a long way off.

Er macht lange Finger.	He's light-fingered; he's a pickpocket.
Er hat eine lange Hand.	He has pull (*or* influence); his influence is far-reaching.

Es war von langer Hand vorbereitet.

The affair was premeditated (or prearranged); it was a foregone conclusion.

Er hat eine lange Leitung.	He's slow to catch on.
Er zog mit langer Nase ab.	He left looking rather disappointed.
Er machte lange Ohren.	He cocked his ears; he sat up and took notice.

Sie machte lange Zähne.

She made a face; she stuck up her nose at it; she didn't like (to eat) it.

Länge:
    Auf die Länge erträgt er das nicht.

He won't put up with that for any length of time.

Die Unterhaltung dehnte sich in die Länge. | The conversation dragged on and on.

längelang:
    Er schlug längelang die Treppe hinunter. — He fell headlong down the stairs.

langen:
    Langt das? — Is that enough?; will that do (*or* suffice)?
    Er langte ihm eine. — He gave him a box on the ear.
    Den Kerl werde ich mir schon langen! — I'll tell that fellow what's what!; I'll give him a piece of my mind!

länger:
    Das habe ich schon länger bemerkt. — I noticed that some time ago.

Langohr:
    Ein Esel schimpft den andern Langohr. — The pot calls the kettle black; one crook accuses another.

langsam:
    Immer langsam voran! — Take it easy!; hold your horses!; not so fast!

längst:
    Der Zug ist längst fällig. — The train is late (*or* long overdue).
    Er ist längst nicht so tüchtig. — He isn't nearly so good.
    Sie wissen es schon längst. — They've known it for a long time.
    Ehrlich währt am längsten. — Honesty is the best policy.

langstielig:
    Er ist ein langstieliger Geselle. — He's a terrible bore.

langweilig:
    Dieser Spieler ist ein langweiliger Peter. — This player is a stick-in-the-mud (*or* slowpoke); he's awfully slow.

Lanze:
    Er legte eine Lanze für sie ein. — He put in a good word for them.

Lappen:
    Hau ihn, daß die Lappen fliegen! — Let him have it;! knock him for a row of pins!; beat him to a pulp!
    Es ist Zeit, daß Sie sich auf die Lappen machen! — You'd better be going!; it's time you were off (*or* on your way).
    Er ist der Polizei durch die Lappen gegangen. — He gave the police the slip; he got away from them.

Lapsus:
    Ihm ist ein Lapsus passiert. — He made a *faux pas* (*or* bad break); he made a mistake.

Lärm:
    Es war nur blinder Lärm. — It was just a false alarm.
    Viel Lärm um nichts. — Much ado about nothing.
    Er droht, deswegen Lärm zu schlagen. — He threatens to kick up a row (*or* make a scene) about it.

lassen:
    Lassen Sie doch! — Stop!; don't!
    Ich lasse ihn bitten. — Please show him in.
    Das läßt alles weit hinter sich. — That beats everything.
    Das läßt sich denken. — I can imagine.
    Er kann es nicht lassen. — He can't stop (*or* keep from doing it).
    Das können Sie tun oder lassen. — Like it or lump it!; take it or leave it!; suit yourself!
    Das muß man ihm lassen. — You have to hand it to him (*or* give him credit).

Lassen:
    Sein Tun und Lassen gefällt ihr nicht. | She doesn't like his attitude (*or* conduct).

Last:
    Er fällt ihnen zu Last. | He's a drag on (*or* burden to) them.
    Man legt es ihm zur Last. | The blame is shoved on him; he gets the blame.

    Der Betrag geht zu seinen Lasten. | It's at his expense; it's charged to his account.

Laster:
    So ein Laster! | Such a hussy!; what a woman!
    Er ist ein langes Laster. | He's a daddy-long-legs.

Lästerallee:
    Sie mußte die Lästerallee passieren. | She was under heavy fire; she had to run the gauntlet of town talk; she had to take a lot of criticism.

lästig:
    Ich möchte Ihnen nicht lästig fallen. | I hate to trouble you.
    Er wurde als lästiger Ausländer abgeschoben. | He was expelled from the country as an undesirable alien.

Latein:
    Ihm ging das Latein aus. | He was at the end of his rope (*or* wits).

Lateiner:
    Er ist ein guter Lateiner. | He's an authority on Latin.

Laterne:
    Er sucht am Tag mit der Laterne danach. | He's looking for a needle in a haystack.

Laternenpfahl:
    Es war ein Wink mit dem Laternenpfahl. | It was a broad hint.

Latsch:
    Man servierte uns zum Frühstück einen schrecklichen Latsch. | The coffee they served us for breakfast was regular dishwater.

Latsche:
    Die beiden passen zusammen wie ein Paar alte Latschen. | They suit each other to a T; they're perfectly matched; they're an ideal couple.
    Das Auto stand auf Latschen. | There was no air in the tires.

Latte:
    Rechnen Sie die Latte zusammen! | Let me have the bill, please!
    Der hat aber eine Latte gefaßt! | He sure is lit (*or* drunk)!

Laube:
    Fertig ist die Laube! | There you are!; that's that!; the job is finished!

Lauf:
    Das ist der Lauf der Dinge. | That's the way it goes; that's the way of the world.
    Er gab seinen Gefühlen freien Lauf. | He gave vent to his feelings.
    Er läßt den Dingen freien Lauf. | He lets things ride (*or* slide); he lets things take their course.

laufen:
    Am Ende läuft es auf eins hinaus. | It's all the same in the end.
    Er weiß darauf zu laufen. | He knows all the tricks; he knows how to get on in the world; he's very resourceful.

Laufen:
Sie werden doch einem alten Hasen nicht das Laufen beibringen wollen?

You don't think you can take in an old-timer with a tale like that?

laufend:
Dieser Anwalt ist auf dem laufenden.

This attorney knows his stuff (*or* business); he keeps well posted on all the latest developments; he doesn't miss a thing.

Lauferei:
Er hatte viel Lauferei damit.

It put him to a lot of bother; it caused him considerable inconvenience.

Laufpaß:
Man gab ihm den Laufpaß.

He was given his walking papers; he was fired (*or* discharged).

Laune:
Es ist nur eine Laune des Glücks.

It's just a freak of fortune (*or* stroke of good luck).

Er spielte mit viel Laune.

He was in good form; he played excellently.

Laus:
Die Laus ist ihm über die Leber gelaufen.

Something's gotten under his skin; he's peeved (*or* vexed); he's out of sorts.

Hier sitzen wir wie die Laus im Grind.

Here we are, snug as bugs in a rug (*or* cozy as can be).

Er hat's im Griff wie der Bettelmann die Laus.

He's a past master at it; he has it down pat; he has the knack of it.

Besser eine Laus im Kohl als gar kein Fleisch.

Anything is better than nothing.

Da haben Sie sich eine schöne Laus in den Pelz gesetzt!

A fine mess you got yourself into!

lausen:
Ich dachte, mich laust der Affe.

I thought I was seeing things; I was quite surprised (*or* taken aback).

Man hat ihn tüchtig gelaust.

He was fleeced (*or* duped).

lauten:
Das Urteil lautet auf Tod.

He's been sentenced to death.

läuten:
Er hat's läuten hören, aber nicht zusammenschlagen.

He's all at sea (*or* in the dark) about it; he can't quite figure (*or* make) it out.

Lautenschlagen:
Er paßt dazu wie der Esel zum Lautenschlagen.

He's like a square peg in a round hole; he isn't suited to it at all.

leben:
Darauf lebe ich!

I'll bet you anything!

So was lebt nicht!

Well, I never!; did you ever!; I don't believe it!

Er ist sein Vater, wie er leibt und lebt.

He's his father all over again; he's the image of his father.

Hier lebt sich's gut.

This is a fine place to live.

Er soll leben!

Here's to him!; three cheers for him!

Leben:
Das Leben und Treiben in der Stadt fiel ihm auf.

He was impressed by the hustle and bustle of the city.

Herr du meines Lebens!

Leaping lizards!; man alive!

Arbeit macht das Leben süß. | No sweet without sweat.

Er nahm sich das Leben. | He committed suicide.

Sie haben Mühe, das nackte Leben zu fristen. | They can hardly keep the wolf from the door; they barely make ends meet.

Er versprach, ein neues Leben anzufangen. | He promised to turn over a new leaf.

Es geht ihm ans Leben. | His life is at stake; it's a matter of life and death.

Er hat das für sein Leben gern. | He's very fond of it.

Er kam mit dem Leben davon. | He had a close shave (*or* narrow escape); he escaped by the skin of his teeth.

Niemand ist ums Leben gekommen. | There were no casualties; no one was killed.

Lebenslicht:

Die Verbrecher bliesen ihm das Lebenslicht aus. | The gangsters rubbed him out; they killed him.

Leber:

Die Laus ist ihm über die Leber gelaufen. | He's peeved (*or* vexed); he's out of sorts.

Er sprach frisch von der Leber weg. | He didn't mince matters; he talked turkey; he spoke his mind frankly.

Leberwurst:

Er markiert die gekränkte Leberwurst. | He's putting on his hurt act; he's pretending to be sore (*or* highly insulted).

lebhaft:

Ich bedaure lebhaft. | I'm awfully (*or* very) sorry; I sincerely regret it.

Lecken:

Vom Lecken wird keiner fett. | That's only a drop in the bucket; that won't get you very far.

Leckermäulchen:

Sie ist ein Leckermäulchen. | She has a sweet tooth; she's fond of sweets.

Leder:

Er schlug zu, was das Leder hielt. | He made the fur fly; he struck out left and right; he fought furiously.

Aus fremdem Leder ist gut Riemen schneiden. | It's easy when you make the other fellow pay.

Er macht in Leder. | He's in the leather business.

Als er frisch vom Leder zog, sprach er vorzüglich. | When he cast aside all reserve (*or* restraint), he spoke excellently.

ledern:

Seine Rede war recht ledern. | His speech lacked snap (*or* punch); it was boring (*or* dull).

leer:

Bei der Besprechung wurde viel leeres Stroh gedroschen. | They wasted a lot of breath at the conference.

Er redete zu leeren Wänden. | He spoke to deaf ears; nobody listened to him.

Leerlauf:

In der Verwaltung gibt es viel Leerlauf. | The working capacity in the administration is not fully utilized.

Lehmann:

Das kann Lehmanns Kutscher auch. | That's as easy as falling off a log; anyone can do that.

Lehre:

Sie können bei ihm in die Lehre gehen.

He can teach you; you can learn something from him.

Lassen Sie sich das zur Lehre dienen!

Let this be a lesson to you!

Lehrgeld:

Er hat schwer Lehrgeld bezahlt.

He paid dearly for it.

Sie können sich Ihr Lehrgeld zurückgeben lassen!

You might just as well get your tuition back!; you haven't learned a (darned) thing!

Leib:

Er opferte Leib und Leben.

He sacrificed life and property.

Er wird die Folgen am eigenen Leib verspüren.

He himself will suffer the consequences.

Es geht ihm an den Leib.

It's a matter of life and death to him.

Er ging der Sache gerade auf den Leib.

He took the bull by the horns; he went straight to the heart of the matter.

Sie hängt sich alles auf den Leib.

She spends every cent on clothes.

Die Rolle ist ihr wie auf den Leib geschrieben.

The part is made (or expressly written) for her.

Er redete sich die Seele aus dem Leib.

He talked his head off.

Das Herz lachte ihr im Leibe.

She was tickled pink (or to death); she was delighted.

Sie standen sich die Beine in den Leib.

They were worn out from standing so long.

Er ist mit Leib und Seele dabei.

He's in it heart and soul.

Bleiben Sie mir damit vom Leib!

Don't bother me with that!

Er ging ihm tüchtig zu Leib.

He gave it to him; he gave him a good thrashing.

leiben:

Er ist sein Vater, wie er leibt und lebt.

He's his father all over again; he's the image of his father.

Leibeskraft:

Er schrie aus Leibeskräften.

He shouted (or yelled) at the top of his lungs.

Leibhaftige:

Er lief, als ob der Leibhaftige hinter ihm wäre.

He ran as if the devil himself were after him.

leiblich:

Er sah es mit seinen leiblichen Augen.

He saw it with his own eyes.

Leiche:

Es war eine große Leiche.

It was a big funeral.

Er geht über Leichen.

He stops at nothing; he lets nothing stand in his way.

Leichenbittermiene:

Machen Sie keine solche Leichenbittermiene!

Cheer up!; keep smiling!; don't look so glum!

Leichenrede:

Halten Sie doch keine Leichenrede!

Don't cry over spilt milk!; let bygones be bygones!

Leichnam:

Er pflegt gern seinen Leichnam.

He likes a good meal; he denies himself nothing; he likes to pamper himself.

leicht:
    Er hat eine leichte Ader.   He has a devil-may-care attitude; he takes life easy; he makes light of everything.

    Sie hat leichtes Spiel damit.   It's child's play to her; she has no difficulty with it.

Leichtfuß:
    Er iſt ein Bruder Leichtfuß.   He's a happy-go-lucky (*or* thoughtless) fellow.

leichthin:
    Er tut ſeine Arbeit nur leichthin.   He does his work after a fashion; he's easy-going (*or* slipshod) on the job.

Leichtſinn:
    Es wäre ſträflicher Leichtſinn, das zu tun.   It would be foolhardy to do that.
    Das ſagen Sie ſo in Ihrem jugendlichen Leichtſinn!   You're not using your head!; you're talking like a greenhorn!

Leid:
    Er tat ſich ein Leid an.   He committed suicide.

leiden:
    Es leidet ihn hier nicht länger.   He finds it impossible to stay here any longer.

Leiden:
    Er ſah aus wie das Leiden Chriſti.   He looked as if he had one foot in the grave; he looked wretched (*or* very miserable).

    Er leerte den Kelch des Leidens bis auf die Neige.   He drained the bitter cup to the dregs.

leidig:
    Wenn nur das leidige Geld nicht wäre!   If it weren't for the filthy lucre!

Leier:
    Es iſt immer die alte Leier.   It's always the same old gag (*or* story).

Leim:
    Das iſt ein elender Leim!   That's a tough break!; that's a real misfortune!

    Er ging glatt auf den Leim.   He was completely taken in.
    Ihre Freundſchaft ging aus dem Leim.   Their friendship was broken off.

leimen:
    Sie haben ihn tüchtig geleimt.   They pulled his whiskers (*or* leg) soundly; they kidded the life out of him; they played an awful joke on him.

Leimſieder:
    Er iſt ein rechter Leimſieder.   He's an awful bore.

Leine:
    Er zog rechtzeitig Leine.   He quit (*or* left) in time.

leiſe:
    Seien Sie, bitte, recht leiſe!   Please keep quiet!; not so much noise, if you please!

    Gehen Sie, bitte, leiſe damit um!   Please handle it with care!; treat it gently (*or* with respect)!

leiſten:
    Sie können ſich das leiſten.   They can afford that.

Leiſten:
    Sie ſind alle über einen Leiſten geſchlagen.   They're all made on the same last; they're birds of a feather; they're all alike.

Leitung:

Er hat eine lange Leitung.

He's slow to catch on.

lendenlahm:

Er brachte eine lendenlahme Entschuldigung vor.

He gave a lame (*or* poor) excuse.

lenken:

Der Mensch denkt, Gott lenkt.

Man proposes, God disposes.

Lenz:

Er zählt zwanzig Lenze.

He's twenty years old.

Lerche:

Das Pferd schoß eine Lerche.

The horse took a tumble.

lesen:

Heute wird nicht gelesen.

No classes (*or* lectures) today.

letzt:

Er wurde noch im letzten Augenblick gerettet.

He was saved in the nick of time.

Er lag in den letzten Zügen.

He was breathing his last; he lay dying.

Letzt(e):

Zu guter Letzt wurde noch ein Walzer gespielt.

They finished up with a waltz.

Leuchtkugel:

Gelt, da staunen Sie bunte Leuchtkugeln!

It surely bowls you over (*or* knocks you flat), doesn't it?

Leute:

Aus Kindern werden Leute.

The youth of today are the men of tomorrow.

Hinterm Berg wohnen auch Leute.

You're not the only pebble on the beach; other people have brains too.

Er kam in der Leute Mund.

He became the talk of the town; he was a sensation.

Kleider machen Leute.

Fine feathers make fine birds; clothes make the man.

Er hat Land und Leute gesehen.

He's been places (*or* around); he's seen the world.

Leviten:

Er hat ihnen die Leviten gelesen.

He lectured them; he laid down the law to them.

Licht:

Jetzt geht mir ein Licht auf!

Now I begin to see!

Er erblickte das Licht der Welt am 1. Februar.

He was born on the first of February.

Er steckte ihnen ein Licht über die Sache auf.

He put them wise; he opened their eyes.

Er ließ sein Licht leuchten.

He put himself into the limelight; he made himself conspicuous.

Er führte sie hinters Licht.

He took them for a ride; he put one over on them.

lieb:

Das weiß der liebe Himmel!

You've got me there; heaven only knows!

Er hat seine liebe Not damit.

He's having a sweet (*or* terrible) time with it; it's giving him plenty of trouble.

Er arbeitet den lieben langen Tag.

He works the livelong day.

liebäugeln:
   Sie liebäugelt schon lange mit dem Gedanken.

She's been playing with the idea; she's had it in mind for a long time.

Liebe:
   Eine Liebe ist der andern wert.
   Dies ist meine brüderliche Liebe.
   Das tut der Liebe keinen Schaden.

One good turn deserves another.
That's my dear brother.
That won't do any harm; it won't change matters any.

   Tun Sie mir die Liebe!

Do me the favor!

liebend:
   Er tat es liebend gern.

He got a big kick out of (doing) it; he loved to do it.

Liebenswürdigkeit:
   Er warf ihnen einige Liebenswürdigkeiten an den Kopf.

He threw some dirty digs (or disparaging remarks) their way; he heaped abuse upon them.

lieber:
   Je mehr, desto lieber.

The more, the merrier.

Lied:
   Wes Brot ich eß', des Lied ich sing'.

I know where my bread is buttered; I never quarrel with those that employ me; I sing my boss' praises.

   Er weiß ein Lied davon zusingen.

He can tell you all about it; he knows from experience.

   Er sang ein hohes Lied zu ihrem Preis.

He sang her praises; he praised her to the skies.

liegen:
   Daran liegt es gerade.
   Wie die Sache liegt.
   Der Wagen liegt gut auf der Straße.
   Er liegt im Sterben.
   Das Fenster liegt nach Osten.

That's just the point.
As matters stand.
The car sticks to (or stays on) the road.
He's dying.
The window faces east.

liegenlassen:
   Er ließ alles andere stehen und liegen.

He dropped everything; he let everything else go.

Lilie:
   Sie stand da wie eine geknickte Lilie.

She looked like the last rose of summer; she was in the dumps; she looked very forlorn (or dejected).

Lineal:
   Der Mensch hat ein Lineal verschluckt.

He's stiff as a poker; he's very strait-laced.

link:
   Sie sind wohl mit dem linken Fuß zuerst aufgestanden!

You must have gotten up on the wrong side of the bed!; my, but you're grouchy today!

   Er kennt sie wie seine linke Westentasche.

He's got their number; he can read them like a book; he knows them inside out.

links:
   Sie lassen ihn links liegen.

They give him the go-by (or cold shoulder); they snub him.

   Kam Ihr Freund, wie verabredet?—Ja, Scheibe links!

Did your friend come as agreed?—Hell, no!; like fun he did!

Lippe:

Er riskierte eine Lippe.	He had the crust (*or* nerve) to say it.
Die Hörer hingen an seinen Lippen.	The audience hung on his words; he held them spellbound.
Kein Wort soll über meine Lippen kommen.	I'll never breathe a word; I'll keep it a dead secret.

Lob:

Er hascht nach Lob.	He's fishing for compliments.
Seine Führung ist über alles Lob erhaben.	His conduct is beyond reproach.
Es gereicht ihm zum Lob.	It does him credit.

loben:

Gute Ware lobt sich selbst.	Quality speaks for itself; good merchandise sells itself.

Loch:

Er säuft wie ein Loch.	He's a regular tank; he drinks like a fish.
Ich werde ihm schon zeigen, wo der Zimmermann das Loch gelassen hat.	I'll give him the air; I'll show him the door.
Lieber lasse ich mir ein Loch ins Knie bohren, als daß ich das tue.	I'd rather be hung than do that.
Er fragte einem ein Loch in den Bauch.	He asked a thousand and one questions.
Ihre Freundschaft hat ein Loch gekriegt.	Their friendship went on the rocks; they've had a falling-out.
Er lachte sich ein Loch in den Bauch.	He nearly split his sides; he nearly died laughing.
Sie stopfen ein Loch mit dem andern.	They rob Peter to pay Paul.
Er pfeift auf dem letzten Loch.	He's done for; he's on his last legs.
Da pfeift es aus einem andern Loch.	That's a horse of a different color; that's another matter.
Er setzte den Fleck neben das Loch.	He fell short of the mark; he did a poor job.

Locke:

Sie fuhren sich in die Locken.	They got into each other's hair; they quarrelled (*or* had quite an argument).

locker:

Er hat ein lockres Handgelenk.	He swings a wicked left; he has a hard punch.

Lockspitzel:

Er dient der Polizei als Lockspitzel.	He's a stool pigeon (*or* spy) for the police.

Löffel:

Regnet's Brei, fehlt ihm der Löffel.	If it were raining five-dollar gold pieces, he'd be in jail; he's always out when opportunity knocks.
Hau ihm eins hinter die Löffel!	Box his ears for him!
Er tut, als hätte er die Weisheit mit Löffeln gefressen.	He's playing the wise guy (*or* know-it-all).
Er hat sie über den Löffel barbiert.	He gypped (*or* cheated) them.

löffeln:

Er hat es immer noch nicht gelöffelt.	He still doesn't get (*or* grasp) it; it doesn't sink in; he can't see the point.

Lohgerber:

Er stand da wie ein betrübter Lohgerber, dem die Felle fortgeschwommen sind.	He was down in the mouth; he looked very despondent (*or* dejected).

Lohn:
Er zeigte sich bald seines Lohnes wert.

He soon proved himself worth his salt; he earned his keep (*or* pay).

los:
Man los!
Der hat was los.

Let's go!; come on!
He knows his stuff (*or* onions); he knows what he's doing.

Was ist los?
Dort ist immer was los.

What's up (*or* the matter)?
There's always something doing (*or* going on) there.

Mit dem ist nicht viel los.

There isn't much to him; he doesn't amount to much.

Los:
Er hat das große Los gewonnen.

He won first prize; he was very lucky.

losballern:
Baller man los!

Fire away!; shoot!; out with it!

lose:
Sie ist ein loses Mädel.

She's a fast one; she's a hussy (*or* loose liver).

loseisen:
Es hielt schwer, sich von den guten Leuten loszueisen.

It was not easy to tear ourselves away from those nice people.

losgehen:
Donnerwetter! Der geht aber los!

By George, he's going it some!; he sure is going at a pretty clip (*or* pace)!

Jetzt geht's los!

There she goes!; now the fun begins!

losgelassen:
Er war wie losgelassen.

He went to town; he carried on like mad; he was in high spirits.

losgondeln:
Laß uns losgondeln!

Let's get a move on!; let's get going!

loslegen:
Endlich legte er los.

He finally cut loose (*or* got going).

losmachen:
Mach los!

Get going!; come on!; make it snappy!

losschlagen:
Er schlug los und traf ihn ins Gesicht.
Es gelang ihm, die Ware loszuschlagen.

He let loose and hit him in the face.
He was lucky enough to sell (*or* get rid of) the article.

losziehen:
Er zog häßlich gegen sie los.

He railed against them; he pitched into them; he bawled them out.

Lot:
Freunde in der Not gehen hundert auf ein Lot.

A friend in need is a friend indeed; when good cheer is lacking, our friends will be packing.

Die Sache ist wieder im Lot.

It's all right (*or* in order) again.

Löwe:
Er war der Löwe des Tages.

He was the big cheese; he stole the show; he got all the attention.

Luchs:
Er paßt auf wie ein Luchs.

He's watching like a hawk.

Luder:

So ein armes Luder!	Poor wretch!
So ein dummes Luder!	What a dope (*or* dumb bunny)!
Er ist ein feines Luder.	He's a regular Jim Dandy; he's a lady-killer; there's class (*or* style) to him.

Luft:

Er ist Luft für sie.	They pretend he doesn't exist; they simply ignore him.
Die Luft ist rein.	The coast is clear.
Dicke Luft!	Danger ahead!; watch your step!
Jetzt hat er Luft zum Arbeiten.	Now he has elbow room to work in.
Er machte seinem Herzen Luft.	He relieved (*or* took a load off) his mind.
Halt die Luft an!	Save (*or* Don't waste) your breath!; be quiet!
Er war so nachlässig im Dienst, daß man ihn bald an die Luft setzte.	He neglected his work so much that he was soon fired (*or* back on the street).
Das ist aus der Luft gegriffen.	That's a lot of hot air; you made that up; that's a pure invention.
Es hängt ein Pferd in der Luft.	Something's up (*or* in the wind); something's going to happen.
Er ging in die Luft, als er davon hörte.	He blew up (*or* lost his temper) when he heard about it.

Luftikus:

Er ist ein Luftikus.	He's a windbag (*or* giddy fellow).

Lug:

Seine Worte sind nichts als Lug und Trug.	There's not a word of truth in what he says; it's nothing but a pack of lies.

Lüge:

Lügen haben kurze Beine.	Cheaters never prosper; a bad penny always turns up; be sure your sins don't find you out!
Er strafte sie Lügen.	He gave her the lie; he called her a liar.

Lügenbeutel:

Er ist ein alter Lügenbeutel.	He's an old liar.

Lulatsch:

Er ist ein langer Lulatsch.	He's a daddy-long-legs.

Lumig:

Er ist ein großer Lumig.	He's a bad egg (*or* big bum).

lumpen:

Er lumpt wieder mal.	He's gone on another binge (*or* spree); he's dissipating again.
Er ließ sich nicht lumpen.	He went the whole hog; he did it in real style (*or* in a big way); he was no piker (*or* tightwad).

Lumpen:

Er schüttelte ihn tüchtig aus den Lumpen.	He bawled him out soundly.

Lumpensammler:

Sie fuhren mit dem Lumpensammler heim.	They went home in the owl car; they came home with the milkman (*or* at dawn).

Lumperei:

Dort herrſcht eine große Lumperei.

Streitet euch doch nicht wegen einer Lumperei!

Lunge:

Er ſchrie ſich die Lunge aus dem Leib.

Schonen Sie Ihre Lunge!

Lunte:

Er roch Lunte.

Lupe:

Den werde ich mir mal unter die Lupe nehmen.

luſchig:

Er hat luſchig gearbeitet.

Luſt:

Er ſchafft, daß es eine Luſt iſt.
Er hat große Luſt dazu.

luſtig:

Nur immer luſtig!
Er machte ſich darüber luſtig.
Das kann ja luſtig werden!

Er iſt ein luſtiger Bruder.

Things are in a bad way there; it's a bad state of affairs.

Don't scrap over trifles!

He shouted (*or* yelled) at the top of his lungs.

Pipe down!; keep quiet!

He smelled a rat; he got wind of it.

I'll put him through the works; I'll give him a stiff (*or* thorough) examination.

He did a sloppy (*or* poor) job.

It's a real pleasure to see him work.
He's very keen on (doing) it; he feels very much like doing it.

Merry is the word!; keep smiling (*or* going)!
He made fun of it.
That's only the beginning!; that promises to be hot stuff (*or* very exciting)!

He's a jolly good fellow (*or* hail-fellow-well-met); he's a good sort.

Mache:

Der Kampf ist lauter Mache.

> The fight is all a put-up job; it's being staged.

Nehmen Sie ihn mal in die Mache!

> Tell him what's what!; lay down the law to him!

machen:

Mach, daß du fortkommst!

> Scram!; get out of here!; off with you!

Mach, mach!

> Step on it!; get a move on!; hurry up!

Mach's gut!

> Good luck!; good-bye!

Ich mach' ja schon!

> (I'm) coming!

Er macht's nun mal nicht anders.

> That's him all over; that's just his way of doing things.

Er macht es nicht mehr lange.

> He won't last (or live) much longer.

Er macht sich nichts draus.

> He should worry; he doesn't let it bother him.

Sie macht sich gut in dem Kleid.

> She looks well in the dress; it's very becoming to her.

Es macht sich schon.

> It'll all come out in the wash; it's sure to turn out all right.

Was macht das?

> How much is that?; what of it?; who cares?

Das macht nichts.

> That's O.K. (or all right); never mind!

Kommen Sie doch mit!—Nichts zu machen!

> Please come along!—Nothing doing!; not a chance!

Macher:

Er ist der Macher vom Ganzen.

> He's the whole cheese (or show); he's the big shot (or leading man); he runs the show.

mächtig:

Er ist des Deutschen mächtig.

> He knows (or speaks) German.

Made:

Er lebt wie die Made im Käse.

> He's in clover; he's got it soft (or easy).

madig:

Er machte sie madig.

> He slammed (or belittled) her.

Magen:

Er ist seinem Magen keine Stiefmutter.

> He likes a square meal; he doesn't stint on food.

Der Kerl liegt mir im Magen.

> He gives me a pain in the neck; I can't stand the sight of him.

mahlen:

Wer zuerst kommt, mahlt zuerst.

> First come, first served.

Mahlzeit:
  Mahlzeit!
  Proſt (die) Mahlzeit!

  Geſegnete Mahlzeit!

Maikäfer:
  Er iſt vergnügt wie ein Maikäfer.

maikäfern:
  Er maikäfert.

Makulatur:
  Red doch keine Makulatur!

mal:
  Kommen Sie mal her!
  Es iſt nun mal nicht anders.

malen:
  Laß dir was malen!

Malen:
  Das iſt zum Malen.

Malz:
  An dem iſt Hopfen und Malz verloren.

man:
  Man ja nicht!
  Das iſt man wenig.
  Er ſoll's man verſuchen.

mancherlei:
  Er weiß immerhin mancherlei.

mangeln:
  Er läßt es ſich an nichts mangeln.

Mann:
  Selbſt iſt der Mann.

  Wollen Sie nicht den vierten Mann machen?
  Er fand ſeinen Mann.
  Das Geſchäft nährt ſeinen Mann.

  Er ſteht ſeinen Mann.
  Er läßt Gott einen guten Mann ſein.

  Wenn Not an Mann kommt.
  Er brachte ſein Talent an den Mann.

  Er brachte die Ware an den Mann.
  Die Koſten betragen drei Mark auf den Mann.
  Sie ſtanden alle für einen Mann.
  Das Schiff ſank mit Mann und Maus.

Hello!; goodbye!

Try and get it!; nothing doing!; that's a fine how-do-you-do (*or* mess)!

Have a good meal!; I hope you enjoy (*or* enjoyed) your meal.

He's merry as a lark; he's feeling very chipper (*or* spry).

He's thinking up (*or* going to make) a (dinner) speech.

Don't be silly!; stop talking tripe (*or* nonsense)!

Come here, will you?

That's the way of the world; there's nothing to be done about it.

Go to hell!

That's pretty as a picture.

He's a hopeless case; he's beyond help.

By no means!; on the contrary!
That's darned (*or* blessed) little.
Just let him try it!

He knows a thing or two.

He denies himself nothing.

If you want a thing done well, do it yourself!; every man for himself!

Won't you be the fourth hand in this game?

He met his match.
The business yields a good income; it nets a good living.

He stands his ground; he doesn't flinch.
He lets things ride (*or* take their course); he doesn't worry about anything.

In case of need.
He showed his stuff (*or* metal); he showed what he could do.

He found a purchaser for his commodity.
The cost is three marks a head.

They stood up for one another.
The ship went down with all hands on board.

Männerchen:
Sie sehen wohl die Männerchen! | You must have bats in your belfry!; you must be seeing things!

Manschette:
Er hat Manschetten vor ihr. | He's afraid of her.

Mantel:
Er dreht den Mantel nach dem Wind. | He watches to see which way the wind blows; he's an opportunist.

Er trägt den Mantel auf beiden Schultern. | He's a handshaker (*or* yes-man); he's on both sides of the fence; he's two-faced.

Er hüllt sich in den Mantel der gekränkten Unschuld. | He puts on an air of injured innocence (*or* righteous indignation).

Mäntelchen:
Er will der Sache ein Mäntelchen umhängen. | He wants to hush up (*or* make light of) the incident; he's trying to smooth it over.

Märchen:
Erzählen Sie keine Märchen! | No spoofing (*or* fooling)!; don't tell us any yarns (*or* fish stories)!

Mark:
Er hat Mark in den Knochen. | He's got brawn (*or* guts); he's a horse (*or* husky fellow).

Der Schreck ging ihr durch Mark und Bein. | Her hair stood on end; she was scared to death.

Marke:
Ist das eine Marke! | What a funny bird!; there's something for your collection!

Markstein:
Das Erlebnis ist ein Markstein seines Lebens. | The experience marks a turning point in his life.

Markt:
Jeder muß seine Haut zu Markte tragen. | Every man (must look out) for himself; no one can fight your battles for you.

marsch:
Marsch, fort! | Away with you!

Marsch:
Er blies ihnen den Marsch. | He called them on the carpet; he gave them a piece of his mind.

Maß:
Das Maß ist erschöpft. | That's the limit (*or* last straw); that's more than enough.

Wenn das Maß voll ist, läuft es über. | When the well is full, it will run over; too much is too much.

Er kann weder Maß noch Ziel halten. | He knows no bounds; he can't control himself.

massenhaft:
Haben Sie genug Bleistifte?—Ja, massenhaft! | Have you pencils enough?—Yes, slews (*or* piles) of them.

maßgebend:

Sein Urteil ist für sie nicht maßgebend.

His opinion cuts no ice (*or* doesn't rate) with her; she puts no stock in it; she doesn't respect it.

Er ist eine maßgebende Persönlichkeit.

He's a big shot; he's a man of influence (*or* authority); his opinions carry great weight.

Mäßigkeitsapostel:

Er ist ein überzeugter Mäßigkeitsapostel.

He's on the water wagon; he's a confirmed teetotaler.

maßlos:

Er war maßlos wütend.

He was madder than a wet hen; he was simply furious.

Matthäi:

Bei ihm ist Matthäi am letzten.

He's down to his last cent.

Mit ihm ist es Matthäi am letzten.

He's a goner; he's beyond help.

Mätzchen:

Machen Sie keine Mätzchen!

Don't be funny!

mau:

Die Arbeit ist man mau.

The work isn't so hot (*or* good); it's a poor job.

Maul:

Alle Mäuler sind voll davon.

It's common talk; it's the talk of the town.

Halt's Maul!

Hang up!; shut your trap!

Er sperrte das Maul auf.

He gaped; he was dumfounded (*or* flabbergasted).

Er hat das Maul auf dem rechten Fleck.

He always has a snappy comeback (*or* ready answer); he's quick at repartee.

Er läßt das Maul hängen.

He's down in the mouth; he's dejected.

Er nahm das Maul voll.

He had a big mouth; he blew off steam; he bragged.

Er kann sich das Maul wischen.

He can whistle for it; he's left holding the bag; he got nothing for his trouble.

Hast du kein Maul?

Can't you speak?

Sie zog ein schiefes Maul.

She made a wry face; she looked dissatisfied (*or* offended).

Er ist nicht aufs Maul gefallen.

He's got the gift of gab; he always has a comeback (*or* ready answer).

Glauben Sie etwa, die gebratenen Tauben fliegen Ihnen ins Maul?

Do you think fortune will come to you in your sleep (*or* be handed to you on a silver platter)?

Er redet, wie es ihm ins Maul kommt.

He always says the first thing that comes into his mind.

Man muß ihm alles erst ins Maul schmieren.

He always has to be coached (*or* prompted).

Er kann alles mit dem Maul.

To hear him talk you'd think he knew everything.

Er ist immer vorweg mit dem Maul.

He has a loose tongue; he's fresh; he talks too much.

Er redet jedem nach dem Maul.

He's a yes-man (*or* parrot); he agrees with everyone.

Sie fuhren ihm übers Maul.

They squelched (*or* silenced) him.

Er schmierte ihr Honig ums Maul.

He soft-soaped her; he wheedled her.

Maulaffe:
Er hielt Maulaffen feil.

He stood there gaping (*or* loafing).

maulen:
Er muß immer erst maulen, ehe er's tut.

He always crabs (*or* complains) before doing it.

Maulspitzen:
Da hilft kein Maulspitzen, es muß gepfiffen werden.

There's no use mincing matters—out with it!; it's no use making a face—it's got to be done!

Maulwerk:
Er hat ein gutes Maulwerk.

He's got a big mouth (*or* the gift of gab); he can talk you deaf, dumb, and blind.

Maulwurf:
Er schläft wie ein Maulwurf.

He sleeps like a log (*or* top).

Maus:
Das ist Maus wie Mutter.

That's six of one and half a dozen of the other; it's all the same.

Das trägt die Maus auf dem Schwanz fort.

That's a mere drop in the bucket; that's very (*or* precious) little.

Da beißt keine Maus den Faden ab.

That's dead sure (*or* final).

Er lebt wie die Mäuse in der Speckseite.

He's in clover; he's on Easy Street; he's living off the fat of the land!

Das ist den Mäusen gepfiffen.

That's a waste of time.

Mit Speck fängt man Mäuse.

Good bait catches fine fish.

Er hat dicke Mäuse.

He has plenty of dough (*or* money).

Das Schiff sank mit Mann und Maus.

The ship went down with all hands on board.

mauscheln:
Mauschel doch nicht so!

Don't talk (*or* act) like a Jew!

Mausen:
Die Katze läßt das Mausen nicht.

What's bred in the bone will come out in the flesh; you can't change human nature.

mausetot:
Diese Auffassung ist mausetot.

This theory is dead as a doornail; it's obsolete.

mausig:
Mach dich nicht so mausig!

Don't be so snooty (*or* uppish)!; none of your airs, please!

Mäuslein:
Daß dich das Mäuslein beiß!

The deuce take you!; go to blazes!

meckern:
Wie der Mensch meckert!

What a horse laugh he has!

Er hat immer was zu meckern.

He's always kicking (*or* complaining) about something.

Meer:
Er hat Schulden wie Sand am Meer.

He's up to his ears in debt.

Meergreis:
Er ist ein Meergreis.

He's a has-been; he's an old fogey (*or* old timer).

mehr:
Er tut es nicht mehr wie gern.

He's only too glad to do it.

Kein Wort mehr!

Not another word!

Und dergleichen mehr.	And the like; and so forth.
Er iſt nicht mehr.	He's dead and gone.
Er iſt kein Kind mehr.	He's no longer a child.
Wer noch mehr?	Who else?
Mehr:	
Er gewann mit einem Mehr von zehn Stimmen.	He won by a majority of ten votes.
mein:	
Ei du mein!	My word!; goodness me!
Er hat mein und dein verwechſelt.	He stole.
meinen:	
Wie meinten Sie?	What did you say?; Sir?
Das will ich meinen.	You bet!; I'll say!; I should say so!
Meinung:	
Er ſagte ihr ſeine Meinung.	He gave her a piece of his mind.
Meiſe:	
Da kannſt du Meiſen ausnehmen.	That won't help; it's a waste of time.
Meiſter:	
Er konnte ſeiner Gefühle nicht Meiſter werden.	He couldn't keep himself in hand (*or* under control); he was unable to restrain his feelings.
Übung macht den Meiſter.	Practice makes perfect.
Er fand ſeinen Meiſter.	He met his match.
melden:	
Bei ihm meldet ſich ſchon das Alter.	He's getting old; he's beginning to show signs of age.
Wen darf ich melden?	What name shall I give?; who shall I say is calling?
Menge:	
Er hat Geld die Menge.	He has piles of money.
mengen:	
Mengen Sie ſich nicht in dieſe Angelegenheiten!	You keep out of this!; this is no affair of yours!
Menkenke:	
Was koſtet die ganze Menkenke?	How much for the whole caboodle (*or* business)?
Mach doch keine Menkenken!	Don't make such a fuss!; don't be funny!
Menſch:	
Sein äußerer Menſch ſieht heruntergekommen aus.	He looks shabby (*or* down at the heel).
Sein ganzer Menſch war ergriffen.	He was thrilled to pieces; he was in ecstasies.
Er hat den alten Menſchen abgelegt.	He turned over a new leaf.
Er hat Knigges „Umgang mit Menſchen" nicht geleſen.	He's never read Emily Post; he has no manners (*or* breeding).
menſchenmöglich:	
Iſt das menſchenmöglich?	For crying out loud!; can it be true?; is it possible?
Menſchenskind:	
Menſchenskind, was haben Sie angeſtellt?	Man alive (*or* My dear fellow), what have you done?

menſchlich:

Das Wetter war einigermaßen menſchlich.	The weather was tolerable.

Menſchliches:

Wenn ihm was Menſchliches zuſtößt.	If anything unforeseen should happen to him.

merken:

Merken Sie ſich! Ich will nichts wieder davon hören!	Now mind you, I don't want to hear about it again!
Er merkt was.	He smells a rat; he suspects something.
Man merkt, daß er lügt.	It's plain that he's lying.
Er ließ ſich nichts merken.	He looked unconcerned (*or* nonchalant).

meſchugge:

Sie ſind wohl meſchugge!	Are you bugs (*or* crazy)?

meſſen:

Sie maß ihn mit verächtlichen Blicken.	She eyed him disdainfully.
Sie kann ſich mit ihm nicht meſſen.	She's no match for him.

Meſſer:

Das Meſſer ſitzt ihm an der Kehle.	He's got a rope around his neck; he's in a bad fix (*or* jam).
Der Vorſchlag iſt ein Meſſer ohne Heft und Klinge.	The suggestion doesn't hold water; it's impracticable (*or* useless).
Die Entſcheidung ſtand auf des Meſſers Schneide.	The decision was hanging fire (*or* in the balance); it was a critical (*or* crucial) moment.
Er gab ſeinem Feind das Meſſer in die Hand.	He cut his own throat; he gave himself into his enemy's hands.
Er führte das große Meſſer.	He put on a big show; he was bragging (*or* showing off).
Auf dieſem Meſſer kann man nach Rom reiten.	This surely is a dull knife; you couldn't cut hot butter with it.

Meter:

Es koſtet drei Meter.	The price is three marks.

Methode:

Er hat ſo ſeine Methode.	He's got his own system (*or* way of doing things).

Methuſalem:

Er iſt ſo alt wie Methuſalem.	He's as old as the hills.

Metzgergang:

Er hat einen Metzgergang gemacht.	He went on a wild-goose chase (*or* useless errand).

mickerig:

Sie iſt noch recht mickerig.	She's still wobbly (*or* weak in the knees).

miemerig:

Du biſt wohl miemerig!	Are you nuts (*or* crazy)?

Miene:

Er machte Miene, es zu tun.	He threatened to do it.
Er machte gute Miene zum böſen Spiel.	He played the game; he grinned and bore it; he made the best of it.
Er tat es, ohne eine Miene zu verziehen.	He did it without wincing (*or* flinching).

mies:

Seine Sache ſteht mies.	The odds are against him.

Miefepeter:
Er ift ein Miefepeter.

He's a softy (*or* weakling); he's a sourpuss (*or* crank).

Miesmacher:
Er ift ein rechter Miesmacher.

He's a regular calamity howler; he's a pessimist.

Milch:
Sie fieht aus wie Milch und Blut.

She looks like peaches and cream; she looks blooming (*or* very healthy).

Er hat nicht viel in die Milch zu brocken.

He has but a small income.

Milchbart:
Er ift noch ein Milchbart.

He's still wet behind his ears; he's nothing but a child.

milchend:
Er ift doch keine milchende Kuh.

He's not a gold mine after all; it's useless trying to mulct him because he hasn't any money.

Milchmädchenrechnung:
Das ift die reinfte Milchmädchenrechnung.

That is just a shot in the dark; that's pure guesswork.

Mimik:
Das ift aber eine dumme Mimik!

That's a nice how-do-you-do!; what a situation (*or* predicament)!

mimen:
Das haben Sie ganz verkehrt gemimt.

You did that all wrong.

mindeftens:
Kommen Sie doch mit!—Mindeftens!

Do come along, please!—Not a chance!; nothing doing!

Mine:
Er ließ alle Minen springen.

He left no stone unturned; he moved heaven and earth; he tried every possible means.

minus:
Wie kamen Sie bei dem Gefchäft davon? —Plus minus null!

How did you make out in this deal?—I just broke even.

Minute:
Es ift fünf Minuten vor zwölf.
Es klappte auf die Minute.

It's high time.
It was perfectly timed; it worked perfectly (*or* like a charm).

mir:
Er kam mir nichts, dir nichts herein.

He dropped in cool as a cucumber (*or* quite nonchalantly).

Heute mir, morgen dir.

Every dog has his day; everyone in his turn; we must all die someday.

Wie du mir, so ich dir.

Tit for tat; an eye for an eye, a tooth for a tooth; I'll treat you to some of your own medicine.

Mißgeburt:
Die Überfetzung ift eine wahre Mißgeburt.

The translation is a monstrosity (*or* fright).

mißlich:
Es fteht mißlich um ihn.

He's in a very bad way; things look very bad for him.

Mist:

Verfluchter Mist! — Dash it all!; doggone it!

Er hat Geld wie Mist. — He has money to burn.

Er weiß einen Mist. — He doesn't know beans (*or* a thing).

Haben Sie je solchen Mist gehört? — Did you ever hear such a line (*or* lingo)?; did you ever hear such tripe (*or* trash)?

Das ist nicht auf seinem Mist gewachsen. — That's not his doing; you can't put that at his door; he can't be blamed for that.

Mistfink:

So ein Mistfink! — What a sloppy (*or* messy) fellow!; he's so uncouth!

mit:

Er ging mit fünf Jahren zur Schule. — He went to school at the age of five.

Das gehört mit dazu. — That belongs to (*or* goes with) it; that's included (in it).

Da kann ich nicht mit. — That's beyond me (*or* out of my reach); I can't do such things; I can't afford that.

Du kannst mit. — You can come along.

mitbringen:

Sie hat nichts mitgebracht. — She had no dowry when she married.

mitgehen:

Der Verkäufer ließ manches mitgehen. — The clerk embezzled (*or* stole) at every turn.

mitgenommen:

Sie sahen mitgenommen aus. — They looked fagged (*or* worn) out.

mitkommen:

Der Junge kommt in der Schule nicht recht mit. — The boy can't catch up with the rest of the class; he can't quite make the grade.

mitmachen:

Sie macht alles mit. — She's a good sport (*or* scout); she coöperates with everyone.

Wenn es einer tut, machen die andern mit. — It's a case of follow the leader; if one does it, the others will follow suit.

Er muß immer alles mitmachen. — He joins every parade; he goes in for (*or* takes part in) everything.

mitreden:

Er hat auch noch ein Wort mitzureden. — He's also entitled to his say; he should be granted a hearing with the rest.

mitspielen:

Man hat ihm übel mitgespielt. — They took him for an awful ride; he was badly mussed (*or* maltreated).

Mittagstisch:

Dort gibt es einen gut bürgerlichen Mittagstisch. — You can get a good plain meal there.

Mittel:

Hier gibt's kein andres Mittel. — There's nothing else to be done in this case; it's the only solution.

Er erhält sich aus eigenen Mitteln. — He's on his own; he's independent.

Er schlug sich ins Mittel. — He acted as a go-between.

mitten:

Der Schi brach mitten entzwei. — The ski broke in two.

Es ging ihm mitten durchs Herz. — It cut him to the quick; it hurt him deeply.

mittenmang:
 Er ist immer mittenmang.

He's always Johnny-on-the-spot; he's always in the thick of the fray (*or* crowd); he's always on hand when something's doing.

Möbel:
 Sie ist ein altes, treues Möbel in unsrer Familie.

She's a permanent fixture (*or* faithful servant) in our family.

möbliert:
 Sie haben einen möblierten Herrn.

They've a star boarder (*or* roomer).

Mode:
 Das ist so seine Mode.
 Das wäre eine neue Mode!

 Er muß immer mit der Mode gehen.

That's him all over; that's his way.
That would be something indeed!; nothing doing!; none of that!
He always follows the crowd; he keeps up with all the latest fads.

Modenarr:
 Er ist ein rechter Modenarr.

He's the last word when it comes to dress; he's a regular fashion plate.

mögen:
 Was ich auch tun mag, es ist ihr nie recht.
 Was mag er dazu sagen?
 Er mochte nicht weiter darüber sprechen.
 Man möchte verrückt werden.
 Daraus möchte wohl nichts werden.

No matter what I do, I can never please her.
I wonder what he'll say to that?
He didn't care to discuss it further.
It's enough to drive one bats (*or* mad).
It's not likely that anything will come of that; it probably won't materialize.

Möglichkeit:
 Ist es die Möglichkeit?

You don't say so!; can it be true?; is it possible?

Möglichstes:
 Tun Sie Ihr Möglichstes!

Do your best (*or* utmost)!

Mohikaner:
 Er gab den letzten der Mohikaner aus.

He spent his last cent.

Mohr:
 Er wollte einen Mohren waschen.

He tried the impossible.

Molle:
 Es goß wie mit Mollen.

The rain came down in sheets (*or* torrents).

mollig:
 Sie ist ein molliges Frauchen.

She's a roly-poly; she's round and rosy; she's chubby (*or* plump).

Mond:
 So ein trauriger Mond!

 Der ist auch drei Meilen hinterm Mond.

 Das sind Schlösser, die im Mond liegen.
 Da kann er in den Mond gucken.

 Ihre Uhr geht wohl nach dem Mond!

What a bore (*or* slowpoke)!; what a bungler (*or* clumsy fellow)!
He's way behind the times; he's very old-fashioned.
Those are pipe dreams (*or* castles in the air).
He can whistle for it; he's sure to get left; he'll not get a thing for his trouble.
Your watch is screwy!; it can't be trusted!

Mondschein:
Er hat bereits einen mächtigen Mond= schein.

He's already very bald.

Der kann mir im Mondschein begegnen.

He can go to hell, for all I care; I'll see him in hell first.

Moos:
Er hat viel Moos.

He has plenty of jack (*or* money).

mopsen:
Er hat sich fürchterlich gemopst.

He was bored to tears (*or* death).

Jemand hat seinen Schlips gemopst.

Somebody swiped (*or* snatched) his tie.

Das wird ihn sehr mopsen.

That will make him very sore (*or* angry).

Moralfatze:
Er ist ein rechter Moralfatze.

He's a regular Boy Scout (*or* goody-goody).

moralisch:
Der Bericht stellt eine moralische Brun= nenvergiftung dar.

The report deliberately misrepresents the facts; it has no foundation in fact and is nothing but a malicious invention.

Moralische:
Er hatte einen Moralischen.

He had a bad conscience; his conscience bothered him.

Mördergrube:
Er machte aus seinem Herzen keine Mördergrube.

He made no bones about it; he was very outspoken.

mörderisch:
Er legte ein mörderisches Tempo vor.

He went at breakneck speed.

mörderlich:
Er fluchte ganz mörderlich.

He swore bloody murder (*or* like a trooper); he cursed heaven and earth.

Mordsangst:
Er hat eine Mordsangst davor.

He has a holy horror of it; he's scared stiff.

Mordsdusel:
Er entwickelte einen Mordsdusel.

He had all the breaks; he was a lucky dog.

Mordskerl:
Er ist ein Mordskerl.

He's a devil of a fellow; he's a crackajack.

mordsmäßig:
Es regnete mordsmäßig.

It rained to beat the band (*or* like fury).

Mordsradau:
Er machte einen Mordsradau, als er davon erfuhr.

He raised hell (*or* a hue and cry) when he learned about it.

Mores:
Ich werde ihn schon Mores lehren.

I'll make him toe the mark; I'll teach him manners (*or* how to behave).

morgen:
Heute mir, morgen dir.

Every dog has his day; everyone in his turn; we must all die someday.

Das läßt sich nicht von heut' auf morgen tun.

Rome was not built in a day; that takes time.

Morgen:
Auf einen trüben Morgen folgt ein heitrer Tag.

Rain before seven, clear before eleven; every cloud has a silver lining.

Morgenluft:
    Er witterte Morgenluft.

He was quick to spot (*or* sense) his advantage.

Morgenstunde:
    Morgenstunde hat Gold im Munde.

The early bird catches the worm; make hay while the sun shines.

Moses:
    Sie haben Moses und die Propheten.

They have what it takes; they've got plenty of dough (*or* money).

Most:
    Der weiß, wo Barthel den Most holt.

He's wise; he's been backstage (*or* around); he knows a thing or two.

Motte:
    Da sind die Motten hereingekommen.
    Du hast die Motten!
    Man hat ihm tüchtig die Motten aus dem Pelz geklopft.
    Du kriegst die Motten!

There's a hitch (*or* catch) somewhere.
You've got funny ideas (*or* queer notions)!
He got a good sound thrashing.

Did you ever!; well, I never!; of all the nerve!; the idea!

    Daß du die Motten kriegst!

Go to the devil!

Muck:
    Er konnte nicht mal mehr „Muck" sagen.

He couldn't even say "boo"; he was speechless.

    Er hat keinen Muck.

He has no guts (*or* spunk); he's yellow (*or* afraid).

Mucke:
    Mit Geduld und Spucke fängt man eine Mucke.
    Er hat Mucken.
    Die Sache hat ihre Mucken.

Everything comes to him who waits!; keep up the good work—you'll get there yet!
He's bats (*or* queer); he's got notions.
There's a hitch to it; it's not so easy as it looks.

Mücke:
    Er macht aus einer Mücke einen Elefanten.

    Man muß nicht nach jeder Mücke schlagen.

He's always making mountains out of molehills; he makes much ado about nothing.
Don't take everything so seriously!

Muckel:
    Na, kleiner Muckel!

Well, sonny (boy)!; well, my little man!

mucken:
    Er tut alles, ohne zu mucken.

He does what he's told without a murmur; he never balks (*or* complains).

Mückenfett:
    Man hat ihn nach Mückenfett geschickt.

They sent him on a fool's errand.

mucksen:
    Mucks dich nicht!

Just you sit tight!; stay put!; don't you budge (*or* move)!

muddelig:
    Es ist eine muddelige Arbeit.

It's a messy (*or* dirty) job.

Mühe:
    Es ist nicht der Mühe wert.
    Der eine hat die Mühe, der andre schöpft die Brühe.

It isn't worth while; never mind!
One man does all the work so the other fellow can have all the fun.

Geben Sie sich keine Mühe! — Don't put yourself out!; don't bother!

Er schaffte es mit Müh' und Not. — He did it with great difficulty; it cost him great effort.

Mühle:

Ihre Mühle steht nie still. — Her tongue is loose at both ends; it rattles incessantly.

Das ist Wasser auf seine Mühle. — That's grist to his mill; that's a feather in his cap; that's just the thing for him.

Er richtet alle Wasser auf seine Mühle. — He's a big goop; he hogs the road; he wants everything for himself.

Das ist noch in der Mühle. — That's still pending (*or* in the air); it hasn't been settled yet.

Mulde:

Es regnete wie mit Mulden. — It rained cats and dogs; it poured for dear life.

Müllerknecht:

Die Müllerknechte schlagen sich. — It's snowing hard.

Müllerschlaf:

Er schläft einen Müllerschlaf. — He sleeps like a log (*or* top); he sleeps very soundly.

mulmig:

Die Sache kommt mir mulmig vor. — It looks fishy (*or* phoney) to me.

Mumm:

Er hat keinen Mumm. — He's a softy; he has no guts (*or* spunk); he's yellow (*or* afraid).

Sie hat keinen rechten Mumm dazu. — She doesn't feel like (doing) it; she lacks the urge (*or* inclination) to do so.

Mummelgreis:

Er ist ein rechter Mummelgreis. — He's a real has-been; he's an old fogy (*or* old-timer).

Mumpitz:

Das ist alles Mumpitz. — That's all humbug (*or* bosh); that's all stuff and nonsense.

Mund:

Er sperrte Mund und Nase auf. — He gaped; he was dumbfounded (*or* flabbergasted).

Tun Sie doch den Mund auf! — Louder!; speak up!

Er läßt den Mund hängen. — He's down in the mouth; he's dejected.

Er redete sich den Mund fusselig. — He was talking his ear off; he talked himself deaf, dumb, and blind.

Man verbot ihm den Mund. — He was shut up (*or* silenced); he was deprived of his voice in the matter.

Verbrennen Sie sich nicht den Mund damit! — Look out that you don't get yourself into hot water!

Sie verzog den Mund. — She pouted (*or* made a face).

Er nahm den Mund gehörig voll. — He talked big; he bragged.

Er darf sich den Mund wischen. — He can whistle for it; he's left holding the bag; he has nothing for it but his trouble.

Er hielt reinen Mund. — He didn't blab; he kept mum; he kept it secret.

Sie ist nicht auf den Mund gefallen. — She always has a snappy (*or* ready) comeback; she's never at a loss for an answer.

Er legte den Finger auf den Mund.	He motioned for silence.
Sie mußten ihm ein Pechpflaster auf den Mund legen.	They cut him short (*or* shut him up); they forced him to keep quiet.
Er war wie auf den Mund geschlagen.	He was struck dumb with amazement; he was simply speechless.
Sie antworteten alle wie aus einem Mund.	They answered as one man.
Er hat es aus ihrem eignen Mund.	He has it from her own lips; she herself told him.
Morgenstunde hat Gold im Munde.	The early bird catches the worm; make hay while the sun shines.
Sie drehte ihm die Worte im Mund herum.	She misconstrued his words.
Er brachte sich in den Mund der Leute.	He became the talk of the town.
Sie legte ihm die Worte in den Mund.	She told him what to say; she gave him an idea of what to say.
Er ist immer mit dem Mund vorneweg.	He always talks out of turn; he's very fresh.
Er redet einem immer nach dem Mund.	He's a mealy-mouthed fellow; he's a yes-man; he agrees with everyone.
Sie fuhren ihm über den Mund.	They squelched (*or* silenced) him.
Sie sparen es sich vom Mund ab.	They save it on food.
Sein Unglück ging von Mund zu Mund.	His hard luck was common talk.
Er nahm ihm das Brot vor dem Mund weg.	He cooked his goose (*or* hash); he killed (*or* ruined) his chances.
Er hat ein Schloß vor dem Mund.	He shuts up like a clam; he's very close-mouthed (*or* reserved).
Er nahm kein Blatt vor den Mund.	He didn't mince matters; he was very plain-spoken (*or* crude).

mundgerecht:

Man hat es ihm mundgerecht gemacht.	They made it easy for him; they adapted it to his taste.

mundtot:

Er ließ sich nicht mundtot machen.	He wouldn't be silenced.

Mundwerk:

Er hat ein gutes Mundwerk.	He's got a big mouth; he's got the gift of gab; he can talk like a politician.

munkeln:

Man munkelt schon lange davon.	It has long been rumored.

Münze:

Er nimmt alles für bare Münze.	He takes everything literally (*or* at face value); he takes it all for Gospel truth.
Er läßt sich sein Können in klingende Münze umsetzen.	He capitalizes (*or* cashes in) on his talent; he exploits it.

mürbe:

Er wird ihn schon mürbe machen.	He'll get (*or* wear) him down; he'll bring him around; he'll make him docile (*or* pliable).

Murmeltier:

Er schläft wie ein Murmeltier.	He sleeps like a log (*or* dead person).

Mus:

Sie hat ihm das Mus versalzen.	She queered (*or* fixed) him all right; she spoiled his fun.
Er hieb den Burschen zu Mus.	He beat that man to a pulp.

Muse:
Die leicht geschürzte Muse beherrschte das Programm. — The program consisted mainly of vaudeville.

Musik:
Da ist Musik drin! — Attaboy!; that's the stuff (*or* way)!; keep up the good work!

Er zog ohne Musik ab. — He took French leave; he left without a word.

Musikant:
Da liegt ein Musikant begraben! — There's the rub!; that's where the shoe pinches (*or* trouble lies)!

müssen:
Er muß wohl daheim sein. — I imagine he's at home.

Muß der Teufel den Menschen auch gerade jetzt herführen! — Why the Sam Hill does he have to show up just now?; he would have to come here now!

Es müßte denn sein, daß er kommt. — Unless he should decide to come.

mustergültig:
Sie benahmen sich mustergültig. — They were on their best behavior; they behaved perfectly.

Mut:
Nur Mut, die Sache wird schon schiefgehen! — Chin up (*or* Don't lose heart), it'll turn out all right!

Als man ihn zur Rede stellte, sank ihm der Mut. — When it came to a showdown, he showed the white feather; he turned tails (*or* capitulated) when he was taken to account.

Mütchen:
Sie versuchten, an ihm ihr Mütchen zu kühlen. — They tried to take it out (*or* vent their anger) on him.

Mutige:
Dem Mutigen gehört die Welt. — Faint heart never won fair lady; fortune favors the brave.

mutmaßlich:
Eine mutmaßliche Berechnung ergab das. — A rough estimate showed that.

Mutter:
Das ist Maus wie Mutter. — That's six of one and half a dozen of the other; it's all the same.

Vorsicht ist die Mutter der Porzellankiste. — An ounce of prevention is worth a pound of cure; a stitch in time saves nine.

Er hat's dort wie bei Muttern. — He's very much at home there.
Sie schliefen bei Mutter Grün. — They slept out of doors (*or* in the open).

Mutterleib:
Er ist so unschuldig wie ein Kind im Mutterleib. — He's innocent as a lamb (*or* babe in arms).

Muttermilch:
Das sollten Sie doch mit der Muttermilch eingesogen haben! — I thought that was second nature to you!

mutterseelenallein:
Er ist mutterseelenallein. — He's all alone (in the world); he hasn't a friend to his name.

Muttersöhnchen:

Er ist das richtige Muttersöhnchen. | He's a mama's boy (*or* darling); he's a spoiled child.

Mütze:

Er hat eins auf die Mütze gekriegt. | He was bawled out (*or* called down); he got a box on the ear.

Das geht ihm ganz nach der Mütze. | That suits him to a T; it suits him fine.

na:

Na!

Na?

Na alfo!

Na ja, ich weiß fchon, aber lieber wäre es
mir doch, wenn . . . .

Na nu!

Na und?

Na und ob!

nach:

Nach meiner Meinung hat er recht.

Es ist zehn nach feiner Uhr.

Er befucht fie nach wie vor.

nacharbeiten:

Er muß die ganze Sache nacharbeiten.

nachbeten:

Er betet alles nach, was andere fagen.

nachdenken:

Denk mal fcharf nach!

nacherzählt:

Dem Schwedifchen nacherzählt.

nachfühlen:

Das kann ich Ihnen nachfühlen.

nachgeben:

Gib nicht nach!

Sie gibt ihm kaum etwas nach.

nachgehen:

Die Sache geht ihm nach.

nachgerade:

Es ist nachgerade Zeit.

Er wird uns nachgerade unangenehm.

nachgetan:

Beffer vorbedacht als nachgetan.

nachhängen:

Häng doch der Sache nicht mehr nach!

Well!; come now!; no!; you don't say so!

Well?; are you coming?; how about it?;
what do you say?

That's the boy!; there you are!; didn't I
tell you?

Yes, I know, but still I'd rather . . . .

Really?; well, I never!; what have we here?;
what's this I hear?; so that's the story!

So what?; is that all?; what happened then?

I should say!; and how!; you bet!

In my opinion he's right.

It's ten by his watch.

He comes to see them as usual.

He has to work (*or* do) it all over.

He's nothing but a parrot; he merely re-
peats the words (*or* opinions) of others.

Try and think back!; think hard and see if
it'll come to you!

Adapted from the Swedish.

I can sympathize with you; I can well understand that.

Keep up the fight!; don't give in!

She's almost as good at it as he is.

He can't put (*or* get) it out of his mind; he
can't forget about it.

Indeed, it's high time.

He's getting on our nerves more and more.

An ounce of prevention is worth a pound
of cure; a stitch in time saves nine.

Don't dwell on the subject any more!; skip
(*or* forget) it!

nachlassen:
Nicht nachlassen! | Never say die!; don't give up!

nachmachen:
Das mach einer mal nach! | Who can beat that?; I'd like to see anyone do better (*or* as well)!

Nachnahme:
Hier ist eine Nachnahme für Sie. | Here's a C.O.D. (=Charge on Delivery) package for you.

nachsagen:
Das dürfen Sie sich nicht nachsagen lassen. | Don't let that be said about you!

nachschießen:
Er schoß einen weitern Betrag nach. | He made another down-payment; he invested more money.

nachschlagen:
Sie schlägt in ihrem Äußern der Mutter nach. | In looks (*or* appearance) she takes after her mother.

nachsehen:
Er sieht ihr vieles nach. | He makes many allowances for her; he overlooks (*or* closes an eye to) many of her faults.

Wollen Sie nachsehen, ob jemand da ist? | Will you go and see if somebody is there?

Nachsehen:
Er hat das Nachsehen. | He's left holding the bag; he can whistle for it; he has nothing for it but his trouble.

nachsenden:
Bitte nachsenden! (auf Briefen) | Please forward! (*referring to letters*).

Nachsicht:
Vorsicht ist besser als Nachsicht. | An ounce of prevention is worth a pound of cure; a stitch in time saves nine.

Nachspiel:
Das geht nicht ohne Nachspiel ab. | We haven't heard the last of it; this isn't the end of the story; there'll be an aftermath.

nächst:
Schreiben Sie bei nächster Gelegenheit! | Write at your earliest opportunity!
Er kommt nächster Tage. | He'll come one of these days.

Nächste:
Jeder ist sich selbst der Nächste. | Charity begins at home; every man for himself.

Ein Teil der Unterhaltung drehte sich um den lieben Nächsten. | A part of the conversation dealt with local gossip.

nachstehend:
Wie nachstehend ausgeführt. | As mentioned below.

Nacht:
Es wurde ihr Nacht vor den Augen. | Everything turned black before her eyes; she fainted.

Sie ist häßlich wie die Nacht. | She's ugly as sin.
Er hat sich die Nacht um die Ohren geschlagen. | He stayed up all night; he got practically no sleep.
Er kommt von einem Ort, wo sich Fuchs und Hase gute Nacht sagen. | He comes from Hickville (*or* the sticks); he's from the country.
Er verschwand bei Nacht und Nebel. | He disappeared in the dead (*or* under cover) of night.

Nachtigall:

Nachtigall, ich hör dir laufen! | Oh, I see!; now I get you!

Was dem einen fin (= fein') Uhl (= Eule) ift, ift dem andern fin Nachtigall. | One man's meat is another man's poison.

Er will die Nachtigall fingen lehren. | He wants to tell the boss how to run his business; he thinks he knows it all.

nachtragen:

Er trägt es Ihnen nicht nach. | He doesn't hold it against you.

nachtfchlafend:

Er kam zu nachtfchlafender Zeit. | He came in the middle of the night.

nachtun:

Wer kann ihm das nachtun? | Who can beat that?; can anyone do as well?

Nacken:

Sie müssen ihm den Nacken steifen. | You must help him keep a stiff upper lip; you must hearten (or encourage) him.

Er fetzte ihm den Fuß auf den Nacken. | He stepped on him; he made him toe the mark; he put him in his place.

Er hat den Schelm im Nacken fitzen. | He's a big tease; he's full of fun.

Die Verfolger faßen ihm im Nacken. | His persecutors were hot on his trail; they were close upon him.

Er warf den Kopf in den Nacken. | He threw back his head.

Nackenschlag:

Er erhielt schwere geschäftliche Nacken= schläge. | He suffered severe financial reverses.

nackt:

Sie haben Mühe, das nackte Leben zu friften. | They can hardly keep the wolf from the door; they barely make ends meet.

Nadel:

Es konnte keine Nadel zur Erde. | People stood sleeve to sleeve; there wasn't room to breathe.

Er fuchte es wie eine Nadel. | He looked for it everywhere; he searched high and low.

Er hat bei mir noch etwas auf der Nadel. | I'll get even with him; he has it coming to him from me.

Nadelftich:

Seine Worte waren scharf wie Nadelftiche. | His words cut like a knife.

Nagel:

Er hat einen Nagel. | He has a pretty good opinion of himself; he's a conceited ass.

Er läßt Nägel auf fich fpitzen. | He takes (or puts up with) everything.

Er hat feinen Beruf an den Nagel ge= hängt. | He gave up his job; he quit (or resigned); he retired.

Die Arbeit brennt ihm auf den Nägeln. | He's being driven (or rushed) on the job; it's a rush job.

nagelfeft:

Die Diebe nahmen mit, was nicht niet= und nagelfeft war. | The thieves took along everything but the fixtures; they cleaned out the place.

nagelneu:

Er hatte einen nagelneuen Hut auf. | He had on a brand-new hat.

Nagelprobe:

Er trank fein Glas bis auf die Nagelprobe aus. | He drained his glass; he drank it down to the last drop.

nagen:
Sie haben kaum zu nagen und zu beißen. — They live on almost nothing; they're very hard up.

nahegehen:
Sein Tod geht ihr sehr nahe. — His death affects her deeply.

nahelegen:
Man hat es ihm nahegelegt. — It has been suggested to him.

näher:
Kennen Sie ihn näher? — Are you a close friend of his?
Bitte, treten Sie näher! — Please step in (*or* up)!
Er ging auf die näheren Umstände ein. — He went into detail.

Naht:
Sie sollten ihm mal auf die Naht gehen. — You should bring pressure to bear upon him; you should sound him out.

Name(n):
Er nannte das Kind beim rechten Namen. — He called a spade a spade; he spoke the plain truth.

Im Namen der Regierung dankte er ihnen. — He thanked them on behalf of the government.

Dann gehen Sie doch in drei Teufels Namen! — Then go, for all I care!; for heaven's sake, go then!

Narr:
Jedem Narren gefällt seine Kappe. — Everyone has his eccentricities; tastes differ.

Am vielen Lachen erkennt man den Narren. — A fool will laugh when he's drowning.
Er hat einen Narren daran gefressen. — He's quite wrapped up in it; he's taken a great fancy (*or* liking) to it.

Narrenhand:
Narrenhände beschmieren Tisch und Wände. — Fools' names are like their faces, often seen in public places.

Narrenseil:
Sie führt ihn am Narrenseil. — She leads him around by the nose; she makes a fool of him.

Nase:
Er sperrte Mund und Nase auf. — He gaped; he was dumbfounded (*or* flabbergasted).

Er begoß sich die Nase. — He drowned his sorrows in drink; he got plastered (*or* drunk).

Sie trägt die Nase hoch. — She's stuck-up (*or* high-hat); she's a snob.
Er wird ihm schon die Nase putzen. — He'll give it to him; he'll give him a punch in the nose.

Sie rümpfte die Nase darüber. — She stuck up her nose at it.
Stecken Sie die Nase ins Buch! — Learn something!; read a book for a change!
Er hat die Nase voll davon. — He's fed up with (*or* sick of) it.
Er hat eine Nase gekriegt. — He was called down (*or* bawled out).
Er drehte ihnen eine Nase. — He took them in; he fooled them.
Er hat eine scharfe Nase. — He has a keen sense of smell; he's quick to spot (*or* sense) danger.

Das kann man ihm an der Nase ansehen. — You can tell that just by looking at him; it's written all over his face.

Zupfen Sie sich an Ihrer Nase!	Go chase yourself!
Er legte den Finger an die Nase.	He fell to thinking.
Er läßt sich auf der Nase herumtanzen.	He lets them run all over him; they can do with him what they please.
Sie liegt auf der Nase.	She's laid up; she's sick in bed.
Das werde ich Ihnen gerade auf die Nase binden!	Catch me telling you!; you won't get that out of me!
Man hat ihm eins auf die Nase gegeben.	He was called on the carpet; he was severely reprimanded.
Er läßt sich den Gewinn aus der Nase gehen.	He lets the profit slip through his fingers.
Er mußte ihnen die Würmer aus der Nase ziehen.	He pumped them; he had to worm (or force) it out of them; he made them tell.
Seine Bemerkung fuhr ihnen in die Nase.	His words burned them up (or made them boil); his remark infuriated them.
Machen Sie sich einen Knoten in die Nase!	Tie a string around your finger!; take it to heart!; be sure to remember that!
Das Angebot stach ihm in die Nase.	The offer attracted him.
Man mußte ihn mit der Nase draufstoßen.	They had to point it out to him; it had to be forcibly brought to his attention.
Er zog mit langer Nase ab.	He left looking rather disappointed.
Immer der Nase nach!	Follow your nose!; (go) straight ahead!
Es gab eine Flasche Bier pro Nase.	There was a bottle of beer for each.
Er hat sich den Wind um die Nase wehen lassen.	He's been places; he's seen the world.
Das werde ich ihm unter die Nase reiben.	I'll rub that into him; I'll throw that up to him.
Er suchte, was ihm vor der Nase lag.	He didn't see the forest for the trees; he was blind as a bat.
Sie schlug ihm die Tür vor der Nase zu.	She slammed the door in his face.
Das ist ihm noch nicht vor die Nase gekommen.	He had never before experienced (or run into) that.
Man hat ihn ihnen vor die Nase gesetzt.	He was placed ahead of them; he was promoted at their expense.

naſe(n)lang:

Der Junge hat alle naselang was andres.	Every two minutes the boy wants something else; he's never satisfied for long.

naß:

Er erhielt es für naß.	He got it dirt-cheap (or for nothing).
Er ist ein nasser Bruder.	He's a tippler (or drunkard).

naſſauern:

Er nassauert bei jeder Gelegenheit.	He's a regular sponger (or moocher); he gets everything for nothing.

Nebel:

Er verschwand bei Nacht und Nebel.	He disappeared in the dead (or under cover) of night.

nehmen:

Er nahm ein trauriges Ende.	He met a tragic death.
Das läßt er sich nicht nehmen.	He won't be talked out of that.

Neid:

Das muß ihm der Neid lassen.	You have to hand it to him; there's no denying it; you have to give him credit.

Neige:	
Der Wein geht zur Neige.	The wine is low (*or* running short).
neigen:	
Bei solchem Wetter neigt man zu Er= kältungen.	One is likely to catch cold in such weather.
nein:	
Nein, so was!	Well, I declare (*or* never)!; the idea!; of all the nerve!
Nein, was es nicht alles gibt!	Who would have thought it possible?
Aber nein!	Says you!; on the contrary!; I should say not!
Nepplokal:	
Keine zehn Pferde bringen mich wieder in dieses Nepplokal!	Wild horses couldn't drag me into this gyp-joint (*or* swell-elegant place) again!
Nessel:	
Setzen Sie sich nicht in die Nesseln!	Keep out of hot water!; don't get into trouble!
Nest:	
Jedem Vogel gefällt sein Nest.	Everyone to his own taste; we each have our own way of doing things.
Diese Stadt ist ein langweiliges Nest.	This burg is a hole; this town is dead (*or* flat).
Die Polizei fand das Nest leer.	The police found that the birds (*or* suspects) had flown; they found the hide-out empty.
Er ist bereits ins Nest gegangen.	He's already turned in (*or* gone to bed).
Auch ein gescheites Huhn legt die Eier neben das Nest.	It's a good horse that never stumbles; no one is perfect.
neugebacken:	
Er ist ein neugebackener Doktor.	He has just received his Ph.D. (*or* doctor's degree).
neugeboren:	
Er fühlt sich wie neugeboren.	He feels like a million dollars; he feels like a new man.
Neune:	
Ach, du grüne Neune!	Whew!; for Pete's sake!; well I'll be darned!; will you look at that!
Neunmalweise:	
Er ist ein Neunmalweiser.	He's a smart-aleck (*or* wise guy).
nichts:	
Er kam mir nichts, dir nichts herein.	He dropped in cool as a cucumber (*or* quite nonchalantly).
Sonst nichts?	Is that all?; anything else?
Nichtsein:	
Es geht um Sein oder Nichtsein.	It's a matter of life or death.
Nickel:	
So ein frecher Nickel!	What a meany (*or* cad)!
Nickerchen:	
Er nimmt gerade ein Nickerchen.	He's taking a little snooze (*or* nap); he's dozing a little.

niedlich:
Das kann ja niedlich werden!

That's only the beginning; that promises to get hot (*or* exciting).

Niere:
Die Sache geht ihm auf die Nieren.

The thing is getting him down; it's getting on his nerves.

Er prüfte sie auf Herz und Nieren.

He gave them the works; he put them to the acid test; he cross-examined them very closely.

niesen:
Dem werde ich was niesen!

I'll tell him to go to hell!

Niete:
Das neue Lustspiel ist eine Niete.

The new comedy is a washout (*or* failure).

nietfest:
Die Diebe nahmen mit, was nicht niet= und nagelfest war.

The thieves took along everything but the fixtures; they cleaned out the place.

Nimm:
Er ist vom Stamme „Nimm.“

He's one of the "gimme" crowd; he's always out for what he can get.

nimmer:
Nie und nimmer!

Never!; not on your life!

Nimmerwiedersehen:
Er verschwand auf Nimmerwiedersehen.

He left for good (and all).

Niveau:
Sein Vortrag hat Niveau.

His lecture has class; it's of a very high order.

nix:
Nix da!

Nothing doing!; nix on that stuff!; you can't get away with that!

nobel:
Nobel muß die Welt zugrunde gehen!
Er hat noble Passionen.

Generous to the bitter end!
He has expensive tastes.

noch:
Noch gestern war er hier.
Gibt es nicht noch andere Mittel?

He was here only yesterday.
Is there no other way?; is there no solution (*or* way out)?

Das muß man noch sehen.
Mag er noch so arm sein.
Der Fluß ist noch einmal so tief.
Er ist deshalb noch lange nicht dumm.

That remains to be seen.
No matter how poor he may be.
The river is twice as deep.
He isn't stupid for all that; nevertheless, he's far from stupid.

Das fehlte noch!

And now that!; what next?; and then that had to happen!

Wer kommt noch?
Und mehr noch.

Who else is coming?
And what's more; and moreover.

nochmal:
Donnerwetter nochmal!

Damn (*or* Hang) it all!; hell and damnation!

nolens volens:
Nolens volens mußte er's tun.

Rain or shine (*or* Sick or well), he had to do it; he had to do it willy-nilly (*or* whether he wanted to or not).

Nolte:
Das mögen Sie machen wie der Pfarrer Nolte.

Do as you please!; suit yourself!; it's up to you!

not:
Es täte not, er käme selbst.

It would be better if he came himself.

Not:
Er hat seine liebe Not damit.

He's having a sweet (*or* terrible) time with it; it's giving him plenty of trouble.

In der Not frißt der Teufel Fliegen.

Anything is better than nothing.

Spare in der Not, dann hast du in der Zeit!

Save your pennies for a rainy day!

Da ist Holland in Nöten!

Man overboard!; S.O.S.!; calling all cars!

Er schaffte es mit Müh' und Not.

He did it with great difficulty; it cost him great effort.

Er kam mit genauer Not davon.

He had a close shave (*or* narrow escape); he got away by the skin of his teeth.

Zur Not kann ich ihm drei Mark geben, aber nicht mehr.

In a pinch, I can give him three marks, but no more.

Note:
Er wurde nach Noten verhauen.

He got an awful licking.

notgedrungen:
Er mußte die Stelle notgedrungen annehmen.

He was forced to take the job; he was hard up for it.

nötig:
Er hat eine Stunde dazu nötig.

It'll take him an hour to do that.

Ein neuer Anzug ist ihm sehr nötig.

He wants (*or* needs) a new suit badly.

nötigen:
Er läßt sich nicht lange nötigen.

He doesn't stand on ceremony; he needs little coaxing.

Notpfennig:
Legen Sie sich einen Notpfennig zurück!

Save your pennies for a rainy day!

nu:
Nu aber!

Is that so?; well, well!

Na nu!

Really?; well, I declare (*or* never)!; what have we here?; what's this I hear?; so that's the story!

Nu:
Er war im Nu da.

He was there in a trice.

nüchtern:
Er trank auf nüchternen Magen.

He drank on an empty stomach.

Nudel:
Er ist eine ulkige Nudel.

He's a funny bird (*or* queer duck).

null:
Wie kamen Sie bei dem Geschäft weg? —Plus minus null!

How did you make out in this deal?—I just broke even.

num:
Es ist rum wie num.

It's six of one and half a dozen of the other; it's all the same.

Nummer:
Er ist eine Nummer für sich. Man weiß nie, was er als nächstes tut.

He's a funny bird (*or* guy)—you never know what he'll do next.

Er ist nur eine Nummer unter vielen.	He's a regular Babbitt; he's just one of many; he has no distinctive personality.
Er hat bei seinem Chef eine gute Nummer.	He's in good with his boss; his boss likes him.
Man hat ihn nach Nummer Sicher gebracht.	They put him under lock and key; he was jailed.

nun:

Nun, wird's bald?	Well, are you coming?
Nun gerade!	All the more!
Nun gut, ich gehe.	All right, I'll go.
Nun, nun!	Come, come!
Wenn er nicht schreibt, nun, dann gehe ich hin.	If he doesn't write, why, I'll go to him.
Wenn er nun käme?	What if he came?; supposing he were to come?
Es ist nun mal nicht anders.	That's the way of the world; there's nothing to be done about it.

nur:

Nur Mut!	Cheer up!; take heart!
Nur zu!	Go to it!; more power to you!; keep going!
Er tut, soviel er nur kann.	He does all that he possibly can.
Er mag ihn nur nicht sprechen hören.	He simply cannot bear to listen to him.
Er schaffte es nur so.	He did it just like that; it cost him no effort at all; it only took him a minute.
Er tut nur so.	He's only pretending (or putting on); he doesn't really mean it.
Er schlug die Tür zu, daß es nur so krachte.	He slammed the door so that the house shook.
Wie erfuhr er das nur?	Where did he ever find that out?
Laß doch nur!	Come now!; do stop!

Nürnberger:

Die Nürnberger hängen keinen, sie hätten ihn denn zuvor.	Don't count your chickens before they're hatched!; first catch your hare!
Man mußte es ihm mit dem Nürnberger Trichter eingießen.	He was so dense (or stupid) we fairly had to pound it into him.

Nuß:

Er ist eine taube Nuß.	He cuts no ice; he's a nobody; he doesn't rate (or count).
Es setzte Nüsse.	The sparks flew; it rained blows.
Ich habe ihn aus der Nuß gehoben.	I set him to rights; I gave him a piece of my mind.
Er ist letzten Winter in die Nüsse gegangen.	He kicked the bucket (or passed away) last winter.
Er tut es nicht um taube Nüsse.	He won't do it for love (or nothing).

Nutz:

Es ist zu seinem Nutz und Frommen.	It's for his own good.

Nützliche:

Er verband das Angenehme mit dem Nützlichen.	He combined business with pleasure.

O:
    Dies ist das A und O des Problems.

This is the problem from A to Z (*or* izzard); this is the whole problem in a nutshell.

ob:
    Ob ich lieber bleibe?

I wonder whether I should stay; would it be better if I stayed?

    Hat es Ihnen gefallen?—Na und ob!

Did you like it?—And how!; you bet I did!; I should say so!

Obacht:
    Obacht geben!

Look out!; watch your step!; take care (*or* heed)!

oben:
    Er scheint oben gut angeschrieben zu sein.

He seems to be well liked by (*or* in good with) his superiors.

    Ihm steht die Sache bis hier oben.
    Er ging nach oben.
    Sie behandelte ihn von oben herab.

He's fed up with it; he's sick and tired of it.
He went upstairs.
She high-hatted (*or* patronized) him; she treated him like a servant.

    Sie musterten ihn von oben bis unten.

They gave him the once-over; they took a good look at him.

obenauf:
    Er ist schon wieder obenauf.

He's back on top; he's weathered the storm.

obendrein:
    Er gab ihnen das obendrein.

He threw that into the bargain; he gave them that to boot (*or* extra).

obenhin:
    Er tat es nur so obenhin.

He did it very lackadaisically; he did it in a slipshod (*or* half-hearted) manner.

obenhinaus:
    Er geht immer gleich obenhinaus.

He always flies right off the handle; he's very hot-tempered.

    Sie will obenhinaus.

She wants to go places (*or* get ahead); she's a climber (*or* very ambitious).

Ober:
    Ober, ein Bier!

Waiter, a glass of beer, please!

oberfaul:
    Die Sache steht oberfaul.

The outcome is very doubtful (*or* uncertain).

Oberste:
    Er kehrte das Oberste zu unterst.

He turned everything topsy-turvy (*or* upside down).

Oberwasser:
    Endlich bekam er Oberwasser.

He finally got the upper hand; at last he got things under control.

obligat:

Er erhielt zu seinem Geburtstag den obligaten Schlips.

He received the customary tie for his birthday.

obsiegend:

Er erlangte ein obsiegendes Urteil.

He secured a favorable verdict.

Obst:

Ich soll das tun? Na, ich danke für Obst und Südfrüchte!

I'm supposed to do that?—Well, you've got another guess coming!; not for me, thanks!; the pleasure's all yours!

Obulus:

Haben Sie schon Ihren Obulus beigesteuert?

Did you chip in?; have you paid your share?

Ochse:

Da steht der Ochs (= Ochse) am Berg!

That's where the shoe pinches!; there's the rub (or difficulty)!

Er stand wie der Ochse vorm Berg.

He was up against a blank wall; he didn't know where to turn.

Er spannte die Ochsen hinter den Pflug.

He put the cart before the horse; he began at the wrong end; he reversed the procedure.

Man kann vom Ochsen nicht mehr verlangen als Rindfleisch.

You can't make a silk purse out of a sow's ear; what else can you expect?

ochsen:

Er ochst schwer.

He's cramming for dear life; he's studying hard.

öden:

Er ödete sie mit seinen alten Geschichten.

He bored them to death with his old stories.

Ofen:

Er wärmt sich am kalten Ofen.

He's barking up the wrong tree; he's got the wrong number; he's come to the wrong door (or party); he won't get anything from that source.

Damit können Sie keinen Hund hinterm Ofen hervorlocken.

That won't get you very far; you'll never get anywhere at that rate.

Den ganzen Tag hockt er hinterm Ofen.

He's a stay-at-home.

offen:

Der Wirt hat offnes Bier.

The innkeeper sells beer on draught (or tap).

Er ist ein offner Kopf.

He has a good head; he's a bright fellow.

Er fand ein offnes Ohr für seine Bitte.

They lent him a ready ear; his request met with a favorable reception.

Mit diesem Vorschlag rennen Sie nur offne Türen ein.

That's carrying coals to Newcastle; that's a waste of time (or energy); that won't get you anywhere.

Er kämpft nicht mit offnem Visier.

He's no square shooter; he's not on the level; he doesn't play fair.

offenbar:

Es ist offenbarer Betrug.

It's a regular racket (or swindle); it's downright fraud.

offenhalten:

Er hält sich offen, dorthin zu gehen.

He reserves the right to go there.

offenstehen:

Es steht ihm offen zu gehen oder zu bleiben. | He's free to come and go.

Öffentlichkeit:

Die Sache wurde unter Ausschluß der Öffentlichkeit verhandelt. | The case was heard behind locked doors.

Er trat die Flucht in die Öffentlichkeit an. | He broke into print; he took refuge in literary expression.

Er hat sich von der Öffentlichkeit zurückgezogen. | He's retired.

offiziös:

Die Meldung ist offiziös. | The report is semi-official.

ohne:

Das ist nicht so ohne. | There's something in (*or* to) that; that's not half (*or* at all) bad.

Ohr:

Machen Sie die Ohren auf! | Get a load of this!; just listen to this!

Er hat die Ohren voll davon. | He's fed up with it.

Halt die Ohren steif! | Keep a stiff upper lip!; grit your teeth!; keep up your spunk (*or* nerve)!

Er hielt sich bei ihren Vorhaltungen die Ohren zu. | He turned a deaf ear to her complaints.

Er machte lange Ohren. | He pricked up his ears; he sat up and took notice.

Hauen Sie sich einen Augenblick aufs Ohr! | Take a cat nap (*or* snooze).

Nehmen Sie ihn mal bei den Ohren! | Take him by the scruff of the neck!; talk to him like a Dutch uncle!; give him a good talking to!

Sie ist verliebt bis über die Ohren. | She's head over heels in love.

Er hat es hinter den Ohren. | He's no dumb bunny; he's very crafty.

Er hat es faustdick hinter den Ohren. | He's a slicker (*or* sharper); he's a clever scoundrel.

Schreiben Sie sich das hinter die Ohren! | Put that in your pipe and smoke it!; let that be a lesson to you!

Er hat Bohnen in den Ohren. | He's deaf as a post; he's stone-deaf.

Er lag mir in den Ohren, daß ich ihm das Buch besorge. | He kept after (*or* pestered) me until I got him the book.

Er hörte mit gespanntem Ohr zu. | He listened attentively.

Man hat ihn übers Ohr gehauen. | He was gypped (*or* cheated).

Er wollte ihnen das Fell über die Ohren ziehen. | He wanted to do (*or* fleece) them.

Er hat viel um die Ohren. | He's up to his neck in work; he has plenty (*or* a lot) on his hands.

Lassen Sie sich erst noch etwas Wind um die Ohren pfeifen! | Better try your wings (*or* get some experience) first!

Er hat sich die Nacht um die Ohren geschlagen. | He stayed up all night; he got hardly any sleep.

Er hat sich die Welt um die Ohren geschlagen. | He's knocked around (*or* traveled) a great deal; he's been places (*or* seen the world).

Er wiederholte es vor unsern Ohren. | He repeated it in our hearing.

Ölgötze:

Er stand da wie ein Ölgötze. | He stood there like a post; he looked blank (*or* stupid).

Olim:

So war es schon zu Olims Zeiten.

That was in the good old days; that's how it used to be.

Olymp:

Sie hatten gerade noch soviel Geld, um sich zwei Sitze auf dem Olymp zu erstehen.

They just managed to scrape up enough money for two seats in the peanut gallery (*or* nigger heaven); they had just enough left for two seats in the second balcony.

Opferwilligkeit:

Der Opferwilligkeit sind keine Schranken gesetzt.

Give whatever you can!; give according to your means!

ordentlich:

Er machte seine Sache recht ordentlich.

He did his work up brown; he made a good (*or* thorough) job of it.

Sie waren ordentlich gerührt.

They were genuinely touched.

ordinär:

Das Buch kostet ordinär zehn Mark.

The publisher's (*or* list) price of that book is ten marks.

Organ:

Dafür hat er kein Organ.

He has no head for that; he can't grasp it.

Orgelpfeife:

Seine Kinder sind wie die Orgelpfeifen.

His children range (*or* come) in steps.

orientieren:

Orientieren Sie sich darüber!

Get a line on it!; find out something about it!

Original:

Er ist ein Original.

He's quite a character.

Ort:

Ein gutes Wort findet einen guten Ort.

A good (*or* kind) word is never lost; it pays to be polite.

Bringen Sie es an Ort und Stelle!

Put it back where it belongs!

Er ist bald an Ort und Stelle.

He'll soon be at his destination.

Tun Sie's hier an Ort und Stelle!

Do it right here and now!

Er ist aus meinem Ort.

He comes from my home town.

Oskar:

Er ist frech wie Oskar.

He's fresh as hell; he's fresh as they come.

Er tat es frech wie Oskar.

He went right ahead and did it (without saying boo to anyone).

Ostern:

Ich hoffe ihn zu sehen, wenn Ostern und Pfingsten auf einen Tag fallen.

Here's hoping I won't see him again till apples bloom on a lilac tree; I hope I'll never see him again.

Er freute sich wie ein Kind zu Ostern.

He was pleased as Punch; he was tickled pink (*or* to death).

℞

℘:
Da werde ich mal gleich ein ℘ vorschreiben.

I'll put a crimp in that right off the bat (*or* from the start); I'll queer (*or* stop) that right away.

paar:
Schreiben Sie ihnen ein paar Zeilen!

Drop them a line!

Paar:
Der Feind wurde zu Paaren getrieben.

The enemy was routed (*or* put to flight).

Pack:
Pack schlägt sich, Pack verträgt sich.

Knaves are foes one minute and friends the next.

Er zog mit Sack und Pack ab.

He left, bag and baggage.

packen:
Pack dich!

Scram!; clear out!; get going!

Wenn Sie sich beeilen, dann packen Sie's noch.

If you hurry, you can still make it (*or* get there on time).

Es hat ihn gepackt.

He was taken sick.

Packung:
Die Mannschaft hat eine tüchtige Packung gekriegt.

The team was badly done in; they took an awful beating.

Pantoffel:
Sie schwingt den Pantoffel.

She wears the pants in that family; she's the boss (*or* head of the household).

Papier:
Papier ist geduldig.

Anything goes!; you can print most anything.

Pappe:
Das ist nicht von Pappe.

That's not half bad; that's not to be sneezed at; you've got something there.

Pappenheimer:
Ich kenne meine Pappenheimer.

I know my men; I know with whom I'm dealing.

Pappenstiel:
Das ist doch kein Pappenstiel!
Er erstand es für einen Pappenstiel.

That's no trifle!; that's quite something!
He got it dirt-cheap (*or* for a mere song).

papperlapapp:
Papperlapapp!

Piffle!; my eye!; fiddlesticks!

Parabel:
Man hat ihn bei der Parabel gekriegt.

He was called on the carpet (*or* taken to task); he was bawled out.

Parade:
Sie fuhren ihm in die Parade.

They held up the works; they spoiled his show (*or* wrecked his plans).

parieren:

Wer nicht pariert, der fliegt! — Fall in line (*or* Toe the mark) or out you go!

Paroli:

Den unsinnigen Forderungen des Abge= ordneten wurde im Senat ein Paroli geboten. — The preposterous demands of the senator were stalled (*or* blocked).

Partei:

Sie nehmen seine Partei. — They take his part; they side with him.
Er hält es mit keiner Partei. — He remains neutral.

Partie:

Sie ist eine gute Partie. — She's a good match.
Er machte eine reiche Partie. — He married (a woman with) money.
Lassen Sie mich mit von der Partie sein! — Count me in, won't you?; may I join you?

Paß:

Er hat ihnen den Paß verlegt. — He put a crimp in their plans; he queered (*or* spoiled) things for them.

Passagier:

Ein blinder Passagier ist an Bord. — There's a stowaway aboard.

Passau:

Er versteht die Passauer Kunst. — There's a tough bird (*or* hard-boiled egg) for you!; he's thick-skinned (*or* immune to everything).

passen:

Das paßt nicht. — That won't do.
Wenn Ihnen das nicht paßt, dann können Sie's bleibenlassen! — Like it or lump it!; take it or leave it!
Das paßt nicht zum Anzug. — That doesn't match the suit.
Er paßt nicht zum Kaufmann. — He'll never make a good businessman; he's not fitted for business.
Das paßt sich nicht. — That's not being done; that's not proper (*or* seemly).

Passion:

Er hat noble Passionen. — He has expensive tastes.

Pastete:

Da haben wir die Pastete! — That's a fine how-do-you-do!; what a fix to be in!; now we're in for it!

Pate:

Er hat ihm die Paten gesagt. — He laid down the law to him; he set him to rights.

patent:

Er ist ein patenter Kerl. — He's a crackajack; he's a good scout (*or* real sport).

Patron:

Das ist mir ein sauberer Patron! — There's a scummy individual (*or* real scoundrel) for you!; what a low-down cad!

Patsche:

Geben Sie mir die Patsche! — Put it there!; shake (hands) on it!
Er half ihnen aus der Patsche. — He helped them over a tight spot; he got them out of the fix (*or* scrape).

patsch(e)naß:

    Sie waren patschnaß. — They were dripping wet (*or* soaked to the skin).

Pauke:

    Er bezog eine Pauke. — He was called down (*or* bawled out).

    Er ist mit Pauken und Trompeten gerasselt. — He flunked (the test) outright.

pauken:

    Er paukt schwer für die Prüfung. — He's cramming (*or* studying hard) for the exam(ination).

Pauker:

    Sein Pauker ist krank. — His prof(essor) is sick.

Paulus:

    Er geht drauflos wie Paulus auf die Korinther. — He's a real go-getter; he's going at it with a vengeance.

    Aus einem Saulus ist ein Paulus geworden. — He turned over a new leaf; he changed for the better.

Pech:

    Die beiden hängen zusammen wie Pech und Schwefel. — They're like the Siamese twins; they're inseparable.

    Er versuchte, sie zu beschummeln, aber er hatte Pech. — He tried to gyp (*or* cheat) them, but it didn't work.

    Er hat Pech an den Fingern. — He's a blunderbuss; he spoils everything he touches.

    Er hat Pech an den Hosen. — He's a sticking plaster; you can't budge him; he doesn't know when to go home.

    Er hatte höllisches Pech. — He had the world's worst breaks (*or* luck); he ran into a heap of trouble.

Pechpflaster:

    Sie mußten ihm ein Pechpflaster auf den Mund legen. — They cut him short (*or* shut him up); they forced him to keep quiet.

Pechsträhne:

    Die Pechsträhne reißt nicht ab. — There's no end to this streak of hard luck.

Pechvogel:

    Er ist ein rechter Pechvogel. — He gets all the tough breaks; the world treats him like a stepchild; he's an unlucky bird.

Pedal:

    Ziehen Sie mal Ihre Pedale ein! — Draw in your dogs!; get your big feet out of the way!

peinlich:

    Er ist in allem sehr peinlich. — He's an old fuss-budget; he's very particular (*or* meticulous) about everything he does.

Pelle:

    Er liegt ihnen den ganzen Tag auf der Pelle. — He hangs around all day long.

Pelz:

    Wasch mir den Pelz, und mach mich nicht naß! — You can't empty the sea with a sieve!; half measures won't do!; it can't be done.

    Er hat ihm den Pelz gewaschen. — He blew him up; he gave him a piece of his mind.

Sie sollten ihm einmal auf den Pelz rücken.	You should pin him down sometime; put it up to him sometime.
Man hat ihm die Motten aus dem Pelz geklopft.	He got a good sound thrashing.
Da haben Sie ihm aber eine schöne Laus in den Pelz gesetzt!	A fine mess you got him into!

pendeln:

Er pendelt zwischen Extremen hin und her.	He can't make up his mind; he can't come to a decision; he wavers back and forth.

Penne:

Er geht noch immer auf die Penne.	He still goes to school.

pennen:

Lassen Sie ihn nur pennen!	Let him sleep!

per:

Bei ihm geht alles gleich per du.	It doesn't take him long to be on familiar terms with a person.

perfekt:

Das Abkommen ist perfekt geworden.	The agreement went into effect.

Perle:

Es wird Ihnen keine Perle aus der Krone fallen.	You can't lose; you won't lose anything by it.

per pedes:

Er kam per pedes.	He hoofed it; he came on foot.

Person:

Ich für meine Person muß jetzt gehen.	I, for one, must go now.

Perücke:

Man ist ihm endlich in die Perücke gefahren.	They finally showed him up (or exposed him).

Pest:

Daß dich die Pest!	Go to blazes!
Ich hasse das wie die Pest.	How I love that!; I hate it like poison.

Peter:

Dieser Spieler ist ein langweiliger Peter.	This player is a stick-in-the mud (or slowpoke); he's awfully slow.

Petersilie:

Was hat Ihnen denn die Petersilie verhagelt?	Who cramped your style?; who had it in for you?; why are you so blue (or down in the mouth)?

Petrus:

Petrus meint's gut.	The weatherman means well; it's a glorious (or fine) day.

Pfahl:

Diese Sache ist ihm ein Pfahl im Fleisch.	That's his weak spot; it's a thorn in his flesh; it's a source of great worry to him.
Er will heute in seinen vier Pfählen bleiben.	He wants to stay home (or in) today; he wants to keep to his own four walls.

Pfanne:

Er hat noch einen guten Witz auf der Pfanne.	He has another good joke on the fire (or up his sleeve).
Er hat ihn nur so in die Pfanne gehauen.	He surely cooked his goose (or killed his chances); he certainly made short work of him; he knocked him out.

Pfarrer:

Der Pfarrer predigt nur einmal.

The cow chews her cud but once; it's the chance of a lifetime; it won't happen again.

Das mögen Sie machen wie der Pfarrer Nolte!

Do as you please!; suit yourself!; it's up to you!

Pfarrerstöchter:

Unter uns Pfarrerstöchtern!

Between you and me and the lamp post!; confidentially!

Pfeffer:

Ich wollte, er wäre, wo der Pfeffer wächst!
Das ist starker Pfeffer.

To hell with him!; I wish he were in Jericho.
That's putting it rather strong; those are hard words.

Da liegt der Hase im Pfeffer!

That's where the shoe pinches!; there's the rub!; there's where the trouble lies!

pfeffern:

Er pfefferte das Buch in die Ecke.

He chucked (or flung) the book into the corner.

Pfeifchen:

Man muß sein Pfeifchen schneiden, solange man im Rohr sitzt.

Make hay while the sun shines!; make the most of your opportunities!

Pfeife:

Er hielt die Pfeife im Sack.

He had nothing to say; he felt glum (or dejected).

Er steckte die Pfeife in den Sack.

He threw up his hands; he gave up the game.

Wer im Rohr sitzt, hat gut Pfeifen schneiden.

It's easy to preach when you're sitting pretty (or you're well off).

Er muß nach ihrer Pfeife tanzen.

He must dance to her tune; he must do as she wishes.

pfeifen:

Ich pfeif' dir was!

Go whistle for it!; no sale!; you're out of luck!

Er pfeift darauf.

He doesn't give a hoot in hell.

Er pfeift nicht mehr lange.

He won't hold out much longer; he's a goner; he's breathing his last.

Da hilft kein Maulspitzen, es muß gepfiffen werden.

There's no use mincing matters—out with it!; it's no use making a face—it's got to be done.

Lassen Sie uns einen pfeifen!

Let's have a drink!

Pfeifendeckel:

Glauben Sie, er wäre gekommen, wie er versprochen hatte?—Ja, Pfeifendeckel!

You think he came as he said he would? —The devil he did!; not he!

Pfennig:

Du kannst mir wohl auch keinen Pfennig wechseln?

You couldn't possibly help me out?; could you lend me two bits?

Sie haben Pfennige.
Er bezahlte auf Heller und Pfennig.

They've got plenty of money.
He paid up to the last cent.

Pferd:

Es hängt ein Pferd in der Luft.

Something's up (or in the wind); something's going to happen.

Das hält kein Pferd aus.	That's (expecting) too much; no one can stand that.
Ihn kriegen heute keine zehn Pferde aus dem Haus.	Nothing in the world could get him to go out today.
Er zäumt das Pferd beim Schwanz auf.	He puts the cart before the horse; he begins at the wrong end; he reverses the procedure.
Er spannt das Pferd hinter den Wagen.	He puts the cart before the horse; he begins at the wrong end; he reverses the procedure.
Mit dem kann man ein Pferd mausen.	He's all right; he's a good sport.
Machen Sie mir nicht die Pferde scheu!	Don't spoil the whole works!
Er wurde auf einem fahlen Pferd gesehen.	He was caught red-handed (or in the act).
Er ist vom Pferd auf den Esel gekommen.	He's come down in the world; his luck has gone back on him.

Pferdearbeit:

Das ist eine Pferdearbeit.	That's a tough (or hell of a) job.

Pferdefuß:

Da guckt der Pferdefuß heraus.	There's the nigger in the wood pile; that's the catch to it.

Pferdekur:

Es war eine Pferdekur, aber ihm wurde geholfen.	It was enough to kill a horse, but it cured him; it would have killed anyone but him.

Pferdenatur:

Er hat eine Pferdenatur.	He's strong as an ox; he's a regular truck horse.

Pferdeverstand:

Er hat keinen Pferdeverstand.	He can't get along with horses.

Pfiff:

Er ließ sich noch einen Pfiff Bier einschenken.	He had another glass of beer.
Er gehorcht ihr auf den Pfiff.	He dances to her tune; he's tied to her apron strings.
Er versteht sich auf den Pfiff.	He's a sly old bird; he knows all the tricks of the trade.

Pfifferling:

Das ist keinen Pfifferling wert.	That's not worth a rap (or straw); it's a lemon.

Pfingsten:

Ich hoffe ihn zu sehen, wenn Pfingsten und Ostern auf einen Tag fallen.	Here's hoping I won't see him again till apples bloom on a lilac tree; I hope I'll never see him again.
Zu Pfingsten auf dem Eis!	Never!; not a chance!

Pfingstochse:

Er war aufgedonnert wie ein Pfingstochse.	He was dressed up to beat the band; he was all decked out.

Pflanze:

Sie ist eine schöne Pflanze geworden.	A fine customer she's turned out to be!; a nice person, indeed!

Pflaster:

Diese Stadt ist ein teures Pflaster.	This city is an expensive place to live in.

Man hat ihm den Charakter eines Gene= | He was given the title of general as hush
rals als Pflaster verliehen. | money (*or* compensation); to smooth over
| the difficulty, he was made a general.

Wo ist Karl?—Er tritt das Pflaster. | Where's Charlie?—He's walking the streets;
| he's out for a walk.

Pflaume:
Das war eine Pflaume! | That was some slam (*or* dirty dig)!; that
| was an awful crack (*or* remark)!

pflegen:
So pflegt es zu gehen. | That's the way of the world; that's always
| the way.

pfleglich:
Behandeln Sie es aber pfleglich! | Take mighty good care of it!

Pflicht:
Es ist seine verdammte Pflicht und | It's his bounden duty.
Schuldigkeit.
Er handelte nach Pflicht und Gewissen. | He handled the matter conscientiously to
| the best of his knowledge.

Pflock:
Er steht wie ein Pflock. | He's a regular stick; he's very clumsy (*or*
| awkward).
Er steckte einen Pflock davor. | He put a stop to it.
Stecken Sie einen Pflock zurück! | Relax (*or* Loosen up) a bit; don't be so fussy
| (*or* particular)!; don't be so stiff (*or*
| proper)!

Pflug:
Er legte die Hand an den Pflug. | He buckled down; he got down to business.
Er spannte die Ochsen hinter den Pflug. | He put the cart before the horse; he began
| at the wrong end; he reversed the pro-
| cedure.

Pfote:
Er schreibt eine schreckliche Pfote. | He writes a terrible scrawl; his handwriting
| is abominable.
Verbrennen Sie sich nicht die Pfoten! | Don't burn your fingers!; don't get yourself
| into trouble!
Er hat eins auf die Pfoten bekommen. | He got his fingers slapped; he was snubbed
| (*or* set to rights).

Pfropfen:
Das ist aber ein dicker Pfropfen! | He's a regular humpty-dumpty (*or* roly-
| poly)!
Laßt die Pfropfen knallen! | Let's celebrate!; let's have champagne!
Er ließ sie am Pfropfen riechen. | He gave them the merry ha-ha; he razzed
| (*or* ridiculed) them.
Er sitzt auf dem Pfropfen. | He's up a tree; he's stumped (*or* stranded);
| he's short of cash (*or* money).

pfropfenvoll:
Der Saal war pfropfenvoll. | The hall was jammed to the rafters.

pfui:
Pfui Tausend! | Ugh!; pugh!; it stinks!
Oben hui und unten pfui! | Fine feathers don't make fine birds; ap-
| pearances are deceiving.

Pfund:
Wuchern Sie mit Ihrem Pfund! | Use your talent!; capitalize on your ability!

pfunbig:
Das ist ja pfunbig!   It's the berries; it's a honey (*or* knockout)!; it's swell!

Pfunbsmotor:
Der Wagen hat einen Pfunbsmotor.   The car has a crack (*or* corking good) motor.

pfuschen:
Er kann nichts als pfuschen.   He bungles (*or* botches) everything; he spoils everything.

phantasieren:
Der Kranke phantasierte die ganze Nacht.   The sick man's mind was wandering all night; he was delirious.

Sie phantasierte auf dem Klavier.   She improvised on the piano.

Philipp:
Setzen Sie Ihren Philipp barunter!   Put your John Henry (*or* signature) to it!; sign on the dotted line!

Philister:
Er ist ein arger Philister geworden.   He's become a regular Babbitt; he's become dreadfully conventional (*or* narrow-minded).

picheln:
Sie pichelten bis spät in die Nacht.   They went on an all-night binge (*or* drinking party).

Piep:
Er konnte nicht mehr Piep sagen.   He couldn't say "boo"; he was struck dumb.

piepen:
Bei Ihnen piept's wohl!   Are you crazy?

Piepen:
Es ist zum Piepen.   It's a scream (*or* riot); it's too funny; I nearly died laughing.

piepsig:
Der Junge ist noch recht piepsig.   The boy is still very shaky (*or* weak).

piesacken:
Der Junge piesackte sie den ganzen Tag.   The boy pestered her all day long.

Pik:
Sie haben einen Pik auf ihn.   They have it in for him; they're down on him; they bear him a grudge.

Pike:
Er hat von der Pike auf gedient.   He started from scratch (*or* the very bottom); he rose from the ranks; he worked his way up from office boy to president.

piksein:
Es sieht piksein aus.   It looks tiptop (*or* first-rate).

pikieren:
Er hat sich darauf pikiert.   He made a point of doing it.

pikiert:
Sie ist sehr pikiert.   She's all hot and bothered; she's very huffy (*or* annoyed).

Pilatus:
Er lief von Pontius zu Pilatus.   He went from pillar to post; he was sent from one to the other.

Pimpelfritz:
Der Junge ist ein rechter Pimpelfritz.

The boy is a spoiled brat.

Pinke:
Ihm ist die Pinke ausgegangen.

He's broke; he's short of cash (*or* money).

Pinkel:
So ein feiner Pinkel!

A regular Jim Dandy!; what a sheik!; isn't he snappy- (*or* smart-)looking though?

Pinsel:
Er ist ein alberner Pinsel!

He's a darned fool (*or* silly ass).

Pipe:
Das ist ihm ganz Pipe.

He doesn't give a hoot; he doesn't care a rap about it.

Pips:
Er hat einen Pips weg.

He's had enough to last him forever; his health is ruined.

Pistole:
Seine Antwort kam wie aus der Pistole geschossen.

He answered right off the bat; his answer came like a shot.

Placet:
Er gab sein Placet.

He gave his O.K. (*or* consent).

plagen:
Ihn plagt der Satan.

The devil is riding (*or* after) him.

Planet:
Ich habe ihm die Planeten gelesen.

I told him where he got off; I laid down the law to him.

Plappermaul:
Sie ist das reine Plappermaul.

She's a born chatterbox (*or* jabberer); she talks incessantly.

platt:
Er war platt, als er das hörte.

He was dumbfounded (*or* taken aback) when he heard that; the news simply floored (*or* amazed) him.

Er ist ein platter Mensch.

He's a yokel; he's thick (*or* dense).

Platt:
Sie sprachen Platt.

They spoke Low German.

Platte:
Der hat aber Platten!

He has the dough, all right!; he's lousy with (*or* rolling in) money.

Putz die Platten!

Scram!; beat it!

Gib ihm eins auf die Platte!

Hit him on the block (*or* head)!; give him a sock!

Das kommt nicht auf die Platte.

That has nothing to do with the price of cheese; that doesn't enter into the matter.

Platz:
Platz da!

Move on!; make way there!

Nehmen Sie Platz!

Have a seat!

Bitte, Platz nehmen! (Eisenbahn)

All aboard!

Zehn Soldaten blieben auf dem Platz.

Ten soldiers were killed.

Seien Sie auf dem Platz!

Be prepared for anything!

Plauze:
Es setzte tüchtige Plauze.

Blows fell hot and heavy.

Er hat es auf der Plauze.	He has pains in his chest.
Er liegt auf der Plauze.	He's laid up; he's sick in bed.

pleite:
Er ist pleite.

He's flat broke; he hasn't a cent.

Pleite:
Das ist aber eine Pleite!

What a mess!; that's bad business!; it's an awful state of affairs!

Plethi:
Er will nichts mit Krethi und Plethi zu tun haben.

He has no use for the rabble (*or* hoi polloi); he'll have nothing to do with Tom, Dick, and Harry.

plötzlich:
Ein Bier, aber etwas plötzlich!

A glass of beer, please, but make it snappy (*or* step on it)!

Nur nicht so plötzlich!

Take it easy!; what's the big hurry?

plump:
Das ist plumper Schwindel.

That's a big racket (*or* swindle).

plus:
Wie kamen Sie bei dem Geschäft weg? —Plus minus null.

How did you make out in this deal?—I just broke even.

Plus:
Das muß als ein Plus für ihn gebucht werden.

He's scored again; you have to hand it to him; you have to give him credit for it.

pochen:
Man hat ihn tüchtig gepocht.

He got a good walloping.

Podium:
Fallen Sie nicht vom Podium!

Don't fall down dead!; don't die (of the shock)!

Polen:
Noch ist Polen nicht verloren!

Never say die!; while there's life, there's hope!

Polente:
Er fiel der Polente in die Hände.

The cops got him; he was arrested.

Polizei:
Er ist dümmer, als die Polizei erlaubt.

It's against the law to be that dumb; he's a perfect moron (*or* numskull).

polnisch:
Die Versammlung war die reine polnische Wirtschaft.

Bedlam reigned at the meeting; everything was topsy-turvy (*or* in a state of confusion).

Pomade:
Das ist mir Pomade.
Er sprach mit der größten Pomade.

What do I care!
He talked with perfect ease and fluency; he had perfect poise.

pomadig:
Er ist ein pomadiger Mensch.

He's a slow coach; he's an easygoing fellow.

Pontius:
Er lief von Pontius zu Pilatus.

He went from pillar to post; he was sent from one to the other.

Popanz:
  Daß dich der Popanz hol'! — The deuce take you!; go to blazes!
  Seine Drohung ist nur ein Popanz für unerfahrene Leute. — His threat is nothing more than a bugaboo (*or* bluff) to scare off the greenhorns.

Porzellankiste:
  Vorsicht ist die Mutter der Porzellankiste. — An ounce of prevention is worth a pound of cure; a stitch in time saves nine.

Porzellanladen:
  Er ist so ungeschickt wie ein Elefant im Porzellanladen. — He's as clumsy as a bull in a china shop; he falls all over himself.

Posemuckel:
  Er ist Arzt in Posemuckel. — He's a country doctor; he's practicing out in the sticks (*or* backwoods).

Possen:
  Ach Possen! — Piffle!; pooh!; nonsense!
  Er tat es ihnen zum Possen. — He wanted to fool them; he did it for fun.

Post:
  Ohne dich fährt die Post auch. — The world will go on just the same without you; you're not so all-important.

Posten:
  Es hat einen hübschen Posten gekostet. — It's cost a pretty penny; it took a small fortune.

  Seien Sie auf dem Posten! — Keep your eye skinned (*or* peeled)!; be on your toes!; be on the alert!

  Ist er wieder auf dem Posten? — Is he well again?; is he back on the job?
  Er ist da auf seinem Posten. — He's the right man for the job.
  Er kämpft auf verlorenem Posten. — He's fighting for a lost cause; he's fighting a losing battle.

Pott:
  Er kann mit der Sache nicht zu Pott kommen. — He can't put it across; he can't get anywhere with it.

potztausend:
  Potztausend! — Great Scott!; leaping lizards!; holy cow!

poussieren:
  Er versuchte, seinen Vorgesetzten zu poussieren. — He tried to handshake (*or* soft-soap) his superior; he tried to sell (*or* promote) himself.

Prä:
  Er hat das Prä. — He's teacher's pet; he always plays first fiddle (*or* base); he gets the preference.

Prachtkerl:
  Er ist ein Prachtkerl. — He's a brick (*or* prince); he's a splendid fellow.

Praktikus:
  Der Einbrecher war ein alter Praktikus. — The burglar was an old hand.

praktisch:
  Er ist praktischer Arzt. — He's a general practitioner.

Pranger:
  Man hat ihn an den Pranger gestellt. — He's been publicly disgraced.

Präsentierteller:
  Er saß wie auf dem Präsentierteller. — He was in the limelight; he was very conspicuous.

Predigt:
Das kommt so gewiß wie das Amen nach der Predigt. — That's as sure as death and taxes.

Preis:
Ohn' Fleiß kein Preis. — No pains, no gains; earn your keep!
Um keinen Preis! — Not for all the world!; not on your life!

prellen:
Der Kellner hat sie gehörig geprellt. — The waiter soaked (*or* overcharged) them good and plenty.

Presse:
Er besuchte eine Presse, bevor er auf die Universität ging. — He attended a prep(aratory) school before entering the university.

pressieren:
Es pressiert nicht. — Take your time!; there's no rush.

Preuße:
So schnell schießen die Preußen nicht. — It won't happen overnight; that'll take time.

preußisch:
Die beiden sind preußisch miteinander. — The two have had a spat (*or* tiff); they're not on speaking terms.

Priesterhandel:
Da haben Sie einen Priesterhandel gemacht. — You've got a real buy (*or* bargain) there.

prima:
Ihnen geht's prima. — They're having a corking good time; they're enjoying themselves hugely.

Prinz:
Das ist mir ein sauberer Prinz! — There's a smoothie (*or* scoundrel) for you!

Prinzipienreiter:
Er ist ein Prinzipienreiter. — He's a stickler for principles; he's very dogmatic.

Pritsche:
Er ist von der Pritsche gefallen. — He took a tumble; he's out of a job.

Probe:
Stellen Sie ihn auf die Probe! — Give him the works (*or* acid test)!; see if he can take it!; try him out!

Probieren:
Probieren geht über Studieren. — The proof of the pudding is in the eating; practice is better than theory.

Prophet:
Sie haben Moses und die Propheten. — They've got what it takes; they've got plenty of jack (*or* money).

Provinz:
Er kommt aus der Provinz. — He comes from the sticks (*or* country).

Prozeß:
Er machte kurzen Prozeß damit. — He made short work of it.

Pudel:

Er zog ab wie ein begossener Pudel.

He slunk off like a dog with his tail between his legs.

Das also war des Pudels Kern!

So that was the gist (*or* crux) of the matter!; so that's how it was meant!

Er hat einen Pudel geschossen.

He pulled a boner; he made a bad break (*or* faux pas).

pudelnärrisch:

Der Junge war ganz pudelnärrisch.

The boy was full of the devil; he was cutting capers (*or* acting silly).

Puff:

Er kann schon einen Puff vertragen.

He can take it; he's thick-skinned; he can stand a good deal.

Er hat seine Püffe weg.

He's been put in his place; he was set to rights.

puffen:

Er lügt, daß es nur so pufft.

He lies like a trooper.

Pulver:

Das ist keinen Schuß Pulver wert.

That isn't worth a darn; it's no good.

Er hat das Pulver nicht erfunden.

He'll never set the world on fire; he'll never be anybody; he's a dumbbell (*or* stupid fellow).

Er kann kein Pulver riechen.

He can't take it; he's lily-livered (*or* chicken-hearted).

Er hat sein Pulver verschossen.

He's at the end of his rope (*or* resources).

Es fehlt ihm an Pulver.

He's short of cash (*or* money).

pumm(e)lig:

Sie ist ein pummeliges Frauchen.

She's a roly-poly; she's a chubby (*or* plump) little thing.

Pump:

Er läßt sich den Anzug auf Pump bauen.

He's having his suit made on credit.

pumpelig:

Er ist alt und pumpelig geworden.

He's grown old and tottery.

pumpen:

Können Sie mir drei Mark pumpen?

Can I touch you for three marks?; will you lend me three marks?

Punkt:

Nun machen Sie aber einen Punkt!

Now do stop (*or* let up) for a while!

In jeder Familie gibt es einen dunklen Punkt.

There's a skeleton in every closet; every family has its ugly duckling.

Das trifft auf den Punkt zu.

That's it to a T; that's exactly right.

Punktum:

Und damit Punktum!

And that's that!; and that's all there's to it!; let that be an end to it!

Puppe:

Das ist einfach Puppe!

That's first-rate (*or* A number one)!; that's the berries!; it's simply swell!

Er ist konservativ bis in die Puppen.

He's conservative to the core; he's a dyed-in-the-wool conservative.

Das geht über die Puppen.

That takes the cake; that's going too far.

Puſſelchen:
  Das Puſſelchen iſt zu poſſierlich.

The little tot (*or* youngster) is just too cute for words; it's the cutest little thing.

Puſte:
  Ihm ging die Puſte aus.

It took his breath away; he was winded.

Puſtekuchen:
  Ich glaubte, es wäre mein Bruder. Aber Puſtekuchen, es war jemand anders.

I thought it was my brother. But shucks, it was somebody else.

puſten:
  Sie wünſchen, daß ich das tue? Darauf puſte ich was!

You want me to do that? Well, you've got another guess coming!

puterrot:
  Er wurde puterrot.

He turned red as a beet.

püttcherig:
  Seien Sie doch nicht ſo püttcherig!
  Ich glaube, der Kerl iſt püttcherig.

Don't be so finicky (*or* particular)!
I believe the fellow is cracked (*or* crazy).

putzig:
  Das iſt aber putzig.

That's funny (*or* queer).

Q

Quadratſchädel:
Er iſt ein furchtbarer Quadratſchädel.

He's stubborn as a mule; he's terribly pig-headed.

Qual:
Wer die Wahl hat, hat die Qual.

Choosing is irksome.

Quälgeiſt:
Er iſt der reine Quälgeiſt.

He's an awful pest.

qualmen:
Bei dem qualmt's aber!

He's foaming with rage; he's rip-roaring mad.

Quark:
Er verſteht den Quark davon.

He doesn't know beans (or the first thing) about it.

Er miſcht ſich in jeden Quark.

He has his finger in every pie; he's always meddling in other people's business.

quaſſeln:
Quaſſel doch nicht!

Cut out the tripe!; don't talk nonsense!

Quaſſelſtrippe:
Er hängt den ganzen Tag an der Quaſſel=ſtrippe.

He's on the phone all day long.

Quatſch:
Ach Quatſch!

Nonsense!; rubbish!

quatſchnaß:
Sie waren quatſchnaß.

They were dripping wet.

Queckſilber:
Er iſt das reine Queckſilber.

He can't sit still a minute; he's a fidgety (or jittery) person.

Quelle:
Er hat die Nachricht aus guter Quelle.

He has the news on good authority (or from a reliable source).

quengeln:
Er quengelte ſo lange, bis ſie nachgab.
Er hat immer was zu quengeln.

He pestered her until she finally gave in.
He's always crabbing (or complaining) about something; he's never satisfied.

quer:
Heute ging alles quer.

Everything went screwy (or wrong) today.

Quere:
Sein Beſuch kam ihnen in die Quere.

His call put a crimp in (or spoiled) their scheme.

Es iſt das intereſſanteſte Buch, das mir je in die Quere kam.

It's the most interesting book I've ever run across.

253

quietſchfidel:
  Sie war quietſchfidel. | She was happy as a lark.

Quirl:
  Sie iſt ein rechter Quirl. | She's a fidgety (*or* jittery) person; she's always on the go.

quittieren:
  Er quittierte die Beleidigung mit einem Lächeln. | He repaid the offense with a smile.

R

Rabe:
 Er ſtiehlt wie ein Rabe.
 Er iſt ein weißer Rabe.
 Ihn werden die Raben freſſen.

He steals like a magpie; he's a born thief.
He's a rare bird; he's one in a million.
He'll end on the gallows.

rabenſchwarz:
 Die Nacht war rabenſchwarz.

The night was pitch-dark.

Rachen:
 Halt den Rachen!
 Er kann den Rachen nicht voll genug
 kriegen.

Can it!; shut up!
He's never satisfied; he can never get
 enough.

Rad:
 Es ſteht Galgen und Rad darauf.

It's a capital offense; the crime is punish-
 able by death.

 Er iſt unter die Räder gekommen.

He's gone to the dogs.

radebrechen:
 Er kann das Engliſche nur radebrechen.

He speaks broken English.

raffiniert:
 Das iſt raffiniert gemacht.

That's cleverly done; that's an ingenious
 device.

Rahmen:
 Eine Erörterung des Problems würde
 den Rahmen dieſer Arbeit ſprengen.
 Seine Rede fiel ganz aus dem Rahmen.
 Im Rahmen des Tragbaren wird er ihren
 Forderungen entgegenkommen.

A discussion of the problem falls beyond
 the scope of this paper.
His speech was quite out of the ordinary.
He'll meet their demands within reason (*or*
 in so far as possible).

rammdöſig:
 Er iſt ganz rammdöſig vom vielen Leſen.

He's quite woozy (*or* groggy) from so much
 reading.

Rampe:
 Ran an die Rampe!

Buckle down!; get to work!

Ramſch:
 Kaufen Sie nur keinen Ramſch!

Whatever you do don't buy any junk!;
 don't get a lot of knickknacks (*or* odds
 and ends).

 Er verkauft ſeine Waren im Ramſch.

He sells his goods at cut-throat prices; he
 undersells everyone else.

ran:
 Ran!

Let's go!; come on!

Rand:
 Halt den Rand!
 Das verſteht ſich am Rande.

Shut up!; hold your tongue!
That goes without saying; that's a matter
 of course.

Er geriet über das Geschenk außer Rand und Band.	He went wild over the present; he was crazy about (*or* thrilled over) it.
Er kommt damit nicht zu Rand.	He can't quite put it over; he can't make a go of it; he can't get it to work right.

Randal:
Hör doch auf mit dem Randal!
    Stop that racket (*or* noise)!

Rang:
Er hat ihnen den Rang abgelaufen.
    He outdid (*or* outwitted) them; he got the better of them.

Ranzen:
Er hat sich den Ranzen gefüllt.
    He's eaten his fill.

Rappel:
Er hatte seinen Rappel, als er jung war.
    He had his fling as a young fellow; he sowed his wild oats when he was young.

rappelköpfig:
Sei doch nicht so rappelköpfig!
    Don't be foolish!; don't get rattled (*or* excited)!

rappeln:
Bei Ihnen rappelt's wohl!
    You must be nutty (*or* crazy)!
Er hat sich wieder hoch gerappelt.
    He snapped out of it all right; he got over it.

rappeltrocken:
Der Wald war rappeltrocken.
    The forest was dry as tinder (*or* dust); it was bone-dry.

Rappen:
Er reist auf Schusters Rappen.
    He rides shank's pony; he trudges on foot.

Raptus:
Mit einem Male bekam er den Raptus, Sekt zu trinken.
    He suddenly had a yen (*or* craving) for some champagne.

Rapuse:
Das Buch ist in die Rapuse gegangen.
    The book went up the flue; it's lost.

rasend:
Er ist rasend hungrig.
    He's hungry as a bear.

rasieren:
Einen Augenblick, Sie werden gleich rasiert!
    Just a minute, you're next!
Wenn er sich nicht fügt, wird er rasiert.
    If he doesn't behave, he'll be scalped (*or* ousted).

Rasse:
Das ist Rasse mit Schlappohren!
    There's quality for you!; this is the real thing!

rasseln:
Er ist in der Prüfung glatt gerasselt.
    He flunked (the test) outright.

Rat:
Dafür ist Rat.
    There's a cure for that; something can be done about it.
Da ist guter Rat teuer!
    It's hard to advise in a case like that; that's a ticklish (*or* difficult) situation to be in!
Geschehene Dinge leiden keinen Rat.
    It's no use crying over spilt milk; what can't be cured must be endured.
Er weiß sich keinen Rat mehr.
    He's at his wits' end; he doesn't know what to do.

Er stand ihnen mit Rat und Tat zur Seite.	He advised and assisted them materially.
Gehen Sie mit sich selbst zu Rat!	Go into a huddle with yourself!; work it out for yourself!; use your own judgment!
Er muß sein Einkommen zu Rate halten.	He has to budget his income.
Man zog den Arzt zu Rat.	The doctor was called in; they consulted him.

raten:

Kommen Sie ja nicht wieder, das rate ich Ihnen!	You'd better not come back (if you know what's good for you)!
Er weiß sich nicht mehr zu raten noch zu helfen.	He's at his wits' end; he doesn't know where to turn.

Ratte:

Er hat eine Ratte im Kopf.	He has bats in his belfry; he's not all there; he's a little touched (or crazy).
Das ist für die Ratte.	You might as well throw it out; that's worthless (or good for nothing).
Die haben für die Ratten.	They're well-to-do; they have more than enough.

Rattenkönig:

Das ist ein wahrer Rattenkönig von Fehlern.	It's full of mistakes.

Ratz:

Er schläft wie eine Ratz.	He sleeps like a log (or top).

ratze(n)kahl:

Er aß alles ratzekahl auf.	He cleaned up the plate; he licked the platter clean.

Raubbau:

Das ist Raubbau an der Gesundheit.	That's burning the candle at both ends; you're ruining your health.

Räuber:

Er ist unter die Räuber gefallen.	He's in a bad way; he was badly done in; he's ruined.

Räuberhöhle:

Bei denen sieht's aus wie in einer Räuberhöhle.	Their place looks like a dump (or pigsty).

rauchen:

Heute raucht's!	Something's going to happen today!; danger ahead!
Er arbeitet, daß es nur so raucht.	Holy smoke, how he can work!; he works to beat the band.

Rauchfang:

Diese Forderung können Sie in den Rauchfang schreiben.	You can kiss that money goodbye; you can charge it to profit and loss; it's a dead loss.

Rauferei:

Die Versammlung endete in einer Rauferei.	The meeting ended in a free-for-all (or scrimmage).

Rauhbein:

Er ist ein altes Rauhbein.	He's an old battle-ax (or hoodlum); he's a tough guy.

Raum:
    Er gab ihrer Bitte Raum.
    He granted her request.

Raupe:
    Er spinnt sich wie eine Raupe ein.
    He draws into his shell; he shuts himself in like a hermit.

    Sie hat ihm Raupen in den Kopf gesetzt.
    She put a bee in his bonnet; she put crazy notions (*or* wild ideas) into his head.

Rausch:
    Er hat sich einen Rausch angetrunken.
    He got plastered (*or* drunk).

rauschend:
    Er empfing rauschenden Beifall.
    He received a thunderous ovation; he was greeted with a burst of applause.

rechnen:
    Er hat Ihnen zuviel dafür gerechnet.
    He overcharged you for it.

Rechnung:
    Man muß der neuen Zeit Rechnung tragen.
    One must adjust oneself to changing conditions.

    Er machte die Rechnung ohne den Wirt.
    He forgot to consider (*or* include) his host.

    Er hat seine Rechnung mit dem Himmel gemacht.
    He's squared up his account with God and man; he's made his peace with the world; he's prepared to die.

    Sind Sie auf Ihre Rechnung gekommen?
    Did it pay (you)?; did you make anything out of it?

    Er machte ihnen einen Strich durch die Rechnung.
    He queered (*or* upset) their plans.

    Sie sollten diesen Faktor in Rechnung ziehen.
    You should take this (factor) into consideration.

recht:
    Da gebe ich Ihnen recht.
    I agree with you there.

    Sie haben recht.
    You said it; you're right.

    Er kam eben recht.
    He came just in time; he came at the psychological moment.

    Da kommt er mir gerade recht!
    He's just the man I'm looking for!; he can't get away with that; just wait till I get him for that!

    Man kann es nicht jedem recht machen.
    One cannot please everybody.

    Das ist mir recht.
    That's O.K. with me; it suits me.

    So ist's recht!
    Attaboy!; that's the stuff; that's the way to do it!

    Alles, was recht ist.
    All that is fair and square; all that's coming to one.

    Ihm ist nicht recht.
    He's not feeling well.

    Das ist so recht etwas für ihn.
    That's the very thing for him; that will just suit him.

    Das ist recht schade.
    It's a pity (*or* shame).

    Er tut das recht gern.
    He gets a kick out of it; he loves to do it.

    Sie sind wohl nicht recht gescheit!
    You must be crazy!

    Glauben Sie, daß er's tut?—Ich weiß nicht recht.
    Do you think he'll do it?—I'm not so sure.

    Wenn ich es recht bedenke.
    Now that I think of it.

    Er wagte nicht recht zu fragen.
    He didn't quite dare ask.

    Was dem einen recht ist, ist dem andern billig.
    What is sauce for the goose is sauce for the gander; what goes for one goes for all.

Das ist nicht mehr wie recht und billig.	It's only fair.
Sie leben schlecht und recht.	They live a simple, honest life.
Er schafft schlecht und recht.	His work is average (*or* fair).
Das geht nicht mit rechten Dingen zu.	Something's rotten in Denmark; it smells fishy; there's something funny (*or* not right) about it.
Er nennt das Kind beim rechten Namen.	He calls a spade a spade; he speaks the plain truth.

Recht:

Recht muß doch Recht bleiben.	Right rules might; right can never be wrong.
Er versuchte, sich selbst Recht zu schaffen.	He tried to take the law into his own hands.
Wo nichts ist, hat selbst der Kaiser sein Recht verloren.	You can't get blood out of a turnip (*or* water out of a stone); nothing ever came of nothing.
Er ließ Gnade für Recht ergehen.	He showed mercy; he was compassionate.
Er tat das mit Fug und Recht.	He had good reason to do so; he was justified in doing it.

Rechte:

Sie sind mir der Rechte!	You're a nice one (to deal with)!; a fine fellow you turned out to be!
Da kam er an den Rechten.	He met his match.

Rechtes:

Er dünkt sich was Rechtes.	He thinks he is somebody; he has a pretty good opinion of himself.
Das ist auch was Rechtes!	A nice mess, this!
Er weiß nichts Rechtes.	He's no shining light; he's not much of a scholar.

rechtschaffen:

Er plagt sich rechtschaffen.	He's working very hard; he's wearing himself out.

Rechtsweg:

Dann muß er eben den Rechtsweg beschreiten.	Then he must take the matter to court.

Rector:

Er ist der Spiritus Rector des Ganzen.	He runs the whole show; he's the moving spirit behind the whole matter.

Rede:

Es geht die Rede, daß	Rumor has it that . . . ; it's been rumored that . . . .
Wenn die Rede darauf kommt.	If the subject should be mentioned.
Wovon ist die Rede?	What are you talking about?
Davon kann keine Rede sein.	That's out of the question; I wouldn't consider it.
Er hat die Gabe der Rede.	He's got the gift of gab; he can talk you deaf, dumb, and blind; he's a born preacher (*or* orator).
Es ist nicht der Rede wert.	Never mind!; forget it!; it's not worth mentioning.
Was ist der langen Rede kurzer Sinn?	What's the long and short of it?; just what is the point?; what is it you're driving at?
Er muß Rede und Antwort stehen.	He has to explain (*or* account for) himself; he has to submit to a cross-examination.

Was steht in Rede?	What's the issue (*or* subject of conversation)?; what are you talking about?
Er fiel ihr in die Rede.	He cut her short; he interrupted her.
Sie stellten ihn dieserhalb zur Rede.	They asked him what he meant by it; they took him to task for it.

reden:

Er läßt mit sich reden.	He's open to reason; he's willing to listen to reason.
Sie macht viel von sich reden.	She gives rise to much comment; she's much talked about.

reell:

Hier werden Sie reell bedient.	Here's where you'll get a square deal; we'll treat you fair.

Reelles:

Das ist doch was Reelles!	That really is something!; that's the real stuff (*or* genuine article)!

Reff:

Sie ist ein altes Reff.	She's an old hellcat (*or* battle-ax).

reflektieren:

Er reflektiert schon lange darauf.	He's had it in mind for a long time; he's been contemplating it for ever so long.

Regel:

Er besiegte ihn nach allen Regeln der Kunst.	He scored on every point; he defeated him in great style.

regen:

Er regt sich tüchtig.	He's very busy.
Er hat sich nicht geregt.	There hasn't been a sign (*or* peep out) of him; he hasn't shown up so far; he hasn't made a move (to pay) until now.

Regen:

Er kam vom Regen in die Traufe.	He fell from the frying pan into the fire; he went from bad to worse.

Regenschirm:

Ich bin darauf gespannt wie ein Regenschirm.	I'm all keyed up (*or* on edge) about it.

Regenwetter:

Er machte ein Gesicht wie vierzehn Tage Regenwetter.	He looked like a bad-weather prophet; he looked very glum (*or* sour).

regieren:

Geld regiert die Welt.	Money is king; money makes the world go round.

Regiment:

Sie führt das Regiment.	She wears the pants in that family; she's the boss (*or* head of the household).

Regiments(un)kosten:

Das geht auf Regimentsunkosten.	That's at the other fellow's expense; the public pays that.

Region:

Sie schwebt immer in höheren Regionen.	She's always living in the clouds; she's forever daydreaming.

Register:

Sie ist ein altes Register.

> She's an old number; she's an old hag (*or* crone).

Er zog alle Register.

> He pulled all his wires; he played all his cards; he tried every possible means.

Dem Kerl gegenüber sollten Sie andre Register ziehen!

> You should try other tactics with that fellow!

Er kommt ins alte Register.

> He's getting old.

Er brachte sie ins schwarze Register.

> He slandered them; he gave them a bad name (*or* reputation).

Reibeisen:

Sie ist ein rechtes Reibeisen.

> She's a born troublemaker.

Er hat eine Stimme wie ein Reibeisen.

> He has a voice like a screech owl; his voice grates on the nerves.

reiben:

Er wollte sich an uns reiben.

> He tried to rub us the wrong way; he tried to tease (*or* annoy) us.

reich:

Er hat reich geheiratet.

> He married money; he married an heiress.

reichen:

Reicht das?

> Will that do?; is that enough?

Darf ich Ihnen etwas reichen?

> May I help you to something?

reifer:

Er steht in reiferem Alter.

> He's reached the years of discretion; he's a mature person.

reiflich:

Überlegen Sie sich's reiflich!

> Go home and sleep on it!; think it over well!

Reigen:

Er eröffnete den Reigen der Ansprachen.

> He delivered the first address.

Reihe:

Es wurde bunte Reihe gemacht.

> They paired off.

Er ist an der Reihe.

> It's his turn.

Sie sind mit ihm noch nicht in der Reihe.

> They still haven't come to terms with him.

Er bringt das wieder in die Reihe.

> He'll fix that; he'll get it to work again.

Die Stühle standen der Reihe nach an der Wand.

> The chairs were arranged along the wall.

reihen:

Eins reiht sich ans andere.

> One thing follows the other.

Reim:

Ich kann keinen Reim darauf finden.

> I can't make head or tail out of it; it doesn't make sense.

reimen:

Wie reimt sich das?

> How do you make that out?; how do you reconcile (*or* account for) that?

rein:

Er wollte sich rein brennen.

> He tried to whitewash (*or* cover) himself; he tried to conceal his guilt.

Das ist rein nichts.

> That's nothing at all; that's a snap (*or* cinch); it's child's play.

Er war rein toll.

> He was mad as a March hare.

Das ist rein unmöglich.

> That's utterly impossible.

Sie sind sich noch nicht im reinen darüber.

> They haven't made up their minds about it yet.

Er sah aus, als wäre er mit der Welt im reinen.	He looked as if he had squared his account with the world; he could look everyone in the eye.
Er brachte es mit einem Federstrich ins reine.	He settled it by a stroke of his pen.
Schreiben Sie das ins reine!	Make a clean copy of it!
Er hielt reinen Mund.	He didn't blab; he kept mum; he kept it secret.
Er schenkte ihnen reinen Wein ein.	He told them the plain truth.

rein(e)weg:

Das ist reinweg zum Tollwerden!	That's enough to drive one crazy!

Reinfall:

Das ist ein böser Reinfall.	That's a tough break; that's a real misfortune.

Reinkultur:

Das ist Kitsch in Reinkultur.	That's pure tripe (or unadulterated trash).

reinlich:

Reinliche Scheidung tut not.	It calls for a divorce (or complete separation).

Reise:

Wohin geht die Reise?	Where are you bound (or headed) for?
Er weiß noch nicht, wohin die Reise geht.	He doesn't know yet where he'll be (or how things will develop).
Er ist auf Reisen.	He's on the road; he's traveling.

Reisende:

Ein armer Reisender stand vor der Tür.	A tramp stood at the door.

Reiseonkel:

Er ist Reiseonkel für Müller & Co.	He's a drummer (or traveling salesman) for Müller, Inc.

Reißaus:

Er nahm Reißaus.	He decamped (or absconded).

reißen:

Er reißt gern Witze.	He likes to wisecrack (or make jokes).
Die Sache reißt ins Geld.	It runs into a lot of money; it gets pretty expensive.
Man riß sich förmlich darum.	There was a mad scramble for it.

reißend:

Die Ware fand einen reißenden Absatz.	The article sold like hot cakes; there was a big (or ready) market for it.

Reißer:

Das neue Lustspiel ist ein Reißer.	The new comedy is a big hit (or success).

reiten:

Der Alp ritt ihn.	He had a nightmare.
Er wird ihn schon reiten.	He'll break him; he'll wear him down.

Reiz:

Das hat keinen Reiz für mich.	That doesn't go over so big with me; I can't go wild over that; that's not so hot (or good) in my opinion.

reizend:

Er ist ein reizender Bengel.	He's a swell guy; he's a good egg (or scout).

rekeln:	
Er rekelte sich auf dem Sofa.	He sprawled all over the sofa.
Rekord:	
Er hat ordentlich Rekord davor.	He treats it with real respect; he's scared to death of it.
Rennen:	
Er gab das Rennen auf.	He threw up the sponge; he gave up (the game).
Renommée:	
Sie steht in schlechtem Renommée.	She has a bad rep(utation); her name is on the black list.
Renommist:	
Er ist ein alter Renommist.	He's an old blow-hard (*or* braggart).
repartieren:	
Lassen Sie uns die Unkosten repartieren!	Let's go Dutch (*or* fifty-fifty)!; let's share expenses!
Repertoire:	
Das Stück hält sich noch immer auf dem Repertoire.	The show is still going strong; the play still draws a full house.
Respekt:	
Das ist, mit Respekt zu sagen, falsch.	Pardon me, but you're mistaken.
Ressort:	
Das ist mein Ressort!	Paddle your own canoe!; that's my business!; you keep out of this!
Rest:	
Das gab ihm den Rest.	That finished him off for good; that ruined him completely.
Er hat sich den Rest geholt.	He got a good dose of it; he fell dangerously ill.
Lassen Sie mich den Rest zur Hälfte tragen!	Let's split the difference!; let me pay half!
restlos:	
Sie sind restlos glücklich.	They're perfectly (*or* ideally) happy.
Retourkutsche:	
Das war eine feine Retourkutsche.	That was a snappy comeback (*or* answer); that was nice repartee.
retten:	
Rette sich, wer kann!	Every man for himself!
reuen:	
Jung gefreit hat noch niemand gereut.	Happy is the wooing that's not long in doing.
Revolverschnauze:	
Er hat die reine Revolverschnauze.	He's always shooting off his mouth; his tongue is loose at both ends.
revozieren:	
Er mußte revozieren.	He had to swallow his teeth; he had to retract his words.
Rezept:	
Er hat ihnen das Rezept verdorben.	He gummed up the works for them; he queered (*or* upset) their plans.

Rhein:

Das heißt Wasser in den Rhein tragen.	That's carrying coals to Newcastle; that's a waste of time (*or* energy).

richten:

Das richtet sich ganz danach.	That all depends.
Es richtet sich gegen ihn.	That's a slam (*or* dirty dig) at him; the remark is meant for him.
Er hat sich nach ihnen gerichtet.	He fell in line; he complied with their wishes.

richtig:

Richtig hat er's vergessen!	Didn't I say he'd forget it?; and sure enough, he forgot!
Er hat nicht richtig gehört, was sie sagte.	He didn't quite catch what she said.
Der Kerl ist richtig.	He's a square-shooter; he's on the level; he's honest and aboveboard.
Es ist nicht ganz richtig damit.	There's something fishy (*or* phoney) about it; something's wrong somewhere.

Richtige:

Das ist mir gerade der Richtige!	He's a fine fellow (to deal with)!; a nice person, indeed!

richtiggehend:

Es war eine richtiggehende Überraschung.	It came as a total surprise.

Richtigkeit:

Damit hat es seine Richtigkeit.	That's quite true; it's a fact.

Richtschnur:

Er hat es sich zur Richtschnur seines Lebens gemacht.	He made it a point (*or* rule).

Richtung:

Geben Sie Ihren Gedanken eine andere Richtung!	Think about something else!; forget it!
Er berührte die mannigfachen Richtungen in der Dichtung.	He touched on the various trends in literature.
Das ist in jeder Richtung verkehrt.	That's entirely wrong.
Er will sich nach keiner Richtung hin festlegen.	He won't commit himself in any way.

riechen:

Er kann den Kerl nicht riechen.	That fellow gives him a pain; he can't stomach (*or* stand) him.
Das konnte ich doch nicht riechen!	How was I to know?

Riecher:

Er hat einen guten Riecher für solche Sachen.	He has a good nose (*or* an instinctive feeling) for things like that.

Riegel:

Er schob dem Gerede einen Riegel vor.	He spiked (*or* squelched) the rumor.
Er sitzt hinter Schloß und Riegel.	They've got him under lock and key; he's behind the bars (*or* in jail).

Riemen:

Aus fremdem Leder ist gut Riemen schneiden.	It's easy when you make the other fellow pay.
Um das Examen zu bestehen, muß er sich sehr in die Riemen legen.	He'll have to knuckle down (*or* get down to brass tacks) in order to pass the exam(ination).

Riese:
Nach Adam Riese stimmt das.

That's right as rain; there's no getting away from it.

riesig:
Sie haben sich riesig gefreut.

They were tickled pink; they were awfully pleased.

Rind:
Der Reiche hat die Rinder, der Arme die Kinder.

Rich men feed and poor men breed.

Rindfleisch:
Man kann vom Ochsen nicht mehr verlangen als Rindfleisch.

You can't make a silk purse out of a sow's ear; what else can you expect?

Ring:
Du kannst mich um den Ring pfeifen!

Go chase yourself!; go to blazes!

ringen:
Er ringt mit dem Tod.

He's in the grip of death.

Rippe:
Man kann sich's doch nicht aus den Rippen schneiden.

You can't draw blood from a turnip; you can't conjure it up.

Er hat's durch die Rippen geschwitzt.

It slipped his mind; he forgot it.

riskieren:
Lassen Sie uns einen riskieren!

Let's blow (or treat) ourselves to a drink!

Riß:
In ihre Freundschaft kam ein tiefer Riß.

Their friendship suffered a severe setback; a gulf arose between them.

Es gab ihm einen Riß.

It gave him a shock; it startled him.

Er trat vor den Riß.

He stepped into the breach; he paid the bill.

Ritter:
Er sah aus wie der Ritter von der traurigen Gestalt.

He looked like Don Quixote himself; he looked very mournful (or woe-begone).

Rock:
Das ist Rock wie Hose.

That's six of one and half a dozen of the other; it's all the same.

Das Hemd ist mir näher als der Rock.

Blood is thicker than water; charity begins at home.

Rocken:
Er hat auch Werg am Rocken.

His hands aren't clean either; he too is implicated (or guilty).

roh:
Er muß wie ein rohes Ei behandelt werden.

He has to be handled with kid gloves; he's a very touchy (or sensitive) person.

Rohbau:
Die Arbeit ist im Rohbau fertig.

The dirty (or rough) work is done; the foundation has been laid.

Rohr:
Er säuft wie ein Rohr.

He's a regular tank; he drinks like a fish.

Er hat etwas auf dem Rohr.

He has his eye on something; he has a prospect in view.

Wer im Rohr sitzt, hat gut Pfeifen schneiden.

It's easy preaching when you're sitting pretty (or well off).

Man muß sein Pfeifchen schneiden, solange man im Rohr sitzt.

Make hay while the sun shines!; make the most of your opportunities!

Rohrspatz:

Sie schimpfte wie ein Rohrspatz.

She railed (*or* scolded) like a fishwife; she was an old nag.

Rolle:

Er spielt eine erbärmliche Rolle.

He cuts a poor figure; he makes a poor showing.

Er spielt eine große Rolle in der Firma.

He's one of the big shots (*or* top men) in the firm.

Geld spielt keine Rolle.

Money cuts no ice; money is no consideration.

Er fiel aus der Rolle.

He forgot to play up; he showed his true character.

Rollen:

Der Stein kam ins Rollen.

Fate took its course; the ball started rolling.

Rom:

Auf diesem Messer kann man nach Rom reiten.

This surely is a dull knife; you couldn't cut hot butter with it.

Das hieße den Ablaß nach Rom tragen.

That would be carrying coals to Newcastle; that's a waste of time (*or* energy).

Los von Rom!

Shake a leg!; get a move on!; hurry up!

Rose:

Sie sind nicht auf Rosen gebettet.

Life isn't all roses (*or* beer and skittles) for them; they're having a hard time of it.

Sie sagte es ihm unter der Rose.

She told him that confidentially; she confided it to him.

Rosine:

Er hat alle Rosinen aus dem Kuchen gepickt.

He kept all the plums (*or* cream) for himself; he took the best for himself and left them holding the bag.

Sie hat große Rosinen im Kopf.

She entertains high-flown (*or* big) ideas; she's very ambitious; she has an excellent opinion of herself.

Roß:

So ein Roß!

What an ass (*or* sap)!

rot:

Heute rot, morgen tot.

Here today, gone tomorrow.

Das werde ich mir rot anstreichen.

I'll make a special note of that.

Der Gedanke zieht sich wie ein roter Faden durch das Buch.

The idea forms the central theme of the book.

Jemand hat ihm den roten Hahn aufs Dach gesetzt.

Someone set fire to his house.

Rotspon:

Lassen Sie uns eine Flasche Rotspon verdrücken!

Let's put away (*or* drink up) a bottle of claret!

Rübe:

Das ist eine freche Rübe.

He's a fresh bird (*or* egg).

Seine Kleider lagen herum wie Kraut und Rüben.

His clothes were scattered all over the place.

Er hat eins auf die Rübe gekriegt.

He got it in the neck; he was called down (*or* bawled out).

Rübchen:
Er schabte ihm ein Rübchen.
He jeered at him; he made fun of him.

Ruck:
Die Wahlen ergaben einen Ruck nach rechts.
The election resulted in a sharp swerve to the Right; it put the conservatives ahead.

Geben Sie der Sache mal einen Ruck!
Give the matter a hand (*or* shove)!; help it along!

Er gab sich einen Ruck.
He pulled himself together; he took himself in hand.

rücken:
Rücke!
Scram!; beat it!

Rücken:
Ihnen juckt wohl der Rücken!
I believe you're itching for a drubbing!; you must be looking for trouble!

Er deckt ihnen den Rücken.
He's backing them up; he's supporting them.

Er hat einen breiten Rücken.
He can take (*or* stand) it; he can put up with a lot.

Er liegt den ganzen Tag auf dem Rücken.
He loafs (*or* lolls) around all day long; he's taking it easy.

Es lief ihr kalt über den Rücken.
It gave her the creeps (*or* shivers); she shuddered.

rückhaltlos:
Er gab es rückhaltlos zu.
He made no bones about it; he admitted it point-blank.

Rückstand:
Er ist mit seiner Arbeit im Rückstand.
He's behind with his work.

rückständig:
Er ist rückständig in seinem Beruf.
He's a back number in his profession; professionally, he's behind the times.

Rückzieher:
Seine Rede war nichts andres als ein Rückzieher.
He swallowed his teeth; his speech was nothing less than a retreat (*or* recantation).

Rudel:
Sie haben ein ganzes Rudel Kinder.
They've a whole string (*or* bunch) of children.

Rüffel:
Er erhielt einen gehörigen Rüffel.
He got a sound bawling-out.

Ruhe:
Ruhe!
Order!; quiet!; silence!

Nur die Ruhe kann es bringen!
Hold your horses!; take it easy!; don't get excited!

Er war die Ruhe selber.
He was cool as a cucumber; he was calm as could be.

Angenehme Ruhe!
Good night!; pleasant dreams!; sleep well!

Er hat nirgends Ruhe.
He never stays put; he's always on the go; he can't settle down.

Er ist nicht aus der Ruhe zu bringen.
He can't be ruffled; he never loses his self-possession.

Überlegen Sie sich's in aller Ruhe!
Go home and sleep on it!; take your time about it!

Immer mit der Ruhe!	Keep your shirt on!; take it easy!; don't get excited!
Er kam endlich zur Ruhe.	He finally calmed down.
Er hat ſich zur Ruhe geſetzt.	He's retired (from business).
Ruheſtand:	
Er iſt in den Ruheſtand verſetzt.	He's been pensioned off.
ruhig:	
Seien Sie deshalb ruhig!	Never mind!; don't let it worry you!
Das können Sie ruhig tun.	You may feel perfectly free to do that; go right ahead!
Ruhig Blut!	Don't boil over!; keep your temper!; take it easy!
Ruhm:	
Den Ruhm muß man ihm laſſen.	You must hand it to him; you must give him credit for it.
Sie haben ſich nicht gerade mit Ruhm bekleckert!	I don't see where you've won any medals!; you haven't done so well by yourself, have you?
Rühmen:	
Er macht nicht viel Rühmens davon.	He doesn't make much fuss about it.
Ruine:	
Er iſt nur noch eine Ruine.	He's a total wreck.
rum:	
Es iſt rum wie num.	That is six of one and half a dozen of the other; it's all the same.
Rummel:	
Er kennt den Rummel.	He's an old hand; he knows the ropes (or tricks).
Sie machen den Rummel nicht mehr mit.	They've called it quits; they're through (with the whole business).
Er verkaufte den ganzen Rummel.	He sold the whole kit and caboodle (or the whole shebang); he sold it lock, stock, and barrel.
rumoren:	
Das Problem der Inflation rumort in vielen Köpfen.	Many people are mulling over (or concerned about) the problem of inflation.
Rumpelkaſten:	
Sein Auto iſt ein alter Rumpelkaſten.	His car is an old tin can.
rund:	
Das iſt ihm zu rund.	That's too deep (or much) for him; that's beyond his comprehension.
Er hat ſich dick und rund gegeſſen.	He's stuffed himself; he's eaten his fill.
Sie machte runde Augen.	Her eyes were like saucers; she was wide-eyed with surprise.
Runde:	
Er ſchmiß einige Runden.	He blew (or treated) the crowd to several drinks.
rundheraus:	
Rundheraus geſagt, ich tue es nicht.	To be perfectly frank (or To put it bluntly), I won't.
rundweg:	
Er lehnte es rundweg ab.	He refused it point-blank.

Runks:
   Das ist ein rechter Runks. | He's a regular hick (*or* farmer).

Rüpelei:
   Es war mehr Rüpelei als Spiel. | The game was more horseplay than anything else.

rupfen:
   Man hat sie gehörig gerupft. | They were badly fleeced (*or* done in).

ruppig:
   Er benahm sich ruppig. | He behaved shabbily.

Ruß:
   Machen Sie keinen Ruß! | Don't make a fuss (*or* scene)!; don't be a fool!; don't start something!

Rute:
   Sie flechten sich da selber die Rute. | You're digging your own grave by doing that; you're cutting your own throat.

rutschen:
   Sie wollen morgen an die Küste rutschen. | They're leaving for the coast tomorrow.

Rutschen:
   Er ist ins Rutschen gekommen. | He's slipping (*or* on the skids); he's going downhill; he's a goner.

rütteln:
   Daran ist nicht zu rütteln. | That's final (*or* settled).

Sache:

Das ist Sache! — Hot dog (*or* stuff)!; swell!; capital!

Nachdenken ist nicht jedermanns Sache. — Thinking is not everyone's line; we're not all philosophers.

Es war beschlossene Sache. — It was a foregone conclusion.

Das ist ganz meine Sache. — That suits me fine.

Das ist seine Sache. — That's his business.

Er ist seiner Sache sicher. — He knows what he's about.

Er ging unverrichteter Sache. — He went as he had come; he left empty-handed (*or* without having accomplished his mission).

Um die Sache kurz zu machen. — To cut a long story short; to get to the point.

Machen Sie keine Sachen! — You don't say!; is it possible?; don't be a fool!; don't start something!

Bleiben Sie bei der Sache! — Stick to the point!; don't evade the issue!

Er ist nicht bei der Sache. — He's absent-minded; his mind isn't on his work.

Was sind das für Sachen! — What is this!; for heaven's sake!

In Sachen des X. — In the case of X.

In Sachen des Geschmacks läßt sich nicht streiten. — There's no accounting for tastes; tastes differ.

Zur Sache! — Question! (*at a meeting*).

Das tut nichts zur Sache. — That makes no difference; that's irrelevant.

sachlich:

Die Arbeit ist sprachlich wie sachlich gut. — It's a good piece of work, both as to form and content.

Sachlichkeit:

Der Bau ist im Stil der neuen Sachlichkeit gehalten. — The building bears all the earmarks of the new modernistic style (functionalism).

sacht:

Das tut sacht. — It does one good.

Sack:

Der Sack ist noch nicht zugebunden. — The issue is still open (*or* undecided); the matter has not yet been settled.

Er schläft wie ein Sack. — He sleeps like a log (*or* top).

Der Himmel ist wie ein Sack. — The sky is overcast.

Er ist grob wie ein Sack. — He's rude (*or* gruff) as a bear.

Er ist voll wie ein Sack. — He's full up to the ears; he's dead-drunk.

Er schlägt den Sack und meint den Esel. — He says one thing and means another.

Er machte eine Faust im Sack. — He gritted his teeth; he steeled himself to it.

Er kauft nicht die Katze im Sack. — He doesn't buy a pig in a poke; he looks before he leaps; he's got his eyes open.

Er hielt die Pfeife im Sack. — He had nothing to say; he felt glum (*or* dejected).

Die Kinder haben Lachen und Weinen in einem Sack.	The children laugh and cry in the same breath.
Es ist dunkel wie in einem Sack.	It's pitch-dark.
Zehn Mann der Fabrik haben in den Sack gehauen.	Ten men walked out of the plant.
Er langte tief in den Sack.	He paid out a lot of money; he paid well for it.
Er steckt jeden in den Sack.	He has everyone under his thumb; he outdoes everyone.
Er steckte die Pfeife in den Sack.	He threw up his hands; he gave up the game.
Er zog mit Sack und Pack ab.	He left, bag and baggage.
Sackgasse:	
Bei den Verhandlungen sind sie in eine Sackgasse geraten.	Negotiations have reached a deadlock; negotiations have hit a snag (or run into difficulties).
sackgrob:	
Er war sackgrob.	He was rude as a bear (or extremely coarse).
Sackstrippe:	
Er war bezecht wie eine Sackstrippe.	He was loaded to the muzzle; he was dead-drunk.
Sackträger:	
Ein Esel schilt den andern Sackträger.	The kettle calls the pot black; one crook accuses another.
Saft:	
Er ist ein Mensch ohne Saft und Kraft.	He's wishy-washy; he's a softy (or spineless creature).
saftig:	
Der Aufstieg war ziemlich saftig.	The climb was pretty tough.
Es war ein saftiger Witz.	It was a dirty joke.
sagen:	
Er gab ihr sage und schreibe drei Mark.	Just think of it, he gave her three marks just like that!
Was Sie sagen!	Well, I never!; you don't say so!
Ich hätte beinahe was gesagt!	Well, I declare (or never)!
Es ist nicht gesagt, daß er nicht wieder gesund wird.	That doesn't mean that he won't recover.
Lassen Sie sich das gesagt sein!	Let this be a warning to you!
Das hat nichts zu sagen.	Never mind!; that's O.K. (or all right); it doesn't matter.
Es ist nicht zu sagen!	Drat it!; it's incredible!
Er läßt sich nichts sagen.	He won't listen to anyone; no one can tell him anything.
Was noch mehr sagen will.	And what's more; moreover.
Was wollen Sie damit sagen?	What do you mean by that?
Ich will nichts gesagt haben.	Don't tell anyone I said so.
Saite:	
Dem sollten Sie einmal die Saiten hochspannen.	You should put him in his place (or set him to rights).
Er droht, andere Saiten aufzuziehen.	He threatens to use other measures.
Salat:	
Da haben wir den Salat!	Now you've got it!; a nice mess to be in!
Machen Sie nur keinen Salat!	Shut up!; keep quiet!; don't make a fuss!

Salbe:

Das ist wie die weiße Salbe.	That can't do any harm.
Er ist mit allen Salben geschmiert.	He knows his onions; he's a sly old fox.

Salm:

Er machte einen langen Salm darüber.	He made a big stew (or fuss) about it.

Salz:

Das Buch hat weder Salz noch Schmalz.	The book is flat (or uninteresting).
Wir beide haben noch keinen Scheffel Salz miteinander gegessen!	Have we ever been introduced?; keep your distance!; don't get familiar!
Damit verdient er nicht das Salz auf die Suppe.	That wouldn't buy him a cup of coffee; he can't get very far on that.
Er hat einen Schinken bei mir im Salz!	I've got a bone to pick with him!; he's got something coming to him from me!; he'll get his yet!
Er liegt schwer im Salz.	He's in a hot (or tight) spot; he's in a real fix.

Sammelsurium:

Seine Wohnung ist ein Sammelsurium von Altertümlichkeiten.	His home is a regular antique shop; he's a collector of antiques.

samt:

Sie wurden samt und sonders hingerichtet.	Every last one of them was executed.

Sand:

Er hat Schulden wie Sand am Meer.	He's up to his ears in debt.
Punktum, streu Sand drauf!	That's that!; let that be final!; that's settled once and for all!
Er streute ihnen Sand in die Augen.	He threw dust into (or pulled the wool over) their eyes; he hoodwinked them.
Er ackert den Sand.	He's beating the air; he's wasting his time.
Er hat ihn auf den Sand gesetzt.	He outdid (or defeated) him.
Sein Eifer verlief sich im Sand.	His zeal petered out; it came to nought.

Sang:

Sein Angebot wurde ohne Sang und Klang abgelehnt.	His offer was turned down unceremoniously (or without discussion); it was refused point-blank.

Sänger:

Darüber schweigt des Sängers Höflichkeit.	Don't let's talk about it!; better say no more about it!

sanglos:

Er verschwand sang- und klanglos.	He took French leave; he slunk away; he disappeared without a word.

satt:

Er hat es satt.	He's fed up with it; he's sick and tired of it.
Sie kann sich nicht satt daran sehen.	She can't feast her eyes enough on it.

Sattel:

Er hob seinen Gegner aus dem Sattel.	He outdid (or supplanted) his opponent.
Er kann sich nicht im Sattel halten.	He can't hold his ground; he's losing out.
Er ist in allen Sätteln gerecht.	He can turn his hand to anything; he fits in anywhere.

sattelfest:

Er wurde bei der Prüfung nicht ganz sattelfest befunden.	He didn't quite make the grade; he just missed passing the exam(ination).

Sau:

Er fuhr sie an wie die Sau den Bettelsack.	He treated them like dirt; he snubbed them.
Er lief davon wie die Sau vom Trog.	He ran off without a word of thanks.
Schon wieder eine Sau im Heft!	Another blot in your notebook!
Wir haben noch nicht die Säue miteinander gehütet!	Have we ever been introduced?; keep your distance!; don't get familiar!
Das ist unter aller Sau.	That's a dirty rotten deal (*or* trick); it's contemptible.

Sauarbeit:

Das ist eine Sauarbeit!	That's a hell of a job!; that's a rotten (*or* nasty) job!

sauber:

Er ist ein sauberes Früchtchen geworden.	He went completely to seed; he went wrong (*or* to the dogs).
Das ist ein sauberes Kleeblatt.	That's a bad lot; they're tough customers; they're a bunch of crooks.
Das ist mir ein sauberer Prinz!	There's a smoothie (*or* scoundrel) for you!

Sauce:

Da sitzen wir in der Sauce!	Now we're in the soup!; a pretty mess to be in!

sauer:

Es kommt ihm sauer an zu bleiben.	It goes against his grain to stay; he can't stomach it.
Das kann ihm noch sauer aufstoßen.	That may have unpleasant consequences for him.
Das Schreiben fällt ihr sauer.	She hates to write.
Das kannst du dir sauer kochen!	Keep the old thing!; it's no good to us.
Machen Sie sich doch das Leben nicht so sauer!	Don't take things so hard!; don't make life any tougher than it is!
Er reagiert sauer.	He's in a bad temper; he doesn't respond.
Er läßt sich die Arbeit sauer werden.	He toils like a Trojan; he works hard.
Er muß in den sauern Apfel beißen.	He has to swallow the bitter pill; he has to take his medicine; he has to suffer the consequences.
Er bot sich an wie sauer Bier.	He was willing to work for a song (*or* practically nothing).

Sauerei:

So eine Sauerei!	What a scummy business!; some mess!

Saufen:

Es war kein Trinken mehr, es war schon Saufen.	They didn't drink, they guzzled.

saugrob:

Er kam ihnen saugrob.	He treated them very rudely.

Sauladen:

Der Frontabschnitt war, auf gut deutsch gesagt, ein Sauladen.	That section of the front was a hell hole, to put it in plain English.

Saulus:

Er ist aus einem Saulus ein Paulus geworden.	He turned over a new leaf; he changed for the better.

saumäßig:

Er hat das saumäßig gemacht.	He did a lousy (*or* rotten) job.
Sie hatten ein saumäßiges Glück.	Their luck was uncanny; they were very lucky.

Sauregurkenzeit:
Seine Ferien fallen gerade in die Sauregurkenzeit.

His vacation comes just during the slack season.

Saures:
Gib ihm Saures!

Give him a good dose of it!; knock the stuffings out of him!

Saus:
Er lebt in Saus und Braus.

He's a high-stepper; he lives fast; he leads a gay life.

sausen:
Der Kopf sauste ihr.

Her ears were ringing (*or* buzzing); her head was in a whirl.

Sauser:
Lassen Sie uns einen Sauser machen!

Let's make whoopee!; let's go on a binge (*or* spree).

Saustall:
Das ist ein schöner Saustall!

A fine kettle of fish!; a nice mess, this!

Sauwetter:
So ein Sauwetter!

What lousy (*or* beastly) weather!

sauwohl:
Ihm ist sauwohl.

He's feeling grand; he's in the best of spirits.

Schabbesdeckel:
Laß doch den Schabbesdeckel daheim!

Leave your lid (*or* hat) at home!

schaben:
Er schabte ihm ein Rübchen.

He jeered at him; he made fun of him.

Schablone:
Die meisten dieser Leute sind Schablonen, keine Menschen.

Most of them are machines (*or* automatons), not men.

schachmatt:
Er ist schachmatt.

He's all in; he's completely worn out.

Schachtel:
Sie ist eine alte Schachtel.

She's an old hen (*or* maid).

schade:
Das ist aber schade!
Dafür ist ihm sein guter Name zu schade.

That's too bad!; what a shame (*or* pity)!
He thinks too well of himself for that; he wouldn't compromise his good name for anything.

Schädel:
Er wird sich den Schädel schon einrennen.
Er will immer gleich mit dem Schädel durch die Wand.

He's sure to come to grief; he'll regret it yet.
He's always knocking his head against a stone wall; he always wants to do the impossible; he's pig-headed.

Schade(n):
Es soll dein Schaden nicht sein.

You won't regret it; you won't lose anything by it.

Wer den Schaden hat, braucht für den Spott nicht zu sorgen.

The laugh is always on the loser.

Durch Schaden wird man klug.

A burnt child dreads the fire; live and learn!; experience is the best teacher.

schaden:
Das schadet nichts.
Das schadet ihm gar nichts.

That's all right; it won't do any harm.
That serves him right.

schädlich:
Was dem einen gut ist, ist dem andern schädlich.

What's one man's meat is another man's poison.

schadlos:
Er wird sich schon schadlos halten.

He'll look after himself all right; he'll see to it that he doesn't get left.

Schaf:
Er ist ein rechtes Schaf.
Er treibt das Schaf aus.
Er hat sich vom Schaf beißen lassen.

He's a big sap (or dumbbell).
He's making a fool of himself.
He was made a sucker; he let himself be taken in.

Schäfchen:
Er hat sein Schäfchen im trockenen.

He's got his little pile (or bank account); he's well off.

Er weiß sein Schäfchen zu scheren.

He knows how to feather his nest; he knows how to make money.

Der Abendhimmel war mit silbernen Schäfchen bedeckt.

The evening sky was lined with fleecy (or cirrus) clouds.

schaffen:
Schaff uns was zu essen!
Das schafft!
Das hätten wir geschafft!
Was haben Sie hier zu schaffen?
Er macht ihnen viel zu schaffen.

Fix (or Get) us something to eat!
Good work!; well done!
Well, that's that!; we did it!
What business have you here?
He keeps them on the go; he gives them a great deal of trouble.

Schaffhausen:
Es war ein Reinfall bei Schaffhausen.

It was a dismal flop (or failure); it was a big letdown (or disappointment).

Schafleder:
Er riß aus wie Schafleder.

He tore (or ran) off like mad.

Schale:
Die Schale senkte sich zu seinen Gunsten.

Fortune was in his favor.

schalten:
Man läßt ihn schalten und walten.

He's given plenty of rope (or freedom); he's allowed to do pretty much as he likes.

Schamade:
Er blies die Schamade.

He came down a peg; he came off his high horse; he gave in.

Schande:
Ich habe es, zu meiner Schande sei es gesagt, ganz vergessen.

I'm ashamed to admit it, but I completely forgot.

Schandfleck:
Er wollte Ihnen gewiß keinen Schandfleck anhängen.

I'm quite sure he didn't mean to cast any aspersions (or reflections) on your character.

Schandgeld:
Er verkaufte das Haus für ein Schandgeld.

He sold the house for a mere song; he sold it dirt-cheap.

Schandtat:
Er ist zu jeder Schandtat bereit. — He's ready for anything; he's a good sport.

Schanze:
Er schlug sein Leben für sie in die Schanze. — He risked his life for them.

schanzen:
Er muß tüchtig schanzen. — He has to work like a dog.

scharf:
Er faßt seine Leute scharf an. — He's very hard on (*or* strict with) his men.
Wenn Sie scharf ausschreiten, können Sie es in einer Stunde schaffen. — If you step on it (*or* hurry up), you'll be able to make it in an hour.
Den habe ich scharf. — I've got it in for him; I hate him.
Er machte die Leute gegen ihren Arbeitgeber scharf. — He set the men against their boss.
Er ist scharf auf Kuchen. — He's after cookies; he has a sweet tooth.
Er hat eine scharfe Nase. — He has a keen sense of smell; he's quick to spot (*or* sense) danger.
Sie hält scharfe Zucht. — She rules with an iron hand.

Schärfe:
Ihn traf die ganze Schärfe des Gesetzes. — He was punished to the fullest extent of the law.
Er sagte das ohne jede persönliche Schärfe. — He said it without personal malice.

Scharte:
Er muß die Scharte wieder auswetzen. — He has to wipe out the score; he must square accounts.

Scharteke:
Sie ist eine alte Scharteke. — She's an old hag (*or* maid).

schaffen:
Schaß dich! — Vamoose!; beat it!
Man hat ihn geschaßt. — He was fired (*or* dismissed).

Schatten:
Sie machen mir Schatten! — You're standing in my light!
Das wirft einen Schatten auf seinen Charakter. — That reflects on his character.
Verlieren Sie nicht über dem Schatten den Kern! — Don't get off the track!; don't lose sight of the main issue!

Schattenseite:
Das sind die Schattenseiten des Plans. — Those are the drawbacks to (*or* disadvantages of) the plan.

Schattierung:
Die Presse aller Schattierungen verurteilt das Abkommen. — Newspapers of every shade of opinion condemn the agreement.

Schau:
Er trug eine gemachte Ruhe zur Schau. — He assumed an air of calm.

schauen:
Schau, daß du weiter kommst! — Get going!; beat it!
Trau, schau, wem! — Look before you leap!; don't trust every Tom, Dick, and Harry!
Schau, schau! — Well, well!; what have we here?
Wie schaut's? — How's tricks?; how's the world treating you?

Schauerroman:
Er las einen Schauerroman.

He was reading a dime novel; he was reading a thriller (*or* detective story).

Schaum:
Träume sind Schäume.

Dreams are mere shadows.

Glauben Sie ihm nicht, er schlägt nur Schaum.

Don't believe him, he's just making conversation (*or* kidding you along); he's just a big bluffer.

scheckig:
Er lachte sich scheckig darüber.

He split his sides laughing.

Er ist bekannt wie ein scheckiger Hund.

You'd spot (*or* recognize) him in the dark; he's known everywhere.

Scheffel:
Wir beide haben noch keinen Scheffel Salz miteinander gegessen!

Have we ever been introduced?; keep your distance!; don't get familiar!

Es goß wie mit Scheffeln.

It rained pitchforks.

Scheibe:
Ist Ihr Freund gekommen, wie verabredet war?—Scheibe links!

Did your friend come as agreed?—Hell, no!; like fun he did!

Schein:
Er besteht auf seinen Schein.

He insists on his claim.

Er behauptet das mit einem gewissen Schein der Berechtigung.

He maintains that with a certain pretense of justification.

Er kam unter dem Schein der Freundschaft.

He came under the guise of friendship.

Scheinfriede:
Es ist nur ein Scheinfriede.

It's only a patched-up (*or* makeshift) peace.

Scheinwerfer:
Er wurde plötzlich von dem Scheinwerfer des öffentlichen Interesses beleuchtet.

He suddenly came into the limelight (*or* public eye).

Scheitel:
Sie ist Dame vom Scheitel bis zur Sohle.

She's every inch a lady; she's a lady from head to foot.

Schelle:
Jeder hat seine Schelle.

Everyone has his hobby.

Er verabreichte ihm ein paar Schellen.

He slapped him in the face.

schellen:
Jetzt hat's aber geschellt!

It's time to call a halt!; that's the limit!; that's going a little too far!

Schellenkönig:
Das geht noch über den Schellenkönig!

That takes the cake!; that beats all!

Man lobt ihn über den Schellenkönig.

He's praised to the skies.

Schelm:
Ein Schelm, der mehr gibt, als er kann!

You can't give more than you have!; you can't expect the impossible!

Ich will ein Schelm sein, wenn ich das getan habe!

You can call me a liar if I did that!

Er ist ein armer Schelm.

He's a poor wretch.

Er hat den Schelm im Nacken sitzen.

He's a big tease; he's full of fun.

Auf einen Schelm gehören anderthalbe.

Set a thief to catch a thief!; pay rogues in their own coin!

Man hat ihn zum Schelm gemacht.

They painted him pretty black; they slandered him.

Schema:
Bei ihm geht alles nach Schema F.

He's a regular rubber stamp (*or* automaton); he does everything by rote (*or* in a routine manner).

schematisch:
Er führte die Anordnung rein schematisch aus.

He carried out the letter rather than spirit of the order.

schenken:
Er schenkte sich den letzten Teil seiner Rede.

He cut (out) (*or* omitted) the last part of his speech.

Man hat ihm das Mündliche geschenkt.

He was excused from the oral exam(ination).

Es soll ihm diesmal geschenkt sein.

I'll let him off this time.

Scherbe:
Bei dieser Aussprache wird es wohl Scherben geben.

This conference may wreck things; it may spell disaster.

Schere:
Er hat ihn in die Schere genommen.

He razzed (*or* censured) him; he set him to rights.

scheren:
Scher dich!

Scram!; beat it!

Er schert sich den Teufel darum.

He doesn't give a damn.

Schererei:
Der Junge macht ihr viel Schererei.

The boy gives her a great deal of trouble.

Scherflein:
Haben Sie schon Ihr Scherflein beigesteuert?

Did you throw in your two-cents' worth?; did you contribute your mite?

Scherz:
Er versteht keinen Scherz.

He has no sense of humor.

Er trieb seinen Scherz mit ihnen.

He poked fun at them.

Machen Sie keine faulen Scherze!

Oh, go on!; you wouldn't kid me?

scherzen:
Er läßt nicht mit sich scherzen.

He's not to be trifled with.

Sie belieben wohl zu scherzen!

You're kidding; you're talking through your hat!; you don't mean it!

Scheu:
Er sprach ohne Scheu.

He spoke without reserve.

Schicht:
Sie haben bereits Schicht gemacht.

They've knocked off; they've called it a day; they've stopped working.

schicken:
Eines schickt sich nicht für alle.

One man's meat is another man's poison; what goes for one does not necessarily go for all.

Schiebung:
Schiebung!

It's a racket (*or* swindle)!; we've been blackmailed!

schiedlich:
Sie haben sich schiedlich, friedlich geeinigt.

They've come to terms amicably.

schief:
Er sah sie schief an.

He gave them a dirty (*or* nasty) look; he scowled at them.

Da sind Sie aber schief gewickelt!	You're all wet!; that's where you're wrong!
Er hat schief geladen.	He's in a drunken stupor; he's had more than his share (of drink).
Nehmen Sie die Sache nicht schief!	Don't take it ill (or amiss)!; don't misunderstand!
Er ist auf der schiefen Bahn.	He's on the skids; he's sliding downhill; he's going to the dogs.
Er ist in einer schiefen Lage.	He's on the spot; he's in a tight place; he's in serious trouble.
Sie zog ein schiefes Maul.	She made a wry face; she looked dissatisfied (or offended).

schiefgehen:

Nur Mut, die Sache wird schon schiefgehen!	Buck (or Cheer) up—it'll turn out all right!

schießen:

Hier wird nicht so schnell geschossen!	Don't try to rush us!; we're in no great hurry.
Er ließ die Sache schießen.	He let the matter go hang; he gave it up.
Er ließ seinen Leidenschaften die Zügel schießen.	He let himself go; he gave full rein to his emotion.

Schießen:

Die Sache ging aus wie das Hornberger Schießen.	The whole thing went up in smoke; nothing came of it.
Das ist zum Schießen!	That's a scream (or riot)!; it's a howler!

Schießhund:

Er paßte auf wie ein Schießhund.	He watched like a hawk; he paid the closest attention.

Schiffbruch:

Das Unternehmen hat Schiffbruch gelitten.	The undertaking went on the rocks; it came to grief.

Schikane:

Das Flugzeug ist mit allen Schikanen der Neuzeit ausgestattet.	The airplane is rigged out with all the latest gadgets (or contraptions).

Schild:

Er führt etwas im Schild.	He's got something up his sleeve; he's up to some mischief.
Er ging aus dem Prozeß mit blankem Schild hervor.	He emerged from the trial with a clean slate; he was exonerated.

Schilda:

Er stammt aus Schilda.	He hails from Nutsville; he's a moron.

Schiller:

Das ist ein Gedanke von Schiller.	That's a bright idea; it's an inspiration.

Schimmel:

Er redete ihm zu wie einem kranken Schimmel.	He coaxed him ever so gently; he did his best to encourage him.

Schimmer:

Sie haben ja keinen Schimmer!	You're ice-cold (or way off)!; you couldn't guess in a million years!; you haven't the faintest idea!

schinden:

Er hat Eindruck geschunden.	He went over big; he made a hit (or good impression).

Laffen Sie uns diese Vorlefung schinden!	Let us sit in on this lecture!
Er muß sich schwer schinden.	He has to toil like a slave.

Schinderei:

Die Arbeit ist eine wahre Schinderei.	It's a hell of a job; it's sheer drudgery.

Schir.bluder:

Er treibt Schindluder mit seinen Leuten.	He's a regular slave driver; he bullies (or razzes) his help unmercifully.

Schinken:

In dem Zimmer hingen einige schreckliche Schinken.	There were some perfectly awful pictures in the room.
Er warf den Schinken nach der Wurst.	He staked everything he had; he risked much to gain little; he took an awful chance.
Er hat einen Schinken bei mir im Salz!	I've got a bone to pick with him!; he's got something coming to him from me!; he'll get his yet.
Er las in einem alten Schinken.	He was reading an old book.
Er warf die Wurst nach dem Schinken.	He cast a minnow to catch a whale; he took no chances.

Schippe:

Sie haben ihm die Schippe gegeben.	They gave him the gate; they chased him out.
Sie verzog den Mund zu einer Schippe.	She pouted; she stuck out her underlip.

Schippchen:

Die Kleine machte ein Schippchen.	The little girl began to sniffle (or sob).

schlachten:

Er schlachtet nach seinem Vater.	He takes after his father.

Schlaf:

Den Seinen gibt's der Herr im Schlaf.	Good fortune comes overnight.

schlafen:

Laffen Sie die Sache schlafen!	Forget (or Skip) it!; drop the matter!

Schlafittchen:

Nehmen Sie ihn mal beim Schlafittchen!	Take him by the scruff of the neck!; rake him over the coals!; tell him a thing or two!

Schlag:

Das Unternehmen war ein Schlag ins Wasser.	The action was a shot in the dark; it was a flop (or failure); it was a vain attempt.
Leute seines Schlages können das tun.	People of his stamp (or caliber) can do that.
Die Studenten beschlossen, einen Schlag zu machen.	The students decided to go out and paint the town red (or make whoopee); they planned to go on a binge (or wild party).
Wollen Sie noch einen Schlag?	Would you like a second helping?
Er ist vom alten Schlag.	He's true-blue; he's of the old school; there's a man for you!
Sie sind alle vom gleichen Schlag.	They're all cut on the same last; they're birds of a feather; they're all alike.

schlagartig:

Die Artillerie setzte schlagartig ein.	The artillery started off with a bang; it went into action all of a sudden.

schleierhaft:
Es ist ihm schleierhaft. — It's a mystery to him.
Er sprach etwas schleierhaft. — He spoke somewhat cryptically (*or* mysteriously).

schleifen:
Er hat sie arg geschliffen. — He gave them the works; he put them to a severe test.

schlendern:
Was man nicht kann ändern, muß man lassen schlendern. — What can't be cured must be endured.

Schlendrian:
Er kommt aus dem alten Schlendrian nicht heraus. — He's in the same old rut; he'll keep it up for the rest of his life.

Schleuderpreis:
Er verkaufte die Waren zu Schleuderpreisen. — He sold the goods at cut-throat prices; he sold them dirt-cheap.

Schleuse:
Er öffnete die Schleusen seiner Beredtsamkeit. — He waxed eloquent; he became talkative.

schlicht:
Er wohnt schlicht um schlicht. — He works for his room and board.
Der schlichte Menschenverstand sagt Ihnen das. — Common sense will tell you that.

Schliff:
Er gibt seiner Arbeit den letzten Schliff. — He's putting the finishing touches on his work.

schlimm:
Ihm ist schlimm. — He doesn't feel well.
Er ist schlimm dran. — He's up against (*or* in for) it; he's in a bad fix.
Das ist nicht weiter schlimm. — That's quite all right; never mind!

Schlips:
Das haut einen auf den Schlips! — Well, I never!; that beats everything!
Du kriegst gleich eins auf den Schlips! — You'll get it in the neck pretty soon!
Mit dieser Bemerkung haben Sie ihm ordentlich auf den Schlips getreten. — You certainly stepped on his toes this time; that remark surely hit home; he was really offended by it.

Schlitten:
Er ist mit ihnen Schlitten gefahren. — He took them for a (sleigh) ride; he gypped (*or* cheated) them.
Er ist unter den Schlitten gekommen. — He's hard-hit; his luck has gone back on him; he's met with many reverses.

Schloß:
Er hat ein Schloß vor dem Mund. — He shuts up like a clam; he's very close-mouthed.
Er sitzt hinter Schloß und Riegel. — They've got him under lock and key; he's behind the bars (*or* in jail).

Schlot:
So ein Schlot! — What an unlicked cub!; what a daddy-long-legs!

ſchlucken:
Er ſchluckt ein Gehalt von fünftauſend Mark das Jahr. — He's pulling down (*or* making) five thousand marks a year.

Schluß:
Schluß der Debatte! — The discussion is closed!; question!
Schluß folgt! — To be concluded (in our next issue).
Laſſen Sie uns Schluß machen und heim= gehen! — Let's call it a day and go home!

ſchlüſſig:
Er kann ſich nicht ſchlüſſig werden. — He can't make up his mind.

Schlußſtein:
Das Geſetz iſt der Schlußſtein einer langen Entwicklung. — The law is the logical outcome of (*or* last step in) a development that extended over a long period of time.

Schlußſtrich:
Er hat den Schlußſtrich darunter ge= zogen. — It's settled as far as he's concerned; he gave his O.K. (*or* stamp of approval).

Schmachtriemen:
Er muß den Schmachtriemen enger ziehen. — He has to pull in his belt a notch; he's hard-up.

ſchmählich:
Es war ſchmählich kalt. — It was beastly cold.

Schmalhans:
Bei ihnen iſt Schmalhans Küchenmeiſter. — They're on short rations; they're on a diet.

Schmalz:
Das Buch hat weder Salz noch Schmalz. — The book is flat (*or* uninteresting).
Er ſitzt im Schmalz. — He's in clover; he's living on the fat of the land.
Das iſt ein Schlager mit Schmalz. — That's a sob (*or* sentimental) story.

Schmarren:
Die neue Operette iſt ein rechter Schmar= ren. — The new operetta is pure trash.

ſchmatzen:
Er ſchmatzt beim Eſſen. — He smacks his lips when he eats; he eats noisily.

ſchmecken:
Schmeckt's? — Taste good?; do you like it?
Das ſchmeckt gut zuſammen. — They go well together; that's a good combination.

ſchmeißen:
Er wird die Sache ſchon ſchmeißen. — He'll put it over; he can do it.

ſchmerzlos:
Machen Sie es kurz und ſchmerzlos! — Get it over with!; make it short and sweet (*or* snappy)!

ſchmettern:
Er hat einen geſchmettert. — He had a glass of liquor.
Laſſen Sie uns einen ſchmettern! — Let's sing a song!

Schmied:
Jeder iſt ſeines Glückes Schmied. — Man is master of his own destiny.

Schmiede:

Gehen Sie nur vor die rechte Schmiede! — Just knock at the right door!; find the right party!

Er kam vor die unrechte Schmiede. — He got into the wrong pew (*or* box); he caught a Tartar; he got worsted.

Schmiere:

Es ist nun alles eine Schmiere. — It's all the same now; it makes no difference now (any more).

Er bezog Schmiere. — He got a licking.

Er stand während des Einbruchs Schmiere. — He was the lookout man during the burglary; he kept watch while the place was being looted.

Er bezahlte die ganze Schmiere. — He footed (*or* paid) the whole bill.

Dieser Schauspieler begann seine Laufbahn bei einer Schmiere. — This actor began his career with a stock company.

Er sitzt schwer in der Schmiere. — He's in Dutch (*or* hot water); he's in serious trouble.

schmieren:

Sie hat ein neues Drama geschmiert. — She dashed off a new play.

Ich werde ihm gleich eine schmieren. — I'll give him a slap in the face right now.

schmierig:

Er hat sich schmierig benommen. — He was a cheap skate; he acted shabbily.

Er hat schmierige Geschäfte gemacht. — He pulled (*or* made) some shady (*or* questionable) deals.

Schminke:

Seine Bescheidenheit ist nur Schminke. — His modesty is only assumed (*or* affected).

Schmiß:

Die ganze Sache hat keinen Schmiß. — The whole thing lacks punch (*or* pep); it lacks fire (*or* spirit).

schmissig:

Es war eine schmissige Musik. — It was catchy music.

Schmöker:

Er bot drei Mark für den alten Schmöker. — He offered three marks for the old book.

Schmollis:

Sie haben Schmollis getrunken. — They drank to friendship; they're chums (*or* pals).

schmoren:

Laß ihn ruhig etwas schmoren! — Let him squirm (*or* suffer) a little!

Schmu:

Er hat Schmu gemacht. — He pulled a fast one; he gypped (*or* cheated).

Schmus:

Red keinen Schmus! — Cut out that applesauce!; don't talk tripe (*or* nonsense)!

Schnabel:

Reden Sie doch, wie Ihnen der Schnabel gewachsen ist! — Speak plain English!; stop talking like a book!

Halten Sie den Schnabel! — Shut up!; keep quiet!

Das ist etwas für seinen Schnabel. — That's something for him; that's what he likes; it would just suit him.

Schnabus:

Lassen Sie uns einen Schnabus trinken! — Let's have a quencher (*or* dram)!

Schnafe:
Er hat nichts als Schnaken im Kopf. — His head is full of nonsense.

schnappen:
Jetzt hat's aber geschnappt! — That's the last straw!; that's more than I can stand!

Schnapsidee:
Es war eine Schnapsidee, bei dem Regen fortzugehen. — It was a crazy idea to leave in the rain.

Schnauze:
Halten Sie die Schnauze! — Hold your tongue!
Er hat die Schnauze voll. — He's fed up with it; he's tired of it.

Schneekönig:
Er freute sich wie ein Schneekönig. — He was gay as a cricket; he was very happy.

Schneid:
Er hat keinen Schneid. — He has no guts (or spunk); he lacks spirit (or initiative).

Schneide:
Die Entscheidung stand auf des Messers Schneide. — The decision was hanging fire (or in the balance); it was a critical (or crucial) moment.

schneiden:
Wenn Sie das erwarten, so schneiden Sie sich aber gewaltig! — You're in for a letdown (or doomed to disappointment) if you expect that!

Schneider:
Er fror wie ein Schneider. — He was chilled to the marrow; he was frozen stiff.
Er ist aus dem Schneider heraus. — He's past thirty.
Er verkehrt nur mit Gevatter Schneider und Schuster. — He's slumming; his friends are all butchers and bakers and candlestick makers.

Schnickschnack:
Ach was, Schnickschnack! — Bunk!; what tripe!; nonsense!

Schnippchen:
Er hat ihnen ein Schnippchen geschlagen. — He put a crimp into their plans; he fooled them.

Schnippelchen:
Er aß seinen Teller bis zum letzten Schnippelchen auf. — He fairly ate the bottom out of his plate; he licked the platter clean.

Schnitt:
Geben Sie mir einen Schnitt Bier! — A small (glass of) beer, please!
Er hat bei dem Geschäft seinen Schnitt gemacht. — He cleaned up (or made a big profit) on that deal.

schnittig:
Das ist ein schnittiger Wagen. — That's a swanky car; it's a slick- (or nifty-) looking car.

Schnitzer:
Er beging einen groben Schnitzer. — He pulled a boner; he made a bad break (or wrong move).

Schnorrer:
Er ist ein alter Schnorrer. — He's an old chiseler (or beggar).

schnüffeln:
Er schnüffelt schon wieder. — He's snooping (or prying) again.

ſchnuppe:
  Das iſt mir ſchnuppe. | It's nothing to me; that's your funeral (*or* lookout); I don't give a hang.

Schnur:
  Man hat ihn in die Schnur genommen. | They roped him in; he was gypped (*or* cheated).

  Er lebt nach der Schnur. | He leads a very methodical (*or* routine) life.
  Er hat über die Schnur gehauen. | He kicked over the traces; he overdid it.
  Sie zehren von der Schnur. | They're living on their principal (*or* savings).

Schnürchen:
  Es geht wie am Schnürchen. | It goes like clockwork; it works beautifully (*or* perfectly).

  Er hat es am Schnürchen. | He's an old hand at it; he has it at his fingertips.

  Sie hat den Jungen am Schnürchen. | She has the boy under her thumb (*or* control).

ſchnurz:
  Das iſt mir ganz ſchnurz. | I don't give a damn.

Schockſchwerenot:
  Schockſchwerenot! | Shucks!; hang it all!

Scholle:
  Die Liebe zur Scholle führte ihn zur alten Heimat zurück. | His love for the mother country led him back home.

ſchon:
  Schon gut! | O.K.!; all right!; that's fine!
  Wie, ſchon wieder? | What, again?
  Schon der Gedanke macht ihn wütend. | The very thought makes him ripping mad (*or* furious).

  Das iſt ſchon wahr, aber . . . . | That's all very well, but . . . .
  Wir könnten hier ſchon bleiben. | We wouldn't mind staying here.
  Das wird ſich ſchon finden. | We'll see when the time comes; time will tell.

  Es wird ſchon gehen. | I'm sure it'll turn out all right.
  Er wollte ſchon gehen. | He was all ready to go.
  Wenn ſchon, denn ſchon! | If it's got to be done, then let's get it over with once and for all!

  Na, wenn ſchon! | So what?; what of it?; what difference does it make?

  Wer nicht will, der hat ſchon! | Like it or lump it!; take it or leave it!
  Da kommen Sie ſchon! | Look, there they come!

ſchön:
  Tun Sie, was ich ſage!—Schön! | Do as I say!—O. K.!; sure thing!; all right!
  Bitte ſchön, würden Sie mir die Zeitung reichen? | Would you please (*or* kindly) pass me the paper?
  Haben Sie vielen Dank!—Bitte ſchön! | Many thanks!—You're welcome!
  Er ließ es ſchön bleiben. | He wouldn't lift his little finger; he did nothing of the kind.

  Sie haben ſich ſchön gewundert. | They were much surprised.
  Das iſt alles recht ſchön, aber. . . . | That's all fine and dandy (*or* very well), but . . . .

Haben Sie schönen Dank! — Thank you ever so much!

Er schickt Ihnen einen schönen Gruß. — He wishes to be remembered to you; he sends best regards.

Das sind ja schöne Sachen! — That's a fine how-do-you-do!; what a mess!

Eines schönen Tages ist er ihnen doch über. — He'll have the whip hand over them one of these days; he'll get the better of them someday.

Dort finden Sie die schöne Welt. — That's where society hangs out; that's where the well-to-do go (or live).

Schöne Worte machen den Kohl nicht fett. — You can't live on promises.

schöner:

Das wäre noch schöner! — That's all that's missing!; that would beat everything!

schönst:

Er ist im schönsten Alter. — He's in the prime of life.

Schopf:

Er nahm die Gelegenheit beim Schopf. — He made hay while the sun shone; he took time by the forelock; he made the most of the opportunity.

Schoppen:

Er sitzt gerade beim Schoppen. — He's over at the bar (or tavern).

Schornstein:

Das Geld können Sie in den Schornstein schreiben. — You can whistle for (or forget about) that money; you can charge it to profit and loss.

Schose:

So geht die Schose nicht. — That won't do (or work); that's not how it's done.

Schoß:

Hier sind wir aufgehoben wie in Abrahams Schoß. — This is pretty soft (or just like home); we're leading the life of Riley; we're living in great comfort.

Es hat keinen Zweck, die Hände in den Schoß zu legen. — There's no sense in giving up (the ghost); you can't lie down on the job now.

Schote:

Er ist ein großer Schote. — He's a big boob (or sap).

Schranke:

Der Opferwilligkeit sind keine Schranken gesetzt. — Give whatever you like!; give according to your means!

Das übersteigt alle Schranken. — That beats everything; that takes the cake; that oversteps all bounds.

Halten Sie sich in Schranken! — Restrain yourself!; calm down!

Er forderte sie in die Schranken. — He took them up on it; he challenged them.

Man wies ihn in die Schranken. — He was put in his place; he was set to rights.

Schraube:

Es ist eine Schraube ohne Ende. — There's no end to it; it goes on and on.

So eine verdrehte Schraube! — What a nut (or crackpot)!

Er stellte seine Worte auf Schrauben. — He weighed every word with the utmost care; he was most particular in his choice of words; his speech was very affected.

schreiben:

Er gab ihr sage und schreibe drei Mark. — Just think of it, he gave her three marks just like that!

Er schreibt sich Müller. — His name is Muller.

Wie schreibt sich das? — How is that spelled?

Schreien:

Es ist zum Schreien! — It's a scream (*or* riot)!; it's a howler!; it's too funny for words!

schreiend:

Sein Schlips war in schreienden Farben gehalten. — He wore a loud (*or* very gay) tie.

Seine Taten stehen in schreiendem Gegensatz zu seinen Worten. — His deeds cry out against his words.

Schritt:

Er kann mit ihnen nicht Schritt halten. — He can't keep up with them.

Er weigert sich, den ersten Schritt zu tun. — He refuses to take the initiative; he won't make the first move.

Bleiben Sie mir drei Schritte vom Leib! — Keep your distance!; don't come near me!

Er behielt sich weitere Schritte vor. — He reserved the right to make further stipulations.

Die Polizei folgt ihm auf Schritt und Tritt. — The police have him covered; they're keeping close tabs on him.

Schrot:

Er ist ein Mann von altem Schrot und Korn. — He's a man of the good old stamp; he's true-blue; there's a real man for you.

Schrulle:

Sie ist eine alte Schrulle. — She's an old shrew (*or* hussy).

Er hat nichts wie Schrullen im Kopf. — His head is full of whims (*or* silly ideas).

schrumm:

Schrumm! — That's that!; now that's over and done with!; it's finished!

Schub:

Man hat den ausländischen Berichterstatter auf den Schub gebracht. — The foreign reporter was forced to leave the country.

Er kam mit dem ersten Schub in den Saal. — He got into the hall with the first group.

Schubsack:

Das hat seine geweisten Schubsäcke. — That's not so simple as it looks (*or* sounds); there are good reasons for it.

schuften:

Er schuftet den ganzen Tag. — He's plugging (*or* working) away all day long.

Schuh:

Umgekehrt wird ein Schuh draus! — You're beginning at the wrong end!; try reversing the procedure!

Das habe ich mir längst an den Schuhen abgelaufen. — I knew that long ago; I learned that from experience.

Er wollte es ihnen in die Schuhe schieben. — He tried to pass the buck (*or* responsibility) on to them.

Schuhputzer:

Sie behandelt ihn wie einen Schuhputzer. — She walks all over him; she treats him like a servant.

Schuhriemen:
  Er ist nicht wert, ihr die Schuhriemen zu lösen.   He isn't fit to wipe her shoes.

Schuhsohle:
  Er hat sich das längst an den Schuhsohlen abgelaufen.   He's known that for a long time; he's learned that from experience.

Schulbank:
  Er drückt noch die Schulbank.   He still goes to school.
  Sie saßen miteinander auf einer Schulbank.   They were classmates.

Schuld:
  Alle Schuld rächt sich auf Erden.   A bad penny always turns up; we must all pay the piper.

schuldig:
  Sie bleibt ihm nichts schuldig.   She gives him tit for tat; she's not afraid to speak up to him.

Schuldigkeit:
  Er ist seine verdammte Pflicht und Schuldigkeit.   It is his bounden duty.

Schule:
  Sein Beispiel hat Schule gemacht.   His example led the way; he set a precedent.
  Nicht aus der Schule plaudern!   Mum's the word!; no snitching (or telling)!
  Er ist hinter die Schule gelaufen.   He played hookey (or truant); he didn't go to school.

Schulsack:
  Er hat auch einen Schulsack gefressen.   He's a walking encyclopedia; he talks like a book.

Schulter:
  Er trägt Wasser auf beiden Schultern.   He's a yes-man (or handshaker); he's on both sides of the fence; he doesn't commit himself.

  Er nimmt alles auf die leichte Schulter.   He takes life easy; he makes light of everything.

schummerig:
  Es war schon schummerig, als sie heimgingen.   It was already growing dark when they went home.

schunkeln:
  Der Kahn schunkelte auf dem Wasser.   The boat was teetering (or rocking gently) on the water.

schupp:
  Schupp, war er draußen!   Bingo, out he was!

Schuppe:
  Da fiel es ihm wie Schuppen von den Augen.   Suddenly he saw the light; his eyes were suddenly opened.

Schur:
  Sie tat es ihm zur Schur.   She did it to annoy him.

schüren:
  Seine Worte schürten das Feuer.   His words added fuel to the fire; they made matters worse.

schurigeln:
Er schurigelt seine Leute.
: He's a regular slave driver; he bullies (or keeps after) his help incessantly.

Schürze:
Er läuft hinter jeder Schürze her.
: He runs after every skirt (or petticoat); he's a ladies' man.

Schuß:
Er hat einen Schuß.
: He's nuts (or crazy); he's drunk.

Das ist keinen Schuß Pulver wert.
: That's not worth a hang (or darn); it's no good.

Wenn er erst mal in Schuß ist.
: Once he gets going; just wait till he gets into the swing of it.

Er hat den Laden schön im Schuß.
: He has the business well under way (or running smoothly).

Er ist weit vom Schuß.
: He's well out of danger; he's on the safe side.

Der Kerl soll mir nur vor den Schuß kommen.
: Let him cross my path!

Schüssel:
Er hat ihnen in die Schüssel gespuckt.
: He queered (or spoiled) their plans.

Sie sitzen vor leeren Schüsseln.
: Their cupboard is bare; they're starving.

schusselig:
Der Junge ist so schusselig.
: The boy is so scatterbrained.

Schuster:
So ein Schuster!
: He's always putting his foot into it!; what a bungler (or botcher)!

Er reitet auf Schusters Rappen.
: He rides shank's pony; he trudges on foot.

Er verkehrt nur mit Gevatter Schuster und Schneider.
: He's slumming; his friends are all butchers and bakers and candlestick makers.

schustern:
Was er wohl jetzt wieder schustert?
: I wonder what he's puttering (or tinkering) with now?

Schutt:
Hier kann Schutt abgeladen werden!
: Pay right here!

Schwabenalter:
Er hat das Schwabenalter noch nicht erreicht.
: He has not yet cut his wisdom teeth; he has still a lot to learn.

Schwachheit:
Bilden Sie sich nur keine Schwachheiten ein!
: Don't fool yourself!

Schwachmatikus:
Er ist im Englischen ein Schwachmatikus.
: He's weak in English.

schwafeln:
Nun haben wir aber genug geschwafelt!
: Now we've chewed the rag long enough!; we'd better not chat (or gossip) any longer!

Schwalbe:
Sie war munter wie eine Schwalbe.
: She was gay as a lark.

Er gab ihm eine Schwalbe.
: He gave him a box on the ear.

Schwamm:
Der ganze Schwamm kostet keine drei Mark.
: The whole caboodle (or business) costs less than three marks.

Schwämmchen:
Da kann man ja die Schwämmchen kriegen! | Confound it!; it's enough to drive one mad!

schwanen:
Mir schwante nichts Gutes. | I had a hunch (*or* feeling) something would interfere (*or* happen).

schwanken:
Die Schreibart dieses Wortes schwankt. | There're several ways of spelling this word.

Schwansfeder:
Ihm wachsen Schwansfedern. | He smells a rat; he has a hunch (*or* suspicion).

Schwanz:
Das glaubt Ihnen kein Schwanz. | No fool would believe that.
Das trägt die Maus auf dem Schwanz fort. | That's a mere drop in the bucket; that's precious little.
Er bindet gern etwas der Elster auf den Schwanz. | He's an old magpie; he likes to spread the dirt (*or* carry tales); he loves to gossip.
Man hat ihm auf den Schwanz getreten. | They stepped on his corns; he feels offended.
Es hieße den Aal beim Schwanz fassen, schenkte man seinen Worten Glauben. | You can't believe a word he says.
Er nahm das Kalb beim Schwanz. | He put the cart before the horse; he began at the wrong end; he reversed the procedure.
Er hat sein Examen mit einem Schwanz gebaut. | He passed his exam(ination)s in all but one subject.
Kommt man über den Hund, so kommt man auch über den Schwanz. | When the main part is done, the rest follows by itself; once the worst is over, the rest is easy going.

Schwänzchen:
Noch ein Schwänzchen, Herr Kapellmeister! | Encore! (*at a concert*)

Schwänzelpfennig:
Er hat Schwänzelpfennige gemacht. | He short-changed them; he pocketed the change.

Schwarm:
Sie ist sein Schwarm. | She's his big moment; he's got a crush on her; he's crazy about her.
Er hat einen Schwarm im Kopf. | He's got a bug; he's eccentric.

schwärmen:
Sie schwärmt für Musik. | She's crazy (*or* wild) about music; she raves about it.
Es schwärmte von Menschen auf den Straßen. | The streets were thronged with people.

Schwarte:
Er arbeitet, daß ihm die Schwarte knackt. | He works his head off; he toils like a slave.
Er hat ihm die Schwarte gegerbt. | He tanned his hide; he gave him a beating.
Wo hat er nur diese alte Schwarte aufgetrieben? | Where in the world did he dig up this old book?

Schwartenwurst:
Der eine ißt gern Schwartenwurst, der andre grüne Seife. | It's all a matter of taste; tastes differ.

schwarz:

Er ärgert sich schwarz.	He's mad as hops.
Er hat es schwarz auf weiß.	He has it in black and white; he has the proof in writing.
Das ist wie schwarz und weiß.	That's a horse of another color; that's entirely different.
Er macht weiß, was schwarz ist.	He'd swear that black is white; he's an awful liar.
Er ist schon wieder schwarz.	He's in the red again; he's broke (*or* short of money) again.
Da kann er warten, bis er schwarz wird.	He can wait till he's blue in the face; let him wait till doomsday; he's out of luck.
Er steht im schwarzen Buch.	Everybody is down on him; he's in general disrepute.
Er hat sie ins schwarze Register gebracht.	He slandered them; he gave them a bad name (*or* reputation).

Schwarze:

Er traf auf hundert Meter ins Schwarze.	He hit the bull's-eye (*or* center of the target) at a distance of a hundred meters.

schweben:

Es schwebte ihm auf der Zunge.	It was on the tip of his tongue.

Schwede:

Wie geht's, alter Schwede?	How are you, old man?

schwedisch:

Er sitzt hinter schwedischen Gardinen.	He's in the pen; he's behind the (prison) bars.

Schwefel:

Die beiden hängen zusammen wie Pech und Schwefel.	They're like the Siamese twins; they're inseparable.

schwefeln:

Er schwefelte schrecklich.	He talked through his hat; he talked a lot of nonsense.

Schwefelsticken:

Nehmen Sie Ihre Schwefelsticken weg!	Draw in your pins (*or* legs)!

Schweigen:

Es war ein beredtes Schweigen.	There was no need for words.
Die offiziellen Stellen hüllen sich in Schweigen.	The authorities keep mum (*or* are silent).

Schwein:

Daraus wird kein Schwein klug.	No one can make anything out of that; no one can understand it.
Da haben Sie aber Schwein gehabt!	You sure were lucky!
Wo haben wir beide denn die Schweine zusammen gehütet?	Have we ever been introduced?; keep your distance!; don't get familiar!

Schweinerei:

So eine Schweinerei!	What a scummy business!; some mess!
Es ist eine bodenlose Schweinerei.	It's a crying shame.

Schweinehund:

Es fiel ihm schwer, den innern Schweinehund zu überwinden.	It was hard for him to overcome his baser instincts (*or* lower nature).

Schweineſtall:
Machen Sie ihm mal den Schweineſtall!

Make it hot for him!; call him on the carpet!; tell him what's what!

Schweinewetter:
Es war ein Schweinewetter.

It was nasty (*or* beastly) weather.

Schweiß:
Das hat viel Schweiß gekoſtet.

That took a lot of elbow grease (*or* energy); it was a tough job.

ſchwenken:
Er wurde wegen Nachläſſigkeit im Dienſt geſchwenkt.

He was fired (*or* discharged) for carelessness.

ſchwer:
Er wird ſich ſchwer hüten, das zu tun.
Er iſt ſchwer von Begriff.

He'll take jolly good care not to do that.
He's a little slow; he doesn't catch on (*or* grasp things) easily.

Sie ſind ſchwer reich.

They're rolling in money; they're millionaires.

Die Polizei faßte einen ſchweren Jungen.

The police caught a bad egg (*or* dangerous criminal).

Schwergewicht:
Er warf ſein ganzes perſönliches Schwergewicht in die Waagſchale.

He brought the full weight of his personal prestige to bear on the matter.

ſchwimmen:
Er ſchwimmt im Geld.
Er ließ die Sache ſchwimmen.

He's rolling in money.
He let the matter ride; he gave it up.

Schwimmen:
Der Rennfahrer kam ins Schwimmen.

The racer began to tread water; he fell behind; he couldn't keep up the pace any longer.

Schwindel:
Was koſtet der ganze Schwindel?

How much for the whole caboodle (*or* business)?

Den Schwindel mache ich nicht mehr mit.

I'll have nothing more to do with that racket (*or* matter).

Schwindelmeier:
Er iſt ein großer Schwindelmeier.

He's a gyp artist; he's a big fraud (*or* bluff).

Schwindſucht:
Da kann man ſich die Schwindſucht an den Hals ärgern!
Er hat die Schwindſucht im Beutel.

It get's my goat; it makes me sick!
He hasn't a nickel in his pocket (*or* to his name).

ſchwingen:
Er muß heute abend eine Rede ſchwingen.

He has to make a speech tonight.

Schwips:
Die ganze Geſellſchaft hatte einen Schwips.

The whole party was lit (*or* drunk).

Schwof:
Laſſen Sie uns zum Schwof gehen!

Let's go to a shindig (*or* dance hall)!

Schwulität:
Er iſt in Schwulitäten.

He's up against it; he's in hot water (*or* a tight spot); he's in difficulties.

Schwung:

Seiner Rede fehlt der rechte Schwung.	His speech lacks fire (*or* punch); it falls flat.
Bringen Sie ihn mal auf den Schwung!	Step on him!; keep after him!
Die Sache kommt langsam in Schwung.	The matter is beginning to perc(olate); it's slowly getting under way.

schwuppdich:

Schwuppdich, hatte er eine im Gesicht!	Bingo (*or* Before he knew it), he'd gotten one in the face!

Sechser:

Haben Sie einen Sechser zur Hand?	Do you happen to have a nickel?; have you a nickel handy?
Er hat auch nicht für einen Sechser Verstand.	He hasn't a spark (*or* particle) of sense.

Sedan:

Er bereitete seinem Feind ein Sedan.	He routed (*or* finished) his enemy; his enemy met his Waterloo; he suffered a crushing defeat.

See:

Sie gehen morgen an die See.	They're going to the coast (*or* beach) tomorrow.
Das Schiff sticht heute nacht in See.	The ship will sail (*or* put out to sea) tonight.

Seele:

Er ist eine Seele von Mensch.	He's a whale of a good fellow; he's a real sport.
Sie sind ein Herz und eine Seele.	They're hand and glove; they're fast friends.
Verwandte Seelen treffen sich zu Wasser und zu Lande.	Birds of a feather flock together.
Er redete sich die Seele aus dem Leib.	He talked his head off.
Er band es ihnen auf die Seele.	He made them give a solemn promise.
Er sprach ihnen aus der Seele.	He voiced their own thoughts (*or* convictions); they heartily agreed with him.
Sie dankte ihm aus tiefster Seele.	She thanked him from the bottom of her heart.
Es tut ihr in der Seele weh.	She regrets it deeply; it makes her heart ache.
Sie ist mit ganzer Seele dabei.	She's sold on it; she's for it heart and soul.

Seelenverkäufer:

Dem Seelenverkäufer vertraue ich mich nicht an.	I won't venture out in that rickety tub (*or* boat).

Segen:

Ist das der ganze Segen?	Is that all (there is to it)?

sehen:

Sieh zu deinen Worten!	Mind your tongue!; (be) careful what you say!
Na, siehst du!	That's the way (*or* stuff)!; there you are!; didn't I tell you?
Sie sieht es gern, wenn man ihr ein paar Blumen gibt.	She likes to receive flowers.
Auf Gehalt wird nicht gesehen.	Salary is no object (*or* consideration).
Er läßt sich nicht mehr sehen.	He doesn't show himself (*or* come around) any more; he's quite a stranger.
Sie kann sich sehen lassen.	She's some looker; she's a stunning girl.

Sehen:

Ihm verging Hören und Sehen.

He was stunned (*or* stupefied); he was struck dumb.

sehr:

Sehr geehrter Herr!

My dear Sir!

Bitte sehr?

Sir?; pardon?; what did you say?

Bitte sehr!

If you please!; that's quite all right; you're welcome.

Seich:

Hören Sie doch auf mit dem Seich!

Cut out that tommyrot!; stop talking tripe (*or* rubbish)!

Seide:

Die beiden spinnen keine Seide.

The two don't pull together; they don't get along together.

Er hat keine Seide dabei gesponnen.

He got nothing out of it; he didn't make much by it.

Seife:

Ab, Seefe (=Seife)!

That's that!; finished!; done!

Der eine ißt gern Schwartenwurst, der andre grüne Seife.

It's all a matter of taste; tastes differ.

Seifenblase:

Seine Pläne sind lauter Seifenblasen.

His plans are all pipe dreams (*or* castles in the air).

Seifensieder:

Jetzt geht ihm ein Seifensieder auf.

Now it dawns on him; now he begins to see (*or* understand).

Sie ist vergnügt wie ein Seifensieder.

She's merry as a lark.

Seil:

Es gelang ihnen, ihm das Seil über die Hörner zu werfen.

They finally roped him in; they outwitted him after all.

Sie ziehen alle am gleichen Seil.

They're all pulling together; they're all working toward the same end.

Er tanzt auf dem Seil.

He's up a tree; he's in a precarious situation.

Seiler:

Er hat des Seilers Tochter geheiratet.

He was hanged.

sein:

Er ist nach Berlin.

He went to Berlin.

Mir ist, als höre ich ihn.

I think I hear him now.

Was nicht ist, kann noch werden.

It can still happen; anything is possible.

Mir fiel eben etwas ein.—Und das wäre?

I've just had an idea.—And what might that be?

Wie wär's, wenn wir jetzt Tennis spielten?

How about a game of tennis now?

Sein:

Es geht um Sein oder Nichtsein.

It's a matter of life or death.

Seine:

Jedem das Seine!

Give credit where credit is due!; to everyone his due!

Den Seinen gibt's der Herr im Schlafe.

Good fortune comes overnight.

seinerzeit:

Ich werde seinerzeit darauf zurückkommen.

I'll come back to that later.

seinesgleichen:
Das sucht seinesgleichen!

It's the limit!; that takes the cake (*or* can't be beat)!; it sets a precedent!

seinetwegen:
Seinetwegen könnte man sterben und verderben.

A person could die, for all he cared; he wouldn't lift a finger to help a fellow in trouble.

Seinige:
Er hat das Seinige getan.
Er ist mit den Seinigen verreist.

He did his part (*or* share).
He's gone away with his family.

Seite:
Das ist seine schwache Seite.
Sie sitzen an seiner grünen Seite.

That's his weak spot (*or* point).
They're in good (*or* on good terms) with him.

Dem ist nichts an die Seite zu stellen.
Er hat die Wahrscheinlichkeit auf seiner Seite.
Er brachte es heimlich auf die Seite.
Man hat ihn auf die Seite geräumt.

It has no parallel; it's unique.
The odds are in his favor.

He lifted (*or* stole) it.
He was taken for a ride; he was bumped off (*or* done away with); he was murdered.

Er hat sich auf die faule Seite gelegt.
Er schlug sich auf ihre Seite.
Er stemmte die Arme in die Seite.
Er quatschte sie von der Seite an.

He's loafing (*or* idling); he's taking it easy.
He sided with them; he took their part.
He stood with his arms akimbo.
He butted (*or* horned) in on them; he intruded upon them.

Man sieht ihn von der Seite an.

He's looked down upon; he's looked at askance (*or* with disapproval).

Sie kamen von allen Seiten.
Ihm stehen gute Freunde zur Seite.

They came from all over.
He has good friends (to back him).

Seitensprung:
Er macht gern Seitensprünge.

He likes to go stepping out (*or* on sprees); he enjoys having affairs.

selber:
Er kam von selber.

He came on his own (hook); he came of his own accord (*or* free will).

selbst:
Selbst seine Freunde glauben es nicht.
Selbst ist der Mann!

Even his friends don't believe it.
If you want a thing done well, do it yourself!; every man for himself!

Er ist die Gesundheit selbst.
Das versteht sich von selbst.

He's the picture of health.
Naturally; that goes without saying.

Selbstbewußtsein:
Es fehlt ihr nicht an Selbstbewußtsein.

She has an excellent opinion of herself.

selig:
Sein Vater selig sagte das immer.
Gott habe ihn selig!
Sie war selig über das Geschenk.

His late father always said so.
God rest his soul!
She was thrilled (*or* delighted) with the present.

Seligkeit:
Bei meiner Seligkeit!

Heavens!; gosh!; my word!

Semester:
Er ist schon ein altes Semester.

He's an old-timer; he's been studying at it for many years.

Semmel:
Die Ware geht ab wie warme Semmeln. — The article sells like hot cakes.

Senf:
Er muß immer seinen Senf dazu geben. — He must always put in his two cents; he always has to have his say.

Machen Sie keinen langen Senf! — Don't make a fuss about it!

Senge:
Er kriegte schwere Senge. — He got an awful beating.

seng(e)rig:
Das kommt ihm sengerig vor. — It looks fishy (or suspicious) to him.
Jetzt wird's aber sengrig! — Things are beginning to get hot!; now the fun begins!

Senkrechte:
Das ist das einzig Senkrechte. — That's the only square (or decent) thing to do.

Sensemann:
Der Sensemann hat ihn geholt. — The grim reaper (or Death) took him away; he's dead.

Sermon:
Halten Sie ihm mal einen Sermon! — Lay down the law to him!; give him a talking-to (or lecture)!

setzen:
Wenn du das nicht tust, setzt's was! — If you don't do it, you'll get something!

sich:
Das fragt sich. — That's a question.
Hat sich was! — Says you!; nothing doing!; you're mistaken!

Es hat nichts auf sich. — It's all right; it doesn't matter.
Er ist nicht bei sich. — He has fainted (or lost consciousness); he's not in his right mind.

Er ist gern für sich. — He likes to be alone.

sicher:
Er nimmt das als sicher an. — He takes it for granted.
Sie rechnen sicher auf ihn. — They're counting on him.

Sicher:
Er kam nach Nummer Sicher. — He was put under lock and key; he was jailed.

sichtlich:
Er verrichtet die Arbeit mit sichtlicher Unlust. — You can tell by his face (or attitude) that he doesn't like the work.

Sie:
Sie da! — Hello, there!

Sieb:
Er schöpft Wasser mit einem Sieb. — He's trying to drain Niagara; he's wasting his time (or energy).

sieben:
Das ist mir ein Buch mit sieben Siegeln. — That's all Greek to me; I can't make head or tail of it.

Er schweigt in sieben Sprachen. — He keeps mum; he doesn't say a word.

Sieben:
Sie ist eine böse Sieben. — She's a shrew (or vixen).

Siebengescheite:
So ein Siebengescheiter! — What a smart-aleck!; he thinks he knows it all!

Siebenkünstler:
Er ist ein Siebenkünstler. — He's a jack-of-all-trades; he can turn his hand to anything.

Siebensachen:
Packen Sie Ihre Siebensachen! — Pull up stakes!; pack up your duds (*or* belongings)!

siebe(n)t:
Das ist einer aus der siebten Bitte. — He's a pain in the neck; I can't stand the sight of him.

sieden:
Da bratet's und siedet's alle Tage. — Every day is a holiday there.

Sieg:
Er trug den Sieg davon. — He won the day.

Siegel:
Darauf gebe ich Ihnen Brief und Siegel. — I'll take an oath on that; you can bank (*or* count) on it.

Das ist mir ein Buch mit sieben Siegeln. — That's all Greek to me; I can't make head or tail of it.

Siele:
Er starb in den Sielen. — He died in harness (*or* on the job).

sinkend:
Er las bis in die sinkende Nacht hinein. — He read far into the night.

Sinn:
Der eigentliche Sinn seiner Worte blieb ihr unklar. — She didn't get the drift (*or* gist) of what he said.

Sein Sinn steht nicht danach. — He's not in the mood to; he doesn't feel like it.

Was ist der langen Rede kurzer Sinn? — What's the long and short of it?; just what is the point?; what is it you're driving at?

Ihr vergingen die Sinne. — She lost consciousness; she fainted.

Er wurde andern Sinnes. — He changed his mind.

Das hat keinen Sinn. — That's silly; there's no point to it.

Sie hat keinen Sinn dafür. — She has no appreciation for it; she takes no interest in it.

Sie können keinen Sinn daraus machen. — They can't make head or tail of it.

Nehmen Sie Ihre fünf Sinne zusammen! — Pay attention!; put your mind on it!

Er beharrt auf seinem Sinn. — He sticks to his guns; he's intent on his purpose; he's pig-headed.

Schlagen Sie sich das aus dem Sinn! — Give up the idea!; forget it!

Sie sind wohl nicht bei Sinnen! — You must be crazy!

Es fuhr mir so durch den Sinn. — It just occurred to me.

Er äußerte sich im gleichen Sinne. — He was of the same opinion; he made the same point; he spoke to the same effect.

Er genügt den Anforderungen in jedem Sinne. — He fulfills the requirements in every respect; he has all the qualifications.

Es war ganz in seinem Sinne gehandelt. — He would have done the very same thing.

Er übte Kritik im weitesten Sinne. — He made a comprehensive critical analysis.

Er erfüllte den Befehl dem Sinne, nicht dem Wortlaut nach. — He carried out the spirit rather than the letter of the order.

Wenn es nach ihrem Sinne ging.	If she had her way.
Das ist ohne Sinn und Verstand.	That's without rhyme or reason; it doesn't make sense.

Sinnen:

Sein ganzes Sinnen und Trachten geht nur auf Gelderwerb aus.	His only interest (*or* concern) in life is to make money.

sinnlos:

Er war sinnlos betrunken.	He was in a drunken stupor; he was dead-drunk.

Sippschaft:

Er jagte die ganze Sippschaft zum Teufel.	He chased the whole gang (*or* bunch).

Sitte:

Das verstößt gegen die guten Sitten.	It's in poor taste; it's bad form.

sittlich:

Ländlich, sittlich.	Every country has its own customs.

Sitz:

Der Anzug hat einen guten Sitz.	The suit is a fine fit.
Er trank drei Glas Bier auf einen Sitz.	He drank three glasses of beer, one right after the other.

sitzen:

So, das sitzt!	There, that ought to stick (*or* stay put)!
Der Mantel sitzt ihm gut.	The overcoat fits him well.
Da sitzen wir!	Now we're in for it!; we've got ourselves into a nice mess!
Das hat gesessen!	That was a grand slam!; that hit home!; that took effect!
Er hat schon gesessen.	He's done time before; he's already been in jail.
Der hat aber einen sitzen!	That fellow is plenty tight (*or* drunk)!

sitzenbleiben:

Der Junge blieb zu Ostern sitzen.	The boy flunked out at Easter; he failed the winter term.
Er blieb auf seiner Ware sitzen.	He was stuck with his wares; he couldn't sell them.
Sie wird noch sitzenbleiben.	She's sure to be shelved (*or* left); she'll be an old maid yet.

sitzenlassen:

Er hat das Mädchen sitzenlassen.	He gave the girl the air; he jilted her.
Er versprach zu kommen, ließ uns aber sitzen.	He promised to come, but left us in the lurch.
Er will den Schimpf nicht auf sich sitzen lassen.	He'll not swallow (*or* put up with) the affront.

Sitzfleisch:

Der Junge hat kein Sitzfleisch.	The lad lacks stick-to-it-iveness (*or* perseverance); he can't sit still (*or* concentrate).

Six:

Meiner Six!	By Jove!; whew!; boy, oh boy!

Skandal:

Die Studenten machten gestern nacht einen großen Skandal.	The students raised hell last night; they made whoopee (*or* painted the town red); they had a wild party.

ſo:

So?	Really?; indeed?
So, nun iſt's aber genug!	Now then, that will do!; no more of that!
So was!	Well, I never!; the idea!; who ever heard the like of it!
So ſind die Menſchen!	People are like that!; that's the way of the world!
So viel es auch koſtet.	Regardless of the cost.
So, ſo!	Well, well!; you don't say!; is that so?
So, ſo, Sie haben das getan?	My, my, so you really did that?; and you actually did it?
Es iſt ſo am beſten.	It's best as it is.
Er ſchreibt ſo alle acht Tage.	He writes every week or so.
Sie hatte ſo eine Ahnung.	She had a hunch (or feeling) that would happen; she suspected something of the kind
Es langt ihnen ſo eben hin.	They manage to get along somehow; they barely make ends meet.
Das hat er ſchon ſo und ſo oft geſagt.	How often has he said that!; he said it time and again!
Das tun ſie ſo wie ſo.	They'll do that anyhow (or regardless).
Sie hatten ſo gut wie nichts an.	They were wearing next to nothing.
Ach ſo!	Oh, I see!; so that's how it is!
Nicht ſo!	Oh no!; that's not the way!
Recht ſo!	Now you've got it!; that's it!; that's quite right!
Eine Zeitlang ſtand es mit ihm ſo ſo; ſchließlich erholte er ſich doch wieder.	For a while it was a case of touch and go (or a matter of life and death) with him, but he finally pulled through.

Socken:

Die Polizei iſt ihm auf den Socken.	The police are hot on his trail; they're right after him.
Machen Sie ſich auf die Socken!	Beat it!; get a move on!

Sohle:

Er hat ſich das an den Sohlen abgelaufen.	He knew that long ago; he learned that from experience.
Machen Sie ſich auf die Sohlen!	You'd better be going!; get a move on!
Sie iſt Dame vom Scheitel bis zur Sohle.	She's every inch a lady; she's a lady from head to toe.
Es brennt ihm unter den Sohlen.	It's high time for him to be going.

Soldatenrock:

Er hat den Soldatenrock ausgezogen.	He's retired from the army.

ſollen:

Du ſollſt ſehen!	Wait and see!; I'll show you!
Was ſoll das?	What's the (big) idea?; what's the meaning of this?
Da ſoll doch gleich der Teufel dreinfahren!	Confound it!
Er ſoll nur kommen!	Just let him come!; let him try it!
Das darf und ſoll nicht ſein.	That must not be.
Es ſoll nicht wieder vorkommen.	It won't happen again.
Sollte er es geweſen ſein?	Could it have been he?

ſonders:
　Sie wurden ſamt und ſonders hinge= | Every last one of them was executed.
richtet.

Sonne:
　Er iſt nicht wert, daß ihn die Sonne | He's absolutely worthless; he's a good-for-
beſcheint. | nothing.
　Die Sonne bringt es an den Tag. | Time will bring it to light; time will tell.
　Er ſtand da wie Butter an der Sonne. | He didn't know where to turn; he was per-
fectly helpless (or hopelessly lost).

Sonnenbruder:
　Er begegnete einigen Sonnenbrüdern. | He met some hoboes (or tramps).

ſonnenklar:
　Das iſt doch ſonnenklar. | That's clear as crystal (or daylight); that's
self-evident (or obvious).

Sonnenſchein:
　Bei denen iſt auch nicht alles eitel Sonnen= | It's not all roses with them either; they're
ſchein. | having a hard time of it.

Sonntag:
　Es iſt nicht alle Tage Sonntag. | Christmas comes but once a year.
　Er verſteht davon ſo viel wie die Kuh vom | He knows as much about it as the man in
Sonntag. | the moon; he hasn't the remotest idea of
it.

ſonſt:
　Er wird ja wohl ſonſt einmal an uns | Perhaps someday he will think of us.
denken.
　Er iſt doch ſonſt nicht ſo. | He isn't usually like this.

Sorge:
　Laſſen Sie das meine Sorge ſein! | That's my funeral (or problem)!; leave it to
me!
　Seien Sie ohne Sorge! | Rest content!; don't you worry!

ſorgen:
　Sorgen Sie dafür, daß es geſchieht! | See to it that it is done!; be sure that it gets
done!
　Sorgen Sie für ſich ſelbſt! | Paddle your own canoe!; shift (or look out)
for yourself!

Sorte:
　Dieſe Kerle, das iſt 'ne Sorte! | What an outfit these fellows are!; what
men!

Span:
　Er arbeitet, daß die Späne fliegen. | He makes the fur fly; he works fast and
furiously.
　Er hat einen Span. | He's cracked (or crazy).
　Er hat Späne. | He has plenty of dough (or money).
　Machen Sie keine Späne! | Come on, now!; don't make a scene (or
fuss)!
　Das geht ihm über den Span. | That's too much for him; it's beyond his
comprehension.

Spanier:
　Er iſt ſtolz wie ein Spanier. | He's proud as a peacock.

ſpaniſch:
　Das kommt mir ſpaniſch vor. | That's funny (or strange); it's all Greek to
me; I can't make head or tail of it.

Sparren:

Er hat einen Sparren. — He's a queer fish; he's eccentric.

Er hat einen Sparren zu viel. — He's got a screw loose; he isn't all there; he's crazy.

Spaß:

Spaß muß sein! — It's all in fun!

Auf Wiedersehn, viel Spaß! — So long—enjoy yourself (*or* have a good time)!

Es macht ihr einen diebischen Spaß. — She gets a big kick (*or* a fiendish delight) out of it; she's tickled pink (*or* to death).

Er versteht keinen Spaß. — He's a poor sport; he can't take a joke; he has no sense of humor.

Machen Sie keine Späße! — Oh, go on!; no fooling!; don't be funny!

spaßen:

Sie spaßen wohl? — No kidding!; you don't mean it!

Mit ihm ist nicht zu spaßen. — He's not to be trifled with.

Spatz:

Ein Spatz in der Hand ist besser als eine Taube auf dem Dach. — A bird in the hand is worth two in the bush.

Wenn der Himmel einfällt, sind die Spatzen alle gefangen. — We're all in the same boat (*or* predicament).

Die Spatzen pfeifen es von allen Dächern. — It's the talk of the town; it's common knowledge.

Sie hat Spatzen im Kopf. — She's stuck-up (*or* high-hat); she's a snob (*or* conceited ass).

Haben Sie Spatzen unterm Hut? — What are you hiding under your hat?; can't you take off your hat?

Er schießt mit Kanonen nach Spatzen. — He's chasing up blind alleys; he's not getting anywhere; he's making no headway.

Speck:

Er sucht Speck in der Hundehütte. — He's in the wrong pew; he's come to the wrong door (*or* party); he won't get anything from that source.

Er hat den Speck gerochen. — He smelled a rat; he got wind of it.

Sie spickt den Speck. — She's laying it on thick; she's overdoing it.

Er geht mit ihnen durch Dreck und Speck. — He sticks to them through thick and thin; he stands by them in fair weather or foul.

Er sitzt im Speck. — He's in clover; he's living off the fat of the land.

Mit Speck fängt man Mäuse. — Good bait catches fine fish.

Speckseite:

Er lebt wie die Mäuse in der Speckseite. — He's in clover; he's on Easy Street; he's living off the fat of the land.

Er warf mit der Wurst nach der Speckseite. — He cast a minnow to catch a whale; he took no chances.

Speiche:

Er fiel ihm in die Speichen. — He put a spoke in his wheel; he cramped his style; he put obstacles in his way.

Greifen Sie mit in die Speichen! — Lend a hand!; help me out!

Speise:

Dem einen ist's Speise, dem andern Gift. — One man's meat is another man's poison.

Spendierhose:

Er hatte die Spendierhosen an. | He was in a generous mood; he was feeling big-hearted; he wanted to treat everyone.

Sperenzien:

Machen Sie keine Sperenzien! | Don't make a scene (*or* fuss)!

sperrangelweit:

Er machte den Mund sperrangelweit auf. | He gaped; his jaw fell; he opened his mouth wide.

Spezielles:

Auf Ihr ganz Spezielles! | Here's to you!; your health!

spicken:

Er hat den Beamten gespickt. | He bribed the officer.
Er hat während der Prüfung gespickt. | He cribbed; he cheated in the test.

Spiegel:

Den Brief wird er sich nicht hinter den Spiegel stecken. | He'll not boast about that letter; he won't want to show that around.

Spiel:

Das Spiel hat sich gewandt. | The tables are turned; luck has shifted.
Es ist ein abgekartetes Spiel. | It's a put-up show; it's a big bluff (*or* farce).
Er trieb falsches Spiel mit ihnen. | He did them dirt; he double-crossed (*or* cheated) them.

Er hatte gewonnenes Spiel. | He held the whip (*or* upper) hand; he won the day.

Er hatte leichtes Spiel. | It was a snap (*or* walk-away); he won with the greatest of ease.

Sein Leben steht auf dem Spiel. | His life is at stake.
Lassen Sie ihn aus dem Spiel! | Don't get him into this!; leave him out of this!

Er hat die Hand im Spiel. | He has a finger in the pie; he's mixed up in the deal.

Eifersucht ist dabei im Spiel. | Jealousy is at the bottom of it; jealousy plays a rôle there.

Das Regiment rückte mit klingendem Spiel in die Stadt ein. | The regiment marched into the town with drums beating.
Er machte gute Miene zum bösen Spiel. | He played the game; he grinned and bore it; he made the best of it.

spielen:

Der Stoff spielt ins Gelbe. | The material is of a yellowish cast (*or* hue).
Er läßt nicht mit sich spielen. | He's not to be trifled with.

spielend:

Die Maschine nahm spielend die Anhöhe. | The car took the grade just like that (*or* like nothing at all).

Spielerei:

Die Arbeit ist eine Spielerei. | The job is a cinch (*or* snap); it's child's play.

Spielraum:

Man läßt ihm freien Spielraum. | He's given plenty of elbow room (*or* freedom).

Spieß:

Hoffentlich dreht er nicht den Spieß um. | I hope he won't turn the tables; I hope he won't cause our downfall.

Er schrie wie am Spieß. | He yelled bloody murder; he yelled for dear life (*or* all he was worth).

Spießer:
Er ist in dem Nest zum Spießer ge= | He's become a regular Babbitt (or Philis-
worden. | tine) in this burg (or town).

Spießrute:
Sie mußte Spießruten durch alle Kritik | She had to take a lot of criticism; she was
laufen. | under heavy fire; she had to run the
| gauntlet of town talk.

Spinne:
Pfui Spinne! | Horrors!; ugh!; how disgusting (or revolt-
| ing)!

spinnefeind:
Er ist ihnen spinnefeind. | He hates them like poison.

spinnen:
Du spinnst wohl! | Are you dreaming (or crazy)?
Er spinnt. | He's doing time (in jail).
Er muß tüchtig spinnen. | He has to buckle down (or work hard).

Spiritus:
Wo hast du deinen Spiritus gelassen? | Have you lost your senses?

Spiritus rector:
Er ist der Spiritus Rector des Ganzen. | He runs the whole show; he's the moving
| spirit behind the whole matter.

spitz:
Er wird die Sache bald spitz bekommen. | It'll soon sink into him; he'll soon catch on.
Er kam ihnen spitz. | He was snappy (or fresh) to them; he in-
| sulted them.

Spitz:
Er hat einen Spitz. | He's pie-eyed (or tipsy); he's drunk.

Spitzbube:
Es regnete Spitzbuben. | It rained cats and dogs.

Spitze:
Die Spitzen der Gesellschaft waren zu= | All the dignitaries (or pillars of society)
gegen. | were present.
Er bot ihnen die Spitze. | He faced (or braved) them.
Sein Humor brach der Peinlichkeit die | His (sense of) humor eased the tension.
Spitze. |
Er trieb die Sache auf die Spitze. | He carried the matter to extremes; he went
| too far; he overstepped the bounds.
Er sagte es mit deutlicher Spitze. | He spoke very pointedly (or in a cutting
| manner); his sarcasm was only too obvi-
| ous.

spitzen:
Er hatte sich so auf den Ausflug gespitzt. | He had been looking forward to the trip; he
| was raring (or all set) to go.

Splitterrichter:
Er ist ein Splitterrichter. | He's a carper; he's always splitting hairs
| (or finding fault).

Sporn:
Er hat sich die Sporen verdient. | He scored his first success.

spornstreichs:
Er ging spornstreichs heim. | He went straight home.

Sportfex:
Er ist ein rechter Sportfex. | He's a real sports fan.

Spott:
Das ist der reine Spott und Hohn. | That's out-and-out mockery; that's sheer spite.

Wer den Schaden hat, braucht für den Spott nicht zu sorgen. | The laugh is always on the loser.

spottleicht:
Das ist spottleicht. | That's as easy as falling off a log; that's a cinch (or snap); it's child's play.

Sprache:
Der Schrecken verschlug ihr die Sprache. | She lost her tongue (or was stricken dumb) from fright.

Die Zahl der Unfälle redet eine deutliche Sprache. | The number of accidents speaks for itself; it's ample proof.

Er schweigt in sieben Sprachen. | He keeps mum; he doesn't say a word.

Er wollte nicht mit der Sprache heraus. | He wouldn't come out with it; he hemmed and hawed.

Der Sprache nach ist er Bayer. | According to (or Judging by) his accent, he's a Bavarian.

Die Sache kam nicht zur Sprache. | The subject didn't come up; it wasn't mentioned.

sprachlich:
Die Arbeit ist sprachlich wie sachlich gut. | It's a good piece of work as to both form and content.

sprechen:
Wir sprechen uns noch. | You'll hear from me; we'll get together one of these days.

Er läßt mit sich sprechen. | He's open to reason.

Ist er zu sprechen? | Is he in?; can he be seen?

Er ist gut auf sie zu sprechen. | He thinks well of them.

sprechend:
Der sprechende Ausdruck des Bildes ist auffallend. | The picture is remarkably lifelike.

springen:
Springen Sie mal schnell zum Metzger! | Run down to the meat market!

Er ließ ein paar Flaschen Bier springen. | He ordered (or treated them to) a couple of bottles of beer.

springend:
Das ist der springende Punkt. | That's the salient (or significant) point.

Spritze:
Er säuft wie eine Spritze. | He drinks like a fish.

Der Arzt hat ihm eine Spritze gegeben. | The doctor gave him a shot (or an injection).

Die Studenten machten eine Spritze. | The students went on a spree (or binge); they made whoopee; they had a gay party.

Er ist der Mann an der Spritze. | He's the big cheese (or shot); he's the boss (or key man).

Er steht bei der Spritze. | He's a fireman.

Spritzfahrt:
Sie sind auf einer Spritzfahrt. | They're on a spree (or joy ride).

Spruch:
  Er klopft gern große Sprüche. | He's an old blow-hard (*or* braggart).

sprudelnd:
  Sie war sprudelnder Laune. | She was bubbling over; she was very exuberant.

Sprung:
  Sie können keine großen Sprünge machen. | They can't do much splurging; they haven't much money to waste.
  Er stand auf dem Sprung abzureisen. | He was on the point of leaving.
  Besuchen Sie ihn mal auf einen Sprung! | Drop in on him sometime!
  Sie halfen ihm auf die Sprünge. | They gave him a boost (*or* helping hand).
  Endlich kamen sie hinter seine Sprünge. | They finally got wise (*or* caught on) to him; at last they found him out.

sprunghaft:
  Die Stadt entwickelt sich sprunghaft. | The town is spreading like a mushroom; its growth is phenomenal.

Spucke:
  Da bleibt mir die Spucke weg! | Well, of all the nerve!; I'll be damned!
  Mit Geduld und Spucke fängt man eine Mucke. | Everything comes to him who waits; patience is crowned with success; keep up the good work—you'll get there yet!

spucken:
  Er spuckt darauf. | He snaps his fingers at it; he doesn't give a rap for it; he holds it in contempt.

Spur:
  Hat er davon gesprochen?—Nicht die Spur! | Did he mention that?—Not once!; not a word of it!
  Er ist keine Spur besser als sie. | He's not a speck (*or* bit) better than she.
  Er kam der Sache auf die Spur. | He got wind of it; he found it out.

spurlos:
  Er ist spurlos in der Versenkung verschwunden. | He dropped completely out of sight.

Staat:
  Es ist ein wahrer Staat, wie der Junge sich gemacht hat. | It's amazing how the lad has developed (*or* progressed).
  Damit können Sie keinen Staat machen. | That's nothing to write home about; you can't make much of a showing with that.
  Er warf sich in Staat. | He put on his glad rags (*or* best clothes); he got all decked out (*or* dressed up).
  Die Wurst ist nicht zum Staat da. | The sausage isn't just to look at; it's there to be eaten.

Stab:
  Brechen Sie den Stab nicht allzu schnell über ihn! | Don't be too hard on him!; don't condemn him too hastily!
  Er geht mit dem weißen Stab. | He goes panhandling (*or* begging).

Stäbchen:
  Darf ich Sie um ein Stäbchen bitten? | May I have a cigarette, please?

Stachel:
  Er fand einen giftigen Stachel darin. | He discovered a fly in the ointment; he ran into unpleasantness (*or* difficulties).
  Es ist nutzlos, wider den Stachel zu lecken. | It's useless to knock your head against a stone wall.

Staffage:
Das ist bei ihr doch alles nur Staffage. — She's only showing off; in her case that's all put on for effect.

stallen:
Die beiden stallen nicht miteinander. — They don't get along together.

Stamm:
Was gibt's heute als Stamm? — What's the blue plate on the menu today?; what's your special (dish) today?

Der Apfel fällt nicht weit vom Stamm. — Like father, like son; he's a chip off the old block.

Er ist vom Stamme „Nimm." — He's one of the "gimme" crowd; he's always out for what he can get.

Stammbuch:
Das können Sie sich ins Stammbuch schreiben! — Let that be a lesson to you!

stammen:
Er stammt aus Sachsen. — He hails from (or was born in) Saxony.
Der Ausdruck stammt von Schiller. — The expression comes from (or was originated by) Schiller.

Stand:
Was ist der heutige Stand der Mark? — What's the exchange rate of the mark today?

Das ist der wirkliche Stand der Dinge. — That's how matters stand; these are the actual facts.

Er hat bei seinem Chef einen guten Stand. — He's in good with his boss; his boss thinks well of him.

Sie hat einen schweren Stand. — She's in a difficult position.

standhalten:
Die Behauptung hält einer näheren Prüfung nicht stand. — The assertion won't bear closer examination; if you examine it more closely, you will find it untenable.

Standpauke:
Er hielt ihnen eine Standpauke. — He laid down the law to them; he gave them a lecture (or calling-down).

Standpunkt:
Sie hat ihm den Standpunkt klargemacht. — She told him what's what; she made it perfectly clear to him.

Stange:
Er hält ihnen die Stange. — He's boosting (or supporting) them; he takes their part.

Er gab eine Stange an. — He was bragging (or talking big).
Das kostet eine schöne Stange Gold. — That will cost a pretty penny.
Bleiben Sie bei der Stange! — Stick to the point (or subject)!
Er hält seine Leute fest bei der Stange. — He has his men well under control; he makes his men toe the mark.

Der Anzug ist von der Stange gekauft. — The suit is a hand-me-down; it's a cheap, ready-made suit.

Star:
Sie haben ihm den Star gestochen. — They put him wise; they opened his eyes.

stark:
Er blutet stark. — He's bleeding copiously.
Sie ist stark erkältet. — She has a bad cold.

Es geht stark auf Mitternacht zu.	It's close to midnight.
Wie stark ist die Auflage?	How large was the edition?; how many copies were printed for this edition?
Er ist stark in den Fünfzigern.	He's in his late fifties.
Es ist noch eine starke Stunde Wegs.	It's a good hour's walk yet.

Stärke:

Geschichte ist seine Stärke.	History is his strong point.
Der Regen hat an Stärke nachgelassen.	The rain has let up a little.

Stärkung:

Er trank einen Whisky zur Stärkung und fühlte sich sofort besser.	He took some whisky as a pick-me-up (*or* bracer) and immediately felt better.

starr:

Sie war einfach starr.	She was dumbfounded (*or* flabbergasted).

Start:

Der Titelverteidiger war nicht am Start.	The champion didn't take part in the match.

Station:

Er hat freie Station.	He gets his room and board free.

Staub:

Die Sache hat viel Staub aufgewirbelt.	The matter stirred up a lot of dirt; it created quite a sensation.
Er hat sich aus dem Staub gemacht.	He flew the coop (*or* skipped); he absconded.
Man hat seine Ehre in den Staub getreten.	His honor was besmirched.

stauchen:

Jemand hat ihm den Hut gestaucht.	Someone swiped (*or* stole) his hat.
Der Chef hat ihn ordentlich gestaucht.	His boss gave him hell; he landed on him good and proper.

Staucher:

Die Wanderung war ein Staucher.	It was a stiff (*or* strenuous) hike.
Er bezog einen Staucher.	He was stepped on (*or* set to rights); he was reprimanded.

Staupe:

Es ist nur eine kurze Staupe.	It's only a shower.

stechen:

Die Sonne sticht.	The sun burns.
Die Farbe sticht ins Blaue.	The color is tinged with blue; it shades into blue; it has a bluish tint.
Das Schiff sticht heute nacht in See.	The ship will sail (*or* put out to sea) tonight.

stecken:

Da steckt er ja!	Why, there he is!
Da steckt's!	There's the rub (*or* hitch)!; that's where the trouble is!
In ihm steckt was.	He has it in him; he has talent.
Er hat es ihnen ordentlich gesteckt.	He sent them flying; he knocked them cold (*or* flat).
Jemand muß es ihm gesteckt haben.	Somebody must have put him wise (*or* told him).

Stecken:

Ihm steht heute kein Stecken gerade.	He's cross (*or* out of sorts) today; nothing suits him today.
Er hat Dreck am Stecken.	He has a guilty conscience.

steckenlaffen:

Laffen Sie Ihr Geld nur stecken! — This is on me!; let this be my treat!

Steg:

Er kennt jeden Weg und Steg. — He knows every cowpath (or fork in the road).

Sie treffen ihn auf Weg und Steg. — They're always bumping (or running) into him; they meet him everywhere.

Stegreif:

Aus dem Stegreif kann ich das auch nicht sagen. — I can't tell you offhand; I don't know at the moment.

stehen:

Hier steht's! — Here it is (in black and white)!; it says so here!

Das steht ihr gut. — That suits her well.

Die Uhr steht. — The clock has stopped.

Das Barometer steht auf Regen. — The barometer points to rain.

Es steht Tod darauf. — It means death; you're taking a horrible chance.

Er steht dafür, daß es gut ist. — He guarantees it.

Wie steht's mit dem Preis? — How about the price?

Sie steht zu ihm. — She sticks to him; she sides with him.

Sie stehen gut miteinander. — They're on friendly terms.

Er kam so, wie er ging und stand. — He came just as he was.

Es kam ihm teuer zu stehen. — It cost him dearly.

stehend:

Er kam stehenden Fußes. — He came straightway (or at once).

stehenlaffen:

Alles stehen= und liegenlaffen! — Let everything go!; drop everything!; stop whatever you're doing!

Stehkragenproletarier:

Das Gesetz nimmt sich auch des Stehkragenproletariers an. — The law also gives a break to the white-collar unemployed; it takes care of the unemployed office workers.

stehlen:

Er stiehlt dem Herrgott die Tage. — He's killing time; he's loafing (or idling).

steif:

Er versicherte es steif und fest. — He stuck to his point; he maintained it obstinately.

steigen:

Er steigt morgen ins Examen. — He's taking his exam(ination) tomorrow.

Die Rennen steigen nächsten Sonntag. — The races will take place next Sunday.

Die neue Stelle ist ihm in den Kopf gestiegen. — The new job went to his head; it gave him a swelled head.

Stein:

Der Stein kam ins Rollen. — Fate took its course; the ball started rolling.

Ihr fiel ein Stein vom Herzen. — A weight was lifted from her mind; her mind was relieved.

Er schlief wie ein Stein. — He slept like a log (or top).

Es fror Stein und Bein. — It was freezing hard.

Er schwor Stein und Bein, daß es so war. — He swore on a stack of Bibles (or by all that is holy) that it was so.

Er hat bei ihr einen Stein im Brett.	He's in good with her; he's in her good graces.
Sie versuchten, ihm Steine in den Weg zu legen.	They tried to put a spoke in his wheel; they tried to cramp his style; they put obstacles in his way.
Es ging über Stock und Stein.	They ran over hedge and ditch; it was a cross-country race.

Stelle:

Die offiziellen Stellen hüllen sich in Schweigen.	The authorities keep mum (or are silent).
Er kommt nicht von der Stelle.	He's a stick-in-the-mud; he doesn't get ahead.
Zur Stelle!	At your service!
Er schaffte es zur Stelle.	He produced (or delivered) the goods.

stellen:

Er stellt sich nur so.	He's just making believe (or putting on); he's only pretending.
Ich bin gespannt, wie er sich dazu stellt.	I'm anxious (or curious) to know what his attitude will be.
Der Preis stellt sich auf drei Mark.	The price is three marks.
Er hat sich der Polizei gestellt.	He gave himself up; he surrendered to the police.
Er kann sich nicht mit ihnen stellen.	He can't fit himself in with them; he can't get on with them.

Stellung:

Wollen Sie nicht dazu Stellung nehmen?	Won't you give us your opinion?; won't you take sides?

Stellungnahme:

Er behält sich seine Stellungnahme vor.	He doesn't commit himself; he's noncommittal.

Stelze:

Ziehen Sie Ihre Stelzen ein!	Draw in your pins (or legs)!

Stengel:

Fallen Sie nicht vom Stengel!	Hold on to your hats!

Sterbenswörtchen:

Sie sagte kein Sterbenswörtchen.	She didn't let on; she never breathed a word.

sterblich:

Er ist sterblich in sie verliebt.	He's hopelessly gone on her; he's desperately in love with her.
Seine sterbliche Hülle wurde beigesetzt.	His remains were laid to rest; his body was buried.

Stern:

Man erhebt ihn zu den Sternen.	They praise him to the skies.
Er greift nach den Sternen.	He's reaching for the moon; he's very ambitious.

sternhagelvoll:

Er ist sternhagelvoll.	He's tight as a drum; he's dead-drunk.

Steuer:

Zur Steuer der Wahrheit möchte ich bemerken, daß	In the interest (or For the sake) of truth, I should like to say that . . . .

steuern:

Er bemüht sich nach Kräften, der Unruhe im Volk zu steuern. — He does his utmost to still (*or* curb) the social unrest.

stibitzen:

Jemand hat ihm das Buch stibitzt. — Somebody swiped (*or* stole) his book.

Stich:

Ein Stich in Zeit erhält das Kleid. — A stitch in time saves nine.

Der Einwand hält nicht Stich. — The argument doesn't hold water; it's not valid (*or* tenable).

Es gab ihm einen Stich. — It cut him to the quick; it hurt him deeply.

Sie haben wohl einen Stich! — Are you crazy?

Das Fleisch hat einen Stich. — The meat is beginning to spoil; it's tainted.

Er hat einen Stich ins Geniale. — He has a streak of genius.

Er ließ sie im Stich. — He left them in the lurch; he deserted them.

Das Kleid ist rot mit einem Stich ins Blaue. — The dress is red with a touch of blue.

Stichblatt:

Er diente ihnen zum Stichblatt. — They made a laughing stock of him; he was the object of their gibes.

stichhaltig:

Diese Theorie ist nicht stichhaltig. — This theory won't hold water; it's not valid (*or* tenable).

Stichtag:

Als Stichtag gilt der 1. Mai. — May 1 is the date set.

Stiefel:

Er quasselte einen Stiefel zusammen. — He talked through his hat; he talked a lot of nonsense.

Er arbeitet seinen Stiefel. — He's plugging (*or* working) away.

Es geht alles den alten Stiefel weiter. — Things go on at the same old pace; it's a humdrum life.

Er verträgt einen guten Stiefel. — He holds his liquor well; he can stand a great deal.

Stiefmutter:

Er ist seinem Magen keine Stiefmutter. — He likes a square meal; he doesn't stint on food.

Stiel:

Plötzlich kehrte er den Stiel um. — Suddenly he turned the tables; he suddenly got the upper hand (*or* advantage).

Er sucht der Axt einen Stiel. — He's looking for a good excuse.

Er wird schon der Hacke einen Stiel finden. — He'll find a peg to fit the hole; he'll fix (*or* manage) that.

Der Ort wurde mit Stumpf und Stiel ausgerottet. — The place was wiped off the map; it was completely destroyed.

Stielauge:

Er machte schöne Stielaugen, als er den neuen Wagen sah. — His eyes fairly popped (out of his head) when he saw the new car.

stiften:

Er ging stiften, als die Polizei nahte. — He gave the police the slip; he had skipped out when the police arrived.

still:

Er denkt im stillen wie wir. — Secretly (*or* At heart) he thinks as we do.

Er ist ein stiller Mann. — He's at rest; he's dead.

stimmen:
 Stimmt! — Correct!; absolutely!; that's quite right!
 Sein Brief stimmte sie fröhlich. — His letter made her happy; it put her in a good frame of mind.

Stimmenfang:
 Er geht auf Stimmenfang aus. — He's on the stump; he's electioneering (*or* canvassing for votes).

Stimmung:
 Die herrschende Stimmung im Volk ist dagegen. — The majority of the people are against it.
 Er lud sie ein, damit sie etwas für Stimmung sorgten. — He invited them to pep (*or* liven) up the party.

Stinkadores:
 Er steckte sich eine neue Stinkadores an. — He lit another stogy (*or* cigar); he took another *el ropo*.

stinken:
 Eigenlob stinkt. — Self-praise is no recommendation.
 Er stinkt nach Geld. — He's lousy with money; he's made of money.

stinkfaul:
 Der Junge ist stinkfaul. — The boy is lazy as hell.

stinkig:
 Er hat eine stinkige Laune. — He's in a vile mood.

Stinkwut:
 Er hatte eine Stinkwut, daß sie nicht kamen. — He was wild with rage at their failure to appear.

Stint:
 Er freut sich wie ein Stint. — He's happy as a clam at high tide; he's feeling very chipper.

Stippvisite:
 Er machte ihnen eine Stippvisite. — He dropped in to see them; he paid them a flying visit.

Stirn:
 Er bot der Gefahr die Stirn. — He met the danger head on; he faced it squarely.
 Er hat die Stirn, es zu leugnen. — He has the crust (*or* nerve) to deny it.
 Sie zog die Stirn kraus. — She frowned (*or* scowled).
 Die Anklage trägt den Stempel der Lüge an der Stirn. — The complaint is obviously unfounded; it's clearly a fake.
 Sie ging mit erhobener Stirn von dannen. — Head up (*or* Nose in air), she made her exit; proudly she left.

Stock:
 Es ging über Stock und Stein. — They ran over hedge and ditch; it was a cross-country race.

stockblind:
 Er ist stockblind. — He's blind as a bat.

stockdeutsch:
 Er ist stockdeutsch. — He's German to the core; he's German as can be.

stocken:
 Es stockt mit der Sache. — The matter is hanging fire.

ſtockfinſter:
Es war ſtockfinſter.
It was pitch-dark.

ſtockmäuschenſtill:
Es war ſtockmäuschenſtill im Zimmer.
The room was so quiet you could have heard a pin drop.

ſtocktaub:
Sie iſt ſtocktaub.
She's deaf as a post.

Stöpſel:
So ein Stöpſel!
What a runt (*or* shrimp)!; he's such a little shaver (*or* fellow).

Storch:
Da brat mir aber einer einen Storch!
Well, I'll be darned!; can you beat that?

ſtoßen:
Stoßen Sie ſich nicht daran!
Don't let that stop you!; don't let it stand in your way!

Daran ſtößt es ſich gerade!
That's just the rub!; that's where the whole trouble lies!

Er ſtieß kürzlich auf eine alte Zeitung.
He came across an old paper the other day.

Stottern:
Er hat ſein Radio auf Stottern gekauft.
He bought his radio on the installment plan.

Strafe:
Das ſollte doch bei Strafe verboten ſein!
There ought to be a law (against that)!

ſtrafen:
Gott ſtrafe mich!
Strike me pink (*or* dead)!; so help me God!

ſträflich:
Es tut ſträflich weh.
It hurts like hell; it's terribly painful.
Es wäre ſträflicher Leichtſinn, das zu tun.
It would be foolhardy to do that.

ſtramm:
Er hat ſtramm gearbeitet.
He buckled down to the job; he worked very hard.

Strandkanone:
Er iſt voll wie eine Strandkanone.
He's tight as a drum; he's dead-drunk.

Strang:
Wenn alle Stränge reißen, dann ſpringt er ein.
If worse comes to worst, he'll help us out.
Sie ziehen alle am gleichen Strang.
They're all pulling together; they're all working toward the same end.

ſtrapaziert:
Der Anzug ſieht recht ſtrapaziert aus.
The suit is beginning to look shabby (*or* frayed).

Straße:
Er hat die Straße gemeſſen.
He kissed the pavement; he fell down on the street.

So eine Ware findet man nicht auf der Straße.
You don't pick up an article like that everywhere.

Wer in der Partei widerſprach, flog auf die Straße.
Dissenters were kicked out of the party.

Er warf ſein Geld auf die Straße.
He threw his money to the winds; he squandered his money.

Er verkauft offenes Bier über die Straße.	He sells beer on draft (*or* tap) over the counter (for home consumption).
Er ist von der Straße aufgelesen.	He's a street urchin; he comes from the slums (*or* dregs of society).

straucheln:

Sie ist in der Großstadt gestrauchelt.	She's gone wrong in the city.

Strecke:

Der Halunke wurde endlich von der Polizei zur Strecke gebracht.	The police finally landed (*or* got) the crook.

strecken:

Er streckte die Waffen.	He struck the flag; he laid down his arms; he gave in.

Streich:

Das war ein rechter Streich!	What a stupid thing (to do)!
Es fällt keine Eiche vom ersten Streich.	Rome wasn't built in a day; that takes time.

Streifen:

Er paßt in den Streifen.	He fits into the picture; he's a good mixer; he gets on well with the rest.
Er lehnte alles ab, was ihm nicht in den Streifen paßte.	He rejected everything that didn't fit in with his plans.

Streit:

Das ist ein Streit um nichts.	That's a tempest in a teapot; it's a case of much ado about nothing.
Sie hat ihren Streit mit ihm beigelegt.	She made up (*or* patched up her differences) with him.
Ohne Streit, das ist recht.	No doubt that's right; that's unquestionably right.

streiten:

Darüber läßt sich streiten.	That's open to question.
Über den Geschmack läßt sich streiten.	Tastes differ; there's no accounting for tastes.

Streithammel:

Er ist ein alter Streithammel.	He's a quarrelsome old cuss.

streng:

Sie ist streng modern angezogen.	She's dressed in the very latest style.

strengstens:

Parken strengstens untersagt!	Positively no parking!

Strich:

Strich darunter!	Forget it!; that's over and done with!; let bygones be bygones!
Sie ist bloß noch ein Strich.	She's a mere shadow of her former self; she's nothing but skin and bones.
Er tat den letzten Strich an seiner Arbeit.	He put the finishing touches to his work.
Er machte ihr einen Strich durch die Rechnung.	He queered (*or* upset) her plans.
Er hat einen dicken Strich unter das Vergangene gemacht.	He turned over a new leaf.
Er hat sie auf dem Strich.	He has it in for them; he bears them a grudge.
Seine Bemerkung ging ihr gegen den Strich.	His remark rubbed her the wrong way; she took exception to it.

Er arbeitet in einem Strich. | He works without a letup; he works incessantly.

Er machte sie nach Strich und Faden herunter. | He raked them over the coals; he gave them hell; he bawled them out soundly.

Der Artikel stand unterm Strich. | The article appeared in the magazine section (of the Sunday paper).

Strick:

Sie sind ja ein Strick! | You're a little rascal!

Wenn alle Stricke reißen. | If worse comes to worst; if everything else fails.

Da kann er sich gleich den Strick nehmen. | Then he might just as well kick the bucket (*or* hang himself).

Er versuchte, ihnen einen Strick zu drehen. | He tried to rope them in; he tried to trap them.

striezen:

Man hat ihm die Decke aus dem Wagen gestriezt. | Someone lifted (*or* stole) the blanket out of his car.

Strippe:

Es regnete Strippen. | It rained pitchforks.

Er hat sie an der Strippe. | He leads them around by the nose; he makes them toe the mark.

Er hängt den ganzen Tag an der Strippe. | He's on the phone all day long.

Stroh:

Bei der Besprechung wurde viel leeres Stroh gedroschen. | A lot of breath was wasted at the conference.

Er hat Stroh im Kopf. | He's a nitwit (*or* dunce).

Er tat Stroh zum Feuer. | He added fuel to the fire; he made matters worse.

Sie sind auf dem Stroh. | They're badly off; they've nothing left.

Strohmann:

Der Führer der Partei ist lediglich Strohmann. | The leader of the party is merely a figurehead.

Strohsack:

Heiliger Strohsack! | Great guns!; holy cow!

Strom:

Der Apparat verbraucht viel Strom. | The apparatus takes a lot of juice (*or* electricity).

Er schwimmt immer gegen den Strom. | He always swims against the tide; he refuses to follow the crowd.

Es goß in Strömen. | The rain came down in sheets (*or* torrents).

Strumpf:

Es ist Zeit, daß Sie sich auf die Strümpfe machen. | It's time you got a move on; you'd better be going.

Stube:

Er möchte die Stube zum Fenster hinauswerfen. | He'd like to cut up (*or* let loose); he feels like kicking over the traces; he's itching for trouble.

Stück:

Es ist noch ein hübsches Stück Weg von hier. | It's still a pretty long way off.

Das nenne ich ein starkes Stück.	I call that laying it on a bit thick; that's putting it mighty strong; that's going a little too far.
Sie hält große Stücke auf ihn.	She thinks the world of him; she has a very high regard for him.
Er tat es aus freien Stücken.	He did it on his own (initiative); he did it of his own free will.
Sie stimmt ihm in vielen Stücken bei.	She agrees with him in many respects.

Studieren:

Probieren geht über Studieren.	The proof of the pudding is in the eating; practice is better than theory.

Stufe:

Sie stehen nicht auf gleicher Stufe.	They're not on the same social level; they're not in the same class.

Stuhl:

Man hat ihm den Stuhl vor die Tür gesetzt.	He was given the gate (*or* shown the door); he was kicked (*or* turned) out; he was fired (*or* discharged).
Er hat sich zwischen zwei Stühle gesetzt.	He lost out on both chances; both opportunities fizzled out (*or* fell through).
Er kommt damit nicht zu Stuhl.	He can't put it across; he can't manage (*or* fix) it.

stumm:

Man hat ihn stumm gemacht.	He was shut up for good and all; he was murdered.
Er wurde stumm wie ein Fisch.	He shut up like a clam.

Stumpf:

Der Ort wurde mit Stumpf und Stiel ausgerottet.	The place was wiped off the map; it was completely destroyed.

Stunde:

Dem Glücklichen schlägt keine Stunde.	Time means nothing to a happy man; time flies when you're enjoying yourself.
Er nimmt deutsche Stunden.	He takes German lessons.

Sturm:

Es ist nur ein Sturm im Wasserglas.	It's just a tempest in a teapot; it's a case of much ado about nothing.
Sein Barometer steht auf Sturm.	He's in a black (*or* vile) mood.

stürmisch:

Er riß die Zuhörer zu stürmischem Beifall hin.	He brought down the house; the audience applauded wildly.

Stürzen:

Es ist zum Stürzen.	It's a scream (*or* riot); it's hilariously funny.

Stuß:

Machen Sie keinen Stuß!	Cut out the funny business!; stop that nonsense!

Subjekt:

Er ist ein übles Subjekt.	He's a bad egg; he's a tough bird (*or* customer).

suchen:

Das hätte ich nicht in ihm gesucht. — I would never have thought (*or* believed) that of him.

Was haben Sie hier zu suchen? — What business (*or* right) have you to be here?; what do you want here?

Südfrucht:

Ich soll das tun? Na, ich danke für Obst und Südfrüchte! — I'm supposed to do that?—Well you've got another guess coming!; not for me, thanks!; the pleasure's all yours!

Suff:

Er hat sich dem stillen Suff ergeben. — He's become a boozer; he's gone in for tippling on the sly.

süffisant:

So ein süffisanter Kerl! — What a conceited ass!

Sumpf:

Er ist in dem Sumpf der Großstadt untergegangen. — He's gone to pot (*or* the dogs) in the city.

Sumpfhuhn:

Er hat sich zu einem Sumpfhuhn entwickelt. — He's become a high-stepper (*or* fast liver); he's become dissipated.

Sums:

Machen Sie keinen Sums! — Don't make such a fuss!

Sündenbabel:

Der Ort ist ein wahres Sündenbabel. — The place is a second Babylon; it's a veritable hotbed of vice.

Sündengeld:

Der Preis ist ein Sündengeld. — The price is exorbitant; it's wholesale robbery.

Sündenmaß:

Sein Sündenmaß ist gestrichen voll. — He's gone the limit; he's done his worst; he's broken all ten Commandments.

Superkluger:

Er ist ein Superkluger. — He's a smart-aleck (*or* wise guy).

Süppchen:

Er kocht sich gern sein Süppchen am Feuer anderer. — He's an old moocher (*or* sponger); he's always taking advantage of the other fellow's good nature (*or* hospitality).

Suppe:

Die Suppe wird nicht so heiß gegessen, wie sie aufgetragen wird. — Nothing is so bad as it is painted; things are always better than they seem.

Nun muß er die Suppe auch ausessen, die er sich eingebrockt hat. — He has to pay the piper; now he must face the music (*or* consequences).

Das macht die Suppe nicht fett. — That won't help matters any.

Er hat ihnen die Suppe versalzen. — He fixed them; he spoiled their fun.

Da hat er sich eine schöne Suppe eingebrockt. — He's in the soup for fair; he surely got himself into a nice mess.

Damit verdient er nicht das Salz auf die Suppe. — That wouldn't buy him a cup of coffee; he can't get very far on that.

Er hat die Brocken aus der Suppe gefischt. — He took the best for himself.

Es hat ihm in die Suppe geregnet. — Someone threw a monkey wrench into his machinery; something queered (*or* spoiled) his plans.

Süßholz:
    Er raspelt Süßholz.

He's flirting with her; he's feeding her a line of sweet nothings; he's heaping compliments upon her.

Szene:
    Er versteht sich in Szene zu setzen.

He knows how to sell himself (*or* make a hit); he puts himself into the limelight.

tabellos:
  Donnerwetter, tabellos!

Hot dog!; great stuff!; it's the berries!; swell!

Tag:
  Nun wird's Tag!

Now I get you!; I catch on!; now I begin to see!

Auf einen trüben Morgen folgt ein heitrer Tag.

Rain before seven, clear before eleven.

Er machte ein Gesicht wie vierzehn Tage Regenwetter.

He was an old sourpuss; he looked very glum (or sour).

Er war der Löwe des Tages.

He was the whole works; he stole the show; he was the center of attraction.

Es ist noch nicht aller Tage Abend.

Time will tell; we haven't seen the last of it.

Man soll den Tag nicht vor dem Abend loben.

Don't crow too soon; praise a fair day at night!

Sie suchen wohl den gestrigen Tag!

You must be dreaming!

Können Sie mir zwei Mark pumpen? —Ja, guten Tag!

Can you lend me two marks?—No, thanks!; nothing doing!

Er hatte mit seinem Vortrag einen guten Tag.

He spoke in his best manner; he delivered an excellent speech.

Machen Sie sich einen guten Tag!

Have a good time!; enjoy yourself!

Es ist nicht alle Tage Sonntag.

Christmas comes but once a year.

Das liegt am Tag.

That's clear as day; it's obvious.

Er sucht am Tag mit der Laterne danach.

He's looking for a needle in a haystack.

Es geschah am hellen Tag.

It happened in broad daylight.

Die Sonne bringt es an den Tag.

Time will bring it to light; it will come out in time.

Sie legt ein bescheidenes Wesen an den Tag.

She's a shrinking violet; she acts very modest (or coy).

Er lebt in den Tag hinein.

He lives from hand to mouth.

Sie schwatzte in den Tag hinein.

She chewed the rag; she rambled (or talked) on and on.

Er kam nach Jahr und Tag.

He came back a full year later.

Er verließ das Haus vor Tau und Tag.

He left the house before dawn.

Er brachte nichts Gescheites zu Tag.

He said nothing relevant (or to the point).

Tagesgespräch:
  Sie ist das Tagesgespräch.

She made the headlines; she's the talk of the town.

Tagesordnung:
  Derartiges ist heute an der Tagesordnung.

Such things are quite common nowadays.

Takt:
  Er gibt in seinem Kreis den Takt an.

He's the leader of his gang (or crowd).

  Ist er wieder im Takt?

Is he back on the job?; is he well again?

taktfest:

Er ist in seinem Fach taktfest.

He knows his business; he has his subject down pat (*or* letter-perfect).

Er ist nicht ganz taktfest auf der Lunge.

His lungs are not at all sound (*or* well).

Er war nicht mehr taktfest.

He wasn't quite steady on his feet; he was a little wobbly (*or* weak) in the knees.

Talent:

Er brachte sein Talent an den Mann.

He showed his stuff (*or* metal); he showed what he could do.

Tamtam:

Der Laden eröffnete mit viel Tamtam.

The store opened with plenty of ballyhoo (*or* display); the opening of the store received plenty of publicity.

Tanz:

Jetzt geht der Tanz los!

Now the fun begins!; the fight's on!

Er machte ihnen einen bösen Tanz.

He blew them up; he gave them hell.

Tanzbein:

Er schwingt gern das Tanzbein.

He likes to foot it; he likes to hop (*or* dance).

Tapet:

Er brachte die Angelegenheit aufs Tapet.

He introduced (*or* broached) the subject.

Taps:

Er ist ein großer Taps.

He's a regular butterfingers; he's a big gawk; he falls all over himself.

Tarantel:

Er fuhr hoch wie von der Tarantel gestochen.

He flew (*or* jumped) up as if stung by an adder.

Tasche:

Er kennt den Ort wie seine Tasche.

He knows the place inside out (*or* like the back of his hand); he could find his way around in the dark.

Er liegt ihnen auf der Tasche.

He's sponging (*or* living) on them; they're keeping (*or* supporting) him.

Er hat sie in der Tasche.

He has them under his thumb; he has complete control over them.

Er mußte tief in die Tasche greifen.

It cost him a lot.

Er steckt alle in die Tasche.

He puts it all over the rest; no one is a match for him.

Taschenmesser:

Er klappte zusammen wie ein Taschenmesser.

He folded up; he collapsed.

Tat:

Er wurde auf frischer Tat ertappt.

He was caught red-handed (*or* in the very act).

Er stand ihnen mit Rat und Tat zur Seite.

He advised and assisted them materially.

tätlich:

Sie wurden bald tätlich.

They soon came to blows.

tatsächlich:

Und tatsächlich!

Believe it or not!; no kidding!; it's a fact!

Tatterich:
 Er hat den Tatterich. He's got the jitters; he's trembling like a leaf.

Tau:
 Er verließ das Haus vor Tau und Tag. He left the house before dawn.

taub:
 Er stellte sich taub zu ihrem Ansinnen. He turned a deaf ear on them; he wouldn't listen to their request.

 Er ist eine taube Nuß. He cuts no ice; he's a nobody.
 Er tut es nicht um taube Nüsse. He won't do it for love (*or* nothing).

Taube:
 Ein Spatz in der Hand ist besser als eine Taube auf dem Dach. A bird in the hand is worth two in the bush.

 Glauben Sie etwa, die gebratenen Tauben fliegen Ihnen ins Maul? Do you think fortune will come to you in your sleep (*or* be handed to you on a silver platter)?

 Sie hat Tauben im Kopf. She has crazy (*or* high-flown) notions.

Taubenschlag:
 Hier geht's zu wie in einem Taubenschlag! They surely keep open house here!; why, this is a regular beehive (*or* hotel)!

Taufe:
 Er half den Verein aus der Taufe heben. He's one of the founders of the club.
 Er hielt das Kind über die Taufe. He stood godfather for the child.

taufen:
 Er hatte den Wein getauft. He had watered the wine.

täuschen:
 Darin täuschen Sie sich! You're all wet!; that's where you're mistaken!

täuschend:
 Es ist eine täuschende Nachahmung. It's a clever reproduction (*or* imitation).

Täuschung:
 Die Schrift erwies sich als eine plumpe Täuschung. It was a clumsy piece of forgery.

Tausend:
 Pfui Tausend! Ugh!; pugh!; it stinks!
 Ei der Tausend! Good heavens!; great guns!

Tausendsasa:
 Er ist ein kleiner Tausendsasa. He's a whizbang (*or* perfect marvel); he's a little genius.

Tausendste:
 Er kam vom Hundertsten ins Tausendste. He couldn't stick to his subject; he talked on and on.

Techtelmechtel:
 Er hat ein kleines Techtelmechtel mit ihr. He's having a little affair (*or* flirtation) with her.

Tee:
 Abwarten und Tee trinken! Wait till the pot begins to boil!; wait and see!; things will soon come to a head.

Teil:

Ich dachte mir mein Teil, als er das sagte.
I kept my tongue in my cheek (*or* my thoughts to myself) when he said that.

Er gab ihnen ihr Teil.
He gave them theirs (*or* what was coming to them); he gave them a piece of his mind.

Tempel:

Kommt das noch einmal vor, dann fliegen Sie zum Tempel hinaus!
If that happens again, out you go!

Tempo:

Nun aber Tempo, Tempo!
Snap (*or* Speed) it up!; step on it!

Er legte ein mörderisches Tempo vor.
He went at a break-neck speed.

teuer:

Das soll ihm teuer zu stehen kommen!
He'll smart (*or* pay) for that!

Da ist guter Rat teuer!
It's hard to advise in a case like that; that's a ticklish (*or* difficult) situation to be in.

Er versicherte hoch und teuer.
He swore on a stack of Bibles; he took a solemn oath.

Er sah aus wie die teure Zeit.
He made a long face; he looked worried.

Teufel:

In der Not frißt der Teufel Fliegen.
Anything is better than nothing.

Er fürchtet das Examen wie der Teufel das Weihwasser.
He's scared to death of the exam(ination).

Der Teufel hat ihn geritten.
He carried on like one possessed; he didn't know what he was doing.

Kein Teufel kann das wissen!
Who'd ever know that?; how was I to know?

Sind Sie des Teufels?
Are you possessed (*or* crazy)?

Dann gehen Sie doch in drei Teufels Namen!
Then go, for all I care!; for heaven's sake, go then!

Malen Sie den Teufel nicht an die Wand!
Don't talk of the devil!; don't invite trouble!

Es müßte mit dem Teufel zugehen, könnte ich das nicht schaffen.
There'd be something wrong with me if I couldn't do that.

Text:

Er hat ihnen den Text gelesen.
He laid down the law to them; he gave them a lecture.

Der Redner kam aus dem Text.
The speaker got muddled (*or* broke down); he lost the thread of his discourse.

Immer weiter im Text!
Go on (with the sermon)!; proceed!

Tezett:

Er kannte seine Rolle bis ins Tezett.
He had his part down pat; he knew it letter-perfect.

Er wiederholte es bis zum Tezett.
He repeated it over and over; he said it time and again.

Theater:

Es war das reine Theater.
It was all a big bluff (*or* put-up job); it was nothing but a farce.

Thespiskarren:

Er zieht mit dem Thespiskarren herum.
He travels around with a stock company; he's a member of an itinerant stock company.

Thron:
Steigen Sie herab von Ihrem Thron! — Get off your high horse!; come down to earth!; don't be so snooty (*or* superior)!

Tick:
Er hat einen Tick. — He's bats (*or* crazy); he's a conceited ass.
Er hat einen Tick auf sie. — He has it in for her; he bears her a grudge.
Sie hat einen Tick ins Große. — She likes to put on airs; she has delusions of grandeur; she thinks she is somebody.

tief:
Das läßt tief blicken. — There's a lot in that; that speaks volumes.
Er ist tief in den Sechzigern. — He's well along in the sixties.

tiefgründig:
Er schrieb eine tiefgründige Abhandlung. — He wrote a profound treatise.

Tiefpunkt:
Die Depression hat ihren Tiefpunkt er= reicht. — The depression has struck rock bottom.

tiefschürfend:
Er stellte tiefschürfende Untersuchungen an. — He made a thoroughgoing investigation.

tiefst:
Sie dankte ihm aus tiefster Seele. — She thanked him from the bottom of her heart.

Tiefstand:
Die Arbeit verrät einen außerordentlichen Tiefstand. — The paper hits a new low; it's extremely poor.

Tier:
Er ist ein hohes Tier. — He's a big shot (*or* gun); he's an important personage.

Tinte:
Das ist so klar wie dicke Tinte. — That's clear as crystal; that's obvious (*or* self-evident).
Du hast wohl Tinte gesoffen! — You must be nuts (*or* crazy)!
Er hat sie in die Tinte geritten. — He got them into a nice mess.

Tippelchen:
Er wußte seine Sache bis aufs Tippelchen. — He had it down to a T; he knew it perfectly.

tippeln:
Sie mußten noch zwei Stunden tippeln, bis sie den Gasthof erreichten. — They had to walk two more hours to reach the hotel.

tippen:
Daran kann er nicht tippen. — That's a peg above him; that's out of his reach; he can't quite make (*or* reach) it.
Daran ist nicht zu tippen. — That leaves nothing to be desired; that's beyond reproach; that's indisputable.

Tisch:
Narrenhände beschmieren Tisch und Wände. — Fools' names are like their faces, often seen in public places.
Er machte reinen Tisch damit. — He made a clean sweep of it; he settled everything.
Er kam nach Tisch. — He came after dinner.
Er steckt gern seine Füße unter andrer Leute Tisch. — He's a moocher (*or* sponger); he imposes on other people's hospitality.

Man ließ das Thema untern Tisch fallen.	The subject was dropped.
Diese Anordnung kommt vom grünen Tisch.	That's a swivel-chair order; it comes from the inner office (*or* big boss).

Tischtuch:
Das Tischtuch ist zwischen ihnen zerschnitten. — They're on the outs; they're not on speaking terms.

Tobak:
Das ist starker Tobak! — That's going some!; that's a pretty strong statement!

Es war anno Tobak. — That was way back; it happened in the year one.

Tochter:
Er hat des Seilers Tochter geheiratet. — He was hanged.

Tod:
Tod und Teufel! — Confound it!; hell and damnation!
Viele Hunde sind des Hasen Tod. — There's no use fighting against great odds.
Er sah aus wie der Tod von Basel (*or* Ypern). — He looked like a ghost; he was pale as death.
Sie sind des Todes! — You're sunk!; you're a goner (*or* dead man)!
Er gab sich den Tod. — He committed suicide.
Es geht auf Tod oder Leben. — It's a matter of life and death.
Sie liegt auf den Tod. — She's on the point of death; she's dangerously ill.
Er ist ihr bis in den Tod verhaßt. — He's anathema to her; she hates him like poison (*or* sin).
Sie hätte sich zu Tode lachen mögen. — She almost died laughing.

Todesgefahr:
Achtung! Todesgefahr! — Danger! 33,000 volts!; stop, look, listen!

tödlich:
Er ist tödlich verunglückt. — He was fatally injured.

todunglücklich:
Sie ist todunglücklich. — She's so unhappy she could die; she's dreadfully unhappy.

Tohuwabohu:
Die Versammlung endete in einem Tohuwabohu. — The meeting ended in a row (*or* state of confusion).

Toilette:
Alle erschienen in großer Toilette. — All appeared in regalia (*or* war paint); all were in full dress.

toll:
Er treibt es gar zu toll. — He's going too far; he's overstepping the bounds.
Er hat sich toll und voll getrunken. — He's tight as a drum; he's dead-drunk.
Er ist ein toller Kerl. — He's a crazy Ike (*or* loon).
Das ist ja eine tolle Wirtschaft! — That's a hell of a mess!; that's a grand mixup!

toller:
Es kommt noch toller. — It gets louder and funnier; you haven't seen anything yet; the worst is yet to come.

Tolpatfch:
So ein Tolpatfch!

What a blunderbuss (*or* dope)!

Ton:
Der gute Ton erfordert das.

Etiquette (*or* Good taste) demands that.

In dem Lager herrfchte ein rauher, aber
herzlicher Ton.

They spoke in the rough, frank language of
the camp.

Sie gibt den Ton an.

She sets the pace (*or* fashion).

Hafte (= Haft du) Töne!

Whew!; gosh!; can you beat that?

Er wurde in allen Tönen gepriefen.

They praised him to the skies.

Er fprach in großen Tönen von feiner
Erfindung.

He boasted (*or* made much) of his invention.

Tonart:
Sie redeten in allen Tonarten auf ihn ein.

They chewed the rag with him; they talked
to him at great length.

Topf:
Kleine Töpfe kochen bald über.

Small pots come to a quick boil; small
people are easily worked up; they're
naturally high-strung (*or* excitable).

Das ift noch nicht in dem Topf, wo's
kochen foll.

It's still in the air; it's still tentative (*or*
unsettled).

Der kocht in allen Töpfen.

He's a jack-of-all-trades; he has his fingers
in every pie.

Er wirft alles in einen Topf.

He makes no distinctions; he treats them
all alike.

topp:
Topp!

O.K.!; it's a go!; that suits me!

Tor:
Das öffnet der Sache Tür und Tor.

That paves the way for it; that leaves the
door open (*or* road clear) for it.

Er ftand da wie die Kuh vorm neuen Tor.

He stood there like a dumb bunny; he
didn't know where to turn; he was at his
wits' end.

Torfchluß:
Er kam gerade noch vor Torfchluß.

He arrived at the eleventh hour (*or* last
minute).

tot:
Heute rot, morgen tot.

Here today, gone tomorrow.

Er ift nicht tot zu kriegen.

He's a die-hard; you can't get him down;
he's indomitable.

Es war ein totes Rennen.

It was a tie; the race ended in a dead heat.

totgeboren:
Der Plan war von Anfang an ein totge-
borenes Kind.

It was an abortive plan from the start; the
plan was predestined to failure.

Totlachen:
Es ift zum Totlachen.

It's a riot (*or* scream); it's hilariously funny;
we nearly died laughing.

totlaufen:
Der Streit hat fich totgelaufen.

The controversy was a fizzle; it petered out.

totreden:
Er redete fie tot.

He talked them deaf, dumb, and blind.

Totſchießen:
Es war zum Totſchießen.

It was a riot (*or* scream); it was screamingly funny; we nearly died laughing.

totſchlagen:
Sie könnten mich gleich totſchlagen, ich kann mich deſſen nicht entſinnen.

Search me!; for the life of me, I can't remember it.

totſchweigen:
Die Sache läßt ſich nicht länger totſchweigen.

The devil will out; the matter can no longer be hushed up.

Tour:
Er arbeitet in einer Tour.

He works straight through (*or* without a letup).

Trab:
Bringen Sie ihn mal auf den Trab!

Step on him!; stick a pin in him!; make him hurry up!

Tracht:
Er bezog eine derbe Tracht Prügel.

He was given a sound thrashing.

trachten:
Er trachtet nach ihrem Geld.

He has his eye on her money; he's out to get it.

Trachten:
Sein ganzes Sinnen und Trachten geht nur auf Gelderwerb.

His only interest (*or* concern) in life is to make money.

Tragbare:
Im Rahmen des Tragbaren will er ihren Forderungen entgegenkommen.

He'll meet her demands within reason (*or* in so far as possible).

tragen:
Soweit das Auge trägt.
Er trägt keine Bedenken, es zu tun.

As far as the eye can see; within view.
He doesn't hesitate to do it; he has no scruples about doing it.

Wer trägt die Schuld?
Sie trägt Sorge dafür.
Er trägt ſich damit.
Es trägt ſich nicht gut.
Sie trägt ſich einfach.

Whose fault is it?
She takes care of that; that's her business.
It's on his mind; he broods over it.
It doesn't wear well.
She dresses simply.

Tran:
Er war im Tran.

He was groggy (*or* in a stupor).

Träne:
Sie weinen ihm keine Träne nach.
Er lehnte mit einer Träne im Knopfloch ab.

They don't mourn (*or* miss) him.
He refused politely (*or* apologetically).

tranig:
Iſt der Menſch aber tranig!

The fellow is slow as molasses!; what a snail (*or* stick-in-the-mud)!

Tranlampe:
Er iſt die reine Tranlampe.

He's a regular slowpoke.

Trara:
Machen Sie nicht ſoviel Trara darum!

Don't make so much fuss (*or* noise) about it!

Tratſch:
Das iſt überflüſſiger Tratſch.

That's bunk (*or* boloney); it's downright trash.

trauen:
 Trau, schau, wem!

Look before you leap!; don't trust every
Tom, Dick, and Harry!

Trauer:
 Sie hat die Trauer noch nicht abgelegt.

She's still in mourning.

Trauerkloß:
 Er ist ein Trauerkloß.

He's a flat tire; he's an awful bore.

Traufe:
 Er kam vom Regen in die Traufe.

He fell from the frying pan into the fire; he
went from bad to worse.

Traum:
 Es fällt ihm nicht im Traum ein, so
 etwas zu tun.

He wouldn't dream of doing such a thing.

träumen:
 Das soll er sich ja nicht träumen lassen!

He has another think (*or* guess) coming!; let
him try and get it!

Traute:
 Der Junge hat keine Traute.
 Sie haben keine rechte Traute dazu.

The boy lacks guts (*or* courage).
They have no confidence in it.

Treff:
 Da ist Treff Trumpf.
 Er hat einen Treff weg.

It's a case of do or die (*or* win or lose).
He has a screw loose; he's not quite right
(in his upper story); he's a little off (*or*
crazy).

treffen:
 Das trifft Sie!
 Wie gut sich das trifft!
 Wann sind Sie zu treffen?

That means you!; that's aimed at you!
What a break!; how lucky!
When will you be in (*or* at home)?

Treffen:
 Wenn's zum Treffen kommt, ist die
 Sache anders.

Of course if it comes to a showdown (*or*
head), that's a different story.

treiben:
 Was treibst du denn?
 Er treibt Sprachen.
 Er treibt es zu weit.
 Wie man es treibt, so geht's.
 Es treibt sie, es Ihnen zu sagen.

What are you doing (*or* up to)?
He studies languages.
He goes too far; he oversteps the bounds.
You reap as you sow.
She feels she ought to tell you.

Treiben:
 Das Leben und Treiben in der Stadt fiel
 ihm auf.
 Er hat das ganze Treiben satt.

He was impressed by the hustle and bustle
of the town.
He's fed up with the whole business; he's
sick and tired of it all.

Treppe:
 Er ist die Treppe hinaufgefallen.
 Sie wohnen drei Treppen hoch.

He was kicked upstairs.
They live on the fourth floor.

treten:
 Treten Sie ihn doch mal!

Remind him!; speak to him about it!

treu:
 Das ist ja treu!

I'll be darned!; of all the nerve!

Treue:
Der Vertrag ist auf Treu und Glauben abgestellt.

It's a gentlemen's agreement.

(Bei) meiner Treu!
In alter Treue!

(Upon) my word!; I say!; well, I never!
As ever!

Trichter:
Sie mußten es ihm mit dem Nürnberger Trichter eingießen.

He was so dense (*or* stupid) they fairly had to pound it into him.

Triller:
Er ging mit einem Triller darüber weg.

He dismissed it with a joke.

Tritt:
Er hat den Tritt gekriegt.
Die Polizei folgt ihm auf Schritt und Tritt.

He was fired (*or* dismissed).
The police have him covered; they're keeping close tabs on him.

Trittchen:
Er hatte neue Trittchen an.

He wore new kicks (*or* shoes).

trocken:
Er sitzt auf dem trocknen.

He's stranded; he's left high and dry; he's hard up (for money).

Das trockne Gedeck kostet vier Mark.

The meal is three marks without drinks.

Trog:
Er lief davon wie die Sau vom Trog.

He ran off without a word of thanks.

Trommel:
Er schlägt eifrig die Trommel für sich.

He's blowing his own horn; he's boosting (*or* praising) himself.

Trommelfeuer:
Das Volk leidet unter einem wahren Trommelfeuer von neuen Steuern.

The people are being subjected to a steady fire (*or* stream) of new taxes.

trommeln:
Er läßt nicht auf sich trommeln.

You can't step all over him; he won't put up with all that.

Trompete:
Er ist mit Pauken und Trompeten gerasselt.

He flunked (the test) outright.

Trost:
Sie sind wohl nicht recht bei Trost!

You must be off your nut!; are you crazy?

trösten:
Trösten Sie sich!
Sie hat sich rasch getröstet.

You should care!; don't fret!; never mind!
She soon got over her loss; she soon married again.

Tröster:
Ohne Tröster kann er nicht mehr auskommen.

He'd be lost without his little drop (*or* bracer) to comfort him.

Trott:
Es geht alles den alten Trott.

It's still the same old routine; everything is just as it always was.

Trottel:
Er ist ein verkalkter trottel.

He's a dried-up prune; he's dead from the neck up; he's got no life (*or* spirit) in him.

trüb:
Er fischt gern im trüben.

He likes to fish in troubled waters; he enjoys stirring up trouble (*or* uncovering a scandal).

Trübsal:
Sie bläst Trübsal.

She has the blues; she's in the dumps; she's feeling low (*or* dejected).

Trübung:
Die diplomatischen Beziehungen haben eine Trübung erfahren.

Diplomatic relations have suffered a rift.

Trug:
Seine Worte sind nichts als Lug und Trug.

There's not a word of truth in what he says; it's nothing but a pack of lies.

Trumm:
Er ist ein Trumm von einem Kerl.
Sie verlor den Trumm.
Er redete in einem Trumm.

He's a regular horse (*or* giant).
She lost the thread of her discourse.
He chewed the rag; he talked on and on.

Trumpf:
Sie wird ihm schon zeigen, was Trumpf ist.
Gesinnung ist Trumpf.
Da ist Treff Trumpf.

She'll show him what's what (*or* who's boss).
It's the principle that counts.
It's a case of do or die (*or* win or lose).

Tuch:
Er wirkt auf sie wie das rote Tuch.

He makes her see red; he gets her goat; he makes her furious.

Das zweierlei Tuch hat es ihr angetan.

She falls for (*or* is attracted to) anything in a uniform; she has a weakness for men in uniform.

Tuchfühlung:
Halten Sie Tuchfühlung mit ihm!

Keep in touch with him!

Tugend:
Jugend hat keine Tugend.

Boys will be boys.

tun:
Tun Sie doch nicht so!

Oh, come on!; don't be like that!; be a good sport!

Er tut nicht gut.
Was tut's?

He's a good-for-nothing (*or* ne'er-do-well).
So what?; what of it?; what difference does it make?

Tut nichts!
Es tut ihm nichts.
Er tut sich.
Wie geht's?—Na, es tut sich.
Es tut sich was dort.
Das können Sie tun oder lassen.

Skip (*or* Forget) it!; never mind!
It won't hurt him.
He gives himself airs.
How are you?—So so!; fair!
There's something up (*or* going on).
Like it or lump it!; take it or leave it!; suit yourself!

Sie werden es mit ihm zu tun kriegen.
Es ist ihr sehr darum zu tun.

You'll have to cope with him.
She's very set on (*or* anxious about) it; it means a great deal to her.

Ihm ist nur um das Geld zu tun.

He's only out for the money.

Tun:
Sein Tun und Lassen gefällt ihr nicht.

She doesn't like his attitude (*or* conduct).

Tüpfelchen:

Das sitzt wie das Tüpfelchen auf dem J.	That fits perfectly; it's a perfect fit.
Er übersieht nicht das Tüpfelchen auf dem J.	He dots his I's and crosses his T's; he's very exacting.
Er geht nicht ein Tüpfelchen davon ab.	He stands by his guns; he doesn't yield an inch.
Er wußte es bis aufs Tüpfelchen.	He knew it to a T (or perfection); he had it down pat.

Tür:

Ihm stehen alle Türen offen.	He has a way with him; he's welcome everywhere; he can get anything he wants.
Das öffnet der Sache Tür und Tor.	That paves the way for it; that leaves the door open (or road clear) for it.
Er wies ihm die Tür.	He sent him about his business.
Damit rennen Sie nur offne Türen ein.	That's carrying coals to Newcastle; that's a waste of time (or energy); that won't get you anywhere.
Er fiel mit der Tür ins Haus.	He blurted out the news.
Weihnachten steht vor der Tür.	Christmas is just around the corner.
Kehren Sie vor Ihrer Tür!	Mind your own business!
Man hat ihm den Stuhl vor die Tür gesetzt.	He was given the gate (or shown the door); he was kicked (or turned) out; he was fired (or discharged).
Er warf ihn zur Tür hinaus.	He turned him out.
Er sagte es ihr zwischen Tür und Angel.	He told her at the last moment (or as he was leaving).

Türklinke:

Er putzt Türklinken.	He goes panhandling (or begging); he begs from door to door.

türmen:

Er versuchte zu türmen.	He tried to slip out (without paying the bill).

Tüte:

Er klebt Tüten.	He's on the rock pile; he's doing time (in jail).
Nicht in die Tüte!	Not on your life!; like hell I will!; catch me doing it!

Tuten:

Er hat keine Ahnung von Tuten und Blasen.	He doesn't know beans about it; he knows as much about it as the man in the moon.

u:
  Er läßt sich kein X für ein U vormachen. | You can't put anything over on him; **he** can't be taken in.

übel:
  Damit wird er übel anlaufen. | He'll get the worst of it.
  Er nimmt leicht etwas übel auf. | He's very touchy; he takes offense easily.
  Er hat nicht übel Lust dazu. | He's rather keen about it; he rather feels like doing it.

über:
  Über kurz oder lang tut er's doch. | Sooner or later he'll do it anyway.
  Das geht über alles. | That's the limit; that beats all.
  Es geht ihm über alles. | He prefers it to anything else.
  Es ging über ihn her. | They ran him down; they dragged him in the mud; they slandered him.

  Er schlief überm Lesen ein. | He fell asleep reading.
  Es ist über acht Tage her. | It's more than a week ago.
  Sie fühlte es die ganze Zeit über. | She felt it all along.
  Eines schönen Tages ist er ihnen doch über. | He'll have the whip-hand over them one of these days; he'll get the better of them someday.

  Es wurde ihr über. | She was fed up with it; she got sick of it.

Überblick:
  Es fehlt ihm an Überblick. | He can't see beyond the end of his nose; he lacks perspective.

Überdruß:
  Das habe ich bis zum Überdruß gehört. | I've heard more than enough of that; I never want to hear of it again.

übereilen:
  Übereilen Sie sich nicht! | Don't kill yourself!; take your time!

überein:
  Sie haben wenig miteinander überein. | They have little in common with one another.

überfliegen:
  Er hat das Buch nur eben überflogen. | He just skimmed over (*or* glanced through) the book.

Überfluß:
  Er hat Geld im Überfluß. | He has money galore; he's rolling in money.
  Zum Überfluß wurde er noch krank. | To cap the climax, he fell sick.

übergeben:
  Geben Sie ihm eins über! | Punch him one!; give him a slap!

übergefahren:
  So ein übergefahrener Mensch! | What a crazy Ike (*or* nut)!; what a silly person!

übergehen:

Die Augen gingen ihr über. | Tears came into her eyes.

Übergewicht:

Er kriegte das Übergewicht. | He lost his balance.

überhaben:

Er hat es über. | He's fed up with it; he's sick of it.

überhaupt:

Suchen Sie uns doch bald auf, überhaupt, wir müſſen uns noch vieles erzählen! | Do look us up soon—we have so much to tell each other!

Wir gehen im Sommer an die See, ſoweit ſich das überhaupt heute ſchon ſagen läßt. | As far as we can tell at this early date, we'll be going to the coast this summer.

Er kann überhaupt nicht mehr ſchlafen. | He can't sleep at all any more.

Was tun Sie jetzt überhaupt? | What are you doing now anyway?

überholt:

Die Verordnung iſt längſt überholt. | The ordinance has long since expired.

überlaufen:

Es überlief ſie kalt. | It gave her the creeps (or shivers); it made her shudder.

überleben:

Das hat ſich überlebt. | That's obsolete (or out of date).

überlegen:

Er gewann die Meiſterſchaft ganz über= legen. | He won the championship by a wide margin.

übermorgen:

Werden Sie ihm das Geld leihen?—Ja, übermorgen! | Are you going to lend him the money?—Like fun I am!; he can wait till doomsday!

übermütig:

Werden Sie nur nicht übermütig! | Don't get cocky (or fresh)!

übernehmen:

Er hat ſich bei der Aufgabe übernommen. | He's bit off more than he can chew; that's more than he can handle.

überquer:

Die Sache ging ihm überquer. | He hit a snag (or ran into difficulties); he was unsuccessful in bringing it about; it got the better of him.

überragend:

Das Problem iſt von überragender Be= deutung. | The problem is of the greatest importance.

überrieſeln:

Es überrieſelte ihn heiß und kalt. | It sent the shivers up and down his spine; it made him hot and cold all over.

überrumpeln:

Sie haben ihn überrumpelt. | They stole a march on him; they took him by surprise.

überſchlagen:

Überſchlagen Sie mal die Koſten! | Make a rough estimate of the costs!

Sie überſchlug ſich faſt vor Liebenswürdig= keit. | She was gushy (or mealy-mouthed); she was amiability personified; she fell all over herself to be nice.

überſchlagen (*adj.*):

Die Temperatur im Zimmer war überſchlagen.

The chill in the room was broken; the room temperature was moderate.

überſehen:

Er überſieht nicht mehr recht das Geſchäft.

He can hardly keep track of the whole business.

Überſicht:

Er will ſich eine Überſicht verſchaffen.

He wants to get a general idea.

überſichtlich:

Das Buch iſt ſehr überſichtlich abgefaßt.

The book affords a very easy orientation in the subject.

überſtehen:

Er hat es überſtanden.

He withstood (*or* got over) it; he recovered; he passed away (*or* died).

überſtürzen:

Die Ereigniſſe überſtürzten ſich.

Events followed one another in rapid succession.

Überſtürzung:

Nur keine Überſtürzung!

Don't be rash (*or* indiscreet)!; take your time!

Übertragung:

Die Übertragung der Rede durch den
Rundfunk findet um neun Uhr ſtatt.

The speech will be broadcast over the radio at nine o'clock.

übertreffen:

Das übertrifft alles Dageweſene!

That takes the cake!; I never heard the like of it!; that's without precedent!

Er übertraf ſich ſelbſt.

He outdid himself.

überwerfen:

Sie hat ſich mit ihm überworfen.

She had a spat (*or* falling-out) with him; she quarreled with him.

überwinden:

Er hat überwunden.

The struggle is over for him; he's dead.

Überwindung:

Es hat ihn viel Überwindung gekoſtet.

That's an antiquated (*or* outmoded) viewpoint; it's obsolete.

überwunden:

Das iſt ein überwundener Standpunkt.

It took a great deal of will power for him to do it; it cost him a great effort.

überzählen:

Er zählte ihm ein paar über.

He gave him a beating.

überzogen:

Er iſt ſehr von ſich überzogen.

He's too big for his boots; he has an exalted opinion of himself.

übrig:

Sie haben übrig genug.

They have plenty of everything; they've got more than enough.

Er hatte niemals etwas dafür übrig.

He never had much use for it; he never liked it.

Sie wollten ein übriges tun.

They wanted to do something extra (*or* more).

übrigens:

Das hätten Sie übrigens selber wissen können! — You might have thought of that yourself, incidentally!

übriglassen:

Seine Antwort ließ an Deutlichkeit nichts zu wünschen übrig. — He hit the nail on the head; his answer was very much to the point; he couldn't have made it plainer.

Uhl:

Was dem einen sin (= sein') Uhl (= Eule) ist, ist dem andern sin Nachtigall. — One man's meat is another man's poison.

Uhr:

Seine Uhr ist abgelaufen. — His hour has struck; the time has come for him to die.

um:

Um so weniger muß er's tun. — All the more reason why he shouldn't do it.

Er betrog sie um eine Mark. — He cheated her out of a mark.

Er braucht so um drei Mark. — He needs about (or approximately) three marks.

Tun Sie es um meinetwillen! — Do it for my sake!

Es ist um, über Frankfurt zu fahren. — It's out of the way to go by Frankfurt.

Es ist schade um ihn. — It's too bad about him; it's a shame (or pity) that had to happen to him.

Er ist um ein Jahr älter als sie. — He's a year older than she.

Sie kamen einer um den andern. — They came one by one.

Er schreibt eine Woche um die andere. — He writes every other week.

Unsre Zeit ist um. — Our time is up; we must go.

umbringen:

Der Stoff ist nicht umzubringen. — The material won't wear out; it wears like iron.

Umbruch:

Er sprach über den geistigen Umbruch unsrer Zeit. — He spoke of the changed spiritual aspect (or outlook) of our time.

umeseln:

Er mußte die Arbeit vollkommen umeseln. — He had to revise the paper completely.

umfallen:

Im letzten Augenblick fiel er um. — He went back on himself at the last moment; he retracted (or capitulated) at the very last.

Umgang:

Er hat Knigges „Umgang mit Menschen" nicht gelesen. — He has never read Emily Post; he has no manners (or breeding).

umgehen:

Sage mir, mit wem du umgehst, und ich sage dir, wer du bist. — Birds of a feather flock together; a man is known by the company he keeps.

Er geht damit um, fortzuziehen. — He is thinking of moving (away from here).

Das läßt sich nicht umgehen. — That can't be avoided; there's no getting around (or out of) that.

Er weiß mit jedem umzugehen. — He's a very easy man to get on with.

umgekehrt:

Umgekehrt wird ein Schuh draus! — You're beginning at the wrong end!; try reversing the procedure!

Der Fall liegt gerade umgekehrt. — The case is just the reverse; it's just the other way around.

umguďen:
　Sie werden sich noch umguďen! | You'll get the surprise of your life!

umkippen:
　Er ist bei den Verhandlungen umgekippt. | He changed horses in midstream; he shifted (*or* reversed) his position during the negotiations.

umklappen:
　Er klappte um. | He pulled in his horns (*or* backed down); he caved in (*or* gave up).

umkommen:
　Laß nichts umkommen! | Don't waste a drop!

Umkommen:
　Die Hitze war zum Umkommen. | The heat was unbearable.

Umlauf:
　Er gab es durch Umlauf bekannt. | He announced it in a circular.

umschmeißen:
　Das schmeißt die ganze Sache um. | That wrecks the whole thing; that upsets everything.

　Der Schauspieler hat umgeschmissen. | The actor forgot his lines.

Umschweif:
　Er sagte es ohne Umschweife. | He made no bones about it; he said it point-blank.

umsehen:
　Er wird sich umsehen, wenn er kein Geld mehr bekommt. | He'll sit up and take notice when the money is no longer forthcoming; he'll be surprised when he no longer gets any money.

umsonst:
　Nicht umsonst wies er darauf hin. | He had his reasons for alluding to it; he mentioned it on purpose.

Umstand:
　Machen Sie keine Umstände! | Don't stand on ceremony!; don't put yourself out!; don't go to a lot of bother!

　Er ging auf die näheren Umstände ein. | He went into detail.
　Sie ist in anderen Umständen. | She's in the family way; she's pregnant.
　Er ist den Umständen nach geborgen. | He's comparatively safe.
　Unter Umständen bleiben sie daheim. | It's possible that they'll stay at home.
　Er muß unter allen Umständen kommen. | He's simply got to come; he must come, regardless.

　Sie will unter keinen Umständen. | She absolutely refuses to do it.
　Er tat es ohne weitere Umstände. | He did it without more ado.

Umstandskasten:
　Sie ist ein rechter Umstandskasten. | She's a regular fuss-budget; she's a stickler for form.

umsteigen:
　Nach Hamburg umsteigen! | Change (trains) for Hamburg!

umstellen:
　Er kann sich nicht umstellen. | He can't adjust himself.

umstoßen:
　Er versprach, sie gelegentlich umzustoßen. | He promised to drop in on them sometime.

Umweg:
　Er erfuhr davon auf Umwegen. | He learned about it indirectly (*or* in a roundabout way).

umwerfen:
Der Sänger hat bei der Aufführung umgeworfen.

The singer got off key during the performance.

Unabänderliche:
Fügen Sie sich ins Unabänderliche!

Play the game!; grin and bear it!; make the best of it!

Unannehmlichkeit:
Bringen Sie sich nicht in Unannehmlichkeiten!

Don't get yourself in Dutch (*or* trouble)!

unbeachtet:
Lassen Sie seinen Rat nicht unbeachtet!

Listen to reason!; you'll take his advice if you know what's good for you!

unbedacht:
Er sagte es in einem unbedachten Augenblick.

He was off his guard when he said it; he said it unthinkingly.

unbenommen:
Das sei Ihnen ganz unbenommen!

Suit yourself!; just as you please!

Unbequemlichkeit:
Machen Sie sich keine Unbequemlichkeiten!

Don't (go to any) bother!; don't put yourself out!; don't inconvenience yourself!

unberufen:
Haben Sie schon einen Automobilunfall gehabt?—Unberufen, nein!
Er mischt sich unberufen in alles.

Have you ever had an automobile accident? —No, but knock on wood!
He pokes his nose into everybody's business.

unbeschrieben:
Er ist ein unbeschriebenes Blatt.

He's an unknown quantity.

unbesorgt:
Seien Sie deshalb unbesorgt!

Don't you fret (*or* worry)!; you may rest assured on that score!

unbewaffnet:
Man kann es mit unbewaffnetem Auge erkennen.

It's visible to the naked eye.

und:
Na und?

So what?; is that all?

uneben:
Das ist gar nicht so uneben!

Not half bad!; that's pretty good!

uneins:
Sie sind uneins geworden.

They had a spat (*or* falling-out); they quarreled.

unendlich:
Er hat es ihnen unendlich oft gesagt.

He's told them a thousand times (*or* time and again).

Wir haben sie unendlich lange nicht mehr gesehen.

It's ages since we saw her.

Unendliche:
Das geht ins Unendliche.

There's no end to it; it goes on and on.

unerhört:
Das ist wirklich unerhört!

Well, I never!; I never heard the like of it!

ungebrannt:
Es gab ungebrannte Asche.

The sparks flew; blows fell.

ungefähr:

Wenn ich nur ungefähr wüßte, was er will.	If only I had some idea of what he wants.
Können Sie mir sagen, wieviel das war, nur so ungefähr?	Can you tell me offhand how much that was?
Es kam so von ungefähr.	It just happened; it came out of a clear sky.

ungehobelt:

Sein Benehmen ist ziemlich ungehobelt.	He acts like an unlicked cub; his manner is rather rough and ready.

ungelegt:

Kümmern Sie sich nicht um ungelegte Eier!	Don't count your chickens before they're hatched!; don't cross your bridges before you come to them!

ungelogen:

Ungelogen, es ist so!	No kidding (or On the level), it's true; that's the truth, so help me!

ungemein:

Das freut mich ungemein.	I'm tickled to death; I'm awfully glad.
Sie haben eine ungemein hohe Meinung von ihm.	They think the world of him; they have the highest regard for him.

ungeniert:

Tun Sie das ungeniert!	Go right ahead and do it!; don't be afraid to do it!

ungenießbar:

Er ist heute ungenießbar.	He's in a bad humor today; he's impossible (or intolerable) today.

ungereimt:

Sie schwatzte ganz ungereimtes Zeug.	She chattered silly nonsense.

ungerupft:

Man kam bei dem Wohltätigkeitsfest nicht ungerupft davon.	The charity bazaar was a regular holdup; everyone was mulcted at the charity bazaar.

Ungeschick:

Ungeschick läßt grüßen!	Butterfingers!; aren't you the helpful Henry?; what a bungler (or clumsy fellow)!

ungewaschen:

Der Kerl hat ein ungewaschenes Maul.	He has a vile (or filthy) tongue; he's absolutely brazen.

ungezogen:

Das ist recht ungezogen von ihm.	That's not at all nice of him.

unglaublich:

Unglaublich, aber wahr!	Strange, but true!
Es ist unglaublich kalt.	It's frightfully cold.
Das ist eine unglaubliche Zumutung!	That's asking too much!; that's an imposition!; it's a preposterous demand!

unglaublichst:

Er macht die unglaublichsten Sachen.	He does the most extraordinary things.

ungleich:

Das ist ungleich besser.	That's ever so much better; there's no comparison.

Unglück:

Unglück über Unglück! — It never rains but it pours!; if it isn't one thing, it's another!

Er saß da wie ein Häufchen Unglück. — He sat there looking as if he had lost his last friend; he looked very forlorn (*or* woebegone).

Um das Unglück voll zu machen. — To cap the climax; to make matters worse.

Bei allem Unglück ist immer noch ein Glück. — Every cloud has a silver lining; everything has its good side.

unglücklich:

Er kam unglücklich zu Fall. — He fell and hurt himself.

Unglücksrabe:

Er ist aber auch ein Unglücksrabe. — He's a regular Jonah (*or* hoodoo); he's a regular croaker (*or* pessimist).

Ungnade:

Er mußte sich auf Gnade und Ungnade ergeben. — He had to make an unconditional surrender.

Ungunst:

Das Urteil fiel zu seinen Ungunsten aus. — The verdict was "guilty"; he was found guilty.

ungünstig:

Sie ist ungünstig gestürzt. — She had a mean (*or* bad) fall.

ungut:

Nichts für ungut! — I'm awfully sorry!; no harm meant!

unheimlich:

Er ist unheimlich gelehrt. — He's awfully learned.

Uniform:

Er hat die Uniform schon lange ausgezogen. — He retired from the army long ago.

Unke:

Er säuft wie eine Unke. — He drinks like a fish.

Sie ist die reine Unke. — She's a regular wet blanket (*or* kill-joy); she's a born croaker (*or* pessimist).

unklar:

Er läßt sie im unklaren darüber. — He leaves them in the dark; he tells them nothing.

unklug:

Das ist recht unklug von ihm. — That's very foolish of him.

Unkosten:

Er hat seine Arbeit ohne eigne geistige Unkosten geschrieben. — He wrote his paper without using his thinking cap (*or* gray matter); he never gave it a thought.

Unkraut:

Unkraut vergeht nicht. — A bad penny always turns up; evil grows apace.

unlieb:

Es ist ihr nicht unlieb, das zu erfahren. — She's glad to hear that.

unliebsam:

Es kam schließlich zu einer unliebsamen Aussprache. — It ended in a spat (*or* quarrel).

Unluſt:
Er verrichtet die Arbeit mit ſichtlicher Unluſt.

You can tell by his face (*or* attitude) that he doesn't like the work.

Unmenſch:
Sei doch kein Unmenſch!

Be a sport!; do say yes!; oh, come on!

unqualifizierbar:
Er benahm ſich ganz und gar unqualifizierbar.

His behavior was impossible (*or* positively disgraceful).

Unrat:
Er witterte Unrat.

He smelled a rat; he scented mischief.

Unrecht:
Er beklagt ſich mit Unrecht.

He has no reason to complain.

Unrechte:
Er iſt an den Unrechten gekommen.

He caught a Tartar; he got the worst of it.

unrein:
Schreiben Sie die Arbeit ins unreine!

Make a rough outline (*or* draft) of the subject; jot down some notes on it.

unſauber:
Es geht bei der Sache unſauber zu.

It's a shady (*or* an underhand) deal; there's crooked business going on.

unſchädlich:
Man hat ihn unſchädlich gemacht.

They put the clamps on him; they put him on the spot; they foiled (*or* fixed) him.

Unſchuld:
Sie iſt die Unſchuld vom Lande.

She's innocence personified; she's straight from the country; she's a simple country lass.

Ich waſche meine Hände in Unſchuld.

I wash my hands of it; I'm not responsible.

unſicher:
Sie machte den Jungen mit ihren vielen Fragen ganz unſicher.

She got the lad all balled (*or* mixed) up with her many questions; she had him rattled (*or* confused).

Er iſt ein unſicherer Kantoniſt.

He's slippery as an eel; you can't pin him down; he's a shifty fellow; he's not dependable.

Unſtimmigkeit:
In der Verwaltung herrſchen Unſtimmigkeiten.

There's friction in the administration.

Bei der Prüfung der Kaſſe fand man große Unſtimmigkeiten.

An investigation into the treasury brought to light great discrepancies.

Untätchen:
An ſeinem Anzug war kein Untätchen.

He was immaculately groomed; his suit was spotlessly clean.

unten:
Er iſt bei ihnen unten durch.

He's in the doghouse; they're through with him; they'll have no more to do with him.

Er hat von unten auf gedient.

He has risen from the ranks; he's worked his way up from office boy to president.

unter:
Unter hundert iſt keiner geeignet.

Not one in a hundred is fit.

Unter uns!

Between you and me; confidentially.

Er fand es unter seinen Büchern.	He found it among (*or* in one of) his books.
Es kam unter die Leute.	It became the talk of the town.
Er gehört unter die Romantiker.	He belongs to the Romantic school; he is a Romanticist.
unterderhand:	
Die Sache wurde unterderhand beigelegt.	The affair was hushed up (*or* smoothed over).
Man gab es ihm unterderhand zu verstehen.	It was intimated to him; they secretly gave him to understand.
Er verschaffte es sich unterderhand.	He succeeded in getting it by hook or by crook; he managed to get it somehow.
unterdrückt:	
Er lachte unterdrückt.	He laughed up his sleeve; he suppressed a laugh; he chuckled quietly.
untergehakt:	
Sie gingen untergehakt.	They went arm in arm.
unterhaltsam:	
Es ist ein unterhaltsamer Abend.	It's a pleasant evening.
unterhauen:	
Er muß noch einen Brief unterhauen.	He has still another letter to sign.
unterkriegen:	
Lassen Sie sich nicht unterkriegen!	Don't let it get you (down)!; never say die!; don't give in!
Unterlage:	
Es gelang ihm, sich die nötigen Unterlagen zu verschaffen.	He succeeded in getting the necessary material.
unterliegen:	
Das unterliegt keinem Zweifel.	There's no doubt about it.
Untermiete:	
Er wohnt zur Untermiete.	He rooms with some family.
unterst:	
Er kehrte das Oberste zu unterst.	He turned everything topsy-turvy (*or* upside down).
unterstehen:	
Unterstehen Sie sich!	Don't you dare!; just try and do it!
unterstreichen:	
Er unterstrich seine Worte durch kräftige Handbewegungen.	He punctuated his words with emphatic gestures.
unterwegs:	
Lassen Sie das unterwegs!	Let it be!; don't!
unumgänglich:	
Behalten Sie das Buch nicht länger, als unumgänglich notwendig ist!	Don't keep the book longer than absolutely necessary!
Unverfrorenheit:	
Was für eine Unverfrorenheit!	Some crust (*or* nerve)!; such insolence!
unverhofft:	
Unverhofft kommt oft.	Things often happen when you least expect them.
unverrichtet:	
Er zog unverrichteter Sache ab.	He went as he had come; he left empty-handed (*or* without having accomplished his mission).

unverrückbar:
Das steht unverrückbar fest.

That's a cinch; that's dead-sure.

unverständlich:
Das ist mir unverständlich.

That's beyond me.

unversucht:
Er ließ kein Mittel unversucht.

He left no stone unturned; he tried every possible means.

unverwüstlich:
Der Kerl ist unverwüstlich.

You can't get him down; nothing bothers him.

unvordenklich:
Es ist so seit unvordenklichen Zeiten.

It's been that way from time immemorial.

unweigerlich:
Es setzt unweigerlich voraus, daß . . . .

It necessarily implies that . . . .

unwiderruflich:
Das sage ich Ihnen unwiderruflich zum letzten Mal.

I tell you once and for all.

unwidersprochen:
Sie können das nicht unwidersprochen lassen.

That calls for a comeback; you can't let that remark pass.

unzugänglich:
Er ist sehr unzugänglich.

He's quite standoffish (*or* unsociable).

üppig:
Werden Sie nur nicht üppig!

Don't get cocky (*or* fresh)!; don't be so snooty (*or* superior)!

urkomisch:
Das ist urkomisch.

That's a scream (*or* riot); that's very funny.

Urlaub:
Er nahm Urlaub auf Krampf.

He played hookey (from school); he sneaked out; he was absent without leave.

Ursache:
Haben Sie vielen Dank!—Keine Ursache!

Many thanks!—You're welcome!; don't mention it!; forget it!

Keine Wirkung ohne Ursache.

Where there's smoke there's fire; there's a reason for everything.

ursprünglich:
Er ist ein so ursprünglicher Mensch.

He's such a natural (*or* an unaffected) fellow; he's so very genuine (*or* sincere).

urwüchsig:
Sein Humor ist urwüchsig bayrisch.

His humor is typically Bavarian.

Valet:
Er hat der Partei Valet gesagt.

He quit the party.

Vaterunser:
Dem kann man das Vaterunser durch die Backen blasen.

He's a skinny ninny; he's nothing but skin and bones.

verabschieden:
Er verabschiedete sich von ihnen.

He said good-bye to them; he took leave of them.

Das Gesetz wurde verabschiedet.

The bill (*or* law) was passed.

verachten:
Das ist nicht zu verachten!

Not (half) bad!; that's not to be sneezed at!; you've got something there!

veräppeln:
Lassen Sie sich nicht veräppeln!

Don't let them razz (*or* ridicule) you!

verballhornen:
Er hat die Sache verballhornt.

He balled it all up; he made a botch (*or* mess) of it; he made matters worse.

verbaut:
Durch sein Verhalten ist jede Verständigung verbaut.

His conduct precludes any agreement; he's making it impossible to reach an agreement.

verbeißen:
Er hat sich in die Anschauung verbissen.

He's sold on (*or* wedded to) the idea; he has his heart set on it.

Sie konnte sich das Lachen nicht verbeißen.

She couldn't help (*or* keep from) laughing.

verbiestert:
Mach den Jungen doch nicht ganz verbiestert!

Don't get the kid all balled (*or* mixed) up; don't get him flustered (*or* confused).

verbieten:
Das verbietet sich von selbst.

That goes without saying.

Verbildung:
Er ist nicht von Verbildung angekränkelt.

Education hasn't spoiled him.

verbimsen:
Er hat viel Geld verbimst.

He blew in (*or* wasted) a lot of money.

verbindlichst:
Verbindlichsten Dank!

Much obliged!; many thanks!

verbitten:
Das möchte ich mir verbeten haben!

I won't have that!; I won't stand for it!

verbleiben:
Dabei verbleibt's!

Leave it (*or* Let it go) at that!; that's final!; we'll say no more about it!

verblühen:
Er ist bereits verblüht. — He skipped; he's gone (*or* left).

verbohren:
Er hat sich darin verbohrt. — It's become a fixed notion with him; he's become obsessed by the idea.

verbohrt:
Er ist ein verbohrter Mensch. — He's an obstinate cuss; he's a pig-headed fellow.

verboten:
Eintritt verboten! — Keep out!; no admittance!
Sie sah in dem altmodischen Kleid verboten aus. — She looked a fright (*or* sight) in that old-fashioned dress.

verbrechen:
Was hat er denn verbrochen? — What has he done (wrong)?; what wrong has he committed?
Sie hat ein Gedicht verbrochen. — She perpetrated (*or* wrote) a poem.

verbumfiedeln:
Er hat die ganze Geschichte verbumfiedelt. — He stalled (*or* gummed up) the works; he spoiled the whole business.

verbummeln:
Sie haben das vollkommen verbummelt. — They've completely forgotten about that.

verbummelt:
Er ist ein verbummeltes Genie. — He's a genius gone to pot (*or* seed); he's an intellectual slacker (*or* loafer).

verbunden:
Würden Sie mir die Zeitung reichen? — Would you pass (*or* hand) me the paper?
Sehr verbunden! — Much obliged!; thank's a lot!
Ich bin falsch verbunden. — I've got the wrong (phone) number.

verbürgt:
Die Nachricht ist verbürgt. — It's straight goods; the news is authentic.

verbuttern:
Er verbuttert sein Geld. — He's squandering (*or* wasting) his money.
Er hat die Sache schon wieder verbuttert. — He botched (*or* spoiled) it again.

verdauen:
Sie können den Menschen nicht verdauen. — They can't stomach (*or* stand) that man.

verdeckt:
Er spielt mit verdeckten Karten. — He doesn't show his hand; he hides his intentions.

verdenken:
Das kann ich Ihnen nicht verdenken. — I can't blame you for that; I sympathize with you.

Verderb:
Sie sind auf Gedeih und Verderb miteinander verbunden. — They'll stick to each other through thick and thin; they're pledged to each other for life.

verderben:
Er will es mit niemand verderben. — He wants to keep on the right side of everyone; he tries to please everyone.
An ihm ist ein Arzt verdorben. — A good doctor is lost in him; he would have made a good doctor.

Er ist längst gestorben und verdorben. | He's long since dead and gone.
Seinetwegen könnte man sterben und verderben. | A person could die, for all he cares; he wouldn't lift a finger to help a fellow in trouble.

Verdienst:
Dem Verdienste seine Krone. | You reap as you sow; honor to whom honor is due.

verdonnern:
Er wurde zu drei Jahren Gefängnis verdonnert. | He was sentenced to three years in jail.

verdonnert:
Sie war wie verdonnert. | She was completely taken off her feet; she was flabbergasted (*or* thunderstruck).

verdreht:
Machen Sie mir doch den Jungen nicht ganz verdreht! | Don't give the lad a bum steer!; don't turn (*or* put ideas into) his head!
So ein verdrehter Kerl! | What a crackpot (*or* fool)!

verdrießen:
Lassen Sie sich's nicht verdrießen! | Never mind!; don't let it get (*or* discourage) you!
Er läßt sich keine Mühe verdrießen. | He goes to no end of trouble; he spares no pains.

verdrücken:
Verdrück dich! | Make yourself scarce!; beat it!
Das werden Sie doch noch verdrücken können! | You'll still be able to get that down, won't you?; I'm sure you can manage to eat that yet!

Verdruß:
Er hat einen kleinen Verdruß. | He's a hunchback; he's deformed.

verduften:
Er hat sich verduftet. | He faded out of the picture; he made himself scarce; he cleared (*or* got) out.

Vereinsmeier:
Er ist der richtige Vereinsmeier. | He's a regular joiner (*or* organizer); he belongs to every club.

verfallen:
Darauf wäre er nie verfallen. | He would never have hit upon this idea; it would never have occurred to him.

verfangen:
Bei dem will nichts verfangen. | He's a bad bet (*or* hopeless case); everything is thrown away on him; nothing impresses him.

verfänglich:
Der Witz war ein wenig verfänglich. | The joke was a little shady (*or* off color); it was risqué (*or* daring).

Verfehlung:
Seine moralischen Verfehlungen wurden bald entdeckt. | His moral lapses were soon noticed.

verflixt:
Verflixt und zugenäht! | Doggone it!; the deuce!

verflucht:
Verflucht noch eins! | Heck!; drat it!; ding bust it!

vergaloppieren:
Da haben Sie sich aber schön vergaloppiert! | You certainly pulled a boner (*or* made a blunder) that time!; that was a bad slip of the tongue!

vergeben:
Sie vergeben sich doch nichts, wenn Sie das tun. | It won't hurt you any to do that; it won't compromise you in any way.

vergehen:
Die Lust dazu wird ihm schon vergehen. | He'll soon lose interest in it; he'll forget all about it in no time.

vergelten:
Vergelt's Gott! | God bless you!

vergipsen:
Sie hat ihnen alles vergipst. | She bungled (*or* spoiled) everything for them.

vergittert:
Er sitzt hinter vergitterten Fenstern. | He's behind the (prison) bars; he's in jail.

vergleichen:
Sie haben sich endlich verglichen. | They finally made up (their differences); they finally came to terms.

Vergnügen:
Viel Vergnügen! | Have a good time!; enjoy yourself!

vergreifen:
Er vergriff sich im Ausdruck. | He used the wrong expression; he confused his terms.

Sie möchte sich lieber nicht an der Sache vergreifen. | She would rather not attempt it.

vergriffen:
Das Werk ist vergriffen. | The book is sold out (*or* out of print).

vergucken:
Er hat sich in sie verguckt. | He fell for (*or* in love with) her.

verhaftet:
Diese Menschen sind der Scholle verhaftet. | These people are rooted in the soil.

verhalten:
Die Sache verhält sich so. | Such is the case; that's how matters stand.
Er verhielt sich still. | He kept quiet; he said nothing.
Sie wissen nicht, wie sie sich verhalten sollen. | They don't know what to do (*or* how to act).

Verhältnis:
Er hat kein inneres Verhältnis zu seiner Arbeit. | His heart isn't in his work.
Sie stehen in gespannten Verhältnissen zueinander. | Their relationship is strained; they're not on good terms.
Er ist mit seinem Verhältnis ausgegangen. | He dated up (*or* went out with) his girl friend.
Sie leben über ihre Verhältnisse. | They live beyond their means (*or* income).

verhängt:
Er kam mit verhängten Zügeln. | He came at a gallop; he came apace (*or* at full speed).

verhauen:
  Er hat das Schriftliche verhauen. — He flunked (*or* failed) the written test.
  Er hat sich in seiner Rede mehrfach verhauen. — He made several slips (*or* blunders) in his speech.

verhauen:
  Er ist ein verhauener Geselle. — He's a queer duck (*or* funny bird).
  Er kam mit verhauenem Gesicht von der Hochschule. — He returned from college with his face all banged up (*or* full of scars).

verheddern:
  Verheddern Sie sich nur nicht in Ihrer Rede! — Don't get balled (*or* mixed) up in your speech!; don't get too involved!

verheerend:
  Das ist ja verheerend! — How perfectly dreadful!; isn't that awful?

verhext:
  Das ist rein wie verhext. — There's something screwy (*or* fishy) about that; the devil must be in that.

verhohnepipeln:
  Er versuchte sie zu verhohnepipeln. — He tried to pooh-pooh (*or* ridicule) her.

verhudeln:
  Er hat das Geschäft ganz verhudelt. — He let the business go to pot (*or* pieces); he let it run down.

verhüten:
  Das verhüte Gott! — Heaven help us!; God forbid!

verhutzelt:
  Sein Gesicht war ganz verhutzelt. — His face was a mass of wrinkles; it was all dried (*or* shrivelled) up.

verjubeln:
  Er verjubelt das Geld. — He's dissipating the money.

verjuxen:
  Sie haben ihr Vermögen verjuxt. — They've squandered their fortune; they spent it all on a good time.

verkalkt:
  Er ist ein verkalkter Trottel. — He's a dried-up prune; he's dead from the neck up; he's got no life (*or* spirit) in him.

verkauft:
  Er sah sich verraten und verkauft. — He found himself sold down the river; he felt utterly helpless.

Verkehr:
  Das ist kein Verkehr für ihn. — That's not the right company for him to keep; he shouldn't associate with that type of person.

verkehren:
  Der Autobus verkehrt alle zehn Minuten. — The bus runs every ten minutes.
  Er verkehrt in diesem Lokal. — He patronizes this restaurant.
  Sie verkehren viel mit ihm. — They pal around with him; they see a good deal of him.

verklapsen:
  Er läßt sich nicht verklapsen. — He won't be bamboozled (*or* made a fool of).

verklatschen:
  Er hat sie verklatscht. — He squealed (*or* snitched); he told on them.

verkloppen:
Er verkloppte seinen Anzug. — He sold his suit; he got rid of it.
Unsre Mannschaft hat den Gegner schwer verkloppt. — Our team gave the other side a good trimming (*or* licking); they beat the other team badly.

verknacken:
Sie haben ihn mächtig verknackt. — They made a laughing stock of him; they razzed (*or* ridiculed) him unmercifully.
Er wurde zu einem Jahr verknackt. — He was sentenced to jail for a year.

verknacksen:
Er hat sich den Fuß verknackst. — He sprained his ankle.

verknallen:
Er hat sich in sie verknallt. — He's gone (*or* stuck) on her; he's crazy about her.

Verkniffenes:
Sein Mund hatte etwas Verkniffenes. — There was a set expression about his mouth; his lips were tightly compressed.

verknöchert:
Er ist ein verknöcherter Bürokrat. — He's an old crab (*or* crank).

verknusen:
Sie kann den Menschen nicht verknusen. — She can't stomach (*or* stand) that man; she can't bear the sight of him.

verkohlen:
Er hat Sie nur verkohlt. — He was only teasing you; he put one over on you.

verkommen:
Die beiden verkommen gut miteinander. — They get along well together.
Er ist ganz verkommen. — He's gone to the dogs; he ended in the gutter; he's gone to rack and ruin.

verkorksen:
Er hat sich den Magen verkorkst. — He got an upset stomach; he spoiled his stomach.

verkrachen:
Sie haben sich verkracht. — They're on the outs; they're not on speaking terms.

verkracht:
Er ist eine verkrachte Existenz. — He's a total flop (*or* failure); he's a wreck.

verkrümeln:
Die Gäste verkrümelten sich bald. — The party soon broke up; by degrees the guests began to leave.

verlangt:
Das ist zuviel verlangt. — That's asking (*or* expecting) too much.

verlassen:
Verlassen Sie sich darauf, das tue ich! — I'll do that, and no mistake!; you can count on my doing it!

Verlaub:
Das ist, mit Verlaub zu sagen, eine Gemeinheit. — You'll pardon me if I venture to say so, but that's a mean (*or* contemptible) thing to do.

verlaufen:

Sein Eifer verlief sich bald. | His zeal (*or* enthusiasm) soon petered out; he soon lost interest.

Wie ist es verlaufen? | What happened?; how did it pan (*or* turn) out?

verlegen:

Sie verlegte sich aufs Bitten. | She resorted to entreaty.

verlegen (*adj.*):

Sie ist nie um eine Antwort verlegen. | She always has a snappy comeback; she's never at a loss for an answer.

Verlegenheit:

Er hat sich gut aus der Verlegenheit gezogen. | He's got out of the difficulty very well.

Er ist in arger Verlegenheit, das zu erklären. | He can't for the life of him account for it; he's quite at a loss to explain that.

verleiden:

Er verleidete ihr die Freude an der Arbeit. | He poured cold water on her enthusiasm; he spoiled her pleasure in the work.

verleugnen:

Sie ließ sich verleugnen. | She was not at home to visitors; she refused to receive callers.

verliebt:

Sie guckte ganz verliebt. | She was flirting (*or* making eyes); she cast amorous glances in that direction.

verlottern:

Er verlottert noch ganz. | He'll go to pot (*or* the dogs) at this rate; he's headed for ruin.

verlohnen:

Es verlohnt sich nicht der Mühe. | It isn't worth while; it's not worth the trouble.

verlöten:

Lassen Sie uns einen verlöten! | Let's have a snifter (*or* drink)!

vermaledeit:

Vermaledeit! | Heck!; blast it!; ding bust it!

vermasseln:

Er vermasselt jedesmal die Pointe eines Witzes. | He misses the point of every joke in the telling.

vermeiden:

Tun Sie's nicht, wenn Sie's vermeiden können! | Don't do it if you can help it!

vermitteln:

Er vermittelte ihnen ein klares Bild von den Vorgängen. | He gave them an accurate account of the events.

vermöbeln:

Er vermöbelt sein Geld. | He squanders (*or* throws away) his money.

Die Kritik hat sein neues Buch gehörig vermöbelt. | The critics panned (*or* attacked) his new book mercilessly.

Er wurde tüchtig vermöbelt. | He was thoroughly thrashed.

vermögen:

Sie vermag viel bei ihm. | She can do anything with him; she wields great influence over him.

Wenn er es über sich vermag. | If he can bring himself to do it.

vernagelt:
Seien Sie doch nicht so vernagelt!   Don't be bull-headed (*or* obstinate)!; don't be so dense (*or* stupid)!

vernarrt:
Er ist ganz darin vernarrt.   He's got a crush on it; he's wild (*or* crazy) about it.

Vernehmen:
Sicherem Vernehmen nach kommt er.   I have it on good authority that he'll come; according to reliable reports, he's coming.

vernichtend:
Die Kritik war vernichtend.   It was a sweeping (*or* devastating) criticism.

Vernunft:
Er handelte wider die gesunde Vernunft.   He acted contrary to common sense.

verpackt:
Der Junge ist aber hart verpackt!   The boy sure is dense (*or* thick); he's awfully slow (in catching on).

verpassen:
Den Fußballspielern wurde die Uniform verpaßt.   The football players were given (*or* fitted for) their uniforms.

verpetzen:
Er weigerte sich, seine Freunde zu verpetzen.   He refused to squeal (*or* snitch); he wouldn't tell on his friends.

verplappern:
Er verplapperte sich beinahe.   He almost spilt the beans (*or* let the cat out of the bag); he nearly gave away the secret.

verp(r)udeln:
Er hat die Sache verpudelt.   He bungled (*or* wrecked) the works; he spoiled the whole thing.

verpuffen:
Die ganze Sache verpuffte.   The whole thing went up in smoke; it fizzled out; nothing came of it.

verpulvern:
Er hat seines Vaters schwer verdientes Geld verpulvert.   He blew in (*or* used up) his father's hard-earned money.

verpusten:
Verpusten Sie sich mal!   Let's call time out!; catch your breath!

verputzen:
Ich kann ihn nicht verputzen.   I can't stomach (*or* stand) him; I can't bear the sight of him.

Der Kerl kann aber viel verputzen!   He certainly can put away a lot!; he's got some appetite!

verraten:
Er sah sich verraten und verkauft.   He found himself sold down the river; he felt utterly helpless; his hands were tied.

verratzt:
Er ist verratzt.   He's a goner (*or* lost soul); he's beyond all help.

verrauchen:
Sein Zorn verrauchte schnell.   His wrath soon blew over (*or* died down); he soon cooled (*or* calmed) down.

Verrecken:
Nicht ums Verrecken! | Nothing doing!; not on your life!

verrennen:
Er hat sich in die Idee verrannt. | That's a fixed idea of his; it's become an obsession with him.

Verrichtung:
Gute Verrichtung! | Good luck!; success (in your undertaking)!

Vers:
Wie geht der Vers? | What was that?; how does it go (*or* read)?; say that again!

Sie kann sich keinen Vers draus machen. | She can't make head or tail of it; she doesn't get (*or* understand) it.

Versager:
Der neue Geschäftsführer ist in jeder Hinsicht ein Versager. | The new manager is a complete washout; he's a total flop (*or* failure).

versagt:
Sind Sie schon für heute abend versagt? | Are you dated up for this evening?; are you doing anything tonight?

versanden:
Die Verhandlungen versandeten. | The negotiations have hit a snag (*or* come to a deadlock).

versauen:
Versauen Sie sich nicht Ihre Laufbahn! | Don't spoil (*or* ruin) your career!

versaufen:
Er hat seinen Verstand versoffen. | Drink went to his head; it's made a mental wreck of him.

verschämt:
Die Dame ist eine verschämte Arme. | The lady is too proud to ask for charity; she's poor but proud.

verschanzen:
Er suchte sich hinter Ausreden zu verschanzen. | He tried to hide behind an alibi; he tried to fortify himself with alibis.

verschärfen:
Die Gegensätze verschärfen sich. | The differences are growing more marked; they're making themselves felt.

verschieben:
Er verschob Waren. | He was bootlegging; he engaged in illegal trading.

verschiedenes:
Da hört sich doch verschiedenes auf! | Well, I'll be darned!; confound it!; that's really too much!

verschimmeln:
In so einem Nest muß der Mensch ja verschimmeln! | A man can't help going to seed (*or* pot) in such a dump!; a place like that would drive anyone to drink!

verschimpfieren:
Das Haus verschimpfiert die ganze Gegend. | The house is a blight on (*or* disgrace to) the whole landscape.

verschlagen:
Was verschlägt's? | So what?; what of it?; what difference does it make?

Es verschlug ihm fast den Atem. | It fairly took his breath away.

verschlamaffeln:
Er hat die Geschichte verschlamaffelt.

He gummed (*or* botched) up the works; he spoiled the whole thing.

verschleiern:
Es läßt sich nicht mehr verschleiern.

The truth will out; it can no longer be concealed (*or* hushed up).

verschleppt:
Er starb an einer verschleppten Lungenentzündung.

He died from a neglected case of pneumonia.

verschließen:
Er hat sich ihrem Rat niemals verschlossen.

He never disregarded her advice.

verschlingen:
Die Reise verschlang viel Geld.

The trip ate up (*or* ran into) a lot of money.

verschlossen:
Das Buch blieb ihr verschlossen.

The book remained a mystery to her; she didn't know what it was all about.

verschmerzt:
Das ist längst verschmerzt.

That's all over and done with; it's long past and forgotten.

verschnupfen:
Sein Benehmen hat sie verschnupft.

She was peeved at (*or* miffed by) his conduct; his conduct offended her.

verschreiben:
Er verschrieb ihnen sein Haus.
Er hat sich dem Teufel verschrieben.

He willed his house to them.
He sold himself to the devil.

verschrieen:
Er ist als Lügner verschrieen.

He's a notorious liar.

verschrumpelt:
Die Alte hatte ein verschrumpeltes Gesicht.

The old woman's face was a mass of wrinkles; it was all wizened (*or* shrivelled up).

verschütt:
Er ist verschütt gegangen.

He's been arrested; he's gone to the dogs.

verschütten:
Er hat es bei ihr verschüttet.

He's in the doghouse; he's in bad with her; he has incurred her displeasure.

verschüttet:
Alle Möglichkeiten zu einer Verständigung sind verschüttet.

All hopes of a reconciliation are gone.

Verschwender:
Er ist ein Geizkragen im kleinen und ein Verschwender im großen.

He's penny-wise and pound-foolish.

verschwiemelt:
Er sah verschwiemelt aus.

He looked washed out (*or* all in); he looked pooped (*or* exhausted).

verschwindend:
Er weiß verschwindend wenig.

He knows blessed little; he knows practically nothing.

verschwistert:
Sie fühlen sich alle wie verschwistert.

They're a congenial crowd; they all feel like one big, happy family.

verſchwitzen:
  Er hatte die Einladung ganz verſchwitzt.
  He had forgotten all about the invitation; it had completely slipped his mind.

verſchwommen:
  Drücken Sie ſich nicht ſo verſchwommen aus!
  Don't be so vague (*or* indefinite)!; make yourself clear!

verſehen:
  Ehe man ſich's verſah, war man ſein Geld los.
  The money just flew; your money was gone before you knew it.
  Deſſen hatte er ſich nicht verſehen.
  He hadn't expected that; he was unprepared for it.

Verſenkung:
  Er verſchwand ſpurlos in der Verſenkung.
  He dropped completely out of sight.

verſeſſen:
  Er iſt ganz verſeſſen darauf.
  He's just nuts (*or* crazy) about it.

verſetzen:
  Dem hat ſie's aber verſetzt.
  She told him where he got off in no uncertain terms; she certainly gave him a piece of her mind.
  Er hat ſein Mädchen verſetzt.
  He stood his girl (friend) up; he failed to keep his date (*or* appointment) with her.

verſilbern:
  Er verſilberte ſeine Uhr.
  He put his watch in hock; he pawned (*or* sold) his watch.

verſohlen:
  Sie haben ihn ordentlich verſohlt.
  They cowhided (*or* flogged) him good and proper.

verſonnen:
  Er iſt ein verſonnener Junge.
  The boy is a dreamer; he's an introvert.

verſorgen:
  Gott verſorge mich!
  For heaven's sake!; so help me God!

verſorgt:
  Sie ſieht verſorgt aus.
  She looks careworn (*or* worried).

verſpielen:
  Er hat bei ihnen verſpielt.
  He's worn out his welcome with them; they're through with him; they'll have nothing more to do with him.

verſpinnen:
  Er hat ſich ganz in den Gedanken verſponnen.
  He's all wrapped up in the idea; he's deeply engrossed in it.

verſprechen:
  Er verſpricht ſich nichts davon.
  He doesn't expect anything from it; he doesn't think anything will come of it.
  Er hat ſich für heute abend verſprochen.
  He has a date (*or* an engagement) for this evening.

verſprochen:
  Die beiden ſind miteinander verſprochen.
  They're engaged.

Verſtand:
  Da ſteht mir der Verſtand ſtill!
  Well, I'll be jiggered (*or* darned)!; can you beat that!; you've got me there!; that's more than I can figure out!

Rauchen Sie diese Zigarre mit Verstand!	Smoke this cigar with relish!; here's a cigar you will appreciate!
Das ist ohne Sinn und Verstand.	That's without rhyme or reason; that doesn't make sense.

verstehen:
Er versteht sich darauf. — He's an expert in such things.
Was verstehen Sie darunter? — What do you mean by that?; how do you interpret that?

Sollen wir jetzt gehen?—Versteht sich! — Shall we go now?—Sure thing!; you bet!; of course!

Er kann sich nicht dazu verstehen. — He can't see his way clear to doing it.
Wir können die Zeit nicht verstehen. — We've no time to waste.
Er gab es ihnen zu verstehen. — He gave them a hint; he intimated it.

Verstehstemich:
Dazu fehlt ihm der Verstehstemich (= Ver-stehst=du=mich). — He doesn't savvy (or catch on); he hasn't the brains for that.

versteifen:
Er versteifte sich darauf. — He clung to it religiously (or obstinately).

versteinert:
Er stand wie versteinert. — He stood stock-still; he was struck dumb.

verstohlen:
Er warf einen verstohlenen Blick nach ihnen. — He stole a glance (or took a peep) at them; he looked at them on the sly.

verstöpseln:
Sie verstöpselte mit ihrem großen Hut die Aussicht. — Her big hat cut off the view.

verstürzt:
Er ist ganz verstürzt darauf. — He goes in for it in a big way; he's a fan; he's wild (or crazy) about it.

Sie sah verstürzt aus. — She looked nonplussed (or crestfallen).

Versuch:
Das käme auf einen Versuch an! — You may just as well try it!

versuchen:
Er will es noch einmal mit ihm versuchen. — He's willing to give him another chance.

versumpfen:
In diesem Kaff versumpft er ganz. — He's going to seed (or pot) in this burg; the place is driving him to drink.

vertobaken:
Den haben sie tüchtig vertobakt. — They gave him a good walloping; they made a big fool of him.

vertrackt:
So eine vertrackte Frage! — Ask me another!; what a sticker!; that question stumps (or gets) me!

Vertrauen:
Er stellte ihn ein im Vertrauen auf seine Zeugnisse. — He hired him on the strength of his references.

vertrauenerweckend:
Er sieht wenig vertrauenerweckend aus. — He looks like a suspicious character.

Vertreter:
Er ist ein feiner Vertreter! — He's a nice one!; what a man!

vertrommeln:
   Sie haben ihn schwer vertrommelt. | They gave him a good beating.

vertütern:
   Er vertüterte sich mehrfach in seiner Rede. | He broke down several times in the course of his speech.

verwachsen:
   Er ist mit der Auffassung wie verwachsen. | He's quite sold on (*or* wedded to) the idea.

verwackeln:
   Sie haben ihn verwackelt. | They gave him a walloping.

verwackelt:
   Die Aufnahme ist verwackelt. | The picture is blurred (*or* out of focus).

verwalken:
   Er wurde gehörig verwalkt. | He got a sound licking.

verwaschen:
   Er gab ihnen eine ganz verwaschene Auslegung von der Sache. | He gave them a very general (*or* indefinite) report on the matter.

verwechseln:
   Er hat mein und dein verwechselt. | He stole.

Verwechseln:
   Sie sehen sich zum Verwechseln ähnlich. | They're like two peas in a pod; they could be taken for twins.

verwenden:
   Er verwandte kein Auge von ihr. | He never took his eyes off her.
   Sie verwandte sich für ihn. | She put in a good word for him; she interceded for him.

Verwendung:
   Er bekam die Stelle auf ihre Verwendung. | He got the position through her influence (*or* recommendation).

   Er wurde der Abteilung zu besonderer Verwendung zugeteilt. | He was assigned special duties in the department.

verwerten:
   Davon ist doch nichts mehr zu verwerten. | That's seen its day; it has done its duty; we have no further use for it.

verwichsen:
   Er verwichste ihn ordentlich. | He gave him a good trimming (*or* beating).
   Er hat das große Vermögen verwichst. | He squandered the huge fortune.

verwogen:
   Sie trägt einen verwogenen Hut. | She wears a snappy (*or* jaunty) hat.

verwünscht:
   Verwünscht, daß er gerade jetzt kommen muß! | Why the blazes (*or* devil) does he have to come just now?

verwursteln:
   Sie verwurstelt alles. | She bungles (*or* makes a mess of) everything.

verzeichnen:
   Er hat einen Erfolg zu verzeichnen. | He's made a hit (*or* sensation); he's scored a victory.

verziehen:
   Verziehen Sie sich! | Scram!; vamoose!; go chase yourself!; get out!

Verzug:

Sie ist der Verzug ihrer Mutter.
She's mother's darling (*or* pet).

Bitte bei Verzug mit neuer Anschrift zurücksenden!
If not delivered, please re-address and return to sender.

verzweifeln:

Nur nicht verzweifeln!
Never say die!; while there's life there's hope.

Vetternstraße:

Er zieht die Vetternstraße.
He's sponging on (*or* living off) his family.

Vieh:

Er säuft wie das liebe Vieh.
He drinks like a fish; he's a regular souse.

vielmals:

Ich bitte vielmals um Verzeihung!
I'm more than sorry!; a thousand pardons!; I beg your pardon!

Grüßen Sie ihn vielmals von mir!
Give him my love (*or* best regards)!

vier:

Er stemmte sich mit allen vieren dagegen.
He resisted it tooth and nail; he fought like a tiger.

Vier Augen sehen mehr als zwei.
Two heads are better than one.

Ich will es Ihnen unter vier Augen sagen.
Between you and me and the lamp post; I'll tell you privately (*or* in confidence).

Er glaubte schon, die Stelle an allen vier Zipfeln zu haben.
He thought he had the job in the bag (*or* his pocket); he was sure he had landed (*or* secured) it.

vierzehn:

Er machte ein Gesicht wie vierzehn Tage Regenwetter.
He looked like a bad-weather prophet; he looked glum (*or* sour).

Er ist in vierzehn Tagen hier.
He'll be here in two weeks.

Visier:

Er kämpft nicht mit offnem Visier.
He's no square shooter; he's not on the level; he doesn't play fair.

Vogel:

Friß, Vogel, oder stirb!
Do or die!; sink or swim!; take it or leave it!

Er sitzt wie der Vogel im Hanf.
He's in clover; he's sitting pretty; he's well off.

Sie ist ein lockrer Vogel.
She's a fast one; she's a loose liver.

Jedem Vogel gefällt sein Nest.
Everyone to his own taste; we each have our own way of doing things.

Er schoß den Vogel ab.
He brought home the bacon; he landed (*or* won) the prize.

Den Vogel erkennt man am Gesang.
Actions speak louder than words.

Er hat einen Vogel.
He has bats in his belfry; he's a crackpot (*or* lunatic).

Die Vögel, die so früh singen, frißt die Katze.
Early ripe, early rotten; don't count your chickens before they're hatched!

Vokativus:

Er ist ein rechter Vokativus.
He's a real slicker (*or* sharper); he's a sly old fox.

Volk:

Er ist ein Mann aus dem Volk.   He's one of the common people; he's a man of the street.

Das ist Kaviar fürs Volk.   That's caviar to the general (*or* public); that's out of their class; it's above them.

Völkchen:

Sie trafen ein lustiges Völkchen an.   They met up with a jolly bunch (*or* crowd).

voll:

Man nimmt ihn nicht voll.   They don't take him seriously.

Es schlug voll.   It struck the full hour.

Er hat sich toll und voll getrunken.   He's tight as a drum; he's dead-drunk.

Er würdigt das voll und ganz.   He appreciates that fully.

Sie wirtschaften aus dem vollen.   They don't have to be economical; they live well.

Es ist sein voller Ernst.   He's in earnest; he really means it.

Er nahm die Kehre in voller Fahrt.   He took (*or* drove around) the corner on two wheels (*or* at top speed).

Er gab sein Geld mit vollen Händen aus.   He spent his money liberally (*or* without giving it a thought).

Sie dankte ihm aus vollem Herzen.   She thanked him from the bottom of her heart.

Er lachte aus voller Kehle.   He laughed heartily.

Sie schrie aus voller Kehle.   She shouted at the top of her voice.

Volldampf:

Er arbeitet mit Volldampf.   He's working at full blast (*or* top speed); he's putting all his strength into the job.

vollenden:

Er hat vollendet.   His race is run; he checked out (*or* passed away); he died.

Vollgas:

Gib Vollgas!   Give her the gas!; step on it!; speed it up!

vollkommen:

Der Mantel ist recht vollkommen.   The overcoat is rather large.

Das ist vollkommener Unsinn.   That's downright nonsense.

Vollständigkeit:

Er erkundigte sich nur der Vollständigkeit halber.   He inquired just to make absolutely sure.

von:

Von mir aus können Sie gehen.   I don't mind if you go; you may go as far as I'm concerned.

Er kam so von ungefähr daher.   He happened (to come) along.

So etwas zu behaupten, das ist doch das Ende von weg!   I call that laying it on a bit thick; that's putting it strong; that's going a little too far.

Hat er das Geld zurückgezahlt?—Ja, von wegen!   Did he pay back the money?—Hell, no!; like fun he did!

vor:

Er sann vor sich hin.   He was lost in thought.

Sie weinte vor Freude.   She wept for joy; she cried because she was so happy.

Sie fürchten sich vor ihm.   They're afraid of him.

Er sah sie vor einer Woche.   He saw her a week ago.

Er kommt nach wie vor.   He comes as usual.

voran:
  Immer langsam voran!

Take it easy!; don't push!; go slow!

vorangehen:
  Gehen Sie voran!

After you, Alphonse!; lead the way!; go on (or ahead)!

  Er ging mit gutem Beispiel voran.

He set a good example.

vorbauen:
  Der kluge Mann baut vor.

It's a wise man who thinks of the future.

vorbedacht:
  Besser vorbedacht als nachgetan.

An ounce of prevention is worth a pound of cure; a stitch in time saves nine.

Vorbehalt:
  Wir geben die Meldung unter Vorbehalt wieder.

We don't vouch for this report.

vorbeibenehmen:
  Er hat sich vorbeibenommen.

He made a break (or faux pas); he made a wrong move.

vorbeigehen:
  Gehen Sie doch heute abend bei ihnen vorbei!

Call (or Drop in) on them tonight!

vorbeigelingen:
  Die Sache ist ihm vorbeigelungen.

He missed out on it; he didn't succeed.

vorbeireden:
  Er redet immer an den Dingen vorbei.

He always talks beside the point; he never sticks to the subject under discussion.

vorbestimmt:
  Es war vorbestimmt.

It was in the cards; fate had decreed it.

vorbildlich:
  Er benahm sich vorbildlich.

He was a perfect brick; he acted perfectly swell; his conduct was exemplary.

vorbohren:
  Aha, der gute Mann bohrt vor!

Well, well, if someone isn't trying to get a stand-in (or place up front)!

Vordermann:
  Er übersprang bei der Beförderung seine Vordermänner.

He was promoted out of turn; he was advanced over his superiors.

vordringlich:
  Er ist als vordringlich vorgemerkt.

He's first on the waiting list; his case will be considered first.

vorfahren:
  Er will heute nachmittag bei Ihnen vorfahren.

He intends to look you up (or drop in on you) this afternoon.

vorflunkern:
  Er flunkerte ihr was vor.

He fibbed (or lied) to her.

vorhaben:
  Er hat andre Dinge vor.

He has other fish to fry; he has other irons in the fire (or things on his mind).

vorkauen:
  Sie haben es ihm, wer weiß wie oft, vorgekaut.

They've threshed it out (or gone over it) with him any number of times.

Vorkenntnis:
Vorkenntnisse nicht erforderlich! — Experience unnecessary!

vorknöpfen:
Knöpfen Sie sich ihn mal vor! — Give him a piece of your mind!; tell him what's what!

vorkommen:
Ich komme morgen mal vor. — I'll drop in tomorrow.

Wie kommst du mir denn vor? — What's the big idea?; how do you get that way?; just what do you mean by that?

Es kommt mir vor, als hätte ich das schon einmal gehört. — I seem to remember having heard that before; where have I heard that before?

Das kommt bei Goethe vor. — This passage comes from (or occurs in) Goethe.

So was ist mir noch nicht vorgekommen! — Of all the nerve!; I never heard the like of it!; such a thing has never happened to me before!

vorlegen:
Legen Sie tüchtig vor! — Fall to!; eat heartily!

vorliegen:
Es liegt weiter nichts vor. — There's no further business; that's all.

vormachen:
Mir können Sie nichts vormachen! — I'm from Missouri!; you can't fool me!; I don't believe it.

vorn:
Da heißt es den ganzen Tag: lieber Karl hinten und lieber Karl vorn. — All day long it's Charlie here, Charlie there, and Charlie everywhere.

Fangen wir wieder von vorn an! — Let's begin all over again!

vornehm:
Vornehm und gering war da. — Rich and poor alike were there.

Sie tut schrecklich vornehm. — She's terribly ritzy (or high-hat); she puts on airs.

vornehmen:
Nehmen Sie sich ihn mal vor! — Tell him what's what!; give him a piece of your mind!

Sie sollten sich nicht zuviel vornehmen! — Don't bite off more than you can chew!; don't take on more than you can handle!

vornehmst:
Es soll meine vornehmste Aufgabe sein. — I'll make it my first duty; I'll attend to that before everything else.

vorreden:
Lassen Sie sich das nicht vorreden! — Don't let anyone humbug (or fool) you!; don't you believe it!

vorrichten:
Er ließ sich ein Zimmer vorrichten. — He made room reservations.

Vorschein:
Er kommt den ganzen Tag nicht zum Vorschein. — He doesn't show up (or come around) all day.

vorschreiben:
Er läßt sich von niemand vorschreiben. — He won't let anyone boss (or dictate to) him; he'll take orders from no one.

Vorschub:
Er leistet ihren Plänen keinen Vorschub. — He won't boost (or back) them; he doesn't support their cause.

vorſchweben:

Es ſchwebt mir ſo dunkel vor. | I vaguely remember.

Ihm ſchwebt eine andre Löſung vor. | He has another solution in mind.

vorſehen:

Vorſehen! | Look out!; take care!

Vorſicht:

Vorſicht! | Danger!; watch your step!; look out!

Seine Angaben müſſen mit einer ge= wiſſen Vorſicht aufgenommen werden. | His statements must be taken with a grain of salt; you can't put any stock in them; you musn't believe everything he says.

vorſintflutlich:

Das ſind ja vorſintflutliche Zuſtände in dieſem Gaſthaus. | Living conditions in this hotel are more than primitive; there are absolutely no modern conveniences in the place.

vorſohlen:

Er wollte Ihnen was vorſohlen. | He tried to pull the wool over your eyes; he wanted to put one over on you.

vorſorglich:

Nehmen Sie vorſorglich Ihren Mantel mit! | Better take your coat along, just in case (of emergency)!

Vorſpann:

Nehmen Sie Vorſpann! | Step on it!; don't dally!; hurry up!

vorſprechen:

Er wird morgen bei Ihnen vorſprechen. | He'll call on you tomorrow.

vorſtellen:

Stellen Sie ſich das nicht ſo leicht vor! | It's not as simple as it looks!; don't think it's easy!

Stellen Sie ſich meine Überraſchung vor! | Just picture my surprise!; you can imagine how surprised I was!

Was ſtellt das vor? | What's the meaning of it?

Sie will immer was Beſonderes vor= ſtellen. | She thinks she is someone; she always gives herself airs.

Vorſtoß:

Er unternahm einen plötzlichen Vorſtoß gegen die Prohibition. | He made a surprise attack on prohibition.

Vorteil:

Er verſteht ſich auf ſeinen Vorteil. | He knows on which side his bread is buttered; he looks out for number one; he knows his best interest.

vorweltlich:

Der Gedanke iſt geradezu vorweltlich. | The idea is impossible (*or* preposterous).

Waage:

Die beiden Dinge halten sich die Waage.	The two things are an even match; one balances the other.
Die Partei bildet das Zünglein an der Waage.	The party holds the balance of power.

Waagschale:

Legen Sie seine Worte nicht auf die Waagschale!	Don't take him too literally!; don't attach too much importance to what he says!
Seine Aussage fällt schwer in die Waagschale.	His statement carries a great deal of weight.
Er warf sein ganzes persönliches Schwergewicht in die Waagschale.	He brought the full weight of his personal prestige to bear in the matter.

Wachtmeister:

Hier ist aber ein Wachtmeister im Zimmer!	You could cut the air with a knife in this room!; my, but the tobacco smoke is dense here!

Waffe:

Er gab seinem Gegner Waffen in die Hand.	He laid himself open to attack; he furnished his opponent with arguments.
Er streckte die Waffen.	He struck the flag; he laid down his arms; he gave in.

Wagen:

Fahr mir nicht an den Wagen!	Keep off!; don't get in my way!
Er spannte das Pferd hinter den Wagen.	He put the cart before the horse; he began at the wrong end; he reversed the procedure.
Er läßt sich nicht vor ihren Wagen spannen.	He won't boost (or back) them; he won't support their cause.

wägen:

Erst wägen, dann wagen!	Look before you leap!; think before you act!

Wahl:

Wer die Wahl hat, hat die Qual.	Choosing is irksome.

Wahn:

Sie ist in dem Wahn, es längst getan zu haben.	She's under the mistaken impression that she did it long ago.

wahr:

So wahr ich lebe!	Upon my word!; as sure as I'm alive!
Er ist hier, nicht wahr?	He's here, isn't he?
Sie sind mir der wahre Jakob!	You're the very man I'm looking for!; you're a fine fellow (to deal with)!
Es ist kein wahres Wort daran.	There's not a word of truth in it.

währen:

Was lange währt, wird gut.	Good work takes time.

wahrhaben:
    Er will es nicht wahrhaben, daß er das gesagt hat. | He won't admit having said it.

wahrhaftig:
    Wahrhaftig? | No kidding!; you don't say so!; not really!
    Wahrhaftiger Gott! | Upon my word!; you bet!; heavens!; good Lord!

Wahrheit:
    Im Wein ist Wahrheit. | Wine loosens the tongue.
    Dem wird er aber die Wahrheit geigen. | He'll tell him what's what; he'll give him a piece of his mind.
    Mit der Wahrheit kommt man am weitesten. | Honesty is the best policy.
    Er nimmt es mit der Wahrheit nicht genau. | His statements aren't any too accurate; he's none too truthful.

Wahrscheinlichkeit:
    Er hat die Wahrscheinlichkeit auf seiner Seite. | The odds are in his favor.

Waisenknabe:
    Gegen sie ist er der reine Waisenknabe. | He doesn't cut any ice (*or* rate) at all next to her; he's a nobody compared to her.

Wald:
    Wie es in den Wald hineinschallt, so schallt es wieder heraus. | As the question, so the answer; you reap as you sow.

walten:
    Das walte Gott! | Amen!; so be it!
    Man läßt ihn schalten und walten. | He's given plenty of rope (*or* freedom); he's allowed to do pretty much as he likes.

Walze:
    Immer die alte Walze! | It's always the same old gag (*or* story)!
    Er hat etwas auf der Walze. | He has something up his sleeve (*or* on the fire); he's got a prospect in view.
    Er ist auf der Walze. | He's on the road; he's traveling.

wälzen:
    Er wälzte sich vor Lachen. | He shook with laughter.
    Er wollte die Verantwortung auf sie wälzen. | He tried to pass the buck; he tried to shove the blame onto them; he tried to hold them responsible.

Wälzen:
    Es ist zum Wälzen. | It's a riot; it's screamingly funny.

Wams:
    Er hat etwas aufs Wams gekriegt. | He got a thrashing.

Wand:
    Hier wackelt die Wand! | There's something up (*or* going on) here!
    Er wurde wie eine Wand. | He turned white as a sheet; he turned pale as a ghost.
    Narrenhände beschmieren Tisch und Wände. | Fools' names are like their faces, often seen in public places.
    Es ist, um die Wände hinaufzuklettern! | It's enough to drive one bats (*or* crazy)!
    Er sprang die Wände hoch vor Freude. | He jumped sky-high for joy.
    Ihn ärgert die Fliege an der Wand. | His nerves are all on edge; everything gets (*or* grates) on his nerves.

Malen Sie den Teufel nicht an die Wand!	Don't talk of the devil!; don't invite trouble!
Er will immer gleich mit dem Schädel durch die Wand.	He's always knocking his head against a stone wall; he always wants to do the impossible; he's pig-headed.
Er redete zu leeren Wänden.	He talked to deaf ears; nobody listened to him.

wandernd:

Er gehört einer wandernden Truppe an.	He belongs to (or travels around with) a stock company.

Wanderschaft:

Er ist auf der Wanderschaft.	He's on the road; he's traveling.

wanken:

Er wankt und weicht nicht.	He sticks to his guns; he stands firm as a rock; nothing can budge (or sway) him.

wann:

Er kommt dann und wann mal.	He comes now and then.

Wanst:

Er hat sich den Wanst vollgeschlagen.	He's eaten his fill.
Er hat eins vor den Wanst bekommen.	He got a drubbing (or beating).

Wanze:

So eine Wanze!	What a pest (or nuisance)!

Wappen:

Er erhält sein Wappen rein.	He keeps his slate (or record) clean.

Ware:

Jeder Krämer lobt seine Ware.	Every cook praises his own dish.

warm:

Den sollten Sie sich warm halten!	You should keep on the right side of him!; he may be useful to you some day.
Der sitzt warm.	He's sitting pretty; he's well off.
Sie sind nie so recht warm miteinander geworden.	They never got to know each other very well; they were never very close (or intimate).

wärmst:

Wärmsten Dank!	Thanks a million!; thanks ever so much!

Warte:

Er sprach von hoher, geistiger Warte.	He spoke with great spiritual insight.

warten:

Warten Sie nur, wie es ihm noch ergehen wird!	Just wait and see what will happen to him!
Er weiß nicht, was seiner wartet.	He doesn't know what's in store for him.
Da können Sie lange warten!	You'll never see the like of it again!; you're out of luck!; you've got a good wait coming!

warum:

Warum nicht gar!	I dare say!; you don't say so!; indeed!

was:

Was ihn betrifft.	As for him.
Was Sie nicht sagen!	For goodness sake!; is it possible?; you don't say so!
Er gilt was bei ihnen.	He's in good with them; they think well of him.

Ach was!	Bah!; bunk!; nonsense!
Na, so was!	Did you ever!; the idea!; of all the nerve!
Hat sich was!	Nothing doing!; oh, no you won't!; you're mistaken!
Das ist so sicher wie nur was.	That's a cinch (*or* sure thing); that's dead-sure.

Wäsche:

Waschen Sie Ihre eigne Wäsche!	Clean up your own dirt!; mind your own business!

waschecht:

Er ist ein waschechter Bayer.	He's a dyed-in-the-wool (*or* native) Bavarian.

waschen:

Das hat sich gewaschen!	It's perfect!; that's capital (*or* first-rate)!
Er schrieb ihnen einen Brief, der sich gewaschen hat.	He wrote them a letter that'll burn them up (*or* make them furious).

Wasser:

Wasser hat keine Balken.	Praise the sea but keep on land!; keep your feet on the ground!; play safe!
Das ist Wasser auf seine Mühle.	That's grist to his mill; that's a feather in his cap; that's just the thing for him.
Das Wasser geht ihm bis an den Hals.	He's up to his neck in debt (*or* trouble); he's in deep (*or* hot) water; he's in straitened circumstances.
Bis dahin fließt noch viel Wasser den Berg hinunter.	That's a long way off yet; it will be a long time before that happens; wait and see!
Er ist ein stilles Wasser.	He's very quiet (*or* reserved).
Er schöpft Wasser mit einem Sieb.	He's trying to drain Niagara; he's wasting his time (*or* energy).
Er schwitzt bei der Arbeit Blut und Wasser.	He's sweating blood; he toils like a Trojan (*or* slave).
Er spricht Englisch wie Wasser.	He speaks English fluently.
Er trägt Wasser auf beiden Schultern.	He's a yes-man (*or* handshaker); he's on both sides of the fence; he doesn't commit himself.
Das heißt Wasser in den Rhein tragen.	That's carrying coals to Newcastle; that's a waste of time (*or* energy).
Er grub ihnen das Wasser ab.	He cut off their water supply (*or* life line); he gave them a dirty deal; he treated them shamefully.
Er pflügt das Wasser.	He's fishing in the air; he's wasting his time (*or* energy).
Er reicht ihr das Wasser nicht.	He couldn't hold a candle to her; he's far beneath her; he's no match for her.
Er richtet alle Wasser auf seine Mühle.	He's a big goop; he hogs the road; he wants everything for himself.
Sie hat nahe am Wasser gebaut.	She's a sob sister (*or* cry-baby); she's always on the verge of tears.
Er war wie aus dem Wasser gezogen.	He was soaked to the skin; he was dripping wet.
Er sitzt bei Wasser und Brot.	He's on a diet of bread and water; he's in jail.
Er ist so gesund wie ein Fisch im Wasser.	He's fit as a fiddle; he's in the best of health.

Die Sache fiel ins Wasser.	The affair went up in smoke; it came to nothing.
Das Unternehmen war ein Schlag ins Wasser.	The action was a shot in the dark; it was a flop (*or* failure); it was a vain attempt.
Hier wird auch nur mit Wasser gekocht.	It's the same the world over.
Er ist mit allen Wassern gewaschen.	He's an old hand; he's been through every type of situation.
Er hält sich so eben über Wasser.	He just manages to get by; he barely makes enough to live on.
Sie halten ihn über Wasser.	They're keeping him (afloat); they're supporting him.
Er ist ein Demokrat vom reinsten Wasser.	He's a dyed-in-the-wool (*or* confirmed) Democrat.
Verwandte Seelen treffen sich zu Wasser und zu Lande.	Birds of a feather flock together.
Die Sache ist zu Wasser geworden.	The affair went up in smoke; it came to naught.

Wässerchen:

Er sieht aus, als könne er kein Wässerchen trüben.	He looks as meek as a lamb; he looks as if he were afraid of his own shadow.

Wasserfall:

Ihr Mundwerk geht wie ein Wasserfall.	She's an old chatterbox; her tongue wags incessantly.

Wasserglas:

Es war ein Sturm im Wasserglas.	It was just a tempest in a teapot; it was a case of much ado about nothing.

wässerig:

Machen Sie ihm den Mund nicht wässerig!	Don't make his mouth water!

Wasserstrahl:

Seine Antwort wirkte wie ein kalter Wasserstrahl.	His answer was like a cold shower; it had a very sobering effect.

Watte:

Er muß in Watte gepackt werden.	He has to be handled with kid gloves; he must be treated gingerly (*or* with care).

Wechselfall:

Wer hat nicht die Wechselfälle des Lebens an sich erfahren?	Who has not had his ups and downs?; we've all had our reverses.

weg:

Kopf weg!	Look out for your head!
Er ist darüber weg.	He's over it; he did it.
So etwas zu behaupten, das ist doch das Ende von weg!	I call that laying it on a bit thick; that's putting it strong; that's going a little too far.
Sie waren ganz weg.	They were swept off their feet; they were wildly enthusiastic.

Weg:

Woher des Wegs?	Where do you come from?
Er kennt jeden Weg und Steg.	He knows every cowpath (*or* fork in the road).
Damit hat es noch gute Wege.	That's still a long way off.
Sie treffen ihn auf Weg und Steg.	They're always bumping (*or* running) into him; they meet him everywhere.

Er ging dem Problem aus dem Weg.	He dodged (or side-stepped) the issue; he avoided it.
Man hat ihn aus dem Weg geräumt.	He was taken for a ride; they bumped him off; he was murdered.
Sie ist nicht gut bei Wege.	She isn't feeling so well.
Er lief uns in den Weg.	We ran into him.
Er leitete die Sache in die Wege.	He took the matter up; he acted on it.
Sie trauen ihm nicht über den Weg.	They don't trust him to the corner (or out of their sight).

wegen:

Wegen mir kann er gehen.	I don't mind (or It's all right with me) if he goes; he may go, for all I care.
Hat er es zurückgebracht?—Ja, von wegen!	Did he bring it back?—Hell, no!; like fun he did!

weggeblasen:

Er ist wie weggeblasen.	He vanished into thin air; there's not a trace of him anywhere.

weggehen:

Gehen Sie mir damit weg!	Oh, go on!; take it away!; I don't want to hear about it!

weghaben:

Das hat er weg.	He has that down pat; he has the knack of it.
Schwuppdich, hatte er eine weg!	Bingo (or Before he knew it), he'd gotten one in the face!
Er hat einen weg.	He's got a screw loose; he's a little off (or crazy); he's had a drop too much.

wegheben:

Heb dich weg!	Scram!; beat it!; go chase yourself!

wegholen:

Er hat sich eine böse Erkältung weggeholt.	He caught a bad cold.

wegkriegen:

Er hat es immer noch nicht weggekriegt, wer ihm den Streich gespielt hat.	He still hasn't found out who played the trick on him.

wegloben:

Er wurde auf einen höheren Posten weggelobt.	They promoted him to get rid of him.

wegmachen:

Er macht einen weg.	He's taking a nap; he's doing time (in jail).

wegputzen:

Die Polizei hat den Verbrecher weggeputzt.	The police did away with the criminal; they shot him.

weh:

Weh, o weh!	Oh dear!; poor me!; alas!

Weh:

Er schrie Ach und Weh, als er das Unglück entdeckte.	He yelled bloody murder (or shouted for help) when he discovered the disaster.
Es war rührend, wie sie um unser Wohl und Weh besorgt war.	It was touching to see how she looked out for our wants (or comfort).

wehleidig:

Er erzählte eine wehleidige Geschichte.	He told a sob (or hard-luck) story.

wehmütig:
Er bat de= und wehmütig um Verzeihung. | He ate humble pie; he begged forgiveness on all fours.

Wehr:
Er setzte sich tapfer zur Wehr. | He put up a stiff fight.

Wehrkraft:
Der Sport stärkt die Wehrkraft eines Landes. | Sports build up the national defense.

Weiblichkeit:
Die holde Weiblichkeit war vollzählig vertreten. | The fair sex was well represented.

Weichbild:
Das Haus liegt noch im Weichbild der Stadt. | The house is still within city limits.

weichen:
Er wankt und weicht nicht. | He sticks to his guns; he stands firm as a rock; nothing can budge (or sway) him.

Weihwasser:
Er fürchtet das Examen wie der Teufel das Weihwasser. | He's scared to death of the exam(ination).

Weile:
Gut Ding will Weile haben. | Haste makes waste.
Damit hat es noch gute Weile. | Take your time; there's no hurry (about it).

Wein:
Er schenkte ihnen reinen Wein ein. | He told them the plain truth.
Im Wein ist Wahrheit. | Wine loosens the tongue.

Weinen:
Auf Lachen folgt Weinen. | Those who sing before breakfast cry before night.

Weise:
Das ist doch keine Art und Weise. | You should be ashamed of yourself; that's no way to do (or be).
Er versuchte es auf alle Art und Weise. | He tried it every which (or possible) way.

Weisheit:
Er tut, als hätte er die Weisheit mit Löffeln gefressen. | He's playing the wise guy (or know-it-all).
Behalten Sie Ihre Weisheit für sich! | None of your lip (or wisecracks)!; mind your own business!
Er ist mit seiner Weisheit zu Ende. | He's at his wits' end; he's in a quandary.

weismachen:
Machen Sie das andern weis! | Tell that to Sweeney!; I'm from Missouri!; I don't believe it!

weiß:
Er macht weiß, was schwarz ist. | He'd swear that black was white; he's an awful liar.
Das ist wie schwarz und weiß. | That's a horse of another color; that's entirely different.
Er hat es schwarz auf weiß. | He has it in black and white; he has the proof in writing.

Er ist ein weißer Rabe.	He's a rare bird (*or* black swan); he's one in a million.
Das ist wie die weiße Salbe.	That can't do any harm.
Er geht mit dem weißen Stab.	He goes panhandling (*or* begging).
Er hat eine weiße Weste an.	His hands are clean; he's innocent.

Weiße:

Man gönnt ihm nicht das Weiße im Auge.	They begrudge him the very shirt on his back.

weit:

Weit gefehlt!	You're way off (*or* all wrong)!; you've missed the point entirely!
Er bringt es noch weit.	He'll go places yet; he's bound to make good (*or* be a big success).
So weit ist es gekommen?	Has it come to that?; is it as bad as all that?
Mit ihm ist es nicht weit her.	He's not so hot (*or* extra special); there's nothing much to him.
Das ist bei weitem nicht so schlecht.	That's not half bad; that's really quite good.
Das liegt noch in weitem Feld.	That's still a long way off.
Er hat ein weites Gewissen.	His conscience doesn't bother him; he's not overly conscientious (*or* scrupulous).

Weite:

Er hat das Weite gesucht.	He cleared out; he made his getaway.

Weite:

Die Weite seines Blicks ist erstaunlich.	His insight is astonishing; he's remarkably farsighted (*or* discerning).
Er zog in die Weite.	He went on a long journey; he went far away from home.

weiter:

Weiter nichts?	Is that all?; anything else?; nothing more?
Es fiel ihr nicht weiter auf.	It didn't strike her particularly.
Es hilft weiter nichts.	It can't be helped; there's no help for it.
Es ist weiter nichts als Spaß.	It's pure fun; it's all in fun.
Es war weiter niemand da.	No one else was there.
Wir wollen nicht weiter davon reden.	Let's skip (*or* forget) it!; let's not talk about it any more!
Immer weiter!	Go on!; keep going!
Nichts weiter!	Not another word!
Was weiter?	Now what?; what next?; anything more?
Hören Sie weiter!	Get the rest of this!; listen to what follows!
Er kam nicht weiter.	He got stuck; he couldn't go on.
Der Skandal zog immer weitere Kreise.	The scandal widened in scope; it spread from mouth to mouth.

weiteres:

Weiteres vorbehalten!	Reserving further details!; to be continued!
Davon belehrt uns die Geschichte eines weiteren.	History gives us further information on that point.
Bleiben Sie bis auf weiteres dort!	Stay there till further notice!
Er tat es ohne weiteres.	He did it without any fuss; he went right ahead (and did it).

weitest:

Mit der Wahrheit kommt man am weitesten.	Honesty is the best policy.
Er übte Kritik im weitesten Sinne.	He made a comprehensive critical analysis.

weitgehend:
    Er fand weitgehendes Entgegenkommen. | He found widespread support.

weitgehendst:
    Der Vorschlag soll weitgehendst berücksichtigt werden. | The suggestion will receive the utmost consideration.

Weizen:
    Sein Weizen blüht. | He's in clover; he's thriving (*or* prospering); luck is with him.

Welt:
    Nobel muß die Welt zugrunde gehen! | Generous to the bitter end!

    Dem Mutigen gehört die Welt. | Faint heart never won fair lady; fortune favors the brave.

    Da ist die Welt mit Brettern vernagelt! | Now we're up against it!; we're stuck (*or* in a rut) for fair!

    Alle Welt war da. | Everybody was there.

    Er erblickte das Licht der Welt am 1. Februar. | He was born on the first of February.

    Er schuldet Gott und aller Welt. | He's up to his ears in debt; he owes everyone.

    Es wird die Welt nicht kosten. | It won't cost a fortune.

    Dort finden Sie die schöne Welt. | That's where society hangs out; that's where the well-to-do go (*or* live).

    Er schaffte die Sache aus der Welt. | He settled (*or* straightened out) the matter; he did away with it.

    Das geht ihn in der Welt nichts an. | That's none of his darned business; it doesn't concern him.

    So geht es immer in der Welt. | Such is life.

    Er tut es nicht um alles in der Welt. | He won't do it at any price.

    Was in aller Welt will er nur? | What on earth does he want?

    Er hat mit der Welt abgeschlossen. | He's done (*or* through) with the world and its concerns; he's retired from active life; he lives in seclusion.

    Er ist mit Gott und der Welt zerfallen. | He's down on the world; he's soured (*or* embittered).

    Wollen Sie das tun?—Nicht um die Welt! | Will you do that?—Not on your life!; not for a million dollars!

    Er ist ein Mann von Welt. | There's class to him; he's a gentleman.

weltbewegend:
    Seine Entdeckung ist nicht weltbewegend. | His discovery won't cause a sensation (*or* set the world afire); it's no seven-day wonder.

Weltgeschichte:
    Da hört doch die Weltgeschichte auf! | That's the last straw!; that beats everything!

wendig:
    Das ist ein wendiger Wagen. | The car responds to the slightest touch; it's very flexible.

wenig:
    Es fehlte wenig, so wäre er gestorben. | He was at the point of death; it wouldn't have taken much to kill him.

weniger:
    Auf Bezahlung wird weniger gesehen. | Salary is no object (*or* consideration).

    Sie ist nichts weniger als glücklich. | She's anything but happy.

wenigſt:
Er ſollte am wenigſten derart reden. | He should be the last one to talk like that; he of all people shouldn't say such things.

wenn:
Na, wenn ſchon! | So what?; what of it?; what difference does it make?

werden:
Wart, dir werd' ich! | Just wait, I'll get (*or* fix) you!
Wird's bald? | Are you coming?; will you hurry up!
Wie wird's? | How's tricks?; how are you coming?; how are things going?

Was nicht iſt, kann noch werden. | It may happen yet; almost anything can happen.

Das muß anders werden. | Something must be done about it; a change must be made.

Werden:
Die Sache iſt noch im Werden. | The matter is still in embryo; it's still brewing (*or* in the making).

werfen:
Die Krankheit warf ſich ihm aufs Herz. | The disease attacked (*or* affected) his heart.

Er hat ſich auf die Muſik geworfen. | He has taken to (*or* gone in for) music.

Werg:
Er hat auch Werg am Rocken. | His hands aren't clean either; he too is implicated (*or* guilty).

Werk:
Etwas iſt im Werk. | There's something up (*or* brewing); something's going on.

Er ſetzte die ganze Sache ins Werk. | He engineered (*or* directed) the whole scheme.

Er ging klug dabei zu Werk. | He proceeded very cleverly.

wertbeſtändig:
Es iſt heutzutage ſchwer, ſein Geld wertbeſtändig anzulegen. | In these days it's difficult to make a good investment.

wertvoll:
Sie iſt ein wertvoller Menſch. | She's a brick (*or* fine person).

Weſen:
Das arme Weſen iſt ganz erſchöpft. | The poor thing is all in (*or* exhausted).
Er macht viel Weſens davon. | He makes a big fuss about it.
Das entſpricht nicht ſeinem Weſen. | That's not at all like him.
Er treibt jetzt ſein Weſen woanders. | He's hanging out somewhere else now; he's gone elsewhere.

Er hat ein beſtechendes Weſen. | He has an engaging (*or* attractive) personality.

Die Idee iſt ihrem Weſen nach gut. | The idea is essentially sound.
Das gehört zum Weſen der Sache. | That's the nature of the thing; that's inherent in it; that's one of its natural properties.

Weſte:
Er hat eine ſaubere Weſte an. | His hands are clean; he's innocent.
Immer feſte auf die Weſte! | Give it to him!; let him have it!; beat him up!

Westentasche:
Er kennt sie wie seine linke Westentasche.

He's got her number; he can read her like a book; he knows her inside out.

Er bezahlte den teuren Wagen glatt aus der Westentasche.

He paid spot cash for the expensive car.

Wette:
Was gilt die Wette?

What will you bet?

Sie sangen um die Wette.

They sang for dear life (*or* all they were worth); they tried to see who could sing the loudest.

wetten:
So haben wir nicht gewettet!

No fair!; that wasn't the agreement!

Wetter:
Wetter noch eins!

Heck!; confound it!; damn it all!

Alle Wetter!

Jumping Jupiter!; good heavens!

Er fuhr wie ein Wetter dazwischen.

He came at them like a cyclone; he flew at (*or* pounced on) them.

Es ist nicht gut Wetter bei ihm.

He's in a vile mood.

Er bat um gut Wetter.

He apologized; he pleaded for a friendly reception.

Wetterfahne:
Er ist wetterwendisch wie eine Wetter=fahne.

He's as changeable (*or* unstable) as the weather.

Wetterwinkel:
Der Balkan gilt als der politische Wetter=winkel Europas.

Politically, the Balkans are considered the danger spot (*or* storm area) of Europe.

wettmachen:
Der Verlust läßt sich nicht so leicht wieder wettmachen.

It's not so easy to make good the loss.

wetzen:
Der kann aber wetzen!

How he can run!

Wichs:
Er warf sich in Wichs.

He donned his best bib and tucker; he got all decked out (*or* dressed up).

Wichse:
Das ist alles dieselbe Wichse.

It's all out of the same bottle; it's all the same thing.

Es setzte Wichse.

The sparks flew; blows fell.

wichtig:
Er kommt sich furchtbar wichtig vor.

He thinks he's the whole show (*or* cheese); he thinks he is somebody.

Wicke:
Das Buch ist in die Wicken gegangen.

The book went up the flue; it's lost.

Wickel:
Er nahm ihn beim Wickel.

He took him by the scruff of the neck; he set him to rights.

widerhaarig:
Er ist ein widerhaariger Geselle.

He's a stubborn mule; he's an obstinate cuss.

Widerspruchsgeist:
Sie ist ein rechter Widerspruchsgeist.

She's a regular contrary Mary; she's very perverse.

widerstreben:
Es widerstrebt ihm, das zu tun. — He hates like sin to do that; it goes against him.

widmen:
Er kann sich Ihnen im Augenblick nicht widmen. — He can't be of service to you at the moment.

wie:
Wie, bitte? — Sir?; pardon?; what did you say?
Wie, schon wieder? — What, again?
Wie gut, daß er es nicht tat! — Good thing (*or* Lucky for him) he didn't do it!
Sie hatten so gut wie nichts an. — They were wearing next to nothing; they had practically nothing on.

wieder:
Er kommt hin und wieder. — He comes now and then.
Er schreibt immer wieder. — He keeps on writing; he corresponds regularly.
Sie zankten sich um nichts und wieder nichts. — They quarreled for no good reason; they quarreled about nothing at all.

Wiedersehen:
Sie feierten ein frohes Wiedersehen. — They had a happy reunion; they celebrated their reunion.
Auf Wiedersehen! — So long!; good-bye!; see you again!

Wiege:
Seine Wiege stand in Frankfurt. — He was born in Frankfurt.
Das ist ihm auch nicht an der Wiege gesungen worden. — People little thought that he would ever come to this.
Das Glück hat ihm schon in der Wiege gelächelt. — He was born with a silver spoon in his mouth; he was born rich.

Wiesel:
Sie ist flink wie ein Wiesel. — She's quick as a wink (*or* flash).

wievielt:
Der wievielte ist heute? — What's the date today?

wild:
Sie ist eine wilde Hummel. — She's a regular tomboy.

Wild:
Er kam sich wie ein gehetztes Wild vor. — He felt like a fox in the chase; he was being hounded (*or* persecuted).

Wilder:
Er schafft wie ein Wilder. — He works like a beaver (*or* horse).
Er stürzte wie ein Wilder davon. — He rushed out like a blue streak; he flew out like mad.

wildfremd:
Er kam wildfremd in dieses Land. — He came to this country a total stranger.

Wilhelm:
Er markiert den dicken Wilhelm. — He puts on airs (*or* the dog); he's strutting (*or* showing off).

Wille(n):
Des Menschen Wille ist sein Himmelreich. — My mind to me a kingdom is.
Tu ihm den Willen! — Do him the favor!; do as he wishes!
Das steht ganz in Ihrem Willen! — That's entirely up to you!; you could if you wanted to!

Er tat es mit Wissen und Willen.	He did it intentionally (*or* on purpose).
Wenn es nach seinem Willen ginge.	If he had his way.
Sie mußte wider Willen lachen.	She had to laugh in spite of herself.

Willkür:

Er ist der Willkür seines Feindes preisgegeben.	He's at the mercy of his enemy.

Wimper:

Er läßt sich nicht an den Wimpern klimpern.	He's not to be trifled with.

Wind:

Es war, als ob es der Wind ihm zuwehte.	It fairly fell into his lap; it came to him out of a clear sky; it cost him no effort.
Ich weiß Wind.	I'm on (*or* wise); I'm in on it; I know all about it.
Er hat sich den Wind um die Nase wehen lassen.	He's been places; he's seen the world.
Lassen Sie sich erst noch etwas Wind um die Ohren pfeifen!	Better try your wings (*or* get some experience) first!
Er machte ihnen lauter Wind vor.	He gave them a lot of hot air; he told them a lot of nonsense.
Er weiß mit jedem Wind zu segeln.	He's very tractable; he adapts himself easily.
Er dreht den Mantel nach dem Wind.	He watches to see which way the wind blows; he's an opportunist.

Windel:

Das Unternehmen liegt noch in den Windeln.	The undertaking is still in its infancy (*or* initial stages).

windelweich:

Er drasch ihn windelweich.	He beat him to a pulp.

Winkelzug:

Er wollte Winkelzüge machen.	He was beating about the bush (*or* evading the issue); he tried to crawl (*or* lie his way) out of it.

Wippchen:

Machen Sie mir keine Wippchen vor!	None of your tricks!; don't try to fool me!; tell the truth!

Wirkung:

Keine Wirkung ohne Ursache.	Where there's smoke there's fire; there's a reason for everything.

Wirtschaft:

Die ganze Wirtschaft taugt nichts.	The whole outfit (*or* lot) is no good.
Die Versammlung war die reine polnische Wirtschaft.	Bedlam reigned at the meeting; everything was topsy-turvy (*or* in a state of confusion).
Man will die Wirtschaft wieder ankurbeln.	They want to start in business again.
Sie führt ihm die Wirtschaft.	She keeps house for him.
Machen Sie keine solche Wirtschaft!	Don't make such a fuss!
Er machte reine Wirtschaft damit.	He made a clean sweep of it; he got it out of the way.

wirtschaften:

Er hat das Geschäft zugrunde gewirtschaftet.	He let the business run down; he let it go to rack and ruin.

Wiſcher:

Er hat einen Wiſcher bezogen. — He was called on the carpet; he was severely reprimanded.

wiſſen:

Ich weiß es von ihm ſelbſt. — He told me so himself.

Glauben Sie, daß er's tut?—Ich weiß nicht recht. — Do you think he'll do it?—I'm not so sure.

Weißt du noch? — You remember?

Er wußte zu entkommen. — He managed to get away.

Ich möchte wiſſen, ob er da iſt. — I wonder if he's there.

Er will nichts davon wiſſen. — He won't hear of it.

Er will nichts von ihnen wiſſen. — He'll have nothing to do with them.

Wiſſen:

Meines Wiſſens iſt es ſo. — As far as I know, it's true.

Er tat es mit Wiſſen und Willen. — He did it intentionally (or on purpose).

Mit ſeinem Wiſſen iſt es nicht weit her. — He's no shining light (or great student); he knows blessed little.

Er handelte nach beſtem Wiſſen und Gewiſſen. — He did his best; he used his best judgment.

wittern:

Er witterte Morgenluft. — He was quick to spot (or sense) his advantage.

Witz:

Das iſt der Witz dabei. — That's the funny part of it.

Das iſt der ganze Witz. — That's just it; that's where the difficulty lies.

Mach keine Witze! — All fooling aside!; do you mean it?

witzig:

Das haben Sie ganz witzig gemacht! — That was very cleverly done!

wo:

Wo werd' ich! — Why should I?

Stimmt das?—I wo! — Is that correct?—Says you!; like fun it is!; I should say not!

Er kommt wo möglich. — He'll come if he can.

Woge:

Er goß Öl auf die Wogen. — He threw oil on troubled waters; he smoothed the matter over.

woher:

Ach woher denn! — I should say not!; not at all!; of course not!

wohl:

Er bat ſie wohl hundertmal darum. — He asked them for it at least a hundred times.

Er kommt wohl gar nicht. — I guess he's not coming at all.

Sehen Sie wohl, daß er recht hatte? — Do you see now that he was right?

Er iſt wohl geſund, aber . . . . — He's healthy enough, but . . . ; he may be healthy, but . . . .

Nichts kann doch wohl leichter ſein. — Surely nothing could be easier.

Es waren ihrer wohl drei. — I should say there were three of them.

Das ſollte ich wohl meinen! — And how!; you bet!; I should jolly well think so!

Wohl:

Es war rührend, wie ſie um unſer Wohl und Weh beſorgt war. — It was touching to see how she looked out for our wants (or comfort).

wohlauf:

  Wohlauf, laßt uns gehen! — All right then, let's go!; here goes then!

wohlergehen:

  Lassen Sie sich's weiterhin wohlergehen! — Good luck for the future!

Wohlfahrt:

  Sie sind in der Wohlfahrt. — They're on relief; they're public charges.

Wohlgefallen:

  Die Sache hat sich in Wohlgefallen aufgelöst. — The affair ended in smoke; it came to naught.

Wolf:

  Er bessert sich wie ein junger Wolf. — He's going from bad to worse; he's growing wilder all the time.

  Mit den Wölfen muß man heulen. — In Rome do as the Romans do.

Wolke:

  Er war wie aus den Wolken gefallen. — He came down to earth with a bang; he was very much taken aback; he was thunderstruck.

Wolle:

  Viel Geschrei und wenig Wolle. — Much ado (or fuss) about nothing; that's all ballyhoo; it's nothing but empty talk.

  Er sitzt in der Wolle. — He's in clover; he's got it soft; he's well off.

  Er geriet mächtig in die Wolle. — He got hot under the collar; he began to tear his hair; he got angry.

wollen:

  Dir will ich! — I'll get (or fix) you!

  Das will ich meinen. — I should say so.

  Das will ich gern glauben. — I readily believe that; I'm sure of it.

  Ich will nichts gesagt haben. — Don't tell anyone I said so!

  Mach, was du willst! — Do as you please!

  Wer nicht will, der hat schon! — Like it or lump it!; take it or leave it!; all right, do without it then!

  Wenn man so will. — If that's the way you want to look at it; if you take it to mean that.

  Das will mir nicht einleuchten. — I don't quite get (or see) that.

  Das will nichts sagen. — That doesn't matter; that's quite all right.

  Er will es selbst gesehen haben. — He claims to have seen it himself.

  Ich tue es, komme was da wolle. — I'll do it in spite of everything.

  Was wollte ich machen? — What was I to do?; what could I do?; how could I help it?

  Was ich noch sagen wollte. — As I was going to say.

  Wir gehen, mag er wollen oder nicht. — We'll go willy-nilly; we'll go regardless (or in spite) of him.

  Du hast gar nichts zu wollen! — You've got nothing to say!; you take what you get!

  Dagegen ist nichts mehr zu wollen. — There's nothing to be done about it.

Wonne:

  Sie schwamm in eitel Wonne. — She was in seventh heaven; she was in ecstasies (or a state of bliss).

Wort:

  Kein Wort ist auch ein Wort. — Silence is consent.

  Das ist ein Wort! — How true that is!; well said!

Das soll ein Wort sein!	It's a go (*or* bargain)!; agreed!
Diese Redensart ist sein drittes Wort.	It's his middle name; it's a pet word (*or* expression) of his.
Schöne Worte machen den Kohl nicht fett.	You can't live on promises.
Sie will es nicht Wort haben.	She won't admit it.
Er schnitt ihr das Wort ab.	He cut her short; he interrupted her.
Sie hat das Wort.	She has the floor; she's doing the talking.
Er richtete das Wort an sie.	He addressed them.
Er führte das große Wort.	He had a big mouth; he talked big; he was bragging.
Hast du Worte!	Knock me down!; I'll be darned!; words fail me!
Mach nicht soviel Worte!	Don't make so much noise (*or* fuss)!; don't talk so much!
Er gehorcht ihr aufs Wort.	He obeys her implicitly (*or* to the letter).
Auf ein Wort!	Just a word!; may I have a word with you?
Man hörte nicht auf seine Worte.	They didn't listen to him; no one paid any attention to him.
Er tat es für Geld und gute Worte.	He did it for money and flattery.
Das läßt sich mit drei Worten sagen.	In a nutshell (*or* word); to put it briefly; to sum it up.
Er bat ums Wort.	He asked for the floor; he asked for permission to speak.
Er konnte nicht zu Wort kommen.	He couldn't get a word in edgewise; he wasn't given a chance to talk.

Wortlaut:

Er erfüllte den Befehl dem Sinne, nicht dem Wortlaut nach.	He carried out the spirit rather than the letter of the order.

wühlen:

Er wühlt nur so im Geld.	He's in the dough; he's just rolling in money.

Wunder:

Ein Wunder, wenn er nicht kommt.	It would be strange if he didn't come.
Er wird noch sein blaues Wunder erleben!	Will he be surprised one fine day!; he'll get the surprise of his life!

Wunsch:

Alles geht nach Wunsch.	Everything is going smoothly (*or* fine).

wünschen:

Das Geschäft läßt zu wünschen übrig.	Business is not so hot (*or* good).

wunschlos:

Sie ist wunschlos glücklich.	She's perfectly happy; she has everything her heart desires.

Wuppdich:

Er tat es in einem Wuppdich.	He did it just like that; he did it in a jiffy (*or* trice).

Würde:

Würde bringt Bürde.	Uneasy lies the head that wears the crown; honor involves responsibility.

würdigen:

Er würdigte sie keines Blickes.	He gave them the go-by (*or* cold shoulder); he ignored them completely.

Wurf:
    Der Wurf ist getan.   The die is cast; the deed is done.
    Das Gemälde hat einen großen Wurf.   The painting has verve (*or* life); it has a lot of spirit (*or* character).

    Da haben Sie einen großen Wurf getan!   That was a good move you made!
    Er setzte alles auf einen Wurf.   He put all his eggs in one basket; he staked everything on a single card (*or* move).

    Er kam ihnen gerade in den Wurf.   He just happened to run into them; he met them in the nick of time.

Würgen:
    Er bestand die Prüfung mit Hängen und Würgen.   He passed the test by the skin of his teeth; he just skimmed by; he barely made (*or* passed) it.

Wurm:
    Ein jeder Mann hat seinen Wurm.   Everyone has his hobby.
    Er mußte ihnen die Würmer aus der Nase ziehen.   He pumped them; he had to worm (*or* draw) it out of them; he made them tell.

wurmen:
    Es wurmt ihn, daß man ihn übergangen hat.   It gripes (*or* galls) him that he was overlooked.

Wurs(ch)t:
    Wurst wider Wurst!   Tit for tat!; you had it coming to you!
    Es ist ihm alles Wurscht.   He doesn't give a hang (*or* damn); it's all the same to him.

    Er will immer eine besondere Wurst gebraten haben.   The best is none too good for him; he always wants to be toadied to (*or* made an exception of).

    Er warf mit der Wurst nach der Speckseite.   He cast a minnow to catch a whale; he took no chances.
    Er warf den Schinken nach der Wurst.   He staked everything he had; he risked much to gain little; he took an awful chance.

    Jetzt geht's um die Wurscht!   Now for a showdown!; now the fun begins!; this is the crucial moment!

Wurstblatt:
    Er gibt irgendwo auf dem Lande ein kleines Wurstblatt heraus.   He edits the local newspaper in some one-horse (*or* hick) town.

wursteln:
    Er arbeitet doch nicht, er wurstelt.   He doesn't work—he just putters around (*or* fools away his time).

    Es wird weiter gewurstelt.   It's the same old routine; everything goes on in the same old way.

Wurstigkeit:
    Er nahm den Tadel mit Wurstigkeit hin.   He accepted the reproach nonchalantly (*or* indifferently).

Wurstkessel:
    Er sitzt im Wurstkessel.   He's in the soup; he's in Dutch (*or* trouble).

Würze:
    In der Kürze liegt die Würze.   Brevity is the soul of wit.

Wurzel:

Er versprach, die Axt an die Wurzel zu legen.

He promised to make radical (*or* drastic) changes.

wurzeln:

Er muß feste wurzeln.

He has to dig away (*or* work hard).

Wüste:

Er wurde in die Wüste geschickt.

He was left out in the cold; he was sidetracked (*or* shelved); he was cast aside.

X

X:
    Er läßt sich kein X für ein U vormachen.

You can't put anything over on him; he can't be taken in.

x-beliebig:
    Geben Sie ihm ein x-beliebiges Buch!

Give him any book you please!

x-mal:
    Er hat es ihr x-mal gesagt.

He's told her time and again.

Y

Ypern:
Er sah aus wie der Tod von Ypern.

He looked pale as death; he looked like a ghost.

zackig:

Der Marsch wurde zackig gespielt.

The march was played with lots of snap (*or* spirit).

Zahn:

Ihm tut kein Zahn mehr weh.

Nothing bothers him anymore; he's dead and gone.

Beißen Sie die Zähne zusammen!

Keep a stiff upper lip!; keep up your spunk (*or* nerve)!; don't lose heart!

Er machte lange Zähne.

He made a face; he stuck up his nose at it; he didn't like (to eat) it.

Sie hat Haare auf den Zähnen.

She's a tough customer; she's a little spitfire; she's not to be trifled with.

Fühlen Sie ihm mal auf den Zahn!

Sound (*or* pump) him!

Er lachte durch die Zähne.

He snickered; he laughed slyly (*or* up his sleeve).

Das ist nur für den hohlen Zahn.

That wouldn't buy you a cup of coffee; that's precious little.

zappeln:

Lassen Sie ihn zappeln!

Keep him on the rack!; keep him guessing (*or* in suspense)!

Zauber:

Das ist fauler Zauber.

That's all humbug (*or* bosh); that's tommy-rot.

Dort ist heute abend großer Zauber.

There's a big affair going on tonight; tonight's a big night.

Den Zauber kennen wir!

That's an old trick!; you can't pull that on us!

Er bezahlte den ganzen Zauber.

He paid for the whole shooting match (*or* business); he paid the entire bill.

Zaum:

Er weiß, wo die Zäume hängen.

He knows the ropes (*or* tricks of the trade).

Halten Sie Ihre Zunge im Zaum!

Keep your tongue in check!

Zaun:

Das ist hinter jedem Zaun zu finden.

That's junk (*or* worthless).

Er brach den Streit vom Zaun.

He picked a quarrel.

Zaunpfahl:

Es ist ein Wink mit dem Zaunpfahl.

It's a broad hint.

Zeche:

Er muß die Zeche bezahlen.

He has to pay the fiddler (*or* price).

zehn:

Er kann durch zehn Bretter sehen.

He can see through a stone wall; he's keen as a whip; he's very observant.

Er leckt alle zehn Finger danach.

He's itching (*or* dying) to get it; he can't keep his fingers off it.

Ihn kriegen heute keine zehn Pferde aus dem Haus.

Nothing in the world could get him to go out today.

Zehnte:
Das weiß der Zehnte nicht.

Most people don't know that.

Zeichen:
Er ist Maurer seines Zeichens.
Die Stadt steht im Zeichen der Messe.

He's a mason by trade.
The city is in the whirl (*or* under the spell) of the fair.

zeigen:
Es wird sich ja zeigen, wer recht hat.

We'll see (*or* Time will tell) who's right.

Zeisig:
Sie ist ein lockrer Zeisig.

She's a high-stepper; she lives fast.

Zeit:
Du liebe Zeit!
Er machte ein Gesicht wie die teure Zeit.
Jedes Ding währt seine Zeit.
Er wußte die ganze Zeit, daß es nicht so war.
Alles zu seiner Zeit.

Gracious!; my word!; well, I never!
He made a long face; he looked worried.
There's an end to everything.
He knew all along that it was not so.

There's a time for everything.

Zeitliche:
Er hat das Zeitliche gesegnet.

He departed this life; he's dead.

Zeitrechnung:
Es ist ein Fehler wider die Zeitrechnung.

It's an anachronism.

zerknittert:
Sie war sehr zerknittert.

She was down in the mouth; she was feeling very blue (*or* dejected).

zerrinnen:
Der Plan zerrann in nichts.

The scheme ended in smoke; it fell through (*or* failed to materialize).

zerronnen:
Wie gewonnen, so zerronnen.

Easy come, easy go.

zerschlagen:
Das Verlöbnis zerschlug sich.

The engagement was broken (*or* called) off.

zerschlagen (*adj.*):
Sie fühlte sich wie zerschlagen.

She was pooped; she felt all washed out (*or* utterly exhausted).

Zetermordio:
Er schrie Zetermordio, als er das Unglück entdeckte.

He yelled bloody murder (*or* shouted for help) when he discovered the disaster.

Zeug:
Er schafft, was das Zeug hält.

He works to beat the band; he works like a slave.

Dummes Zeug!
Er hat das Zeug dazu.

Bunk!; boloney!; nonsense!
He's got what it takes; he's cut out (*or* made) for it; he can do it.

Sie wollte ihm was am Zeug flicken.

She wanted to show him up (*or* find fault with him).

Er ist gut beim Zeug.

He's in good form (*or* shape); he's feeling well.

Er ging tüchtig ins Zeug.

He snapped into it; he went (to work) at it with a vim.

Er legte sich für sie ins Zeug.

He came to their aid.

Zeugnis:
  Wir können ihr nur das beste Zeugnis ausstellen. | We cannot speak highly enough of her.

Zicke:
  Mach keine Zicken! | Don't be funny!

Ziege:
  Sie ist neugierig wie eine Ziege. | She's curious as a cat; she's dying of curiosity.

  So eine alte Ziege! | What an old hag!

ziehen:
  Dieser Grund zieht bei ihm nicht. | This argument cuts no ice with (*or* doesn't impress) him.

Ziel:
  Er kann weder Maß noch Ziel halten. | He knows no bounds; he can't control himself.

  Er schoß übers Ziel. | He went too far; he overstepped the limits (of propriety).

  Er ist weit vom Ziel. | He's quite beside the mark; he's far afield.
  Die Verhandlungen führten nicht zum Ziel. | The negotiations fell through (*or* failed).

Zielbewußtes:
  Er hat etwas Zielbewußtes in seinem Auftreten. | He has a very determined approach; he's very aggressive.

ziemlich:
  Er ist so ziemlich in deinem Alter. | He's pretty much your own age; he's about as old as you are.

  Es waren ziemlich viel Leute da. | A good many people were there.

zieren:
  Zieren Sie sich doch nicht! | Don't be such a prude!; don't stand on ceremony!

Zieten:
  Er kam wie Zieten aus dem Busch. | He popped up from nowhere; he came like a bolt out of the blue.

Zigarre:
  Er hat eine Zigarre verpaßt bekommen. | He got a bawling-out.

Zimmermann:
  Ich werde ihm schon zeigen, wo der Zimmermann das Loch gelassen hat. | I'll give him the air; I'll show him the door.

Zimt:
  Machen Sie nicht solchen Zimt! | Don't make such a fuss!
  Er bezahlte fünf Mark für den ganzen Zimt. | He paid five marks for the whole outfit (*or* business).

Zinken:
  Sie hat ihm den Zinken gestochen. | She told him where he got off; she gave him a good piece of her mind.

  Er hat einen mächtigen Zinken. | He has an awful red beak; he's got some beer nose.

Zinshahn:
  Sie wurde rot wie ein Zinshahn. | She turned red as a beet.

Zipfel:

Er glaubte schon die Stelle an allen vier Zipfeln zu haben.	He thought he had the job in the bag (*or* his pocket); he was sure he had landed (*or* secured) it.
Er faßte die Arbeit beim rechten Zipfel an.	He tackled the job from the right angle; he went at it in the right way.

Zitterwoche:

Nach den Flitterwochen kommen die Zitterwochen.	Life is not all roses (*or* one sweet song); even lovers must come down to earth again.

Zivilcourage:

Es fehlt ihm an der nötigen Zivilcourage.	He won't stick to his guns; he hasn't the courage of his convictions; he's afraid to stand up for his rights.

Zopf:

Er räumte mit dem alten Zopf auf.	He did away with the red tape (*or* petty formality).

zu:

Nur zu!	Shoot!; go to it!; come on!
Er steckte es zu sich.	He put it in his pocket.
Sie waren zu dreien.	There were three of them.
Er kommt ab und zu.	He comes occasionally (*or* once in a while).

zubringen:

Damit hat er lange zugebracht.	It took him a long time (to do it).

zubrocken:

Er hat nicht viel zuzubrocken.	He has only a small income.

Zucht:

Verfluchte Zucht!	Damn it all!

Zucker:

Sie gaben ihrem Affen Zucker.	They made whoopee (*or* cut loose); they were going strong (*or* making merry).

zudecken:

Die Mannschaft wurde schön zugedeckt.	The team took an awful trimming (*or* beating).

zudenken:

Das Übrige mögen Sie sich zudenken!	I leave the rest to your imagination.

Zufall:

Der Zufall fügte es, daß wir uns trafen.	We happened to run into each other.

Zufälligkeit:

Das Gelingen hängt von tausend Zufälligkeiten ab.	Success is purely a matter of luck.

zufassen:

Würden Sie, bitte, mal zufassen?	Will you lend me a hand, please?

zufliegen:

Die Gedanken fliegen ihm nur so zu.	Ideas come to him just like that (*or* out of a clear sky); he gets hunches (*or* inspirations).

zufrieden:

Er gab sich damit zufrieden.	He put up with it.
Lassen Sie ihn zufrieden!	Leave him alone!

Zug:

Da ist Zug drin.	It has snap (*or* dash).
Das ist der Zug der Zeit.	That's the trend of the times.
Es ist ein schöner Zug von ihr.	It's very nice (*or* decent) of her.
Er folgte dem Zuge seines Herzens.	He let his heart rule his head; he followed his impulses.
Er hat einen guten Zug am Leibe.	He drinks like a cow; he surely can gulp it down.
Sie sind am Zug!	It's your move (*or* turn)!
Er hat sie auf dem Zug.	He has it in for them; he bears them a grudge.
Er leerte das Glas auf einen Zug.	He emptied the glass at one draught.
Er hat seine Leute gut im Zug.	He has his men well under control.
Er las das Buch in einem Zug.	He read the book at one sitting.
Der Erzähler war im besten Zug, als er unterbrochen wurde.	The narrator was in full swing when he was interrupted.
Er trank den Wein in bedächtigen Zügen.	He sipped his wine deliberately.
Sie schilderte den Vorfall in knappen Zügen.	She gave a rough outline (*or* brief account) of the event.
Er lag in den letzten Zügen.	He was breathing his last; he lay dying.
Sie genossen die Ferien in vollen Zügen.	They enjoyed their vacation to the fullest extent.
Es ist ein Geschäft Zug um Zug.	It's a cash proposition.

Zugabe:

Bei dem Kauf des Anzugs erhielt er den Schlips als Zugabe.	When he bought the suit, he received the tie to boot; with the purchase of the suit, the tie was thrown into the bargain.
Das Publikum verlangte stürmisch eine Zugabe.	The audience clamored for an encore.

zugänglich:

Er ist vernünftigen Erwägungen immer zugänglich.	He's always open to conviction; he's always willing to listen to reason.

zugehen:

Es müßte seltsam zugehen, wenn er das nicht fertig brächte.	It would be strange if he couldn't do that.

zugeknöpft:

Er war den ganzen Abend zugeknöpft.	He was very reserved all evening.

Zügel:

Nehmen Sie den Kerl mal an die Zügel!	Take that fellow in hand!; make him toe the mark!
Er kam mit verhängten Zügeln.	He came at a gallop; he came apace (*or* at full speed).

zugenäht:

Verflixt und zugenäht!	Doggone it!; hang it all!

zugreifen:

Greifen Sie zu!	Dig in!; help yourself!

zugrunde:

Der Behauptung liegt nichts zugrunde.	There's no basis for such a contention.

zugute:

Sie sollten ihm seine Jugend zugute halten.	You should make allowance for his youth.

| Seine Erfahrung kommt ihm zugute. | His experience comes in handy; it stands him in good stead. |
| Er tut sich nicht wenig darauf zugute. | He's very proud of it. |

zuhaben:

| Sie möchten bei dem Geschäft wohl noch etwas zuhaben? | You probably want a commission on the deal? |

zuhalten:

| Halten Sie sich zu! | Hurry up!; get a move on! |

zukommen:

| Es kommt ihm nicht zu, dies zu sagen. | It's not for him (*or* his place) to say this; he has no business to say it. |
| Lassen Sie ihnen doch auch was zukommen! | Do let them have some too! |

Zukunft:

| Er ist ein Mann der Zukunft. | He's up and coming; he's making a name for himself; he'll be famous some day. |
| Das ist der Zukunft vorbehalten. | Time will tell; that remains to be seen. |

Zukunftsmusik:

| Das ist Zukunftsmusik. | That's still indefinite (*or* in the dim and distant future); those are pipe dreams (*or* castles in the air). |

zulande:

| Bei uns zulande ist das anders. | That's not customary here. |

zulangen:

| Langen Sie zu! | Dig in!; help yourself! |
| Wollen Sie mir bitte die Zeitung zulangen? | Will you please hand me the paper? |

Zulauf:

| Der Arzt hat großen Zulauf. | The doctor is very much in demand; he has a large practice. |

zulegen:

| Er legte bei dem Handel zu. | He lost money on the deal. |
| Sie haben sich einen Wagen zugelegt. | They bought (*or* got themselves) a car. |

zumachen:

| Sie müssen zumachen, wenn Sie den Zug noch erreichen wollen. | You'll have to hurry up if you want to catch that train. |

zumute:

| Ihr war gar nicht lächerlich zumute. | She was in no joking mood; she was very serious; she felt depressed. |

zumuten:

| Muten Sie das mal jemand zu! | Can you feature (*or* picture) that?; just imagine that! |
| Er hat sich zuviel zugemutet. | He bit off more than he could chew; he attempted too much; he overdid. |

Zumutung:

| Das ist eine starke Zumutung! | That's going it strong; that's expecting (*or* saying) a good deal! |

Zunder:

| Gleich gibt's Zunder! | You'll get it pretty soon! |

Zunft:

| Das ist eine saubere Zunft! | That's a nice gang (*or* outfit)! |
| Er ist von der Zunft. | He knows the ropes; he knows his business. |

zünftig:
   Er ist ein zünftiger Jäger. | He's a real hunter.

Zunge:
   Die Zunge klebte ihm am Gaumen. | He could have spit cotton; he was dry as a gourd.

   Er trägt das Herz auf der Zunge. | He wears his heart on his sleeve; he's very outspoken.

   Es schwebte ihm auf der Zunge. | He had it on the tip of his tongue.
   Sie biß sich rechtzeitig auf die Zunge. | She stopped just in time.

Zungenfertigkeit:
   Er verfügt über eine große Zungenfertigkeit. | He talks like a politician; he's got the gift of gab; he has a big mouth (or ready tongue).

Zünglein:
   Die Partei bildet das Zünglein an der Waage. | The party holds the balance of power.

zunutze:
   Machen Sie sich das zunutze! | Take advantage of it!; make the most of it!

zupaß:
   Es kamen ihnen sehr zupaß. | It suited them fine.

zuraten:
   Er riet ihnen weder zu noch ab. | He advised them neither one way nor the other.

zurechtzimmern:
   Sie hat sich eine eigenartige Weltanschauung zurechtgezimmert. | She has concocted (or worked out) a peculiar philosophy of life for herself.

zurichten:
   Er wurde bei dem Unfall böse zugerichtet. | He was badly injured in the accident.

zurückbleiben:
   Seine Leistungen blieben hinter ihren Erwartungen zurück. | His work fell short of their expectations.

zurückgeben:
   Dem haben Sie's aber gut zurückgegeben! | That was telling him!; that was a fine comeback (or retort)!

zurückgehen:
   Das Geschäft geht zurück. | Business is falling off (or going downhill).
   Die Verlobung ist zurückgegangen. | The engagement has been broken off.

zurückstehen:
   Sie müssen leider zurückstehen! | I'm very sorry, but you'll have to wait (or forgo it).

zusammenhängen:
   Wie hängt das zusammen? | How is that?; how do you figure that out?

zusammenhauen:
   Man sieht sofort, daß die Arbeit zusammengehauen ist. | It's obvious that the paper is just a hodgepodge (or patchwork).

zusammenläppern:
   Es läppert sich so zusammen. | It runs into money; the expense mounts up.

zusammenlegen:
   Sie beschlossen zusammenzulegen und gemeinsam zu reisen. | They decided to pool expenses and travel together.

zufammennehmen:

Nehmen Sie fich jetzt zufammen! — Watch your step!; careful now!; be on your guard!; I warn you!

Er nahm fich zufammen. — He pulled himself together; he got himself under control.

zufammenreimen:

Wie reimt fich das zufammen? — How do you make that out?; how do you account for (*or* reconcile) that?

zufammenfchlagen:

Er hat's läuten hören, aber nicht zufammenfchlagen. — He's all at sea (*or* in the dark) about it; he can't quite figure (*or* make) it out.

zufammenfchließen:

Die beiden Banken haben fich zufammengefchloffen. — The two banks merged.

zufammentreffen:

Das trifft nicht ganz mit feinen Erwartungen zufammen. — That doesn't quite come up to his expectations.

zufchanden:

Er arbeitet fich noch zufchanden. — He'll work himself to death yet.

Hoffnung läßt nicht zufchanden werden. — While there's life there's hope.

zufchanzen:

Er fchanzte ihm die Stellung zu. — He got him the position.

zufchreiben:

Das haben Sie fich felber zuzufchreiben. — You can lay that at your own door; you have yourself to thank for that; it's your own fault.

Zufchuß:

Gleich gibt's Zufchuß! — You'll get it in the neck pretty soon!

zufchuftern:

Er fchufterte ihm die Stelle zu. — He got him the job.

Zufehen:

Sie hatten das Zufehen. — They were left holding the bag; they got left (*or* nothing out of it).

zufetzen:

Die Krankheit fetzte ihm fehr zu. — The illness was very hard on him.

Er hat bei dem Gefchäft viel zugefetzt. — He lost quite heavily on the deal.

zufpitzen:

Die Lage fpitzt fich immer mehr zu. — The situation is drawing to a head (*or* becoming more and more critical).

zufprechen:

Er fpricht der Flafche eifrig zu. — He hits the bottle; he's an inveterate drinker.

Der Preis wurde ihm zugefprochen. — He was awarded the prize.

Zufpruch:

Der Anwalt erfreut fich eines großen Zufpruchs. — The attorney has a large clientele.

Zuftand:

Hier herrfchen Zuftände! — What a mess (*or* mixup)!; what an awful state of affairs!; conditions here are terrible!

Sie hat ihre Zuftände. — She's having one of her spells; she's in one of her moods.

zuſtatten:

Seine Erfahrung kommt ihm zuſtatten. — His experience comes in handy; it stands him in good stead.

zuſtecken:

Er ſteckte ihm eine Mark zu. — He slipped him a mark on the q.t. (*or* sly).

zuſtehen:

Es ſteht ihm nicht zu, darüber zu urteilen. — It's not his place (*or* up to him) to decide.

Ihm ſtehen noch zwei Mark zu. — He still has two marks coming to him.

zuſteuern:

Er ſteuerte fünf Mark zu. — He chipped in (*or* contributed) five marks.

zuſtoßen:

Hoffentlich ſtößt ihm nichts zu! — I hope nothing happens to him!

zutragen:

Sie trägt alles zu, was ſie hört. — She's a regular tattletale; she carries tales.

Wie hat ſich das zugetragen? — How did that happen?

zutrauen:

Das hätte ich ihm nie zugetraut! — I would never have thought (*or* believed) that of him!

zutreffen:

Das dürfte wohl nicht ganz zutreffen. — That's not quite correct; that wasn't quite how it happened.

Zutun:

Ohne ſein Zutun hätten ſie das nicht erreicht. — They could never have succeeded without his help.

zuvorkommen:

Er kam ihnen darin zuvor. — He stole a march on (*or* got ahead of) them.

zuwälzen:

Er wälzte ihr die Verantwortung zu. — He passed the buck to her; he laid the blame at her door.

zuwege:

Er bringt das nicht zuwege. — He can't put that across; he can't get away with that.

Er iſt gut zuwege. — He's doing (*or* feeling) fine.

zuzüglich:

Das Buch koſtet fünf Mark zuzüglich der Portoſpeſen. — The book costs five marks plus the postage.

Zwang:

Bitte, tun Sie ſich keinen Zwang an! — Don't stand on ceremony!; make yourself at home!

zwanglos:

Kommen Sie heute zum Abendbrot, aber ganz zwanglos, bitte! — Come and have supper with us tonight— but please, make (*or* let's have) it informal!

zwar:

Er kam zwar, doch war es ſchon zu ſpät. — He did finally come, but it was too late then.

Er hat zwei Kinder, und zwar einen Sohn und eine Tochter. — He has two children, (namely) a son and a daughter.

Sie kamen, und zwar pünktlich. — They came, and what's more, on time.

Er trinkt, und zwar nicht zu knapp. — He drinks, and none too sparingly at that.

Zweck:

Es hat keinen Zweck. — It doesn't pay; it's no use.

zwei:
Seine Familie steht nur noch auf zwei Augen.

There's only one member of his family left.

zweideutig:
Er nahm eine zweideutige Haltung ein.

He straddled the issue; he was noncommittal.

Sie machten zweideutige Witze.

They told off-color jokes; they told jokes that had a double meaning.

zweierlei:
Das zweierlei Tuch hat es ihr angetan.

She falls for (*or* is attracted to) anything in a uniform; she has a weakness for men in uniform.

Zweig:
Er kommt nie auf einen grünen Zweig.

He'll never get ahead in the world.

zweischneidig:
Die Begründung ist zweischneidig.

The argument cuts (*or* holds) both ways; there are two sides to the argument.

Zwerchfell:
Er erschütterte ihnen das Zwerchfell.

He made them split with laughter.

Zwickmühle:
Er sitzt in der Zwickmühle.

He's on the spot; he's in a real fix.

zwiebeln:
Sie zwiebelten ihn so lange, bis er nachgab.

They made it hot for (*or* kept at) him until he yielded.

zwingen:
Er kann's nicht zwingen.

He can't make the grade; he can't do it.

Zwirn:
Sie hat Zwirn im Kopf.

She's got brains; she's no fool.

Zwirnsfaden:
Er stolpert über einen Zwirnsfaden.

He's too scrupulous (*or* fussy).

zwölf:
Nun hat's aber zwölf geschlagen!

That's enough!; that's the last straw!; let's call it a day!

Es ist fünf Minuten vor zwölf!

It's high time!

zwölft:
Er kam in zwölfter Stunde.

He came at the eleventh hour (*or* last minute).